TROUBLED
TIMES

TROUBLED TIMES

U.S.-Japan
Trade Relations
in the 1990s

EDWARD J. LINCOLN

BROOKINGS INSTITUTION PRESS
Washington, D.C.

Copyright © 1999
THE BROOKINGS INSTITUTION
1775 Massachusetts Avenue, N.W., Washington, D.C. 20036
www.brookings.edu

Library of Congress Cataloging-in-Publication data

Lincoln, Edward J.
    Troubled times : U.S.-Japan trade relations in the 1990s /
Edward J. Lincoln.
        p.   cm.
    Includes index.

    ISBN 0-8157-5268-7 (alk. paper)
    ISBN 0-8157-5267-9 (pbk. : alk. paper)
    1. United States—Commerce—Japan.   2. Japan—Commerce—United
States.   3. United States—Foreign economic relations—Japan.   4.
Japan—Foreign economic relations—United States.   I. Title.
    HF3127   .L56   1999
    381'.0973052—dc21   98-58144
                                                                                            CIP

                                    9 8 7 6 5 4 3 2 1

The paper used in this publication meets minimum requirements of the American
National Standard for Information Sciences—Permanence of Paper for Printed
                    Library Materials: ANSI Z39.48-1984.

                                    Typeset in Minion

                        Composition by Harlowe Typography
                                Cottage City, Maryland

                        Printed by R.R. Donnelley & Sons
                            Harrisonburg, Virginia

ⒷTHE BROOKINGS INSTITUTION

THE BROOKINGS INSTITUTION is an independent organization devoted to nonpartisan research, education, and publication in economics, government, foreign policy, and the social sciences generally. Its principal purposes are to aid in the development of sound public policies and to promote public understanding of issues of national importance.

The Institution was founded on December 8, 1927, to merge the activities of the Institute for Government Research, founded in 1916, the Institute of Economics, founded in 1922, and the Robert Brookings Graduate School of Economics and Government, founded in 1924.

The general administration of the Institution is the responsibility of a Board of Trustees charged with maintaining the independence of the staff and fostering the most favorable conditions for creative research and education. The immediate direction of the policies, program, and staff of the Institution is vested in the president, assisted by an advisory committee of the officers and staff.

In publishing a study, the Institution presents it as a competent treatment of a subject worthy of public consideration. The interpretations and conclusions in such publications are those of the author or authors and do not necessarily reflect the views of the other staff members, officers, or trustees of the Brookings Institution.

Foreword

The Brookings Institution's record of research and analysis on Asia stretches back to the 1930s. This new book continues the tradition, tackling an important problem in the bilateral relationship with Japan. Overall, the relationship between Japan and the United States has been extremely close during the past half century. The two countries are linked by a mutual security pact, and economic ties have grown. Nevertheless, U.S.-Japan trade relations have often been tense. Certainly during my tenure as U.S. ambassador to Japan, difficult trade issues occupied many of my waking hours.

At the root of many of these trade-related problems is the persistent perception by American corporations and industries that access to Japanese markets is unusually difficult. How true are these allegations? How should U.S. government policy be shaped to deal with them? Ambassadors and other busy government officials rarely have time to step back from the overwhelming press of daily business on individual issues to think about these questions more broadly.

In this book, Edward J. Lincoln analyzes market access and policy options for coping with it. This study extends and broadens his previous Brookings book on market access, *Japan's Unequal Trade* (1990). A decade ago, Japanese merchandise trade was characterized by distinctive patterns, such as a very low penetration of the economy by imports of manufactured goods relative to the situation in other countries. This new book

vii

shows that the wide distinctions in trade behavior between Japan and other industrial countries continued in the 1990s, although the disparities have narrowed somewhat since the middle of the decade. Service sector trade does not show the same lopsided patterns, but examples of obstacles to access to the Japanese market abound. The evidence on persistent price differentials reinforces the analysis for both manufactured goods and services, with prices far higher in Japan than in other countries. Low levels of direct investment in Japan by foreign corporations further confirms the evidence. Direct investment is important because it usually has a complementary relationship with manufactured goods trade and is a vital component of market access in many service industries. Japanese domestic markets are certainly not "closed" to foreign firms in most cases, but the evidence in this book supports the claim that, in comparison with other nations, access to Japan's market is generally more difficult.

What policies the U.S. government should pursue in addressing this situation has been the subject of great debate during the past two decades. Lincoln argues that the problems and tension cannot be swept away with easy answers. Neither special arrangements such as a bilateral free trade area, nor large negotiating initiatives such as the Framework Agreement, promise to solve access problems quickly. Lincoln suggests several modest changes to enhance the process but says the United States must be resigned to prolonged and sometimes difficult negotiations to advance the goal of more open access. The result is that my successors at the American Embassy are likely to find themselves wrestling with market access problems for some time to come.

As this book goes to press, Japan's economy is being buffeted by a major recession and a worsening of a bad debt problem in the banking sector. Much of the malaise in the economy is macroeconomic, but some of the problem is structural. Just as foreign goods and services have been important in driving the American economy to greater efficiency in the past several decades, easier access to Japanese markets would have a beneficial impact on Japan's economy. Unfortunately, trade concessions have often been regarded in Japan as a matter of national sacrifice.

Economic distress in Japan has reached a point at which some of the investment problems identified by Lincoln may be easing somewhat. Acquisitions by foreign firms in the financial sector that would have been unthinkable a year or two ago have now materialized. But too little time has passed to know whether a trend is under way that will yield a larger role for foreign firms in Japan. This book also identifies factors that still militate against rapid or extensive regulatory or structural change. Given the positive impact greater market openness would have on forcing beneficial change for the Japanese economy, though, one can at least hope that in another decade some of the conclusions of this book will no longer be valid.

The author is grateful to Robert Angel, Hugh Patrick, Mark Tilton, and Ambassador Walter Mondale for comments on the first draft of this study. Excellent research assistance was provided by Kaori Lindeman and staff assistance by Mica Kreutz. Theresa Walker edited the manuscript and guided the publication process. Takako Tsuji verified the factual content, Carlotta Ribar proofread the book, and Julia Petrakis compiled the index.

Funding was provided by the Carnegie Corporation of New York, the John D. and Catherine T. MacArthur Foundation, and the Rockefeller Brothers Fund.

The views expressed in this book are those of the author and should not be ascribed to any of the persons whose assistance is acknowledged above, or to the trustees, officers, or other staff members of the Brookings Institution.

MICHAEL H. ARMACOST
President

April 1999
Washington, D.C.

Contents

CHAPTER ONE

Introduction

In the spring of 1995, the governments of the United States and Japan were engaged in tense negotiations over access to the markets for automobiles and automobile parts in Japan. Negotiations failed to move toward resolution, and the U.S. government threatened to impose punitive 100 percent tariffs on luxury cars imported from Japan. The two countries appeared in the press to be on a collision course as the deadline for collection of the tariff approached.

But the auto negotiations resulted in a bilateral agreement at the end of June, just hours before the threatened sanctions were to be activated. Far from representing the onset of heightened stress, in the bilateral trade relationship, resolution of the auto dispute marked the end of decade-long, high-profile, aggressive trade negotiations. Trade issues continued on the government agenda and sometimes erupted in public (as was the case briefly in the fall of 1997 when negotiations over restrictive practices in Japanese ports stalled), but overall these issues were relegated to a much lower level of priority and proceeded more quietly.

By the late 1990s American attitudes toward Japan had shifted substantially. Bilateral trade issues no longer commanded attention. In contrast to the view of Japan's economy as a competitive challenge or threat to American firms, recent images are of a diminished, weakened Japan beset with serious economic problems. After the collapse of the speculative bubble in real estate and stock prices, the Japanese economy grew slowly in the 1990s, and a mountain of bad debt burdened the financial system. In 1998 the nation was experiencing a serious recession, with a shrinking economy and soaring bankruptcies. Japan no longer fit the popular stereotypes of the late 1980s. The problems in its economy are substantial, and solutions have been elusive. Simultaneously, American self-images improved with the prolonged economic expansion of the 1990s and accompanying drop in unemployment. Much greater confidence prevailed in the resiliency and success of the U.S. economy. Concern that Japanese firms could or would grab global market share from American firms while remaining protected from American competition in their own home market clearly diminished.

In this changed environment, why focus on bilateral trade relations? If the supposed juggernaut of the 1980s has proved illusory, why should any-one care about questions of access to Japanese markets? If restricted access to markets in Japan did not give Japanese industries any special advantage in growth or efficiency, then why should government become immersed in arcane, detailed, and often murky investigations and negotiations over the details of access problems?

This study argues that dismissing the importance of trade relations with Japan is premature. Despite slow growth and difficulties in the finan-cial sector, leading manufacturers in Japan remain serious global competi-tors in many industries. More important, many Japanese industries (both those that are internationally competitive and those that are not) retain ample protection from foreign firms within their home market. Some pos-itive change has occurred in international access to Japanese markets, but many problems remain. Access to the Japanese market—second largest in the world—still matters to any multinational firm that intends to be a global competitor. This large market is also very affluent, meaning that it con-sumes the kinds of goods and services American firms produce. In any industry characterized by extensive economies of scale, Japanese firms can reap some benefit in international competition from restricting access to their home market, creating profits at home to subsidize expansion abroad. The past decade suggests that access problems in Japan are generally not life and death issues for American corporations, but neither are they trivial.

The decade from 1985 to 1995 had been one of rising momentum in American efforts to improve access to Japanese markets, with increasing numbers of trade negotiations and heavier American pressure exerted on Japan. For the late 1990s this history raises several questions. How much has this decade of activism changed the rules of access, behavior patterns in Jap-anese markets, and attitudes toward openness in Japan? Was the pressure and tension worth the effort? Have the 1990s brought more self-initiated change in Japan that diminishes the need for negotiations? More generally, where should American policy be headed now?

Japan has certainly moved farther away from its heavily protectionist developing country legacy of the early postwar period. From the end of the 1940s until the 1970s, Japan maintained a mutually reinforcing pattern of very stiff formal import barriers (quotas and tariffs) and severe investment controls that made access difficult or impossible for many foreign companies. In the 1970s and early 1980s, therefore, one could view much of Japanese behavior as the lingering legacy of these strong protectionist policies put in place in the early postwar period. Those policies were part of a determined economic nationalism, with the goal of building an industrially advanced nation owned and operated by Japanese nationals. Having achieved that goal by the 1970s, the protectionist policies that were part of it lingered on.

Optimists argued in the early 1980s that within time those policies would wither away. Protectionism may have been useful as part of Japan's determined development strategy but was not consistent with the needs and desires of a developed country. Negotiation with Japan should have, therefore, dovetailed with domestic interests favoring a general opening of markets that would be in the best economic interests of Japan. The succeeding decade of negotiations, with periodic episodes of extreme tension and drama, belied that optimistic image. Many have deplored the frequency of these disputes, the media attention focused on them, the raucous nature of the negotiating process, and the possible collateral damage to other aspects of the bilateral relationship. Despite the dismay, the record of the Reagan, Bush, and Clinton administrations was one of a series of negotiations aimed at both individual industries and more generic or "structural" issues. In the late 1990s, sufficient time has passed to ask what has been accomplished. Is Japan really more open or more "international" than a decade ago? And, depending on the answer, what should be the policy of the United States toward Japan now? This book takes up these questions.

Bilateral economic relations are broad and complex. The two nations are intertwined through trade, sales by firms with direct investment in the other country, technology and other licensing arrangements, and financial markets. Each item presents a different set of issues. Earlier in the postwar period, much of the bilateral dialogue concerned the terms on which Japanese firms could enter the U.S. market, with a number of American industries attempting to use trade law to restrict or slow the competitive pressures from Japanese firms. That era is largely gone, and attention became increasingly directed to the terms of access to Japanese markets. This study, therefore, examines this aspect of the bilateral economic relationship—access to Japanese markets in both manufacturing and nonmanufacturing sectors through trade and investment.

This analysis builds upon my earlier book, *Japan's Unequal Trade* (Brookings, 1990), which made use of data through 1988. At that time, Japan's trade patterns were distinctly different from those of other industrialized countries, differences that could not be explained away on the basis of economic factors. The picture that emerged from that study was of a country whose markets were relatively less open to foreign goods than markets of other industrial nations were. Since that time relatively little new research has appeared concerning the negotiations and changes of the 1990s. The Japanese government has vociferously claimed that whatever impediments may have existed in the past are now gone and, therefore, that foreign complaints about market access are unjustified. Certainly the possibility exists that the picture of access to Japanese markets in the late 1990s could be quite different than it was a decade earlier.

The conclusion of this study, however, is decidedly cautious. A variety of statistical evidence shows that the presence of foreign firms and their products has not increased in Japan very much over the past decade and remains remarkably low in comparison to other countries. Those increases are insufficient to suggest that Japan is no longer distinctive. In many ways the contrast between Japan and the rest of the world remains startling.

These data do not imply that Japan's markets are "closed" while those of the United States and other countries are "open." Everything is relative; Japan's markets are less open or more difficult to penetrate than those of other countries on average. Furthermore, much variation exists across industries. Some success stories do exist. But the fact that some firms or industries have been successful in participating relatively easily in Japanese markets does not negate the broader conclusion of access being more difficult than in other nations.

Ease of access varies greatly across sectors. Raw materials do not face any serious barriers today (as Japan gradually abandoned support for its own few raw material industries—mainly coal and timber). Agricultural products from abroad have faced a mixed situation with markets for grains relatively open (except for continued stiff controls on rice) while previously protected markets for meat, fruits, and vegetables gradually became more open during the 1980s and 1990s. Most of them, however, still face barriers of varying severity. Markets for foreign manufactured goods should be open, as tariffs are generally (though not universally) low. But problems stemming from manipulation of standards and testing procedures, as well as state-tolerated (or even encouraged) collusion among domestic firms, presented serious problems in several industries that remain in the late 1990s. Service sector access also varies widely, with fairly few problems in some areas (such as accounting services or architecture) and serious issues stemming from regulation and collusion in others (such as airline services, legal services, and insurance). Commercial banking and investment banking, two areas of finance in which foreign institutions had been kept to a minor role, showed some signs of improvement in the late 1990s. Service problems within the domestic financial sector led the government to view foreign institutions somewhat more favorably as a means to rescue and restructure the tattered domestic industry.

Over time emphasis on certain sectors may also be shifting, with the traditional stress on agricultural and manufacturing goods diminishing as trade in services and negotiations on barriers affecting service industries gained relative importance. Nevertheless, problems of access do remain, and at least for manufactured goods (where data are the most readily available), access to Japanese markets still lags behind that in other countries.

Furthermore, even if access to Japanese markets were comparable to the situation in many other countries, efforts to reduce barriers would still be justified. Japan is the second largest economy in the world, representing 18 percent of global gross domestic product (GDP) in 1995. Government negotiators cannot deal with all issues in all countries simultaneously. Japan (and the increasingly unified EU market) is a logical focus of bilateral negotiating effort. That Japan is also a more difficult market to gain access to in many industries strengthens this point—it behooves the U.S. government to prevent Japan from serving as an example to other countries of how far a nation can deviate from the ideal of open markets.

The process of dismantling the convoluted and obscure market barriers remains difficult and often contentious. Resolving these access problems may be even more difficult than a decade earlier because the easier issues have been handled and because attitudes in the Japanese government and private sector have hardened. The negotiating record of the 1990s belies the optimistic belief that self-generated change would accelerate the pace of change. This conclusion is at odds with the image Japan has projected in the 1990s of reform and deregulation—administrative reform, deregulation, and the Big Bang in financial deregulation were all highly visible issues in Japan after 1993. However, active discussion far exceeded the reality of change. Some deregulation is occurring and will continue in Japan, but the political process driving it forward is weak in comparison to what has occurred in other countries (the United States, Britain, or New Zealand, for example). Even the rest of Europe—known for extensive economic regulation, appeared to be moving forward faster and with greater resolve than Japan in the 1990s. Some of the most significant Japanese deregulation measures of the 1990s came only as the result of contentious negotiations with the United States (as was the case in deregulation of the insurance sector) and not simply as the result of domestic dynamics.

These conclusions about the continuation of access problems and the weakness of the domestic deregulation movement imply that trade disputes will continue. American and other foreign firms will meet access obstacles that they cannot resolve on their own and that appear to be at odds with Japanese government rhetoric or Japanese obligations under existing international agreements. How then should such problems be resolved?

During the past three decades, American efforts to open markets in Japan relied on both the multilateral General Agreement on Tariffs and Trade (GATT) and separate bilateral negotiations. The multilateral negotiation rounds within the GATT—the Kennedy Round, Tokyo Round, and Uruguay Round—provided an opportunity to press tariff and some other issues. GATT dispute resolution procedures were also useful for some issues (such as getting Japan to convert from quotas to tariffs on beef and citrus fruit). But much of the negotiating process proceeded on a bilateral basis, backed periodically by American threats of retaliation against Japanese economic interests in the United States as a tactical bargaining tool.

In 1995 the GATT was transformed into the World Trade Organization (WTO). Resentful of American bilateral pressures, the Japanese saw the WTO as a useful arena to resolve disputes. The WTO offers some hope in dealing with disputes, but its usefulness in dealing with the often informal and opaque dilemmas in Japan remains in doubt. The initial American test on color film of WTO applicability to informal trade barriers (consisting of government encouragement or even direction of collusive behavior among domestic firms to inhibit access by foreign firms) was not successful. Furthermore, some industries and practices remain outside the purview of existing WTO rules, and some bilateral disputes deal with getting Japan to make new commitments rather than with behavior under existing ones. The U.S. government should certainly make vigorous use of the WTO dispute resolution mechanism whenever possible, but no one should anticipate that this will offer a solution in all cases.

Given these limitations on the applicability of the WTO to access problems in Japan, there is little alternative to continuation of a lengthy and often frustrating process of chipping away at access problems through bilateral negotiations. In that process, bargaining leverage is critical, but the levers available to U.S. negotiators are now somewhat limited. In particular, the option of unilateral sanctions (that is, retaliatory action by the United States not specifically sanctioned by the WTO) is less viable under the WTO than it was under the GATT. This constraint implies that the bilateral trade negotiating process is destined to remain a frustrating one. Progress will probably be slow and often disappointing. The negotiations are worth pursuing, and leverage should be used when available, but expectations about significant changes in access should remain modest.

Focus

This study focuses exclusively on access by foreign firms to Japanese markets for both goods and services through trade or investment. Neither Japanese access to the U.S. market nor macroeconomic balances receives any treatment. This choice deserves some explanation.

The media commonly assume that macroeconomics dominates the bilateral economic relationship. When trade imbalances worsen (with either Japan's global current-account surplus rising or the bilateral trade imbalance deteriorating), bilateral relations seem to worsen. However, although trade figures provide convenient numbers for the media and some politicians to seize upon, their real relationship to bilateral issues is not entirely obvious. Trade and current-account imbalances are largely the product of macroeconomic factors—domestic savings and investment imbalances and government fiscal and monetary policy actions. Those factors may be affected by microeconomic developments, but the connections are complex and ambiguous in impact (a serious import barrier, for example, could reduce a nation's current-account balance with the world under certain circumstances).

Macroeconomic issues matter a great deal, since nations can and do pursue macroeconomic policies that prove unsustainable and result in global or bilateral problems (as was the case with Mexico in 1995 and Thailand and other Asian nations in 1997). Similarly, macroeconomic developments in Japan and the United States matter from the standpoint of sustainability or sensibility. Fiscal and monetary policies pursued by both countries in the 1980s drove them in opposite directions: the United States into sharp current-account deficits and Japan to high surpluses. And a core piece of the bilateral relationship in the 1990s has concerned American and other G-7 nation pressure on Japan to alter its macroeconomic policies. Beset with prolonged stagnation, a dangerous overhang of nonperforming loans, and muddled policymaking, the Japanese government faced strong pressure from the U.S. government to provide additional stimulus and resolve the problems in the financial sector. But those issues deserve their own analysis and are not the subject of this book.

Macroeconomic imbalances, though, may well provide a background for increased politicization of trade issues. Trade numbers resulting from macroeconomic forces have certainly been convenient fodder for criticism, mainly in the form of pressure on Japan to open its markets because it has a large surplus. This criticism seems to be exacerbated if the U.S. economy is slowing down (or in recession), with corporate profits falling and unemployment rising. Sometimes such rhetoric claims that barriers must be lowered because they have caused the trade imbalance, a proposition that is generally untrue (since the imbalances are primarily macroeconomic in nature). Sometimes the logic is one of "fairness"; nations that have large surpluses presumably are economically successful and, therefore, do not need to protect domestic industry. They should play a positive leadership role in multilateral efforts to lower barriers. Japan offends foreign observers because it does not fit this model. Despite a decade and a half of large current-account surpluses, Japan continues to be a difficult place for foreign firms to do business in, and it has certainly not been a leader in multilateral processes. In these ways, Japan's large surpluses have helped shape the overall negative atmosphere in which trade and investment disputes occur, but this study gives more attention to the substance of market access barriers than to the macroeconomic-inspired political environment in which they are discussed.

Similarly, this book does not deal with access to the U.S. market. From the early 1950s through the early 1980s, much of bilateral discussion concerned the terms of access to the U.S. market for Japanese firms. Beginning with textiles, and then moving through steel, color televisions, automobiles, motorcycles, and other products, American industries sought to protect themselves from an onslaught of imports from Japan, alleging unfair practices as defined in U.S. dumping and other trade laws. Fearful of damaging its overall political relationship with the United States, the Japanese government was often willing to agree to "voluntary" export restrictions that conveniently sidestepped multilateral rules against quotas. The high-water mark came at the beginning of the 1980s, with a bilateral agreement that restricted the shipment of automobiles from Japan to the United States for several years.

But that era of informal political deals to limit Japan's access to American markets is largely over. Most American industries have adjusted to competition from Japan and recognize that the benefits from pursuing protectionist agendas are often slow and uncertain. Firms do not always win their trade cases in Washington, and even when they do, the resulting protectionist benefits are usually modest. Occasionally, visible issues still crop up, such as the somewhat controversial decision to investigate dumping of Japanese supercomputers in the United States in 1997 that led to imposition of very high dumping duties (454 percent for the NEC Corporation).[1] But even this case was mostly the result of charges brought by a frustrated Cray Research (now a division of Silicon Graphics), which had faced exclusionary practices in Japan. Thus the desire to reduce access to the U.S. market was a retaliatory move within the context of attempts to increase access to Japanese markets rather than a simple protectionist move. The reality remains that relatively few American industries have found trade law remedies to be either easily forthcoming or satisfactory in providing protection from international competition. Access to the American market is not entirely open, but at least in the case of competition with Japan attempts to reduce access have diminished, and most of the informal "voluntary" restrictions of the past have lapsed. With new WTO rules in place, and a more assertive Japanese government, a return to an era of proliferating "voluntary" export restrictions affecting Japanese exports to the United States is unlikely, although the issue of restraining Japanese steel exports was back on the bilateral agenda by 1999.

As the question of access to the U.S. market has waned in importance, access to the Japanese market has become the central focus of bilateral trade relations. Both American firms and the U.S. government may have been somewhat slow to comprehend the problems involved in access to Japanese markets. During the 1960s and 1970s, emphasis remained on reduction of formal tariff, quota, and direct investment barriers. In both multilateral forums (the Kennedy Round and Tokyo Round of GATT negotiations) and bilaterally, the U.S. government pursued this traditional route with the expectation that reductions in formal barriers would lead to increased real access to Japanese markets. During the 1980s, however, came the realization that this formal opening of markets often failed to produce anticipated changes in the market place. From the early 1980s, attention has focused on understanding the nature of these nontariff access problems and attempting to engage the Japanese government in negotiations to remove restrictions. Many access problems have been informal and opaque, complicating the process and necessitating greater analytical and negotiating effort.

Furthermore, the emerging emphasis on access to Japan was related to competition from Japanese firms in the United States and in third markets. To the extent that the theory of strategic trade policy has some validity, then Japanese firms operating in a protected home market have the potential of generating excess profits that can be used to subsidize penetration of foreign markets, including the United States. If this is true, rather than seeking temporary relief from competition in the United States directly through restrictions on access to the U.S. market, a better corporate strategy is to eliminate the source of the competition's ability to pursue such predatory practices. As more American manufacturing firms have viewed their markets in global terms, they appear to have moved toward this strategic view of corporate policy.

As a result, the core of bilateral trade issues has shifted decisively to the question of access to Japanese markets, and enough problems exist to warrant the exclusive focus of this book on access to Japanese markets. The United States is not completely without blame on trade protectionism, but attitudes and policies in the United States deserve a separate study.[2]

Access to markets is a complex issue. Several aspects of access to Japanese markets form the basis of the analysis in this study.

First is the fundamental question of the extent to which access to Japanese markets deviates from the situation in other countries. No nation practices complete free trade and investment policies, although most countries have undergone a broad and substantial lowering of barriers in the past half century. The relevant question is, just how different is Japan from other markets? Are markets in Japan less accessible for foreign firms than the markets of other industrial countries? This concern goes beyond the traditional notion of trade barriers.

As posed, this question is about corporate access to markets, not simply about import barriers. Traditionally economists and government officials have concentrated on cross-border trade barriers: policies (tariffs, quotas, and standards) that prevent or limit the ability of foreign goods to enter into the country. However, firms can compete in a foreign market through exports but may also be involved through investment. In a nation with high barriers at the border, investment can be a means to circumvent them. Often, though, trade and investment are inextricably intertwined; real market access often requires investment for sales and service even if the products come from abroad. Therefore, the broad picture of access to markets in Japan through both trade and investment is the appropriate focus.

Second, do the problems facing American and other foreign businesses really matter? That is, even if the problems of market access are real, do they deserve to be on the foreign policy agenda of the United States? Some argue that access issues do not deserve to be on the agenda because barriers in Japan simply hurt the efficiency of the Japanese economy, or because the internal debate over deregulation in Japan will accomplish American policy goals on its own without the need for contentious trade negotiations. These views, though, can be challenged.

Third, if access to Japanese markets is less open than in other countries, and if those barriers do deserve attention, what should the policy approach of the U.S. government be? Do the problems warrant special attention from the U.S. government or a policy approach that departs from principles of free trade? Many business people have argued over the past decade that Japan's economy is sufficiently different from that of the United States that only a managed trade approach would work to offset restricted access. That is, rather than negotiating over tariffs, standards, and other rules, the object should be to simply specify a market share for foreign products. The rationale is that many markets in Japan fail to operate on open market principles, so rewriting rules of access (standards, testing procedures, and bidding procedures among others) fails to make markets more open. Did the Clinton administration move in this direction? Is this the only way to make progress? What else can be done?

Overview

The measurement of access to Japanese markets can be approached in several ways. One is to measure an estimated cost of limited access to Japanese markets in terms of the value of blocked imports, or to calculate other statistical measures of the extent to which Japan's trade and investment patterns deviate from other nations.[3] Another is to provide a catalogue of problems by sector, as does the Office of the U.S. Trade Representative (USTR) in its annual report to Congress, and the American Chamber of Commerce in Japan in its occasional white papers.[4] Or one can approach the subject in a chronological fashion, describing the history of the Bush and Clinton administrations' approach to Japan. Each of these individual approaches has been adopted by other observers. This book follows an eclectic yet comprehensive approach, exploring both the quantitative analysis of the issue and a review of the policy issues of the 1990s without being either explicitly chronological or sectoral.

Chapter 2 begins the task with a discussion of Japan's evolving merchandise trade patterns, answering questions about how distinctive those patterns are relative to other countries. The answer is decidedly mixed. Japan experienced a sizable spurt in imports in 1995–96 when the yen was very strong—a spurt that suggested on the surface that access conditions had improved. However, the simple ratio of manufactured imports to gross domestic product (GDP) has exhibited little sustained change—rising modestly in the late 1980s, subsiding in the early 1990s, and then rising again in the mid-1990s. The index for intra-industry trade (an indicator of the extent to which a nation engages in both exports and imports in different product areas), on the other hand, did move upward from the late 1980s to the mid-1990s, and the gap between Japan and other countries closed modestly. But even with a modest improvement in the extent of intra-industry trade, Japan still lagged far behind most other industrial nations on these indicators. Trade data for the service sector do not show the same pattern of lopsided surpluses for Japan as do manufactured goods trade data, but certainly there is evidence of problems in some areas. Meanwhile, a pattern of much higher retail prices for goods and services in Japan compared with the United States and other countries continued unabated in the 1990s, differences that ought to have engendered substantial arbitrage in fully open markets (with entrepreneurs buying goods abroad and selling them in Japan). All of the trade and price indicators show a picture of a nation that continued to be less accessible on average to foreign firms than is the case for other nations.

Chapter 3 analyzes the investment dimension of the relationship. As noted earlier, investment can either complement or substitute for trade. Viewed as a substitute, much of the distinctiveness of Japan explored in chapter 2 could be offset if foreign firms simply preferred to invest in production within Japan rather than exporting to Japan. However, this is not the case. Investment into Japan has also been low relative to investment into the United States or other countries, although the data for measuring those differences are not very accurate. In fact, investment is more of a complement than a substitute for trade. Even manufacturing investment is generally positively related to trade; local production brings in imported components and may lead to establishment of local distribution channels that then handle additional imported products of the same firm. The importance of investment is all the more obvious when one moves beyond the traditional concern over merchandise trade to consider access in service industries, where the nature of the business often demands a local presence. The complementarity of investment and trade implies that the distinctively low level of investment is an important part of the explanation for the distinctiveness of Japanese trade patterns.

Chapter 4 turns to the record of trade negotiations with Japan in the 1990s, touching on the Bush administration and more extensively on the Clinton administration. The Bush administration highlighted an intense discussion of broad structural issues called the Structural Impediments Initiative (SII). The Clinton administration pursued a broad set of negotiations on structural and sectoral issues defined by the Framework Agreement of 1993. The Clinton administration was widely accused of adopting a managed trade approach toward Japan, and of creating unnecessary tension in the bilateral relationship through its series of very noisy trade disputes in the 1993–95 period. This chapter argues that the criticism was largely undeserved, although the administration was slow to define what it wanted in the negotiations and did a poor job of public communication. In its second term, the Clinton administration adopted a lower profile for trade negotiations with Japan and emphasized a continuing dialogue on deregulation. Throughout this time, Japanese negotiators vigorously resisted changes intended to make markets more open, resistance occurring when the rhetoric in Japan was dominated by notions of deregulation. The record of both the Bush and Clinton administrations was one of only modest success.

Chapter 5 takes up the issue of the ways in which Japan is changing on its own. The 1990s brought unprecedented problems for Japan—a collapse of asset prices and prolonged relative stagnation. Average annual growth from 1992 through 1997 was only just over 1 percent a year. These ills spawned an energetic debate about the need for deregulation and for broadly reducing government intrusion in the economy. The appearance of incipient change was reinforced in 1993 when Morihiro Hosokawa became the first prime minister since 1955 from outside the Liberal Democratic Party. His accession and the invigorated debate over deregulation led to a perception in the United States that real and substantial change was under way or was about to begin. That perception motivated some of the criticism of the Clinton administration; if Japan was embarking on a process of change that would result in more accessible markets, why should the United States engage in such contentious trade disputes? However, this chapter argues that the process of deregulation and decontrol in the 1990s was rather weak.

Although the rhetoric in favor of deregulation was often strong, real support in Japan was mixed, and the process put in place seriously flawed. Outcomes through 1997 were disappointing, and the prospects for vigorous deregulation were not bright. Poor economic performance through the remainder of the decade may cause sufficient domestic concern or frustration to inject a bit more vigor into the process, but even in this case the implications for foreign firms are unclear. The goal of deregulation and reform is to improve the performance of Japanese firms. Ample opportunity exists to pursue this goal without greatly increasing opportunities for foreign firms to participate in domestic markets. The one major exception to this general picture is the market for financial services, where disarray in the industry reduced obstacles to foreign investment banks and commercial banks.

The final chapter of the book focuses on appropriate American policy toward Japan. Are access issues worth pursuing? Yes. Japan's size in the global economy is very large (the second largest in the world), and the nation is very affluent. As a result, the Japanese consume large quantities of the goods and services in which American firms specialize. The Japanese market should loom large for any American firm that is seriously engaged in global markets, and, therefore, should be concerned about access barriers. Furthermore, for several industries, Japan is the home of major global competitors to American firms. As a matter of corporate strategy these firms should be in their competitors' home market, and if access is blocked, those competitors may gain global advantage from the excess profits generated at home. These issues also matter because of the example Japanese behavior sets in the global effort to lower trade and investment barriers. And finally, these issues matter politically; the domestic political support for open trade in America depends in large part on the belief that major trading partners like Japan are also open or becoming more open.

Can we improve upon the process that has so often resulted in noisy and tense bilateral disputes in the past? The answer in chapter 6 is very cautious. There are no easy solutions—and proposals such as creation of a bilateral dispute resolution mechanism should be rejected. Nevertheless, the negotiating approach can be refined in some ways. This chapter offers a variety of suggestions, beginning with the need to use the WTO more aggressively. However, the WTO is no panacea. Some problems with Japan concern industries that remain outside the purview of the WTO (such as commercial aviation). Other issues involve complex and opaque aspects of industrial policy that are difficult to prove convincingly in the legalistic setting of the WTO. As happened in the case about access to the market for color film, the WTO has proved ill-suited for dealing with the informal nature of business-government ties in Japan. Furthermore, some issues involve American requests for new commitments from Japan rather than disputes about existing rules and commitments. Sometimes such requests can be integrated in multilateral negotiating rounds, but these are infrequent and lengthy. The WTO expects nations to work out bilateral agreements, with the stipulation that the resulting agreements be applicable on a most favored nation basis.

With its limitations, the WTO cannot possibly be the forum for resolution of all bilateral economic problems between the United States and Japan. The process of bilateral negotiation must continue. On several occasions, the U.S. government has chosen high-profile themes for intense negotiating schedules, including the Market-Oriented Sector Selective (MOSS) negotiations of 1985–86, the SII talks, and the Framework negotiations. This approach should be discouraged; these episodes raise unrealistic expectations and often fade away before complex issues can be resolved. Themes are not harmful if they serve solely as an organizing mechanism for a collection of negotiations, but when highlighted as a means for producing substantial results, they can be a liability. Certainly the MOSS, SII, and Framework negotiations led to agreements, but short time frames (one year for both the MOSS and SII episodes) limited what could be accomplished. What is needed is a more constant level of negotiating and monitoring effort, flexible enough to cope with the wide variety of sectoral and structural problems that arise as American firms pursue Japanese markets. Within this effort, greater attention should also be given to public information; far too often the U.S. government has been disadvantaged by aggressive Japanese public relations campaigns designed to undermine political support within the United States for the administration's negotiating initiatives.

In pursuing a bilateral trade agenda, though, what form of leverage can or should the U.S. government exercise? Retaliatory imposition of barriers to Japanese access in the United States as a negotiating lever without approval by the WTO is now problematical in many cases. Nevertheless, retaliation should not be completely abandoned as a tactic. The lack of real deregulation and the continued stiff stance of Japanese trade negotiators imply that occasional use of such leverage is justified.

Use of the WTO when possible and pursuit of bilateral negotiations require human resources to deal with analysis of problems, negotiations, preparation of WTO cases, and monitoring of existing agreements. Trade relations with Japan have never had the necessary human support in the U.S. government, and at least modest staffing increases would be helpful.

But the final conclusion is relatively pessimistic. Japan is a sovereign nation, and opportunities to exercise leverage in negotiations are fairly limited. The process of bringing about greater market access will remain slow and frustrating. Domestic opposition to true deregulation and liberalization will conflict with American ideals and goals. Generally the direction of change has been positive; negotiations have produced better market access in many sectors over the past decade. And domestic pressures have moved Japan along a path of deregulation. But the pace has been slow and the process difficult. Sadly, the most important result is the need to lower American expectations about what can be accomplished.

CHAPTER TWO

Evolving
Trade Patterns

Merchandise trade is the most stud-
ied element of access to Japanese markets, producing a debate in the 1980s
over the extent to which Japan was "different." Firms can participate in markets of other countries by shipping goods from factories in their own country or in third countries. Governments have collected data on the flow of
goods for many years with detailed classifications by industry or product, a
result in large part of the existence of import tariffs. Analysis of these trade
data can help answer questions about the penetrability of national markets. Since direct investment provides an alternative mechanism for penetration—with complex connections to trade flows—analysis of trade patterns does not provide a complete picture. This chapter deals with trade,
and chapter 3 takes up the investment dimension.

Japan's Unequal Trade told how Japan's trade patterns differed from
those of other industrial nations in ways difficult to justify simply as the
consequences of economic variables.[1] This distinctive pattern of trade did
much to explain why foreign firms felt unusually hampered in entering Japanese markets. The analysis explored two principal dimensions of trade: the
overall penetration of manufactured imports in the economy and intra-
industry trade.

The penetration of manufactured imports was unusually low through
the mid-1980s. Whether measured by the ratio of manufactured imports
to GDP or to apparent domestic consumption of manufactures, Japan has

had one of the lowest levels of import penetration in the world. Furthermore, between 1970 and the mid-1980s, this ratio did not rise for Japan, in contrast to the experience of other nations. Generally overall manufactured import penetration has risen as nations lowered their trade barriers, but this was not the case for Japan.

Related to this distinctive feature was Japan's record on intra-industry trade. Trade among industrialized nations has become increasingly characterized by a pattern in which nations both import and export products within the same industry categories, in contrast to what one would expect from a simple model of comparative advantage. However, the statistic for measuring the extent of intra-industry trade showed that Japan had a much lower proclivity to engage in such trade than did most other nations. In particular, Japan tended to import very little in those industries characterized by high exports, in sharp contrast to other industrial nations.

These two peculiarities explained why foreign firms would feel frustrated in exporting to Japanese markets. Overall, the Japanese economy was absorbing fewer imports relative to the size of its economy, another way of saying that the market was more difficult to penetrate than those of other countries. And industries used to a competitive situation characterized by substantial exports and imports in other national markets found Japan especially resistant to imports in those industries characterized by strong Japanese exports.

One objective of this chapter is to analyze what has happened to these dimensions of merchandise trade over the past decade. The broad comparative picture in *Japan's Unequal Trade* includes data through 1985, supplemented by some additional data for Japan and the United States through 1988. Much may have changed—a position often argued by Japanese analysts—and the data need to be revisited.

Another aspect of trade considered in *Japan's Unequal Trade* is price differences. In a perfectly competitive world with no trade barriers, prices in any market should be the same, plus transportation costs. With no entry barriers, markets with prices higher than justified by transportation costs will attract an inflow of cheaper products from abroad. When a nation does exhibit much higher prices than the rest of the world for a sustained period, therefore, the distinct possibility exists that some form of trade barrier underwrites the difference. In the late 1980s, Japan had prices for many tradable consumer goods that were much higher than in other markets, a fact that reinforced the conclusion that something other than normal economic factors was restricting the inflow of foreign products. Since that time exchange rates have moved considerably, and Japan has experienced falling retail prices for some products, a development termed *bukka hakkai* (price destruction) by the Japanese media. This raises the question of the status of price differences in the mid-1990s. Have price differences diminished, or do they persist?

A dimension of trade that was not discussed in *Japan's Unequal Trade* is trade in services. The measurement of import penetration and intra-industry trade applies only to merchandise trade. However, trade in services has been rising very rapidly and deserves separate consideration, especially since this is an area of presumed competitive strength for American firms. Analysis of trade in services is complicated by the disparate nature of the service sector and the fact that sale of services in foreign markets often involves direct investment rather than exports from a home base (or that this form of participation in foreign markets is more prevalent than for manufactured goods).

This chapter reaches a mixed conclusion. Some change has occurred in Japan. Import penetration has risen somewhat, intra-industry trade has increased somewhat, and the picture for service trade is quite different than for merchandise trade. However, modest change has not significantly erased the distinctiveness of Japan. Manufactured import penetration continues to be far below that of other countries even though the gap narrowed a bit in the mid-1990s; intra-industry trade continues to be quite low; and prices remain high. After a brief period of improvement in import penetration from 1986 to 1990, the ratio of manufactured imports to GDP then stagnated, a stagnation that helps to explain the continued frustration of businesses and policymakers in the early 1990s when the Clinton administration came into office. The rise of penetration levels after 1993 may also help explain why the Clinton administration did not continue a high-profile, aggressive trade policy in the second term.

The topic of market access also relates closely to investment. Since the question of direct investment into and out of Japan is a large subject, it is the topic of chapter 3. Data in that chapter will largely confirm the picture presented here.

The Primary Sector

International merchandise trade includes raw materials, agricultural products, and manufactured products. Each of these broad areas has its own set of market access issues. The main focus of this chapter will be on manufactured goods. However, some comments on raw materials and agriculture are also necessary.

Raw materials have generally faced few barriers in the Japanese market. The Japanese economy has long been dependent on imports of some raw materials because of an absolute lack of domestic sources (including petroleum, rubber, and bauxite). In some other cases, domestic sources involve high extraction costs relative to imports, such as coal. Given the need for raw material inputs for the manufacturing sector, few barriers affect foreign products. Some exceptions to this general pattern exist, such as subsidizations of domestic coal production, but these have been relatively few. Foreign firms involved in raw material extraction and trade have generally found few problems in selling to Japan.

Agriculture presents a more complex picture. In general, Japan has an inefficient, high-cost agricultural sector that is highly subsidized. Trade barriers are also part of the support for domestic agriculture, but the pattern is very uneven. Some products, including wheat, corn, and soybeans, are almost entirely imported and barriers are minimal. At the other extreme, the market for rice was completely closed in the postwar period until the government made a minor market opening concession in the Uruguay Round of multilateral trade negotiations in 1994. Other products fit in between these two extremes, facing tariff, quota, or other nontariff barriers that have restricted or prevented their ability to enter Japanese markets. Often these barriers have taken the form of phytosanitary standards that have been much stricter than in other countries and without sufficient scientific justification. As with raw materials, some items are imported because no domestic supply capability exists (including fish and shellfish that do not exist in Japanese waters or tropical fruits and vegetables that do not grow in Japan).

Agriculture, as subdivided in international trade, is a mixture of farm and fishery products, plus processed or manufactured food products. One could argue that products such as whiskey—a highly differentiated product with strong brand-name characteristics—is more properly included in manufactured goods than agriculture. Most of the rest of this chapter will focus on manufactured goods, which inadvertently exclude this kind of processed food and beverage products.

Overall, reliance on imported food has grown over time, as shown in figure 2-1. On a value basis, food imports expanded from only 6 percent of domestic food consumption expenditures in 1965 to 41 percent by 1993. On a caloric basis the shift is from a 27 percent reliance on imports in 1965 to

Figure 2-1. *Imports as a Share of Food Consumption*

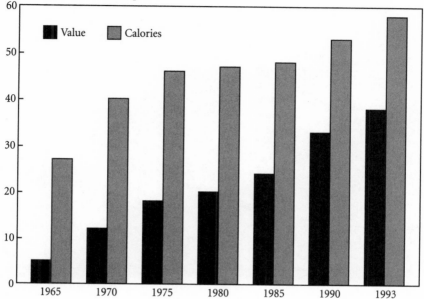

Percent of domestic consumption

Source: Statistics Bureau, Management and Coordination Agency, *Japan Statistical Yearbook, 1998* (Tokyo, 1997), p. 276.

63 percent by 1993. In very broad terms, therefore, imports responded to the growing relative inefficiency or higher cost of domestic agricultural products. Both the ratio of foreign agricultural products to domestic consumption and the sustained rise in that ratio stand in stark contrast to evidence on manufactured products presented in this chapter.

Much of the growth in agriculture imports has come in the higher value-added processed products. The parts of the market that had been open and had already largely replaced domestic sources of supply, such as wheat and soybeans, faced relatively slow growth in the 1990s, since basic foodstuffs tend to be relatively price and income inelastic. Figure 2-2 indicates what has happened to total agricultural imports, as well as several categories of prepared or processed food products.

Total agricultural imports rose at a relatively steady pace, with some acceleration after 1993. But the several categories of prepared or processed products rose much faster, especially after 1991. The one uneven pattern is

Figure 2-2. *Growth of Agricultural Imports, 1988–96*

Index (1988 = 100)

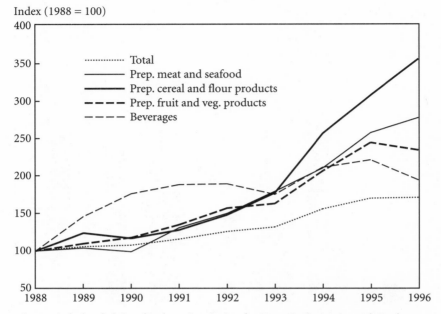

Source: Author's calculations based on Organization for Economic Cooperation and Development, *International Trade by Commodities Statistics, H.S. Rev. 1 1988–1996* (Paris, 1997), on CD-ROM.

for imported beverages, affected by the boom in imported wine in the "bubble economy" years of the late 1980s and the temporary inroads of foreign beer in 1994–95 (with beer imports doubling in value from 1993 to 1994, and then dropping by almost 45 percent by 1996).[2] This more rapid rise of prepared or processed products was of particular interest to American business, eager to move to higher value-added food exports to Japan.

The general trend in the role of imported food does not negate the importance of trade barriers. At any point in time, the role of foreign products would have been even higher if the market were more open. But what appears to have been happening over the past three decades is that the government was fighting a rearguard action. Knowing that domestic agriculture was inefficient, but desiring to protect the politically well-organized farmers, the government provided import protection as long as possible before acceding to international demands for change. Unlike the situation in a number of manufactured-good negotiations, changes in the rules of access made a real difference in market outcomes. Retail chains and food distributors do not appear to have blocked imported food products once overt barriers were lowered, or at least they did not do so in any sustained manner.

By the late 1990s, the situation for food products continued to present a mixed picture, with some product areas still facing considerable obstacles. But as chapter 6 explains, a new code on phytosanitary standards was part of the Uruguay Round agreement, and that code provided a stronger tool for pushing the Japanese government to alter its standards on food products. Only a few products faced high tariffs or quotas by the late 1990s, but those that did still had far to go. High tariffs still applied to beef and citrus fruits, while the permissible imports of rice were minuscule. This record implies that although the overall picture of agriculture sector products has been encouraging, trade issues will remain for years to come.

Manufactured Import Penetration

Economists have long recognized that the penetration of manufactured imports into countries varies considerably. Population, economic size, level of economic development, and raw material endowment can all affect total import penetration. Small countries have incomplete manufacturing sectors; realistically they can specialize in only a few industries, and they rely on imports for the rest of domestic demand. It makes no sense, for example, for Luxembourg to have a domestic automobile industry given the large economies of scale in auto manufacturing. More affluent countries tend to have higher import penetration because they have abandoned labor-intensive manufactures and because imports satisfy the broader tastes for more sophisticated and varied consumer goods. Furthermore, import penetration has generally risen in the past half century as nations have lowered trade barriers.

What has happened to Japan? Figure 2-3 shows manufactured imports as a share of gross domestic product (GDP) for Japan and several other countries from 1980 to 1996. Since Japan is reliant upon imports for some raw materials, especially oil, manufactured imports are a more relevant basis of comparison than total imports (a choice for comparison explored later in this chapter). On this basis, Japan has had a low import penetration ratio that changed little in the fifteen years from 1980 to 1993, remaining close to 3 percent. From 1986 to 1990 a modest increase appeared to be under way, with the ratio rising to almost 4 percent in 1990, but thereafter it drifted back during the first half of the 1990s. By 1993 the ratio was no

Figure 2-3. *Manufactured Imports as a Share of GDP, 1980–96*

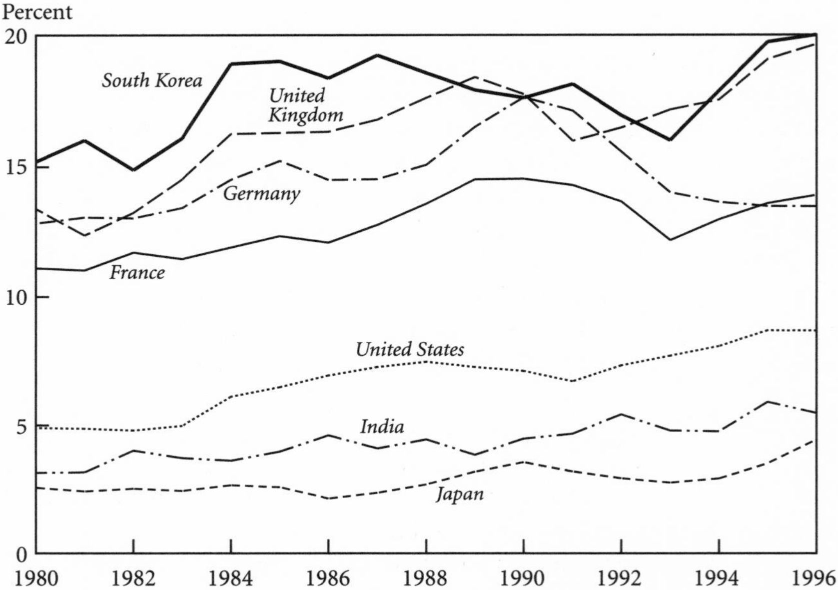

Percent

Sources: Data before 1993 are from World Bank, *World Tables* (Washington, various years); and 1993–96 data are from World Bank, *World Development Indicators* (Washington, 1998), on CD-ROM.

higher than in 1980. This evenness contrasted with the slowly rising trend for the United States. Most other countries experienced increases and decreases in import penetration, probably because of market responses to exchange rate fluctuations. But even with some fluctuation, most had higher levels of import penetration in 1993 than back in 1980.

The countries in this sample are mostly other industrial nations. The European countries have high levels of manufactured import penetration, given their geographical proximity to one another and the existence of an increasingly open intra-European market. But figure 2-3 also includes South Korea, a neighbor to Japan that lacks raw materials and maintains significant trade barriers. Korea, though, has a much higher and rising level of manufactured import penetration, going from 15 percent of GDP in 1980 to nearly 20 percent by 1996. India is also in the sample—a continental nation with a large population and stiff trade barriers. That combination of factors gives India a low manufactured import penetration level but still slightly higher (about 5.5 percent of GDP in 1996) than that of Japan.

Only after 1993 did foreign manufactured imports begin to rise again as a share of Japanese GDP. From 1993 to 1996, the ratio rose from 2.8 percent to 4.2 percent, above the previous peak of 3.6 percent in 1990. This sudden rise came as the result of rapidly rising imports in a largely stagnant economy, motivated by both the appreciation of the yen (making imports more price competitive with domestic products) and the outcome of the previous decade of market-opening negotiations. In the late 1990s, the new question was whether the rise in manufactured import penetration would remain at this higher level or recede as it did in the early 1990s. Given the rapid depreciation of the yen after the spring of 1995 (from a peak of ¥80 per dollar in April 1995 to ¥145 by the summer of 1998), and economic recession in 1998, imports were likely to lose ground in the economy.

Even with the rise in the ratio of manufactured imports to GDP in Japan, figure 2-3 shows that Japan is still below the other countries in the sample. This disparity between Japan and the United States narrowed modestly, but the United States and other countries have also experienced rising (though unevenly) ratios of manufactured imports to GDP.

Virtually no other nation in the world has a manufactured import penetration ratio as low as Japan's. Of 98 countries reporting the necessary data to the World Bank for 1990, only Brazil and Argentina had ratios lower than Japan's.[3] As an affluent, industrially advanced nation, it is startling that imports continued to be such a small part of the economy in Japan. It is equally startling that the decade of the 1980s, with all the trade negotiations pursued by the Reagan and Bush administrations, yielded so little discernible impact on overall import penetration in Japan.

One important caveat should be kept in mind. The data in figure 2-3 are affected by movements in the exchange rate. If a nation's currency rises in value, that nation can buy imports at a cheaper price in terms of its domestic currency. Therefore, for the same percentage of GDP it can obtain a larger real amount of goods from abroad. Masaru Yoshitomi, a Japanese economist formerly with the government's Economic Planning Agency, explains the failure of the nominal ratio of manufactured imports to GDP to rise as a result of this effect of the exchange rate. He notes that over a long period from 1975 to 1992, the price index for manufactured imports relative to the GNP deflator dropped by half. Thus, he argues, the real increase in manufactured goods imports was larger than shown by the nominal data.[4] With the nominal ratio remaining relatively constant, the real presence of imported manufactures should have roughly doubled.

Certainly the volume of imports in Japan increased in the 1990s, and casual observation leads one to believe that foreign-made consumer products were much more visible in the mid-1990s than they were a decade earlier. This real change is borne out by crude data on the volume of manufactured imports. According to Japanese data, the volume of manufactured imports rose 41 percent from 1990 to 1996 (for an annual growth of 5.9 percent), while the yen value of these imports rose only 12 percent over the same time period.[5] Nevertheless, over a decade or more, other nations also experienced swings both up and down in exchange rates without erasing the general trend of rising import penetration. That import penetration in Japan has been much lower than in virtually any other country and failed to converge with other industrial nations over the period from 1980 to 1996 remains a distinctive and startling fact.

Another way to refine the comparison is to look at manufactured imports as a share of apparent domestic consumption of manufactures. Nations produce both goods and services, and a more accurate measure of import penetration comes from observing how imports fare in comparison to total domestic sales of manufactured goods. In statistical data available across countries, apparent domestic consumption of manufactured goods can be estimated as domestic manufacturing production, minus exports, and plus imports. That is, what is consumed domestically is that portion of domestic production that is not exported, plus imports. The "apparent" qualification is because part of domestic supply goes to inventories rather than being consumed and because some imports might be re-exported rather than being consumed domestically. The role of manufactured imports in the economy is best reflected as a ratio to this quantity. Figure 2-4 shows the trend in this ratio since 1980 for the same set of countries as in figure 2-3.

The result is essentially the same as in the previous comparison. After reaching a temporary peak of 16 percent in 1990, this ratio sagged until 1993 and then moved up to 18 percent by 1995. Comparison to the United States and other countries is hampered somewhat by data availability, but the conclusions drawn from figure 2-3 also apply here. The rise in manufactured imports as a share of apparent domestic consumption after 1993 probably narrowed the gap between Japan and the United States but still left Japan far below (with Japan at 18 percent in 1995 and the United States at 37 percent in 1993). Even India had a ratio of 31 percent in 1996, and the European countries plus South Korea were all well over 50 percent.

Figure 2-4. *Manufactured Imports as a Share of*
Apparent Consumption

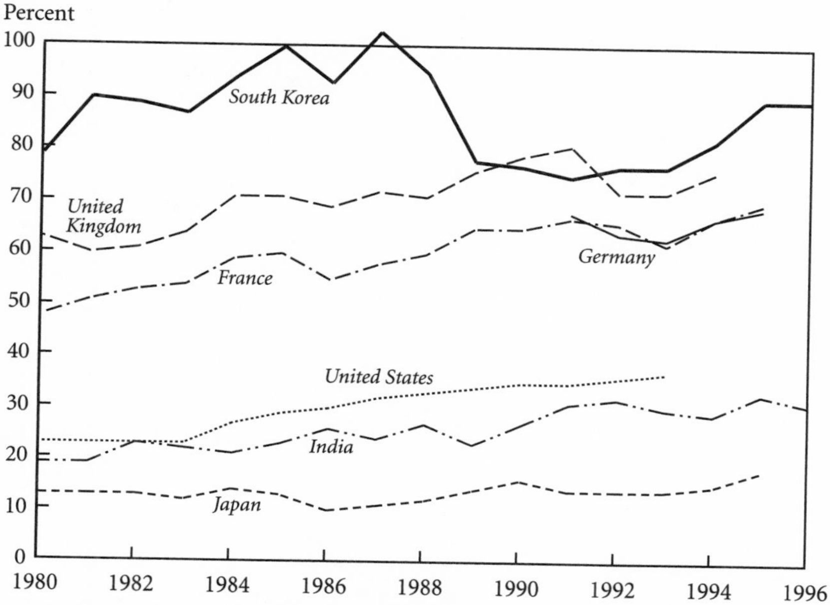

Percent

Sources: Data before 1993 are from World Bank, *World Tables;* and 1993–96 data are from World Bank, *World Development Indicators,* on CD-ROM.

If one looks at a broad cross-section of nations, the same generalizations result. Out of a sample of seventy-seven countries that reported all the necessary data to the World Bank for 1990, only three (Argentina, Brazil, and Estonia) had a penetration level lower than that of Japan. Indeed, most industrial nations were well above the U.S. level as well.[6]

The data presented above could have a variety of explanations. Some unusual economic factors might explain why manufactured imports are lower in Japan than most other countries. Or market barriers could explain this outcome. Economists have wrestled with the causes of Japan's low manufactured imports for a number of years. Most economists have been unable to explain these low levels as just the result of economic factors (labor and capital endowment, population, or level of per capita GDP), so that trade barriers are generally part of the explanations.[7]

The conclusion that these low import penetration levels partly reflect protectionism has been challenged by Japanese government officials and academics. They argue that the economy has no room for manufactures given heavy raw material imports. Nations that must import raw materials should not be expected to import as many manufactured goods as other nations. This argument assumes that a nation faces the world with something akin to a budget constraint; given its foreign exchange earnings from exports, a nation can allocate those earnings to raw materials or manufactures. Nations have little choice in the purchase of raw materials when they have an absolute domestic lack of those materials (as is the case for oil and a few other raw materials in Japan). Thus nations that must allocate a large portion of their foreign exchange earnings to the necessary purchase of raw materials will import fewer manufactured goods. Furthermore, if the price of raw materials goes up (as it did in the 1970s), then the share of foreign exchange funds that can go to manufactures declines. In the vocabulary of economics, the demand for raw material imports is less price elastic than that for manufactures (at higher prices, nations do import fewer raw materials—at least in the long run—but the short-run drop in demand is less than in the case of most manufactured goods). Since Japan is generally regarded as poorly endowed with raw materials and heavily reliant on their import, this logic becomes an explanation for the low level of manufactured imports.

This logic is flawed. No economic theory justifies this simple notion of budget constraints on buying manufactured imports. Nations can run prolonged surpluses or deficits on international trade. The story of Japan in the 1980s and 1990s was one of continuous trade surpluses, implying that the nation was exporting more than enough to pay for imports of all kinds. Thus the lack of raw materials is not a convincing explanation for Japan's low level of manufactured imports.

Another way the same argument could be phrased is that the nation's current-account and trade surplus or deficit are determined by macroeconomic factors. Given the size of the surplus, and given global demand for the nation's exports, then the level of imports is determined and the inelastic demand for raw materials will shape the level of manufactured imports. But this does not save the budget constraint argument. A nation's trade surplus is a net figure—Japan could have the same trade surplus with a low level of both imports and exports or a high level, so long as the difference between them is the same. If Japan's exports were seriously constrained by trade barriers in the rest of the world, imports would also be constrained (everything else being equal). But the notion of serious binding constraints on Japan's global exports does not reflect reality, even though some of its exports to some markets have been restrained at certain times (such as auto-mobile exports to the United States in the 1981–85 period). Nor does the causality necessarily flow from exogenous macroeconomic factors (such as savings and investment), to the current-account and trade balances, to the level of manufactured imports. In a more open market, in which manufac-tured imports were higher, the rest of the variables could well shift to accommodate the higher demand for imports.[8]

Furthermore, this logic of constrained manufactured imports supposes that nations have no choice on the import of raw materials if they have an absolute lack of domestic endowment. This ignores possibilities for substi-tution, conservation, and imports of manufactured goods using the raw material (such as importing aluminum products rather than bauxite). Even nations with a lack of major raw materials such as oil find ways to adjust their import of it given their additional desire to import manufactured goods. The short-term price elasticity of raw materials may be low, but the long-term price elasticity is higher because of these possible means for adjustment. In Japan, from the early postwar period through at least the mid-1980s, import policies were skewed in favor of raw material imports. Whereas markets might have produced more imports in the form of man-ufactures embodying raw materials, government policy worked against this outcome.[9]

Another frequent rebuttal to the conclusion that manufactured imports are unusually low is that the ratio of manufactured imports to total imports has increased in Japan from the beginning of the 1980s to the mid-1990s, and that this change demonstrates increased manufactured import pene-tration.[10] This hypothesis is illogical since the denominator is total imports rather than any measure of the economy, but for the sake of argument, consider what has happened to this ratio. In 1980 manufactured imports were only 22 percent of total imports (with the rest being raw materials and agricultural products), but the ratio almost tripled to 63 percent by 1996.[11] This ratio is a function of both a real rise in manufactured imports and the price of raw materials. Japan is not more open just because the price of raw materials falls and, therefore, the relative share of manufactures in total imports rises. When oil prices rose sharply in the 1970s, the share of raw materials in total imports rose. As a result, manufactured goods repre-sented 30 percent of total imports in 1973 but only 22 percent in 1980. Then during the decade of the 1980s the price of raw materials fell, especially for oil. This trend was furthered by the sharp appreciation of the yen after 1985, making raw materials even less expensive in yen terms. Taking just imports of crude petroleum, the yen cost per kiloliter dropped 70 percent between 1980 and 1996. Japan imported 3 percent more crude petroleum in 1996 than in 1980 but spent only 30 percent as much to do so. Had the yen-denominated cost of petroleum been as high in 1996 as in 1980, then the ratio of manufactured imports to total imports would have been 51 percent rather than 63 percent, all else equal.[12] Adjusting in similar fashion for yen-denominated price changes in several other major raw materials brings the ratio of manufactures to total imports down to 46 percent. This is still much higher than the 22 percent value of 1980 but demonstrates the importance of price changes in affecting the nominal ratio.

An alternative measure of import penetration popular with the Japanese government is imports per capita rather than per unit of GDP or per unit of apparent consumption of manufactures. On a per capita basis, for example, Japanese individuals import as much or more from America as Americans import from Japan. Therefore, according to this logic, the Japanese market must be as open as American markets despite the data on the ratio of imports to GDP. As expressed in one comparison, Japan's average annual per capita imports from the United States in the 1990–92 period were $380, while the reverse flow (average annual American purchases from Japan) were just slightly lower at $376.[13] Japan's Ministry of Foreign Affairs has adopted this approach in its public relations effort to explain the relatively low level of manufactured imports in Japan. According to their analysis for 1993, per capita imports into Japan from the United States came to $444, while the reverse flow was a slightly lower $421.[14] If one believes that this comparison is sensible, then the bilateral U.S.-Japan trade imbalance is simply a result of the differing size of the populations.

If this simple logic were true, then all nations with large populations would be condemned to run trade deficits with the rest of the world (since most or all of their trading partners would have smaller populations). As appealing as the notion might be that "fairness" consists of equality of per capita imports, international trade simply does not work this way. Nations with large populations tend to import less on a per capita basis than those with small populations. The same is true of geographical area; large continental nations tend to import less on a per capita basis than smaller ones. And nations with higher per capita income levels import more than those with lower incomes. Equality of per capita import levels would actually lead to a profoundly unfair or inefficient outcome. Small nations want or need to import more goods on a per capita basis to make up for the small size of their manufacturing sectors (which, as discussed earlier, cannot produce as wide a range of products as efficiently as the manufacturing sectors of large nations). They would be denied this opportunity if global trade were to operate on the basis of equality of per capita imports.

As a nation with a small geographical area, smaller population than the United States, and higher nominal per capita income level than the United States in 1993, Japan's per capita imports from the United States into Japan should have been much higher than the reverse flow. The Japanese government's use of this notion of per capita import equality as part of its public relations campaign is simply wrong. Besides, one could equally make the argument for equality of per capita exports. Shouldn't nations have the right to export equal per capita amounts to one another? Japan's per capita exports to the United States are about four times higher than the reverse flow. Both ideas are equally silly, and the Japanese government should desist from using the per capita import argument.

The fact remains that imports are a function of a variety of economic factors. Careful studies that have attempted to explain imports as a share of GDP as a function of these factors have generally found Japan to be an outlier on the low side. That is, population size, geographical area, natural resource endowment, distance from markets, and level of per capita income cannot fully explain the low level of manufactured imports in the Japanese economy.[15] Since the import penetration level in Japan was the same in the mid-1990s as in 1980, this conclusion remained in the mid-1990s. The 1994–96 import increase narrowed the gap between Japan and other countries modestly. However, to view this change optimistically, the increases would have to be only the beginning of a sustained increase in the penetration of foreign manufactures. With a depreciating yen after the spring of 1995, and then a descent into recession in 1997–98, the prognosis was not good.

Intra-Industry Trade

Intra-industry trade refers to the export and import of products within industry categories. The simple theory of comparative advantage in international trade states that nations will export products of those industries in which they have a comparative advantage relative to other nations, and import products in industries in which they have a comparative disadvantage. Developing countries with abundant labor export labor-intensive products and import capital- and technology-intensive ones, while advanced industrial nations do the reverse. But the actual pattern of international trade demonstrates that nations also both export and import products within relatively narrow industry categories, seemingly at odds with the prediction of comparative advantage theory.

The theoretical reasons for why such trade occurs were addressed in *Japan's Unequal Trade*.[16] Principally the explanation involves product differentiation (not all products within an industry are identical) and economies of scale. Industries within a country exposed to international trade cede certain parts of the product range to their foreign competitors, and by concentrating on a narrower range of products themselves, achieve economies of scale that enable them to successfully export those products to the home countries of their competitors. The theory of intra-industry trade does not negate comparative advantage; capital-intensive, high-wage countries do concentrate in capital-intensive industries requiring skilled labor and import low-skill, labor-intensive products. But intra-industry trade explains why so much of the world's trade is among nations that have similar endowments of labor and capital.

Economists have also discovered that intra-industry trade varies in relatively predictable ways. Larger nations and nations with higher levels of per capita income tend to engage in more intra-industry trade, and such trade also rises as trade barriers fall. Higher levels of income enable people to demand and afford wider varieties of goods or indulge in brand-name products. And larger nations (in terms of population) are also likely to have wider variations in consumer taste. Falling trade barriers imply that consumers can achieve their desire for a broader range of differentiated products through increased imports. This story has emphasized consumer goods, but something similar can occur for industrial products, with rising demand for specialized equipment or components that must be met with imports as the manufacturing sector becomes larger or more sophisticated.

Japan's Unequal Trade, however, demonstrates that these characterizations of intra-industry trade behavior did not apply to Japan's experience from 1970 to the mid-1980s. Japan was characterized by very low levels of intra-industry trade that did not rise appreciably as the nation became more developed, and as official trade barriers fell. Therefore, intra-industry trade was one important dimension in which Japan's behavior differed from other nations in the 1980s in a way likely to generate negative reactions among its trading partners.

The conclusions of *Japan's Unequal Trade* were criticized by both Japanese academics and government officials who claimed that economic factors could explain low levels of intra-industry trade. The Japanese government endeavored to contradict evidence that Japan was "different," or that statistical data implied Japanese markets were more difficult to gain access to than has been true in other countries. At one level, this effort meant denial of the validity of specific trade complaints. At a broader level, it meant analyzing intra-industry trade. Mitsuo Hosen, a career official of the Ministry of International Trade and Industry (MITI) was the principal analyst working on this issue.[17] Hosen acknowledged that Japan engaged in far less intra-industry trade than most other industrial nations and attempted to explain the differences through variations in factor endowment. As noted above, economists have long argued that the tendency to engage in intra-industry trade will increase with the size of the economy and with increasing similarity in factor endowment (since, for example, nations that have similar capital intensities are likely to be competitive in roughly the same manufacturing industries). He then attempted to demonstrate through econometric analysis that another aspect of factor endowment—the relative lack of land and energy raw materials—explained Japan's low intra-industry trade patterns. Kazumasa Iwata, an economist at the University of Tokyo, basically supports the points made by Hosen in a somewhat different analysis.[18]

The analyses of both Hosen and Iwata are seriously flawed, though for somewhat different reasons. First, Hosen estimated his equations with a group of only ten countries. This is an extraordinarily small sample size with which to estimate an equation. With only ten observations and four independent variables, the equations have only six degrees of freedom, quite low for any serious econometric exercise. Furthermore, the small sample size relative to the large number of countries in the world opens the way for an arbitrary, biased sample.

Second, Hosen chose to measure intra-industry trade across all traded products rather than just manufactured goods. All economists agree that land and energy endowment are critical determinants of whether a nation imports or exports agricultural and energy products. Therefore, it is not at all surprising that he finds much of the low level of Japan's intra-industry trade is because of low endowment of land and energy. His finding was enhanced by having included in the small sample of countries in the equation two that are at the extreme ends of the spectrum in per capita land endowment—Japan (with a low ratio of land per person) and Australia (an entire continent with a small population). For energy endowment, Hosen focuses on petroleum. Since crude petroleum is only imported, producing no intra-industry trade, the sizable share of oil imports in Japan's overall trade structure necessarily pulls down the measurement of intra-industry trade. Furthermore, the increased share of oil in total Japanese imports in the 1970s because of crude oil price increases explains why the measurement of intra-industry trade fell. Hosen's analysis is factually correct but answers an uninteresting question—the variation in the level of intra-industry trade across all sectors including raw materials. No one would challenge the notion of low intra-industry trade for raw materials since product differentiation is low. The important question is manufactures. A lack of land and energy resources does not explain the large variations between the trade patterns of Japan and other countries in manufactured goods. Manufactured products are not land intensive, and energy intensity applies mainly to certain basic manufactures (such as aluminum refining). The puzzle for Japan is why the economy exhibits less intra-industry trade within the manufacturing sector.

Iwata tries to come to grips with this more significant question, but his approach is flawed too. He argues that energy intensity does vary across manufacturing industries and can explain the lack of intra-industry trade. This leads him to the conclusion that a nation with a low endowment of energy will have less overall intra-industry trade because its lack of competitiveness in energy-intensive industries leads to lopsided imports of products in those industries. This is akin to saying that industrialized nations engage in extensive intra-industry trade among themselves, but less so with developing nations, with whom trade patterns reflect the broader comparative advantages in capital- or labor-intensive products. In similar fashion, an industrial nation might exhibit a pattern of broad comparative advantage rather than intra-industry trade driven by its comparative disadvantage in energy-intensive products.

This model sounds as though it might be a rational explanation for Japan's low intra-industry trade, but it makes two major mistakes. First, energy is not a factor endowment like labor, capital, or land. Those factors are geographically specific; the labor force, for example, is largely confined to those people who grew up in Japan (especially with the limited inward migration of foreign workers to Japan). But major forms of energy are globally traded commodities (oil, natural gas, uranium). If Japan does not have petroleum, it can buy what it needs on global markets at a global price. The high prices in Japan for some forms of energy do not reflect a lack of domestic primary energy reserves. Japan has high electricity costs, for example, but this pricing has more to do with inefficiency and high profits protected by government regulation than with high petroleum costs. Similarly, Japan has high gasoline prices, owing to a combination of high gasoline taxes and very inefficient domestic refineries. Therefore, insertion of an energy variable in equations to explain national variations in intra-industry trade for manufactures is unconvincing.

Second, Iwata's model assumes that, as an energy-deficient nation, Japan should be a heavy importer of energy-intensive goods. But other than aluminum ingots, one is hard pressed to find examples where Japan is a heavy importer. Cement, steel, and other energy-intensive processing industries are characterized by both low imports and extensive exports (even though domestic prices are often higher than on global markets).[19]

Even if the conclusion stands that Japan's pattern of intra-industry trade in the 1980s was unusually low, what has happened in the 1990s? Much has occurred in the decade since the mid-1980s—further trade negotiations, discussion of deregulation, and further yen appreciation in the mid-1990s. Did any of this have an impact on intra-industry trade?

Intra-industry trade is commonly measured by a statistic scaled to vary from zero to one hundred. If a country exports a product but does not import it at all (or the reverse), then no intra-industry trade occurs, and the index number is zero. If a country exports exactly the same amount of a product as it imports, then complete intra-industry trade occurs and the index number equals one hundred. These index numbers for each industry can be summed across all products or industries, weighted by the importance of each industry to total trade, to produce an average index number that also varies between zero and one hundred. Further detail on the calculation of this statistic is contained in appendix A.

Consider first the comparison between the United States and Japan over the 1988 to 1996 period, shown in figure 2-5. U.S. global trade was characterized by high and gradually rising levels of intra-industry trade with the overall index number for intra-industry trade drifting up from 71.5 in 1990 to 75.1 by 1996. This increase for the United States occurred on a slow but rather steady basis. For Japan no consistent change occurred from 1989 through 1994, after an earlier brief jump from 1985 to 1988.[20] From a level of 33.2 in 1989, the index number was 35.8 in 1994. However, it then rose sharply in 1995 and 1996, reaching 46.9. Something new and different was occurring, reducing some of the gap between Japan and the United States. This sudden, substantial upward movement in the index number for intra-industry trade raises two dilemmas in interpretation. First, was the reduction in the gap between Japan and the United States significant, or should emphasis remain on its continued existence? Second, was this two-

Figure 2-5. *United States and Japan, Intra-Industry Trade*

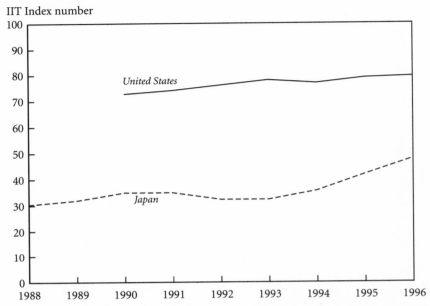

IIT Index number

Source: Author's calculations based on OECD, *International Trade by Commodities Statistics, H.S. Rev. 1988–1996,* on CD-ROM.

year jump the beginning of a trend, or would the economic recession and weaker yen of 1997–98 reverse some of the gains? The change was certainly a positive development and may reflect a structural improvement in access to Japanese markets, but a longer upward trend would be necessary to make Japanese trade patterns less distinctive.

Despite the upward shift, Japan still had a level of intra-industry trade below that of most other countries. Table 2-1 presents intra-industry trade index numbers for all countries reported by the Organization for Economic Cooperation and Development (OECD) in 1988 and 1996. Of all thirty countries reported by the OECD for 1996, only five others had an overall IIT index number lower than Japan's: Australia (41), Greece (36), Iceland (19), New Zealand (34), and Turkey (40). These five countries can be relatively easily explained. They have small populations that limit the scope of the manufacturing sector (especially Iceland), have abundant natural resource processing industries (with less product differentiation and, therefore, low intra-industry trade) that have developed at the expense of other

Table 2-1. *Intra-Industry Trade Index Numbers*

Country	IIT index number 1988	IIT index number 1996
Australia	28.2	41.2
Belgium/Luxembourg	79.3	85.8
Canada	66.0	68.5
China	. . .	55.5
Czech Republic	. . .	75.2
Denmark	16.4	77.1
Finland	55.2	63.1
France	85.6	89.0
Germany	69.3	75.5
Greece	34.0	35.5[a]
Hong Kong	. . .	86.4
Hungary	. . .	74.3[a]
Iceland	13.2	19.0[a]
Ireland	70.6	66.8
Italy	70.4	72.9
Japan	31.0	6.9
Korea	. . .	59.3[a]
Mexico	. . .	77.2
Netherlands	81.9	88.1[a]
New Zealand	. . .	33.5[a]
Norway	50.7	57.1
Poland	. . .	50.8[a]
Portugal	41.0	60.0
Spain	71.8	76.5
Sweden	77.7	74.2
Switzerland	70.7	70.6
Taiwan	. . .	64.8
Turkey	. . .	40.3[a]
United Kingdom	78.8	86.6
United States	72.0[b]	75.1

Source: Author's calculations based on Organization for Economic Cooperation and Development, *International Trade by Commodities Statistics, H.S. Rev. 21* (Paris, 1997), and *1988–1996* (1997), data on CD-ROM.

a. 1995 IIT index number.

b. 1990 IIT index number.

domestic manufacturing industries (especially Australia), have an over-whelming comparative advantage in agriculture that developed at the expense of manufacturing (such as Denmark or New Zealand), have strong protectionist policies (Turkey), or are still low-income countries with poorly developed manufacturing sectors (such as Greece and Turkey). None of these characteristics applies to Japan, a large, mature economy with a well-developed manufacturing sector and a large population. These are all characteristics that should push Japan's intra-industry trade to higher levels but have not.

This point can be explored more rigorously. As noted earlier, the eco-nomic theory of intra-industry trade argues that the propensity to engage in such trade rises as population increases and as industrial development reaches higher levels. An analysis by an Australian economist using an econo-metric model testing these propositions with data from the late 1980s con-cluded that factor endowment could not fully account for Japan's low intra-industry trade. His analysis involved levels of intra-industry trade among the 231 bilateral pairs of nations reported in OECD, pooling these cross-section observations over time (1965–85). The results confirmed the usual hypothe-ses about intra-industry trade, which rose as factor endowments converged and as nations grew in economic size. Other factors, including common land borders and membership in the then-European Economic Community, were also important in increasing intra-industry trade. He also includes both land and natural resource endowment among the factor endowment variables (with greater difference in land and resource endowment between a pair of nations reducing intra-industry trade as Hosen and Iwata argued). However, even accounting for all these possible sources of variation in intra-industry trade, intra-industry trade in bilateral pairs involving Japan remained signif-icantly lower than for other countries.[21]

Was this still true in the mid-1990s? Consider the following simple test on the data in table 2-1. GDP per capita provides a rough proxy of eco-nomic development and complexity of manufacturing sectors (some mod-els, such as the one by Hosen discussed earlier, attempt to measure the ratios of capital to labor, but such efforts are fraught with major measurement problems that offset the added theoretical sophistication of the model). Then:

$$Intra\text{-}Industry\ Trade = f(population,\ GDP/population).[22]$$

This simple model can be modified to include dummy variables for the distinctiveness of Japan. The index of intra-industry trade is the dependent variable, with the log of population, log of GDP per capita, and a dummy variable for Japan as the independent variables. The resulting equation does suggest that population size and per capita GDP are not sufficient to explain the low level of intra-industry trade for Japan in 1996. The dummy coefficient to identify Japan is negative as expected and is significantly different from zero at a 98 percent confidence level.

These results help explain why dissatisfaction and tension concerning access to Japanese markets continued in the early to mid-1990s. Not only was the pattern of intra-industry trade much lower than for the United States, the flat trend through the early 1990s was in conflict with patterns elsewhere and with American expectations about the nature of needed change in Japan. Even in 1995 Japan appeared to be distinctively below the level of intra-industry trade expected for a nation of its size and industrial sophistication. These differences affect what businesses experience in the market. Although even successful American firms face substantial competition at home from imports, and compete in other countries on a somewhat similar basis, they continued to face a situation in Japan that involved a more lop-sided imbalance, generally in the form of markets with high exports and low imports. This is the kind of market outcome that leads to business frustration.

At the bilateral level, the picture concerning relations with Japan is more complex. A high level of intra-industry trade characterizes U.S. trade with major European countries, as shown in figure 2-6. At the end of the 1980s, intra-industry trade with Japan (31.7) was only half the level of that with these European nations, and little change occurred in the pattern with Japan until 1994. The sudden and strong upward trend with Japan for 1994–96 (reaching 47.6 in 1996) brought the level of intra-industry trade closer to the level with the European countries, which ranged from 67 to 72 in 1996. This narrowing of the gap suggests that something was happening to alter the structure of bilateral trade, paralleling the trend in Japan's global trade. The substantial increase in 1995 and 1996 may help explain why the Clinton administration chose to place less emphasis on trade negotiations with Japan in its second term. If the rise in bilateral intra-industry trade meant that American firms experienced rising sales in Japan and a less lopsided trade pattern, they would have been less interested in seeking U.S. government negotiating assistance.

Even with the improvement in the level of intra-industry trade with Japan, the situation by 1996 was still somewhat discouraging. Consider the increase in U.S.-Korean intra-industry trade, which rose steadily from 36.4

Figure 2-6. *U.S. Bilateral Intra-Industry Trade, 1989–96*

Intra-industry trade index number

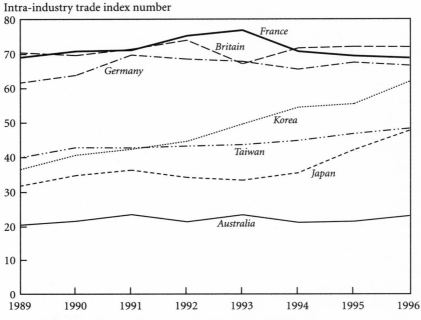

Source: Author's calculations based on data from *World Trade Atlas* database.

in 1989 to 61.8 by 1996. In this case, rapid economic growth in Korea (broadening the manufacturing base in a way to enable more opportunities for product differentiation and two-way product flow) and reduction in trade and investment barriers made a much stronger difference in the pattern of trade than in the case of Japan. Furthermore, even in 1996, the level of intra-industry trade with Japan was only as high as that with Taiwan (48.2), a country with a population only 17 percent the size of that of Japan, a less-developed manufacturing sector, much lower per capita income levels, and obvious import and investment barriers.[23] These are all factors that should imply a lower level of bilateral intra-industry trade than in the case of U.S.-Japan trade. If the increase in intra-industry trade between the United States and Japan were to level off after the increases in 1995 and 1996, therefore, American firms would eventually notice once again the disparity in their experience in Japan compared with other nations.

How much of the change with Japan occurred simply because of a shift in trade in automobiles? Since autos are a large part of two-way trade and were subject to serious trade negotiations intended to make Japan's market more open, much of the increase in measured intra-industry trade between the two countries could possibly have occurred because of this single industry. However, the data imply that the improvement is much broader than this single industry.

At the two-digit industry level, trade in vehicles (HS 87, vehicles, not railway) equaled 23 percent of the total bilateral two-way trade flow in 1996. And this industry category did exhibit a strong increase in intra-industry trade, from a very low 6.7 in 1989 to 24.5 by 1996. All of the change is because of a strong rise in U.S. vehicle exports to Japan (from only $1 billion in 1989 to $4 billion by 1996) while imports from Japan stagnated. The rise in American vehicle exports to Japan was a combination of rising sales by both American firms and the Japanese transplants. Recalculating the bilateral intra-industry trade index number without vehicles, though, still shows a considerable gain in the 1990s (from 39.7 in 1989 to 41.6 in 1994 and 53.4 by 1996). Therefore, the gains in intra-industry trade are certainly broader than just the vehicle industry. Over this period, 30 of 70 two-digit industry categories exhibited rising intra-industry trade levels, including the key industries of machinery (up 6.7 points) and electric machinery (up a large 24.7 points). These data imply, therefore, a rather broad-based change in trade patterns in a direction of a stronger two-way flow of products within industry categories. This movement is encouraging since the automobile sector was so politicized that the improvement in the 1990s could have been a politically motivated aberration from broader trends. Increased exports of vehicles from Japanese transplants back to Japan, for example, appeared to be largely a politically motivated development rather than an economic one.

Another way to consider the impact of intra-industry trade patterns is through the experience of major U.S. export industries. Table 2-2 shows that, in general, the top U.S. exports to the world are in industries where the United States also imports heavily. The table lists, in descending order, the top fifteen U.S. export categories at both two-digit and four-digit industrial classification levels. For each of these categories, the table reports global intra-industry trade index numbers and those for bilateral trade with Japan. These industries exhibit very high intra-industry trade levels on a global basis, indicating that the most successful American export industries have not operated from a protected U.S. market. But some of these exports face a different situation in trade with Japan. Consider the top three exports to Japan. American machinery products exhibit a global intra-industry trade index number of 97, compared with 49 in trade with Japan, while for electric machinery the global index number is 92 compared with 53 bilaterally, and for vehicles the comparison is 70 compared with 25. In all three cases, the lower bilateral intra-industry trade index number results from a flow in which U.S. imports from Japan are much larger than exports. That is, while these industries generate the largest amount of exports to the rest of the world of any industries in the United States, they export relatively low amounts to Japan in comparison to imports. In only a few cases does the generally lower level of intra-industry trade work in the favor of American exporters. The United States imports virtually no wood products from Japan, a situation that, to a lesser degree, characterizes trade in precious stones, paper, and pharmaceutical products.

Two-digit industry categories are quite broad, but the above point is true for more narrowly defined industries too, as shown in the bottom portion of table 2-2. Even at a detailed four-digit HS classification, the categories that generate the largest U.S. exports on a global basis are generally industries where the United States also imports heavily, resulting in high intra-industry trade index values. But of the top fifteen exports, American industries experience higher degrees of intra-industry trade on a global basis than bilaterally with Japan in eleven cases. And for ten out of fifteen categories, bilateral trade with Japan involves imports that are larger than exports. That is, whereas the most successful American exports to the world also face substantial imports, the record with Japan is one of exports that are usually much lower than imports. The most important exceptions are aircraft, aircraft parts, and nonelectrical medical equipment. With aircraft, U.S. industry benefits from this skewed pattern, since Japan did not export aircraft to the United States in 1996. But with aircraft parts, bilateral trade exhibits a higher intra-industry trade index number (mainly because Boeing has chosen to incorporate substantial parts inputs from Japan for its planes) than is the case for global trade.

This comparison can be broadened by a look at the global export patterns of Japan and the United States. Figure 2-7 shows the percentage of the exports of each country by the degree of intra-industry trade in 1995. Each point in the figure indicates the percentage of total manufactured exports exhibiting an intra-industry index number in the range shown on the x axis (where each number on the axis indicates the top of a range; so that 10 indicates a range of greater than five and less than or equal to 10). This depiction of trade gives some notion of how successful export sectors fare; do a nation's exports come mainly in industry categories where the nation also has large imports (producing a high intra-industry trade index number) or not (producing a low index number)?

Figure 2-7 indicates that in 1996 half of Japan's exports are in industries in which the extent of intra-industry trade is 50 or less; relatively few U.S. exports are in industry categories with such low levels of intra-industry trade. For Japan 51 percent of its exports were in industries characterized by a degree of intra-industry trade of 50 or less, whereas only 11 percent of American exports were in industries exhibiting this low a degree of intra-industry trade. In sharp contrast, a high percentage of U.S. exports are in industries with very high levels of intra-industry trade; 71 percent of American exports were in industries showing a degree of intra-industry trade greater than 70 (with 41 percent in the category of 90 or higher), whereas only 6 percent of Japanese exports were in industries exhibiting this high a level of intra-industry trade. This contrast between the two countries is less sharp than a decade earlier, but the distinction remained large in 1996.[24] The general conclusion remains; successful American industries (defined as those producing a significant portion of American exports) also face large imports, while successful Japanese export industries do not.

To see this comparison in the bilateral context, look at figure 2-8. It indicates the contrast between the 1996 U.S. global pattern of trade and its bilateral trade with Japan, using the same separation of exports by ranges of intra-industry trade as in figure 2-7. In sharp contrast to the high share of U.S. global exports in categories with high levels of intra-industry trade, only a small share of U.S. manufactured exports to Japan are in such categories. Only 22 percent of U.S. exports to Japan were in products of industries with intra-industry trade index numbers higher than 70, less than one-third the share of U.S. global exports occurring in industries characterized by intra-industry trade in these high ranges. Similarly, a small portion of bilateral trade was still characterized by very low levels of intra-industry trade (with 21 percent of U.S. exports in categories with a degree of intra-industry trade of 30 or less, in contrast to only 1 percent of U.S. global exports).

Even though figures 2-7 and 2-8 illustrate substantial differences between the trade patterns of Japan and the United States, at least Japan's trade patterns shifted somewhat in the 1988–96 period. Figure 2-9 shows the distribution of Japan's global exports by the level of intra-industry trade in 1988 and 1996. In 1988 the dominant portion of exports was in industries characterized by intra-industry trade levels in an interval of 10 to 30, accounting for 76 percent of all exports. By 1996 the dominant portion of

Table 2-2. Top U.S. Exports

HS[a]	Description	Global			With Japan			Differences (Global-Japan)	Exports >imports?
		Exports	Imports	IIT[b]	Exports	Imports	IIT[b]		
Two-digit industries									
84	Machinery	123.1	130.1	97.2	10.2	31.6	49.0	48.3	No
85	Electrical machinery	97.6	114.6	92.0	9.2	25.3	53.2	38.8	No
87	Vehicles, not railway	56.2	104.4	70.0	4.0	29.0	24.5	45.5	No
88	Aircraft, spacecraft	32.4	7.6	38.2	3.0	0.8	40.7	-2.5	Yes
90	Medical instruments	30.5	23.8	87.6	4.9	7.5	78.4	9.2	No
39	Plastic	20.3	13.0	77.9	1.1	1.5	88.0	-10.1	No
98	Special other	19.7	20.5	98.0	1.1	1.4	89.8	8.2	No
29	Organic chemicals	16.2	16.5	99.1	1.4	2.3	76.4	22.6	No
71	Precious stones, metals	12.2	17.2	82.8	0.6	0.2	49.6	33.2	Yes
48	Paper, paperboard	10.3	11.8	93.1	0.9	0.3	49.0	44.1	Yes
38	Misc. chemical products	8.5	3.4	56.7	1.0	0.9	94.6	-37.9	Yes
73	Iron or steel products	7.5	9.5	88.0	0.3	1.4	33.4	54.7	No
44	Wood	7.3	11.6	77.2	3.3	0.0	0.4	76.8	Yes
30	Pharmaceutical products	5.6	4.9	93.5	0.6	0.3	70.2	23.3	Yes
40	Rubber	5.3	8.1	79.1	0.4	1.4	42.2	37.0	No
Four-digit industries									
8542	Integrated circuits	32.9	33.5	99.1	4.0	7.7	69.0	30.1	No
8471	Computers+components	25.3	39.4	78.2	3.3	9.4	52.1	26.1	No
8708	Auto parts	24.7	20.4	90.4	1.1	6.4	29.2	61.2	No
8802	Powered aircraft; spacecraft	20.2	4.2	34.2	1.5	0.0	0.0	34.2	Yes

8473	Office machine parts	18.7	21.3	93.5	2.3	4.5	67.5	26.0	No
8703	Passenger motor	17.5	66.2	41.8	2.5	20.2	21.7	20.1	No
8803	Aircraft parts	11.9	3.4	44.3	1.5	0.8	68.4	−24.1	Yes
8411	Gas turbines	9.1	6.1	79.9	0.7	0.2	49.6	30.3	Yes
8479	Individual functions[c]	7.6	3.1	57.6	1.2	1.4	90.9	−33.3	No
8431	Nonelectric machinery parts	7.6	2.3	46.1	0.1	0.5	46.8	−0.7	No
9081	N-el med/surg/etc ins[d]	7.2	3.3	62.4	1.4	0.7	68.4	−6.1	Yes
8517	Electric apparatus	6.5	7.2	94.7	0.9	1.3	82.6	12.1	No
8704	Motor trucks	6.0	10.4	73.2	0.3	0.8	50.0	23.2	No
7108	Gold	5.8	2.6	62.5	0.1	0.0	5.6	56.9	Yes
8525	Transmission apparatus[e]	5.4	6.3	91.8	0.4	2.7	23.4	68.5	No

Source: *World Trade Atlas Annual Summary*, U.S. ed. (1989–1996) (Global Trade Information Services, 1997), on CD-ROM.
a. Harmonized system classification.
b. Intra-industry trade index.
c. Machines and mechanical appliances having individual functions.
d. Instruments and appliances for veterinary, medical, surgical, dental work; other electromedical apparatus.
e. Transmission apparatus for radio-telephony radio broadcasting; television camera.

Figure 2-7. *Exports, by Level of Intra-Industry Trade Index*

Percent of total exports

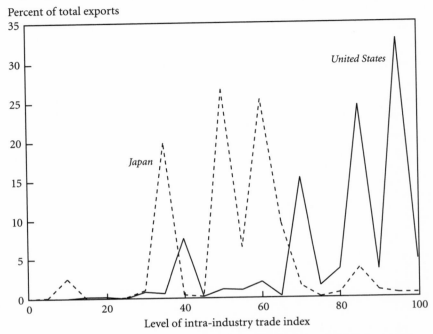

Level of intra-industry trade index

Sources: Author's calculations based on OECD, *International Trade by Commodities Statistics, H.S. Rev. 1, 1988–1996,* on CD-ROM.

Note: Total manufactured exports as used in this figure for calculating the share of exports in each level of intra-industry trade includes 2-digit industry categories 28 through 97, excluding miscellaneous products in categories 98 and 99 (because they do not correspond to the concept of an industry).

exports has shifted upward to an interval of 50 to 60 (accounting for 58 percent of all exports). This shift occurs largely because of increased intra-industry trade in two industries: nonelectric machinery (which rose from an interval of 25–29 in 1988 to 45–49 in 1996) and electric machinery (which rose from an interval of 20–24 to 55–59). These industries include products of great interest from a bilateral standpoint, including computers and semiconductors, but also include many products that Japanese firms moved to overseas production (television sets, video cassette recorders, and other electrical appliances).

What does all this evidence imply? Variations in the extent of intra-industry trade can have many causes. An industry in one country might develop a strong competitive position across a broad range of individual

Figure 2-8. *U.S. Exports, by Intra-Industry Trade Index Intervals*

Percent of exports

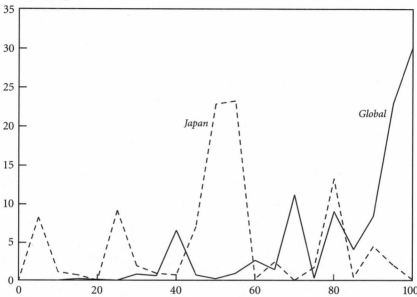

Source: Author's calculations based on data from *World Trade Atlas Annual Summary*, U.S. ed. (Global Trade Information Services, 1997).

products, yielding a low level of intra-industry trade. Some analysts, like Hosen and Iwata, have tried to explain the variation as the result of a strong comparative advantage in all manufacturing. Could Japanese manufacturing have developed such broad international competitiveness across a broad array of industries in such sharp contrast to all other large, mature industrial nations? One could argue that the Japanese economy has a comparative advantage in manufacturing relative to agriculture or services and that the implication of this comparative advantage is an unusually lopsided set of surpluses in manufacturing. For whatever reason, manufacturing (relative to agriculture and services) could have attracted more capital and the most talented managers and engineers. Having done so, foreign manufacturers, even those of other advanced industrial nations such as the United States, cannot compete on price or quality. But is such an explanation plausible?

Figure 2-9. *Japanese Exports, by Intra-Industry Trade Index Intervals*

Percent of total exports

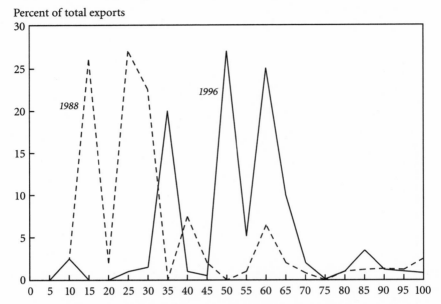

Source: Author's calculations based on OECD, *International Trade by Commodities Statistics, H.S. Rev. 1, 1988–1996,* on CD-ROM.

Note: Total manufactured exports as used for calculating the share of exports on each level of intra-industry trade includes two-digit industry categories 28 through 97, excluding miscellaneous products in categories 98 and 99 (since they do not correspond to the concept of an industry).

If Japanese manufacturing had a broad comparative advantage over all foreign competitors, then one would expect that the ratio of manufactured exports to domestic manufacturing output would be high in international comparison. Figure 2-10 provides evidence on this ratio. The ratio of exports to manufactured output was higher than that of the United States in the 1980s, but below that of major European countries, and the distinction between the United States and Japan was gone in the 1990s. Were it true that Japanese manufacturing had a broad and strong comparative advantage in manufacturing, then this comparison ought to show a more persistent disparity and a ratio closer to that of European nations.

Could Japanese manufactured exports to the world be seriously constrained by protectionism? Some Japanese exports to some countries at some periods of time have been constrained, but it is difficult to believe that global constraints on Japanese products could be so pervasive across prod-

Figure 2-10. *Ratio of Exports of Manufactures to Manufacturing Output*

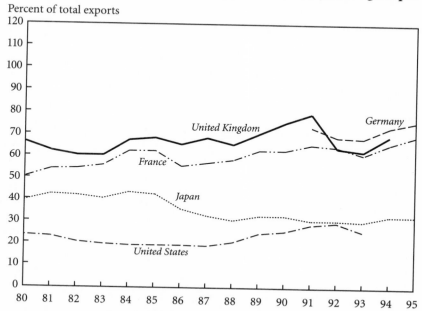

Percent of total exports

Source: Data before 1993 are from World Bank, *World Tables;* and 1993–96 data are from World Bank, *World Development Indicators,* on CD-ROM.

ucts and countries to yield the results in figure 2-10. If protectionism has not seriously constrained Japanese exports, then figure 2-10 implies that Japanese manufacturing does not have a distinctive, broad comparative advantage, especially in the 1990s.

An alternative way to approach this question is through the distribution of exports across industry or product categories. Nations with only a narrow range of competitive products or industries ought to have an export structure in which just a handful of products dominate. Nations with a strong comparative advantage across the whole manufacturing sector ought to have an export structure that is less reliant on only a few products. To be sure, different products or industries have varying global market sizes. Exports of automobiles should be larger than those of telescopes because the global market is much larger. Nevertheless, if Japanese manufacturing had broad comparative advantage, exports ought to be less concentrated on a few products than is the case for other industrial nations (since if Japanese

Figure 2-11. *Concentration of Exports, 1996*

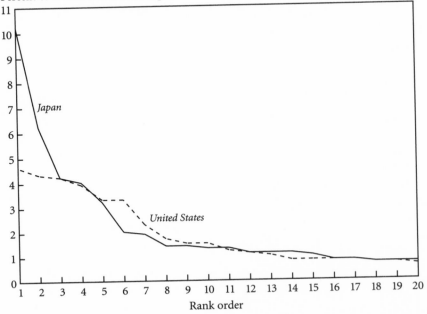

Percent of total manufactured exports

Rank order

Source: Author's calculations based on OECD, *International Trade by Commodities Statistics, H.S. Rev. 1, 1988–1996,* on CD-ROM.

manufacturing had a comparative advantage, the manufacturing sectors of other industrial nations must have a comparative disadvantage, or at least less comparative advantage than Japanese industry). Figure 2-11 addresses this question with a comparison of the export structure of Japan and the United States in 1996.

The data show the percentage of total manufactured exports accounted for by the largest four-digit product categories in four key two-digit industries—nonelectric machinery (two-digit industry category 84), electric machinery (85), automobiles (87), and aircraft (88). Why present the data this way instead of using all four-digit product groups in manufacturing? First, these categories include the ones in which Japanese manufacturing appears to be the most competitive and yield the largest four-digit level exports, and, therefore, provides the most interesting bilateral comparison (with aircraft added because it is an area of large American exports). Second, the electronic OECD trade data set software does not permit easy extraction of all four-digit categories (since they can be viewed only for a single two-digit industry at a time).

What figure 2-11 shows is that at a detailed four-digit product level, Japanese exports are somewhat more concentrated than those of the United States. The top two exports at this level of industry detail account for 16.5 percent of total Japanese manufacturing exports, while the top two American exports acount for 8.9 percent of manufacturing exports. Beyond these top two products, the shares look remarkably similar, leaving a conclusion that Japanese export structure is a bit more concentrated than that of the United States.

This comparison can be put in another way. Just five four-digit product categories account for 25 percent of Japanese manufactured exports, while it takes seven categories to account for 25 percent of American manufactured exports. And twenty-nine categories account for 50 percent of Japanese manufactured exports, while it takes fifty-five categories to reach 50 percent of the total for American manufactured exports. The distinction is somewhat less noticeable when the comparison is more narrowly restricted to the shares of just the subset of manufactured products in this group of four industries. The top three four-digit groups exceed 25 percent of Japanese exports in this set of industries, compared with four for the United States. And for both countries nine four-digit groups account for 50 percent of exports in this subset.

What does all this mean? Two conclusions flow from these data. First, American comparative advantage extends more broadly across manufacturing than does that of Japan. The four leading industries used in this subset account for a smaller share of American manufactured exports than is the case for Japan. Second, within these four leading industry groups, American competitiveness is distributed about as broadly as that of Japan. This provides evidence against the notion of a broad comparative advantage across manufacturing for Japanese industry as an explanation for low intra-industry trade levels.

The far more likely explanation for low intra-industry trade lies in Japanese trade barriers, at least in part. The low level of intra-industry trade in the various comparisons just presented is consistent with the perception of difficult market access in Japan relative to the situation in other countries that is often voiced by American businesses.

The low level of intra-industry trade, and the lack of any rise from 1988 to 1993, is also consistent with the sense of frustration among American businesses and government officials. If businesses see a market situation in Japan that differs sharply from that at home in the United States or in third countries, then they are likely to be frustrated. If their industry is characterized by competition from imports at home and a sense of openness in the markets of other countries as seen through relative balance in exports and imports, then a Japanese market characterized by low imports and high exports is understandably frustrating. Although for any particular industry, the explanation for the situation in the Japanese market may involve ordinary issues (language, consumer taste, cost, and others), the situation often includes perceptions of trade barriers. When firms cannot resolve their market access problems on their own, they go to Washington to seek assistance from government. Therefore, the intra-industry trade analysis helps explain why American business and government frustration was high in the early 1990s.

Nevertheless, the above analysis also demonstrates that some change occurred in Japan in the two years of 1995 and 1996. Some of the most stark differences between Japan and other industrial nations have narrowed. No matter how one analyzes the intra-industry trade data, changes over this short period are evident. This two-year shift suggests that a real structural change may have been under way in the direction of easier market access. This was also a time of an extraordinarily strong value of the yen against the dollar. Along with the many trade negotiations that made the rules of access easier, the rise in the yen may have broken some of the collusive or nationalistic commitments in the market place that had obstructed imports in the past. If that were the case, then the question for the late 1990s was how robust this structural change would be. Would intra-industry trade remain on its higher level, or would the depreciation of the yen from 1995 to 1998 reverse the trends?

Regardless of the answer, the developments in 1995 and 1996 help to explain the decline in the high-profile nature of trade negotiations after 1995. If American firms faced increased sales in Japan, their perception of opportunities and problems was at least temporarily altered. Until they bumped up against another set of barriers or faced declining market share, their frustrations in the Japanese market were eased.

Service Trade

In the past, economists generally analyzed only trade in goods. But trade in service industries has grown rapidly in the past several decades. That trade is sufficiently large that it must be included in any analysis of Japan's trade patterns. If one can argue that American industry has a comparative advantage in international trade in services (relative to manufactures), and if the American firms have been successful in exporting to the Japanese market in these industries, then the focus on only merchandise trade flows would be somewhat misplaced. However, although it is broadly true that the United States has a bilateral surplus in its service sector trade with Japan, many problems of market access exist in this sector too. The surplus exists despite those barriers because of the lack of international competitiveness of most Japanese service sector firms.

The importance of service trade has been recognized by those involved in U.S. policy toward Japan. The Advisory Committee on Trade Policy and Negotiations (ACTPN) private sector committee established to advise the U.S. Trade Representative (USTR) noted in 1993 that "services issues were dealt with in the previous ACTPN report only as adjuncts to 'goods' issues. Yet, as in the United States, services make up the largest share of economic activity in Japan."[25] Besides representing an increasingly important area of economic activity and trade, many bilateral negotiations have concerned service sector industries. In the past decade, bilateral negotiations and agreements have occurred in civil aviation, construction services, computer services, insurance, other financial services, intellectual property rights (patents, trademarks, and copyright protection), legal services, telecommunications services, and the retail sector.

As the list of negotiations suggests, the service sector consists of a wide array of industries. Unlike goods trade, however, the classification of industries is not as detailed, so the kind of intra-industry analysis done in this chapter with manufactured goods trade is not feasible. Indeed, the detail was only recently increased in the Japanese data.

Further complicating the analysis of service sector trade is the fact that trade data do not capture transactions in all service industries. The balance of payments data for services include travel (expenditures by individuals traveling abroad for food, lodging, local transportation, and so on), passenger airfares, other transportation (international freight transportation), royalties and licensing fees, and other private services. "Other" includes separate listings for education, financial services, insurance, telecommunications, business consulting, and other professional or technical services. These categories capture much of U.S. trade with Japan in service sectors, but by no means all. For example, in the amusement park industry, Disney corporation receives all of its earnings from Tokyo Disneyland in the form of royalties and fees (because it has no equity stake), which do appear in the balance of payments data as a service transaction. But if Tokyo Disneyland were a subsidiary of Disney, then its income would appear as repatriated investment earnings. In neither case, though, would the earnings of Disney be visible as an amusement or entertainment industry category since the data are not subdivided in this manner. Furthermore, the meaning of royalty and license payments does not entirely correspond to the common notion of service industry activity since it includes payments to manufacturing firms for product and process technologies. Many other service industries are similar to the amusement park example because the service activity must occur locally. Unlike a manufactured good that can be produced in one country and moved to another, a service often must be "produced" where it is consumed. As a result, the international income flow will appear primarily in the form of either fees and royalties or earnings on investment (depending on the ownership arrangements for overseas operations) rather than as a service sector transaction. Some industries that would fit in this category include financial services, hotels, advertising, personnel supply (Korn Ferry and other management search agencies have offices in Tokyo to deal with the local market), data processing (EDS and other companies have offices in Japan), motion picture theaters (for example, profits earned by Sony Theaters in the United States), video tape rental (Blockbuster is setting up outlets in Japan), commercial sports (Japanese investors own several sports teams in the United States, including Tampa Bay Lightning ice hockey team), auditing (the major American accounting firms have offices in Tokyo to handle local work), and management consulting (A. D. Little and other major consulting firms have offices in Japan).[26]

Even market involvement for merchandise involves this dilemma, since firms can either export from abroad or invest in production locally, as discussed in chapter 3. But this relationship of market participation to investment without generation of a noticeable trade flow is even more characteristic of service industries. As a result, the balance of payments data should be viewed with considerable caution since they provide such incomplete coverage of international activity in service industries.

Reflecting the growing importance of trade in services, Japan has revised the presentation of its balance of payments data, providing more detail and separating investment income from the service sector account. This is a positive step, but none of the new detail is available before 1992. The longer-term picture, therefore, depends on the earlier categories. With these caveats in mind, table 2-3 provides data on Japan's service trade accounts under the former accounting procedures (excluding investment income, which was lumped into service transactions under the old accounting framework but is excluded here since no industry detail is available, and much of those flows represents earnings on manufacturing investments or portfolio financial investments). Overall, Japan has had a rising deficit on its service account. After fluctuating around $12 billion in the first half of the 1980s, the deficit on service industry trade ballooned after 1985. By 1990 the net deficit was $46 billion, and by 1997 it was $54 billion.

What drove this process? The most noticeable element has been the behavior of individual Japanese consumers, who chose to travel abroad in droves (while foreigners did not reciprocate), motivated by the dramatic appreciation of the yen against the dollar since 1985. The net balance on passenger fares and travel went from a small deficit of $4.9 billion in 1980 to $35.1 billion by 1997. Passenger fares and travel receipts (spending by visitors to Japan) rose during this seventeen-year period from $1.1 billion to $6.1 billion, while payments (spending by Japanese on fares and travel abroad) exploded from $6.1 billion in 1996 to $41.3 billion in 1997, with all of the growth after 1985 (eventually stagnating or falling after 1995 because of yen depreciation and economic recession that dampened demand for overseas travel).

One of the implications of these data is that services that might be considered nontradables have become tradable. Hotel rooms, car rentals, taxi fares, and retail store markups are so much lower outside of Japan (including in the United States) that Japanese consumers began to shift their leisure and vacation expenditures abroad. These are industries in which American exports to Japan actually take place in the United States, often with no special effort or recognition that an international transaction is occurring as these travelers spend their money.

To the extent that the balance of payments data reflect overall trends in actual service sector trade, the change over time suggests a rising comparative disadvantage for Japan. In 1980 Japan's service sector exports were 16 percent the size of merchandise exports; by 1997 this level remained virtually unchanged at 16.9 percent. On the import side, service imports in 1980 were 26 percent as large as merchandise imports, while in 1997, they had grown to 40 percent the size of merchandise imports.[27] These data imply some deterioration in Japan's comparative advantage in service industries relative to manufacturing over the course of the 1980s and 1990s. And at 40 percent the size of merchandise imports, services are a sufficiently

Table 2-3. Japan's Service Sector Trade

Billions of U.S. dollars

Item	1980	1981	1982	1983	1984	1985	1986	1987	1988	1989	1990	1991	1992	1993	1994	1995	1996	1997
Receipts (exports)	20.4	24.0	22.8	22.0	23.4	23.4	24.6	30.4	36.9	42.1	43.6	47.9	51.8	56.1	61.3	65.5	67.7	69.3
Transportation	13.0	15.4	13.3	12.2	12.9	12.4	11.3	13.0	15.5	18.1	18.1	19.6	20.3	20.7	22.2	22.6	21.6	21.8
Freight	7.2	8.1	7.2	6.8	7.4	7.4	6.7	7.5	8.2	9.0	9.1	9.9	9.9	9.7	10.3	11.5	13.0	13.5
Passenger	0.5	0.5	0.6	0.6	0.5	0.6	0.7	0.9	1.1	1.5	1.3	1.3	1.3	1.4	1.5	1.7	1.7	1.8
Travel	0.6	0.7	0.8	0.8	1.0	1.1	1.5	2.1	2.9	3.1	3.6	3.4	3.6	3.6	3.5	3.2	4.1	4.3
Other	6.7	7.9	8.7	8.9	9.5	9.8	11.8	15.3	18.5	20.8	22.0	24.9	28.0	31.9	35.6	39.7	42.0	43.2
Royalties	0.4	0.5	0.6	0.6	0.7	0.7	0.9	1.3	1.6	2.0	2.5	2.9	3.1	3.9	5.2	6.0	6.7	7.3
Management fees	0.6	0.7	0.9	0.9	1.1	1.2	1.5	2.3	2.9	3.2	3.6	4.3	5.4	5.4	5.7	n.a.	n.a.	n.a.
Payments (imports)	32.6	36.8	34.3	34.2	35.4	35.4	39.0	52.8	69.2	81.0	89.1	92.3	98.2	101.5	111.6	122.8	130.0	123.4
Transportation	17.3	18.5	16.7	15.5	15.9	15.1	13.9	19.1	23.0	25.9	27.6	29.9	30.3	31.9	34.8	35.9	33.6	31.1
Freight	3.8	3.4	3.4	3.5	3.8	3.7	4.0	6.9	7.3	7.0	7.2	7.8	7.3	8.4	9.5	11.9	17.4	16.4
Passenger	1.5	1.7	1.7	1.7	1.9	1.9	2.3	3.6	4.8	6.5	7.3	7.5	8.6	8.9	9.5	10.2	9.7	8.3
Travel	4.6	4.6	4.1	4.4	4.6	4.8	7.2	10.8	18.7	22.5	24.9	24.0	26.8	26.9	30.7	36.8	37.1	33.0
Other	10.7	13.7	13.5	14.2	14.8	15.5	17.9	22.9	27.6	32.7	36.6	38.5	41.0	42.7	46.1	50.0	59.3	59.4
Royalties	1.3	1.7	1.8	2.0	2.3	2.4	3.2	3.8	5.0	5.3	6.0	6.1	7.2	7.2	8.3	9.4	9.8	9.6
Management fees	1.2	1.5	1.7	1.8	1.9	2.1	2.3	3.4	4.0	4.5	5.4	6.0	5.9	5.7	5.9	n.a.	n.a.	n.a.

Net balance	−12.2	−12.8	−11.6	−12.2	−12.0	−12.0	−14.4	−22.4	−32.3	−39.0	−45.5	−44.4	−46.3	−45.4	−50.3	−57.3	−62.3	−54.1
Transportation	−4.3	−3.2	−3.4	−3.3	−3.0	−2.6	−2.5	−6.1	−7.4	−7.8	−9.5	−10.3	−10.0	−11.2	−12.6	−13.4	−12.0	−9.3
Freight	3.4	4.7	3.9	3.3	3.5	3.7	2.7	0.7	0.9	2.0	1.9	2.1	2.6	1.4	0.8	−0.4	−4.9	−2.9
Passenger	−1.0	−1.2	−1.2	−1.2	−1.3	−1.3	−1.7	−2.7	−3.7	−5.1	−6.0	−6.2	−7.2	−7.5	−8.0	−8.5	−8.0	−6.5
Travel	−3.9	−3.9	−3.4	−3.6	−3.6	−3.7	−5.8	−8.7	−15.8	−19.3	−21.4	−20.5	−23.2	−23.3	−27.2	−33.6	−33.0	−28.6
Other	−3.9	−5.8	−4.8	−5.3	−5.3	−5.7	−6.1	−7.6	−9.1	−11.9	−14.6	−13.6	−13.1	−10.9	−10.5	−10.4	−17.3	−16.2
Royalties	−1.0	−1.2	−1.2	−1.4	−1.6	−1.6	−2.3	−2.5	−3.4	−3.3	−3.6	−3.2	−4.2	−3.3	−3.1	−3.4	−3.2	−2.3
Management fees	−0.6	−0.8	−0.9	−0.9	−0.8	−0.9	−0.8	−1.1	−1.0	−1.3	−1.9	−1.7	−0.5	−0.3	−0.2	n.a.	n.a.	n.a.
Other fees	−2.1	−3.4	−3.1	−2.6	−2.7	−2.5	−2.5	−3.3	−3.7	−5.0	−5.6	−6.4	−6.0	−5.5	−4.7	n.a.	n.a.	n.a.

Source: Bank of Japan, *Balance of Payments Monthly*, various issues.

Note: Before 1995, Japan's balance of payments data were reported on a dollar basis and since 1995 on a yen basis. Data for 1995, 1996, and 1997, are converted based on International Monetary Fund average annual exchange rates.

n.a. Not available

large component of Japan's imports to justify serious attention at a policy level.

Studies of global service trade reach the conclusion that services have been a relatively steady 20 percent of total (merchandise plus services) global trade.[28] If one expresses Japan's service trade in similar fashion, service exports were 14 percent of total merchandise plus service exports, while service imports were 26 percent of total imports in 1997. With exports far below the global average and imports considerably above, the notion of a revealed comparative disadvantage in services is reinforced.

The new detail available for 1992–97 paints a somewhat more nuanced picture of Japan's global service trade. Table 2-4 shows yen- and dollar-denominated service trade under the new accounting framework, providing a more detailed listing of service industries. As with merchandise trade, the strengthening of the yen from 1993 to 1995 made foreign services increasingly price competitive, and Japanese service exports less competitive. On the merchandise side of trade, this shift in price competitiveness contributed to the strong increase in imports discussed earlier. But for services the picture is decidedly mixed. As covered above, travel expenditures show a clear trend, with the net deficit expanding 23 percent from $23.2 billion in 1992 to $28.6 billion by 1997. Air transportation, though, remained in a narrow $4.6 billion to $5.0 billion range from 1992 to 1996 and then shrank suddenly in 1997 to only $3.3 billion as travel demand fell. In the heavily regulated, price-fixing world of international airline transportation to and from Japan, the effect of the exchange rate in the mid-1990s was not as strong as one would expect with a free market. Most of the modest deterioration in the 1992 to 1996 period was actually an exchange-rate effect; Japanese passengers purchased somewhat more transportation on foreign airlines, but because of the movement in the exchange rate, spent fewer yen to do so (¥1.08 trillion in 1992, down very slightly to ¥1.06 trillion in 1996 and a bit more to ¥1.01 trillion in 1997).

Other services are mixed. In dollar terms, Japan's deficit on telecommunications services fell, as did those on financial services, royalties and license fees—all movements opposite the direction one might expect given the appreciation of the yen. Perhaps the demand for foreign technologies in Japan is price inelastic (so that the higher yen did not induce additional licensing transactions). Telecommunications services have been highly regulated, and foreign entry in Japan limited so that the higher yen is not reflected in pricing of international telecommunications services. However, deficits rose (or surpluses shrank) for construction, insurance, "other" business services, and personal, cultural, and recreational services and government services, as expected. Despite the general conclusion of increasing comparative disadvantage in services over time, therefore, the experience of individual sectors varies widely.

One factor that may have helped some Japanese service sector exports is the existence of close business ties with Japanese manufacturing firms investing overseas. Japanese firms building factories abroad tend to use Japanese construction firms, rely on Japanese trading companies, buy insurance from Japanese insurance companies, and conduct business through Japanese financial institutions. As a result, those service exports grow as overseas operations of Japanese manufacturers expand regardless of changes in price competitiveness of Japanese service providers. Presumably there exists an exchange rate at which these loyalties fray (similar to the situation with *keiretsu* parts suppliers in the manufacturing sector), but *keiretsu* ties are certainly an important part in explaining Japanese service sector exports in the 1990s. With more firms relocating manufacturing production abroad as the yen rose in the 1993–95 period, these service exports benefited.

Other service transactions may be affected by intra-corporate transfers. The balance on sea transportation deteriorated (from a deficit of $4.1 billion in 1992 to $7.0 billion in 1996). But some of this movement may represent increased payments to the Panamanian and Liberian subsidiaries of Japanese shipping companies to gain the labor-cost advantage of "flags of convenience," paralleling the trend of American shipping firms. If Japanese firms had not already switched heavily to flags of convenience, then yen appreciation may have included a further shift. Trends on royalties, license fees, and other business services are also muddied since these transactions can be a means to extract payments from subsidiaries abroad other than through repatriation of profits (and thereby lowering tax liabilities abroad). This also helps explain why the deficit on royalties and fees fell when the yen rose.

Nevertheless, the broad trend appears real. Service sector imports in several categories increased more rapidly than exports, and the size of those imports was sufficiently large by the mid-1990s to justify attention. The trend of increasing service imports might be accelerated if barriers were removed or lowered in service industries such as civil aviation (including both passenger and freight), telecommunications, construction, insurance, and financial services.

What happens when service trade is viewed from the American side? Table 2-5 provides data from U.S. balance of payments data. As was done

Table 2-4. Japan's Service Trade—New Balance of Payments Framework

Billions of yen

	Receipts (exports)						Payments (imports)						Net balance					
	1992	1993	1994	1995	1996	1997	1992	1993	1994	1995	1996	1997	1992	1993	1994	1995	1996	1997
Total	6208	5916	5958	6157	7366	8388	11779	10696	10856	11547	14145	14931	-5571	-4780	-4898	-5390	-6779	-6542
Transportation	2338	2103	2074	2123	2350	2640	3438	3205	3233	3379	3656	3760	-1100	-1103	-1159	-1256	-1307	-1120
Sea transport	1592	1402	1359	1394	1570	1754	2112	2002	2037	2166	2327	2473	-520	-600	-678	-772	-757	-719
Freight	1087	923	871	891	1209	1396	824	815	834	956	1713	1821	262	108	37	-65	-504	-425
Air transport	746	701	715	729	777	884	1326	1203	1196	1213	1324	1278	-580	-502	-481	-484	-547	-394
Passenger	167	153	155	157	184	223	1083	986	975	961	1059	1009	-916	-833	-820	-804	-875	-786
Freight	172	157	176	187	206	240	102	111	132	158	177	167	71	46	44	28	28	73
Other	407	391	384	385	387	421	141	107	90	94	88	102	265	284	295	291	300	319
Travel	455	394	355	305	445	524	3396	2976	3132	3464	4033	3989	-2941	-2582	-2776	-3160	-3588	-3465
Business	116	119	111	98	134	152	594	547	579	693	801	771	-478	-429	-468	-595	-668	-619
Personal	339	275	245	207	311	372	2803	2429	2553	2772	3232	3218	-2463	-2154	-2308	-2565	-2920	-2846
Other	3416	3420	3529	3730	4571	5225	4945	4515	4491	4703	6456	7181	-1529	-1095	-962	-974	-1884	-1957
Telecommunication	24	24	48	47	150	165	101	82	81	80	203	208	-76	-58	-32	-32	-53	-43
Construction	614	541	508	620	645	950	284	235	238	302	524	660	331	306	270	318	121	290
Insurance	-22	8	37	28	53	42	114	210	263	235	208	246	-136	-202	-226	-207	-155	-204
Financial	18	26	19	29	309	224	141	128	58	44	324	324	-123	-102	-39	-14	-16	-100
Computer and information					133	171					266	422					-133	-251
Royalties and license fees	388	430	529	567	726	884	911	800	848	888	1068	1163	-523	-370	-318	-321	-343	-279
Other business services	2198	2203	2220	2302	2391	2619	3248	2913	2863	3003	3590	3861	-1050	-710	-643	-700	-1199	-1242
Personal, cultural, recreation	12	10	11	13	19	28	57	58	49	52	132	132	-44	-48	-38	-39	-112	-103
Government	183	178	156	123	146	141	90	90	92	101	140	166	93	88	63	22	6	-25

	Billions of U.S. dollars[a]																	
Total	49.0	53.2	58.3	65.5	67.7	69.3	93.0	96.2	106.2	122.8	130.0	123.4	−44.0	−43.0	−47.9	−57.3	−62.3	−54.1
Transportation	18.5	18.9	20.3	22.6	21.6	21.8	27.1	28.8	31.6	35.9	33.6	31.1	−8.7	−9.9	−11.3	−13.4	−12.0	−9.3
Sea transport	12.6	12.6	13.3	14.8	14.4	14.5	16.7	18.0	19.9	23.0	21.4	20.4	−4.1	−5.4	−6.6	−8.2	−7.0	−5.9
Freight	8.6	8.3	8.5	9.5	11.1	11.5	6.5	7.3	8.2	10.2	15.7	15.1	2.1	1.0	0.4	−0.7	−4.6	−3.5
Air transport	5.9	6.3	7.0	7.7	7.1	7.3	10.5	10.8	11.7	12.9	12.2	10.6	−4.6	−4.5	−5.1	−5.1	−5.0	−3.3
Passenger	1.3	1.4	1.5	1.7	1.7	1.8	8.5	8.9	9.5	10.2	9.7	8.3	−7.2	−7.5	−8.0	−8.5	−8.0	−6.5
Freight	1.4	1.4	1.7	2.0	1.9	2.0	0.8	1.0	1.3	1.7	1.6	1.4	0.6	0.4	0.4	0.4	0.3	0.6
Other	3.2	3.5	3.8	4.1	3.6	3.5	1.1	1.0	0.9	1.0	0.8	0.8	2.1	2.6	2.9	3.1	2.8	2.6
Travel	3.6	3.5	3.5	3.2	4.1	4.3	26.8	26.8	30.6	36.8	37.1	33.0	−23.2	−23.2	−27.2	−33.6	−33.0	−28.6
Business	0.9	1.1	1.1	1.0	1.2	1.3	4.7	4.9	5.7	7.4	7.4	6.4	−3.8	−3.9	−4.6	−6.3	−6.1	−5.1
Personal	2.7	2.5	2.4	2.2	2.9	3.1	22.1	21.8	25.0	29.5	29.7	26.6	−19.4	−19.4	−22.6	−27.3	−26.8	−23.5
Other	27.0	30.8	34.5	39.7	42.0	43.2	39.0	40.6	43.9	50.0	59.3	59.4	−12.1	−9.9	−9.4	−10.4	−17.3	−16.2
Telecommunication	0.2	0.2	0.5	0.5	1.4	1.4	0.8	0.7	0.8	0.8	1.9	1.7	−0.6	−0.5	−0.3	−0.3	−0.5	−0.4
Construction	4.9	4.9	5.0	6.6	5.9	7.9	2.2	2.1	2.3	3.2	4.8	5.5	2.6	2.8	2.6	3.4	1.1	2.4
Insurance	−0.2	0.1	0.4	0.3	0.5	0.3	0.9	1.9	2.6	2.5	1.9	2.0	−1.1	−1.8	−2.2	−2.2	−1.4	−1.7
Financial	0.1	0.2	0.2	0.3	2.8	1.8	1.1	1.1	0.6	0.5	3.0	2.7	−1.0	−0.9	−0.4	−0.2	−0.1	−0.8
Computer and information					1.2	1.4					2.4	3.5					−1.2	−2.1
Royalties and license fees	3.1	3.9	5.2	6.0	6.7	7.3	7.2	7.2	8.3	9.4	9.8	9.6	−4.1	−3.3	−3.1	−3.4	−3.2	−2.3
Other business services	17.4	19.8	21.7	24.5	22.0	21.6	25.6	26.2	28.0	31.9	33.0	31.9	−8.3	−6.4	−6.3	−7.4	−11.0	−10.3
Personal, cultural, recreation	0.1	0.1	0.1	0.1	0.2	0.2	0.5	0.5	0.5	0.5	0.5	1.1	−0.4	−0.4	−0.4	−0.4	−1.0	−0.9
Government	1.4	1.6	1.5	1.3	1.3	1.2	0.7	0.8	0.9	1.1	1.3	1.4	0.7	0.8	0.6	0.2	0.1	−0.2

Source: Bank of Japan, *Balance of Payments Monthly*, no. 366 (January 1997), and no. 382 (May 1998), pp. 9, 10, 13, 14, 17, 18, in both issues. For exchange rate, IMF, *International Financial Statistics*.

a. Conversion based on IMF average annual exchange rates.

Table 2-5. *U.S. Trade in Services*

Billions of dollars

	Global			With Japan		
Year	Exports	Imports	Net balance	Exports	Imports	Net balance
1986	86.4	81.8	4.6	n.a.	n.a.	n.a.
1987	98.6	92.3	6.3	n.a.	n.a.	n.a.
1988	111.1	100.0	11.1	14.4	9.0	5.5
1989	127.2	104.2	23.0	17.2	8.9	8.3
1990	147.9	120.0	27.9	19.4	10.1	9.3
1991	164.3	121.2	43.1	24.7	12.7	12.0
1992	177.0	119.6	57.4	26.1	13.5	12.6
1993	186.4	125.7	60.7	27.4	14.1	13.4
1994	201.4	136.2	65.2	30.4	15.1	15.3
1995	219.8	146.0	73.8	34.5	15.0	19.5
1996	238.8	156.0	82.8	33.7	14.2	19.5
1997	258.3	170.5	87.8	34.6	15.5	19.1

Sources: For U.S. data, Department of Commerce, *Survey of Current Business,* vol. 78 (July 1998), p. 69; and for Japan data, *Survey of Current Business,* various issues.
n.a. Not available.

with the Japanese, these data are exclusive of repatriated earnings of foreign investments since they are not necessarily transactions in service industries. Before 1986 American statistics were widely considered to underestimate service sector trade transactions (owing to faulty survey techniques). A major effort to revise the data collection procedures began in 1988, with a sharp upward jump in measured transactions starting in 1986.[29] Because of this revision in measurement techniques, compatibility of pre-1986 numbers with those from 1986 to the present is questionable. Therefore, table 2-5 includes data only for the 1986–97 period. U.S. service exports to the world rose from $86.4 billion in 1986 to $258.3 billion by 1997. With Japan, U.S. service exports rose from $14.4 billion in 1988 to $34.6 billion by 1997.

With rapid growth of both global and bilateral service exports, they became more significant relative to the size of merchandise exports. On a global basis, the U.S. ratio of service exports to merchandise exports rose from 22 percent to 38 percent from 1988 to 1997. Meanwhile, in U.S. bilateral trade with Japan, the same ratio rose from 38.8 percent in 1988 to almost 54 percent by 1997. This is a startling change.[30]

Furthermore, trade in services has been an area of growing U.S. global and bilateral surplus. On a global basis, the U.S. surplus on private services rose from $19 billion in 1988 to nearly $83 billion by 1997. On a bilateral basis with Japan, the surplus jumped from $6 billion in 1988 to $19 billion by 1997.

Do these data imply that the United States has a comparative advantage in service industries relative to manufactures? Yes. Do they imply that Japanese markets (and global markets) are open to American exports in service industries since U.S. bilateral exports and surpluses expanded rapidly? No.

American success in some service industries has little to do with conventional notions of market access barriers. Two important areas of expanding American surplus with Japan have been education and travel, brought about by an explosion of Japanese travel to the United States after 1985, and a similar jump in the number of Japanese studying at American universities. This major shift was a product of an increasing sense of affluence in Japanese society (with travel abroad a highly income-elastic good), movements in the exchange rate with strong yen appreciation after 1985 (making Japanese travel and education in the United States less expensive for Japanese, and travel or education in Japan more expensive for Americans) combined with a high price elasticity of demand for foreign travel by Japanese individuals, and shifting social attitudes about the value of a foreign university degree. What matters is that this export of travel and educational services is unconnected to possible market barriers in Japan; the travel and education occurs in the United States. Inefficiency, poor quality, and high prices in Japan hurt the reverse flow; fewer foreigners choose to travel to Japan or obtain education in Japan. Perversely, the notion of barriers (such as visa difficulties or high airfares imposed by the Japanese government) become export barriers in this case; by discouraging a flow of foreigners to Japan, travel and educational service exports (receipts from foreigners traveling or studying in Japan) are diminished. These are areas where inefficient domestic industries have been unable to protect themselves behind market access barriers.

Some other service industries also seem to represent areas of American strength relative to Japanese firms in head-to-head competition. Airlines, telecommunications, university education, architecture, accounting, legal services, management consulting, retailing, financial services, and other service-sector industries appear to be more advanced in the United States than Japan. But competitive strength and even favorable movements in balance of payments data do not necessarily imply that markets are open.

A number of these service industries have been seriously constrained by trade barriers in Japan, including international airline travel, telecommunications, retailing, insurance, other financial services, and legal services.

Airlines represent an excellent example of both the success and continuing problems in gaining access to Japanese markets. U.S. passenger fare exports to Japan (representing payments to American-owned airlines by Japanese traveling internationally) rose from $1.9 billion in 1988 to $5.4 billion by 1997, representing a 12 percent average annual growth. Meanwhile, U.S. imports of air travel from Japan (payments by Americans to ride on Japanese-owned airlines) were low and growing slowly over the same period—rising from $465 million in 1988 to only $757 million by 1997. The U.S. bilateral surplus on passenger fares, therefore, grew more than 200 percent from $1.4 billion in 1988 to $4.7 billion by 1997.[31]

On the surface, these numbers suggest that markets worked, with efficiency and movements in the exchange rate greatly expanding the American market share in this bilateral trade. In real terms, the proportion of passengers to and from Japan traveling on Japanese-owned airlines slid from 52 percent in 1985 to about 39 percent by 1997, suggesting that Japanese airlines generally lost competitiveness to all foreign carriers.[32] In a bilateral context, a similar shift occurred with trans-Pacific travel gradually shifting in favor of U.S. carriers. From 51 percent in 1981, the share of trans-Pacific passengers between the United States and Japan traveling on Japanese carriers fell slowly to 34 percent by the 1990s.[33] Certainly one factor behind this shift has been the lagging price competitiveness of the Japanese airlines, known for their high cost structures. Overt price competition on routes between the United States and Japan has been limited owing to the Japanese government's desire to maintain price controls. But even with the high, controlled level of fares, Japanese airlines appear to have been unable to maintain sufficient profits to maintain flights authorized under the bilateral civil aviation treaty, leading to the deterioration in their market share.

If the civil aviation market were truly open, the American firms would have performed even better. In theory, the 1952 treaty that governs bilateral airline travel granted four airlines (Japan Airlines [JAL], Northwest Airlines, and United Airlines—originally Pan Am, and Flying Tiger—now Federal Express) unlimited access to both countries, leaving the governments to negotiate over the flights and frequencies of other airlines. This freedom to pick routes and frequencies would suggest that markets were only partially fettered. But for all of the 1980s and 1990s, landing capacity in Japan has been constrained, and the Japanese government (Ministry of Transport) has had total control over the allocation of landing slots and gate assignments. Furthermore, the government pursued a regime of price control that made flying between Japan and the United States much more expensive than between the United States and other Asian countries. Controlled prices diminished the ability of the American-flag carriers to compete fully on the basis of price in the Japanese market. At lower, more competitive prices, Japanese-flag airlines would have had even more trouble competing in the trans-Pacific market.

Harassment has even extended to airport services; when the new terminal opened at Narita Airport in late 1992, the Japanese airlines and some minor foreign ones moved to the spacious new terminal, leaving the two incumbent American-flag carriers, Northwest and United, in the aging, cramped original facility. At least these two airlines should have benefited from lessened crowding as the other airlines moved out of the old terminal, but the Ministry of Transport announced a renovation plan for the vacated half of the building—originally scheduled to take ten years!

Rather than talking about competition, the Japanese government has preferred to emphasize the unfairly biased rights built into the 1952 treaty governing bilateral aviation. Since the United States had two incumbent passenger carriers (Northwest and United) to Japan's one (JAL) and two incumbent freight carriers (Federal Express and Northwest) to Japan's one (JAL), the balance seemed to favor the Americans. A new agreement reached in 1998 extended incumbency to All Nippon Airways (ANA), a move that the Japanese government had long desired to "balance" the relationship. As part of its charge of imbalance, the Ministry of Transport was fond of showing that U.S. carriers flew to far more points in the United States from Japan than did Japanese carriers, flew beyond Japan to far more points in Asia than Japanese-flag carriers did from the United States (since the Japanese had only one passenger route—beyond Los Angeles to Brazil, and two cargo routes on to Canada from Chicago and New York), and operated more flights across the Pacific. Perhaps most interesting, they point out that while 75 percent of the passengers on U.S.-Japan routes were Japanese nationals in 1994, Japanese-flag carriers were moving only 34 percent of the passenger load.[34] The obvious implicit implication of this last comparison is that citizens should be moving on the carriers of their own country (or would do so if the market were "fair").

The Japanese government's notion of fairness was very peculiar. As long as it could exercise strict control over landing slots at the principal international airports in Japan (Narita, and in the 1990s, the new Kansai International Airport in Osaka) as well as impose severe restrictions on pricing, the original designation of incumbent carriers bore little relationship to actual ability to gain market share. Furthermore, even though American carriers flew beyond Japan to other Asian destinations, the Ministry of Transport limited the number of passengers these flights could pick up in Japan. The history of the 1980s and 1990s was one of almost continuous and often bitter negotiations over allocation of new routes and flights for ANA and the nonincumbent American carriers, and disputes over flights continuing beyond Japan to other destinations (known as "beyond rights"). In particular, the Ministry of Transport attempted to limit the number of passengers American carriers could pick up in Japan for these flights continuing to other destinations in Asia. One could easily argue that the increased American market share in the trans-Pacific route came despite these many restrictions rather than as a result of any unbalanced treaty.

This example of airline services illustrates the difficulty in assessing the nature of competition in the service industry. Similar problems of access exist in other areas such as legal services, financial services, and construction. In some respects, American and other foreign firms do appear to have had a competitive advantage that led to increased sales in the Japanese market and a rising bilateral service trade surplus in favor of the United States. But the microeconomic evidence of specific problems in many service industries is extensive. Although some of those problems eased somewhat over the years, the picture in the late 1990s is certainly not one of a largely open market.

Price Differentials

When prices in one market differ from those in another, an incentive exists for businesses to move products to the higher-priced market. In a perfectly competitive world, this arbitrage should eliminate or minimize price differences across markets. Obviously, transportation costs or other specific costs (such as advertising) may leave small differences. The point remains, though, that price differences create profit incentives for businesses to engage in arbitrage. Therefore, when large price differences between countries exist for prolonged periods, the clear question is why. The answer is often the existence of market barriers.

Analyses attempting to explain away low levels of manufactured good penetration or intra-industry trade as the result of standard economic variables would be more believable if prices in Japan and the rest of the world were comparable. However, considerable evidence demonstrates that prices for many goods and services are, on average, much higher in Japan than the rest of the world, strengthening the conclusion that market obstacles remain. Ideally, one would like to measure all prices for goods and services. But transaction prices for many producer goods are difficult to obtain. What economists can observe and measure, therefore, is limited largely to the retail price for consumer goods and services. Japanese concerns that their businesses operate in a high-cost domestic environment suggest that producer goods and services are also higher priced in Japan than in other countries. The following discussion, though, sticks to consumer prices.

The Ministry of International Trade and Industry (MITI) acknowledges that domestic prices are much higher than American prices. Assuming that prices were equal between the two countries in 1973, MITI estimated that prices were 80 percent higher in Japan than the United States by 1994, a startling disparity. This comparison was based on combining the trends in the GDP deflator and exchange rates, giving a very broad view of price movements in the economy. But it was also dependent on the startling assumption that prices were comparable in 1973—a time when prices for various nontradable services were probably lower than in the United States (because Japan still had lower wages than the United States at that time), but those for a variety of agricultural and manufactured goods were higher even at the much weaker yen exchange rate of that time.[35]

The Economic Planning Agency (EPA) of the Japanese government has provided its own simple relative price analysis based on a comparison of the cost of a basket of goods and services purchased by the typical consumer. The EPA concluded that Tokyo prices were 52 percent higher than New York prices in 1994, declining to 33 percent higher by 1996 because of the depreciation of the yen.[36] This tendency to compare the two countries on the basis of New York and Tokyo prices produces a downward bias in the price disparity. Many goods and services in New York are much more expensive than elsewhere in the country, whereas this is not true to the same extent in Japan. To deal with this possible distortion, the EPA survey does include a Kanazawa–St. Louis comparison, yielding a higher price difference of 57 percent in 1996.

The EPA approach is susceptible to the choice of goods and services in the basket and the actual measurement of the prices. For example, in another study the government's advisory panel on price stabilization found golf course greens fees 3.85 times higher in the Tokyo area than in the New York area in 1995, but a MITI survey two years later in 1997 (when the yen was weaker) put the spread at 5.64 times.[37]

Averages of this sort, even if they are at all accurate, provide only an incomplete picture. Some goods and services do move freely and exhibit only small price differences across countries. In other cases the price disparities are shockingly large. In 1997, for example, the government admitted that the price of pacemakers, a product subject to bilateral negotiations over the years, was as much as 6.9 times more expensive in Japan than in the United States, a remarkable difference.[38]

Comparisons can also be complicated by questions of availability and choice in ways that might understate the real differences, as suggested above in the example of the golf course. Often identical products are not even available if little or no trade takes place, or consumers face a wide variety of differentiated products that make a single product comparison an inadequate data point. For example, if a consumer walked into a store in Japan looking for a refrigerator in 1994, the array of products and prices would be quite different than in the United States. In Tachikawa Topos, a discount store in the Tokyo suburb of Tachikawa, thirty-one models of refrigerators with differing sizes and amenities were on display in the spring of 1994, ranging in price from ¥56,900 ($542 at then current exchange rates) to ¥249,000 ($2,371), with an average price of ¥119,371 ($1,137). Down the street, Dai-Ichi Kaden, a specialist discount appliance retailer, offered twenty-eight models ranging in price from ¥69,800 ($665) to ¥248,000 ($2,362) for an average of ¥152,446 ($1,452). In a Sears store in the suburbs of Washington, D.C., that same spring, a consumer would see eighteen models of full-size refrigerators ranging in price from $600 to $1,350. On average the price was 28 percent higher at Topos than at Sears and 63 percent higher at Dai-Ichi Kaden (with the difference between the two Japanese stores largely attributable to the presence of several rather small models at Topos for a price of less than ¥60,000 but a storage capacity of only 200 liters or less—roughly 7 cubic feet). Besides being much higher in price on average, Japanese consumers obtained less storage capacity for their money. Not a single American refrigerator was as small as the largest Japanese one in these stores. If price is calculated in terms of price per liter of capacity, prices in Japan were 2.2 times higher in Japan. Recognizing that Japanese houses have less space (skewing demand toward smaller refrigerators) and that the manufacturing process may involve economies of size (since all refrigerators need the same mechanisms) some disparity in sizes available and relative price is understandable. But what happens when one compares refrigerators that are reasonably close in size? The two Japanese stores offered four "large" models of 450 to 455 liters while the five smallest models offered by Sears were in a 500–530 liter range, only slightly larger than the Japanese subsample. For this small sample, the average price was a startling 3.3 times higher in Japan![39] This example illustrates the difficulty in calculating price differences—especially in markets where there are few comparable products—and the fairly clear indication that prices can be far wider than averages would suggest.

After the spring of 1995, the yen depreciated against the dollar. One could argue that the price disparities in 1994 (when the exchange rate was ¥105 per U.S. dollar) overstated the differences. As the yen appreciated rapidly from 1993 to 1994, retailers did not adjust prices continuously, owing to lags between contracts and delivery of goods (so that the current exchange rate does not reflect that built into the contract), or because of disbelief among retailers that the new exchange rates represented a long-term shift.

But in the refrigerator example, price differences could not be attributed to the unusually strong yen of 1994. From the spring of 1994 to the summer of 1998, the yen depreciated from ¥105 per dollar to a temporary low of ¥140. If retail prices in Japan and the United States remained constant, then a 33 percent reduction in price differentials would have occurred. But a similar comparison of refrigerators in the summer of 1998 revealed the average price at a major discount store in Akihabara (Ishimaru Denki) to be 22 percent higher than at Sears and the average price per cubic unit of interior space to be 1.9 times higher. The comparison of the smallest models in Sears to the largest in Ishimaru yielded an average price difference of 2.9 times, and a price per cubic unit of space of 2.9 times. With changes in price, and changes in the product mix on display, the very large price differences remained little changed (even when calculated by using the low point in the yen-dollar exchange rate in 1998).[40]

Price differences are by no means confined to manufactured goods; services are part of the internationally high cost of living in Japan. Some services are not readily tradable (such as the proverbial haircut industry) and are peripheral to the question of why goods prices differ so much between Japan and other countries. The EPA study found some services far higher in Tokyo than New York—72 percent higher for utility prices, 35 percent for transportation, and 74 percent for housing.[41] Another government report in 1997 admitted the retail price of electric power in Japan was 2.2 times higher than in the United States on average (including 2.5 times higher for power generation costs and 5.0 times higher for power distribution).[42] Such a price difference for electric power may have many causes (including inefficient and excessive investment in facilities), of which one factor may be that the electric power industry has preferred domestic equipment suppliers over lower-cost American and other foreign suppliers of generating equipment, cable, and other products.[43]

To its credit, the Japanese government has at least carried out price surveys of the sort cited earlier, and the media have emphasized them. Having the government recognize high prices as a problem is at least a step forward. This focus on prices began in the late 1980s in the form of a joint U.S.-Japan government survey of prices, but it has continued in the 1990s on the part of the Japanese government with a variety of agencies producing annual reports.

But not all economists in Japan accepted the notion that price differentials might be related to market access impediments. Masaru Yoshitomi, former chief economist at the government's Economic Planning Agency and then with the Long-Term Credit Bank, argued in the 1990s that the overall higher level of prices in Japan was driven by the high productivity of the tradable goods sector relative both to nontradables and to other countries. With productivity in the tradable goods sector rising faster than in other countries, the yen appreciated against other currencies. But this process left prices for nontradables high when converted into foreign currencies for comparison. Thus he argued that the overall perception of high prices was the result of success in driving down costs and prices in the export goods manufacturing sector. Price differentials for tradable goods themselves he dismissed as small in general, and sometimes the result of strong brand-name appeal for particular foreign products (so that Japanese consumers were willing to bid up prices for these goods beyond the level in other countries).[44]

An identical argument appeared in the government's annual white paper on trade, noting that for industrial nations in general, productivity growth tends to be higher in the tradable sector than nontradables. The white paper also argues that price differences can simply be the result of movement in the exchange rate since even the process of international arbitrage takes time to respond to the trade opportunities presented by a currency's appreciation.[45]

Although interesting and logical, this argument about tradables versus nontradables is not credible, and several objections can be raised. First, many goods and services considered to be nontradables can be traded (construction, leisure services such as resort hotels, and so on). As discussed in the previous section, some of these tradable service sectors exhibit major barriers to entry. Second, although average tradable goods price differentials may be smaller than those for nontradables, tradable goods price differences are too large and too broad to be ascribed to the peculiarities of brand-name appeal. Differences of 30 to 100 percent or more as indicated in the earlier discussion ought to be sufficient to generate more vigorous arbitrage activity. And nothing other than trade barriers can justify the finding of a 6.9 times differential in pacemaker price or a 3.3 times differential for refrigerators.

Nevertheless, the desire of Japanese economists to explain away price differentials has been strong. Another economist argued that comparisons at nominal exchange rates are invalid, since nominal exchange rates can deviate from "equilibrium rates." His novel approach was to compare the price of goods to family income; since nominal family income was higher in Japan than the United States (at then-current exchange rates) in the mid-1990s, higher nominal prices in Japan did not necessarily mean that families had to spend a greater share of their incomes to purchase those goods and services. He claimed, for example, that the retail price of rice was 32 percent lower in the United States than in Japan (by his calculation, which surely understated by a wide margin the actual retail price difference), but it was actually 8 percent more expensive in the United States when adjusted for family income levels.[46] This approach is simply absurd, and comparisons to family income are irrelevant. Although the comparison of family cost may be ludicrous, it matters because respectable Japanese economists writing in widely read business and economics publications continue to push such views, and they find a receptive audience.

A much better and broader way to consider price differences broadly defined is to look at the difference between GDP per capita when measured at nominal and purchasing power parity (PPP) exchange rates. Think of nominal rates as the exchange rates at which exporters are able to price their products to meet global prices. PPP rates equate the broad basket of goods and services consumed in the economy to the prices abroad. This estimate is basically a crude expansion of the more detailed basket price comparisons carried out by the Japanese government. This comparison manages to encompass the variation in price for both goods and services, both of which are more expensive in Japan than elsewhere. In 1996, for example, Japan's GDP per capita was 31 percent higher than that of the United States when the comparison is made at nominal exchange rates, but 16 percent lower when made at PPP exchange rates.[47]

The more important issue is arbitrage; the obvious response to wide international price differentials is the movement of goods and services. If differentials are wide, then in an open world firms would buy in the cheap country and sell in the dear. Therefore, persistence of differentials raises questions of barriers; what is preventing arbitrage from taking place? The process of arbitrage depends on the differences that exist at nominal prices and nominal exchange rates.

If the existence of wide price differentials suggests that market impediments exist, then reduction in those differentials should imply a reduction in barriers. Much attention was generated by a decline in some retail prices in the early to mid-1990s, yielding the popular phrase *kakaku hakkai* (price destruction). MITI attributed some of this trend to the relaxation of controls on large-sized stores in 1992 and rising imports. In fact, MITI explicitly admitted a connection between imports and large stores, stating that discount stores were able to cut retail prices and markup margins on the basis of both greater productivity (relative to small retail outlets) and use of lower-priced imported products.[48] To have the government formally recognize this obvious connection was helpful, since the U.S. government had argued for years that the restrictions on expansion of large stores had a detrimental impact on imports.

Another government study measured the change in wholesale and retail prices in the 1990s for a variety of goods. On average, the retail-wholesale margin shrank a bit as change and greater competition began to characterize the distribution sector. They concluded that on average, families saved ¥22,000 a year ($202 at 1996 exchange rates) from these changes.[49] The intent of this report, however, was to tout greater efficiency in distribution (wholesaling, transportation, and retail) rather than greater competition from foreign goods and services.

This evidence on retail margins suggests that something was happening to reduce retail prices. But the focus on efficiency gets at only part of the issue. Retail price markups have been high because of collusion among distributors or between distributors and manufacturers to keep prices high. Foreign consumer products that enter this collusive world also end up with higher prices, often to the delight of foreign manufacturers who find that their small market share in Japan can be very profitable. Large chain stores are important because they have more bargaining power to resist the collusive desires of domestic manufacturers, not just because they are more efficient.

The evidence on price differences is an important part of the argument that access to Japanese markets is obstructed. Many manufactured products exhibit price gaps sufficiently high that an open market ought to generate a strong inflow of foreign products. When the foreign consumer products that do enter Japanese markets end up with similarly high prices, the explanation lies either in foreign firms who leave distribution in Japan to a Japanese distributor or who have gleefully joined a high-price, high-profit game. One should not be surprised that foreign firms behave in such a manner, but the important issue is that Japanese markets enable such collusive behavior.

The wide price disparities of the 1994–95 period could be attributed to the strength of the yen. As noted earlier, the lag between contracts and delivery of goods can cause price adjustments to lag. But the decline in the yen after 1995 did not erase the differences. Japanese government price surveys indicate a decline in the price gap, with the November 1997 survey showing a price gap of only 18 percent with New York (down from the 52 percent in 1994 mentioned earlier).[50] But the evidence on refrigerators in 1998 presented earlier (which could be extended to a range of other consumer products such as television sets, microwave ovens, and others) indicates continuing large price gaps for consumer products even at the weak exchange rate (¥140 per U.S. dollar) that prevailed temporarily in the summer of 1998. And for 1998 as a whole, nominal exchange rates will not be much different from 1996 (since the yen strengthened after the summer), when there was the large gap between nominal and PPP per capita GDP.

Conclusion

The Japanese market is not "closed" to foreign products and services in any strict sense for most goods and tradable services. Nevertheless, a variety of indicators suggest strongly that Japan does not absorb as many products from abroad as other nations, and that this fact cannot be explained away with simple economic variables. The statistical evidence on manufactured imports, while not outright proof of market access problems, is highly consistent with the anecdotal evidence.

In some dimensions, access problems appear to have eased over the past decade. Certainly the propensity to engage in intra-industry trade increased sharply in the 1995–96 period. And even though the nominal ratio of manufactured imports to GDP has not risen consistently, one could argue that the real penetration of imports has increased somewhat. These are encouraging developments. Nevertheless, a decade of change left Japan still lagging far behind most other countries in the mid-1990s on both the overall penetration of foreign products and the extent of intra-industry trade.

Furthermore, wide price differentials continued to exist throughout the 1990s. Differentials were sufficiently wide that they should have generated vigorous arbitrage if markets were open. This price evidence is consistent with the trade evidence. If manufactured imports are low in international comparison, and domestic prices are high, then market barriers are the only logical answer.

Access to service sector markets is more difficult to assess since so much of market participation involves investment rather than trade, but the evidence suggests that serious problems exist in this sector too. Price differences also exist in the service sector, although some of these are for services not considered tradable. More telling, several service industries are subject to overt regulation that creates a collusive outcome excluding or minimizing the market share of efficient foreign firms. Although this chapter focuses on civil aviation as an example, similar stories of heavy regulation and obstructed entry exist for many other services. With the rising importance of the service sector in bilateral economic ties, these market access problems have become more important.

The evidence of this chapter, therefore, broadly supports the conclusion that Japanese markets for both goods and services continued to be characterized by market-access problems in the 1990s. The upward shift in the indicators for manufactured goods trade in 1995–96 is suggestive of an improvement but still left a wide disparity between Japan and other countries. Three main conclusions follow from the analysis of this chapter.

First, the stagnation in the upward movement of the statistical indicators of manufactured goods trade helps explain the frustration of American firms in the early 1990s. That frustration was transmitted to Washington, leading to the pressure on the Bush administration and then the incoming Clinton administration to actively pursue trade negotiations to make Japanese markets more open.

Second, the upward movement in the trade statistics in 1995–96 helps explain the declining emphasis on trade negotiations in the second term of the Clinton administration. As discussed chapter 4, trade negotiations continued in the second Clinton term but without the sense of political priority that characterized the first term. Rising sales to Japan made American firms less frustrated, and as new market conditions unfolded, perhaps they became more willing to wait as new market conditions unfolded before making further judgments.

Third, problems of market access continued into the late 1990s. The period of strong yen appreciation and rising imports in the mid-1990s reduced the distinctiveness of Japanese trade patterns but did not erase it. High prices for consumer goods and services relative to other countries abated as the yen fell against the dollar after 1995 but were not fully erased, and very large differentials remained for some goods and services. In the service sector evidence remained strong of regulatory controls affecting foreign market access. Once American firms adjust to the changes of the mid-1990s, many of them will once again realize that they face a more difficult environment in the Japanese market than elsewhere in the world.

The Investment Dimension

Trade tells only part of the story about access to markets. Firms can participate in international markets through trade, direct investment, or both. Put in the simplest terms, a firm can export products from its home market to the world or build those products in the market where they are sold. In reality, involvement in international markets generally means a combination of trade and investment, which are related in complex ways. This chapter explores the investment dimension of access to Japanese markets.

One possibility is that investment is a substitute for trade; when investment is local, products from the local plant substitute for products that had been supplied from the firm's home country. Although the very simple notion of investment as a substitute for trade may be true for certain cases, economists generally see a more complementary relationship between trade and investment. Even if a manufacturing firm exports products from a domestic production base, it often must invest locally to facilitate sales and provide after-sales service for its customers in order to successfully participate in a market. And rather than substituting local production for exports, foreign direct investment may well generate additional trade. Manufacturing investment abroad may create flows of parts into markets where trade barriers at the border (quotas or tariffs) prevented imports of the finished products (so that a positive flow of parts results where there had been no trade previously). Manufacturing plants in a foreign market may manufacture only one product out of the array that the firm produces, and creation of local distribution channels for that product may motivate exports of other products from home. In the reverse direction, firms might also choose to locate production abroad and import back to their home country for reasons of cost. In all these cases, direct investment increases trade rather than reducing it.

For the service sector, chapter 2 pointed out that investment is a more critical aspect of market participation, since services often have to be produced where they are consumed. But even in this case investment may be complementary with trade. A service sector firm may have to invest locally (such as airline investment to provide local sales, terminal staff, and maintenance) while generating transactions that do show up as service trade (receipts for international air travel from people in the local market).

These many possibilities concerning investment as a means to gain access to markets abroad lead to many questions concerning Japan. This chapter addresses two important questions:

First, is evidence on relatively low levels of manufactured imports offset by high levels of foreign investment in Japan? That is, has investment been a substitute for trade, so that foreign firms have actually been quite active in Japanese markets despite the impression given by the trade data? For example, the Japanese government has virtually banned the import of most refined petroleum products until very recently, but American petroleum companies have had major investments in oil refining in Japan since the 1950s. If this pattern is generally true, then Japanese markets are more easily accessible than implied by the evidence in chapter 2.

Second, has the large increase in Japanese manufactured imports in the past decade come primarily from independent foreign firms or from the rapidly expanding foreign subsidiaries of Japanese manufacturing firms? All industrial nations have firms shipping products back home from foreign production bases, and for Japan to move in this same direction is neither wrong nor remarkable. The decade after 1985 was characterized by rapid Japanese direct investment abroad. Some of it involved factories producing products for shipment back to Japan. This does raise an important question, though, about the openness of Japanese markets. Japanese firms have an inherent advantage over independent foreign firms in bringing products back into Japan. If access problems within Japanese markets have to do with collusion or blocked entry to distribution, then the existing Japanese firms within the industry are already inside the system and can import their own products easily. If access problems involve customs procedures, Japanese firms may have political connections that enable them to manipulate the system to their advantage in getting their own products into the country. Or, if access problems involve standards and testing procedures, Japanese firms can produce their already certified and tested products abroad without facing the hurdles that confront non-Japanese firms. Therefore, if the bulk of the increase in imports from the mid-1980s through the mid-1990s came from the subsidiaries of these firms, then the rise in imports or increase in intra-industry trade does not imply that markets necessarily became more open. Independent foreign firms could have continued to face the same barriers as in the past.

Both of these investment issues have become important because a web of earlier postwar restrictions on direct investment—both into and out of Japan—had been swept away in a series of steps from the late 1960s to the early 1980s. This decontrol presumably made investment by foreign firms into Japan much easier. After 1985 the large and rapid shift in the exchange rate then motivated a massive increase in Japanese direct investment abroad.

This chapter looks at both of the issues raised by the investment dimension. The task is complicated by the poor quality of the data available on investment into or out of Japan. Any conclusions drawn from the data must be tempered by a word of caution about these major data problems, the detailed nature of which is discussed later. Nevertheless, for foreign firms, the overall conclusion is that even if investment could be a substitute for trade, investment in Japan has been insufficient to offset the low levels of imports analyzed in chapter 2. Indeed, not only is Japan characterized by distinctively low levels of imports, but low levels of inward direct investment as well. Although the data are very imperfect, even a generous estimate leaves the presence of foreign firms in Japan far lower than in other industrial nations. If one assumes that investment is complementary to trade, then the low level of investment helps to explain the low level of imports into Japan.

On the question of Japanese investments abroad and their impact on imports into Japan, the picture is also discouraging. At least in the first half of the 1990s, crude estimates discussed later in this chapter imply that almost a third of the increase in Japan's imports came from Japanese-affiliated firms abroad rather than from independent firms. This explains why foreign firms would continue to feel that they faced market barriers in Japan despite rising imports into Japan in these industries.

Investment into Japan

For many years, one of the striking characteristics of Japan has been the low level of inward foreign direct investment. Early in the postwar period, the government established very stiff investment barriers that kept out investments by most foreign firms. Those barriers were dismantled between 1967 and the early 1980s. Even after official barriers fell, though, investment did not rise as rapidly as one might expect. The importance of foreign investment into Japan in explaining economic tensions with the United States and causes for the low level of investment were the subject of seminal work by Mark Mason and Dennis Encarnation.[1] But in the decade since the late 1980s, the situation could have changed. The following analysis, however, indicates that since the 1980s overall foreign direct investment in Japan has remained low. Any analysis of the issue is complicated by the poor quality of the official data, but this conclusion stands even after attempts are made to adjust for probable biases in the data.

A partial recent exception to this overall picture of low investment may be finance and distribution. The extreme distress within the financial sector in the late 1990s opened up new opportunities that would have been unthinkable as recently as 1996. In distribution, pressure from the U.S. government during the Bush administration opened the way for American retail chains to enter Japan (principally Toys R Us). But as considered later in this chapter, how far these new trends would go was uncertain in 1998.

Certainly many foreign firms do have manufacturing, sales, and service facilities in Japan. The American Chamber of Commerce in Japan listed 1,553 member firms in 1997, representing American firms that maintain offices or subsidiaries in Japan.[2] If manufacturing firms choose to manufacture in Japan rather than export, then the foreign participation in Japanese markets is larger than is indicated by the manufactured good trade data analyzed in chapter 2. And if service sector firms participate mainly through investment rather than transactions from their home countries, the same could be true of foreign participation in services. Therefore, it is important to examine the data on the investment and sales of foreign firms in Japan.

Some allege that the sizable number of foreign firms with subsidiaries in Japan implies markets are more open than outside observers believe.

James Abegglen, a long-term business consultant residing in Japan, has been a vocal advocate of this position. His consulting firm publishes an annual list of the 100 largest non-Japanese firms with subsidiaries operating in Japan. The top 100 foreign firms operating in Japan in 1994 had sales of $155 billion, with half the companies and two-thirds of the sales coming from subsidiaries of American firms. He argues that the data provide "little support for the view that Japan's economy and markets are closed."[3]

Abegglen certainly raises a valid point, but the selective data provided do not prove that foreign firms have unimpeded access to markets in Japan. Sales by foreign-owned companies (composed of a mix of products or services they produce in Japan, import from their home countries, and produce in third countries for shipment to Japan) are certainly larger than suggested by import data. However, investment flows into all countries, and the question remains as to how Japan compares with the foreign penetration of other markets through investment. Broader evidence based on official statistics shows that Japan compares badly.

Official data on foreign direct investment flows into Japan are presented in figure 3-1, showing the annual flow of investment into and out of Japan. The first striking fact is the large disparity between inflows and outflows. Although the large outflow in 1989 was affected by the "bubble" in the economy (when Japanese firms were flush with cash and had developed a new interest in foreign real estate), direct investment overseas began rising again after 1992 and was $51 billion in fiscal 1995. Meanwhile, inward investment flows hovered around $4 billion in the 1990s and were $7 billion in fiscal 1996. These data only imperfectly measure investment flows because the Ministry of Finance counts only notifications of investment. Firms intending to invest abroad or foreign firms intending to invest in Japan must notify the Ministry of Finance of their intent. Subsequently the firms might invest less than announced or might postpone or cancel investments altogether. Furthermore, notification only applies to investment; disinvestment (the decision of firms to withdraw from previous investments) is not recorded. Regarding the observed gap between inflows and outflows, the contrast should remain valid if the general disparity between notifications and real investment affects both inflows and outflows more or less equally.

As a result of the low inflows of direct investment, the cumulative amount of inward direct investment was only $45 billion on March 31, 1997. In stark contrast, the rapid rise in outward flows resulted in a cumulative total of direct investment abroad by Japanese firms of $564 billion.

Figure 3-1. *FDI Flows: Into and Out of Japan*

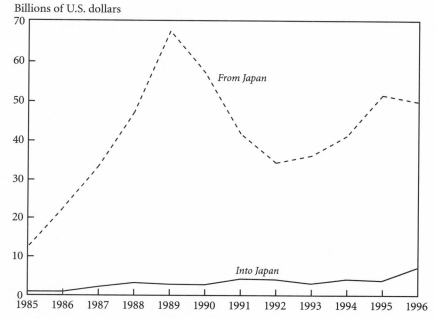

Billions of U.S. dollars

Source: Ministry of Finance, Ōkurashō Kokusai Kin'yūkyoku Nempō, no. 13 (1991), pp. 457, 482; no. 16, (1992), pp. 479, 504; and "Statistical Profile: International Transactions of Japan in 1996," *JEI Report* no. 45A (December 5, 1997), pp. 16, 17.

Thus cumulative investment abroad was thirteen times larger than investment into Japan, an enormous disparity.[4]

In sharp contrast to this picture of Japan, foreign firms added $69 billion to their direct investments in the United States in 1996, almost ten times larger than the flow into Japan. For year-end 1996, cumulative foreign investment in the United States totaled $630 billion, more than twelve times larger than the amount reported by Japan for the end of March in 1996. Furthermore, the value of foreign direct investment in the United States was not far different from the value of American direct investment abroad. At the end of 1996, American direct investment abroad totaled $796 billion, or only 26 percent larger than the stock of foreign direct investment in the United States. Even if the data are adjusted to reflect current market value of

Table 3-1. *U.S. Direct Investment Position Abroad*

Year-end stock position

	Amount (billions of dollars)			Shares of total (percent)		
Year	Total	Japan	Europe	Rest of world	Japan	Europe	Rest of world
1980	213	6.3	96	112	2.9	44.8	52.2
1981	227	6.8	101	119	3.0	44.6	52.4
1982	222	6.9	99	115	3.1	44.9	52.0
1983	226	8.1	102	116	3.6	45.3	51.1
1984	213	7.9	92	113	3.7	43.2	53.1
1985	233	9.1	107	117	3.9	45.9	50.2
1986	260	11.5	121	128	4.4	46.5	49.1
1987	308	14.7	146	147	4.8	47.5	47.8
1988	327	16.9	152	158	5.2	46.6	48.3
1989	382	19.9	189	172	5.2	49.6	45.2
1990	427	22.5	213	191	5.3	50.0	44.8
1991	461	24.9	233	203	5.4	50.6	44.0
1992	487	26.2	239	221	5.4	49.2	45.4
1993	564	31.1	286	247	5.5	50.6	43.9
1994	613	34.1	297	282	5.6	48.5	46.0
1995	699	37.3	345	317	5.3	49.3	45.4
1996	777	35.7	382	281	5.1	54.7	40.2
1997	861	35.6	421	321	4.6	54.2	41.3

Sources: Department of Commerce, *Survey of Current Business*, various issues.

corporate assets rather than historical cost, American investment abroad is only 22 percent higher than foreign investment in the United States.[5]

Of the very modest direct investment inflows in Japan, American firms have been the primary source. At the end of March 1997, American-sourced investments totaled $17.8 billion, or 40 percent of the total.[6] These data suggest that at least relative to firms of other nations, American firms are somewhat more successful or active in using investment as part of their strategy to enter the Japanese market.

However, these investments should be viewed in the context of overall American overseas direct investment. Seen in context, the amount invested in Japan is trivial. Table 3-1 shows that in 1997 the cumulative stock of American investment in Japan was only 4.6 percent of U.S. global investment.

Attracted by the dismantling of controls on inward direct investment, which was virtually complete by the beginning of the 1980s, American investment in Japan did expand during the 1980s. Cumulative investment had been only 2.9 percent of the global investment abroad by American firms in 1980 and expanded to 5.2 percent by 1988 (with the fall after 1994 a result of the decline of the yen, decreasing the dollar-denominated value of yen-based local investments in Japan). But this share subsequently remained stagnant. Thus the share of American direct investment in Japan relative to U.S. global investment remains well below what one would expect given the size and affluent nature of the market (implying consumption patterns closer to those of the United States). In 1995 Japan represented 18 percent of global GDP at nominal exchange rates, and even deflating that share for the overvaluation of the yen in that year would still leave Japan representing a share of the global economy far in excess of the share of American foreign direct investment it has attracted.[7]

People often think of foreign direct investment as flowing to low-wage developing countries to produce goods for shipment back home and to the rest of the world. Japan in the 1990s was certainly not an attractive base for American manufacturing in this sense. But even American manufacturing firms needed investments within Japan to manage distribution, after-sales service, and research (such as consumer preference research to design products for the local market). In the remainder of this chapter, all data referring to manufacturing sector investment in Japan represent investments by foreign manufacturing *firms*, which may not always involve investment in manufacturing *factories*. And as argued in chapter 2, service-sector firms are even more likely to need a local presence to sell their services than manufacturers. In addition, Japan is the home country of many leading competitors of American firms in both manufacturing and services, implying a strategic reason for American firms to invest in Japan. Thus, once capital controls were officially lifted in Japan, the logical result would have been an even more rapid increase in the American presence as firms adjusted their low actual investment position in the market toward a much higher desired level reflecting the economic size and importance of the Japanese market. For a variety of reasons considered later this did not happen.

More detailed information on foreign firms in Japan comes from an annual survey conducted by the Ministry of International Trade and Industry (MITI). This survey has severe limitations since it is based on voluntary returns to a questionnaire. All the data reported by MITI are only for the surveyed firms, with no attempt to adjust the sample results to esti-

Table 3-2. *Shares of Foreign-Affiliated Firms in the Japanese Economy according to the Ministry of International Trade and Industry*

Percent

Item	1980	1990	1995
Share of employment			
Total	0.8	0.5	0.5
Oil	22.0	16.7	16.7
Manufacturing	1.6	1.2	1.2
Nonmanufacturing	0.2	n.a.	0.2
Share of sales			
Total	2.2	1.2	1.2
Oil	38.1	26.9	28.3
Manufacturing	4.7	2.6	2.9
Nonmanufacturing	1.0	n.a.	0.6
Share of assets			
Total	2.1	0.9	0.9
Oil	33.7	23.7	23.7
Manufacturing	4.5	2.2	2.4
Nonmanufacturing	0.8	n.a.	0.3

Sources: Ministry of International Trade and Industry, *Gaishikei Kigyō no Dōkō, 15th ed.* (Tokyo), pp. 29, 35; 25th ed., p. 40; 30th ed., p. 106.
  n.a. Not available.

mate the total picture. Nevertheless, the MITI survey represents virtually the only detailed data on operations of foreign-affiliated firms (defined as those with more than 33 percent foreign ownership).

According to these data, presented in table 3-2, assets of foreign-affiliated firms in fiscal 1995 represented only 0.9 percent of total corporate assets (2.4 percent in manufacturing), 0.5 percent of total employment (1.2 percent in manufacturing), and 1.2 percent of total corporate sales (2.9 percent in manufacturing). Nonmanufacturing (that is, service-sector firms) were especially low, representing only 0.2 percent of domestic employment in the sector and only 0.6 percent of sales in 1995. The only exception is the petroleum industry (not part of "nonmanufacturing" in this survey). Foreign-affiliated oil companies are a much higher 16.7 percent of employment, 28.3 percent of sales, and 23.7 percent of assets in this industry, mainly in the form of 50-50 joint ventures formed in the 1950s (at a time when the Japanese economy was shifting to oil as an energy source but lacked technology in both extraction and refining).

If one makes the assumption that firms not responding to the survey had the same size characteristics as those that did (though those not responding are likely to be concentrated at the bottom end in terms of assets, personnel, and sales on the assumption that smaller firms are less likely to bother filling out voluntary surveys) and adjusted the survey results accordingly, the percentages would still be very low. In fiscal 1995, 52 percent of firms responded to the survey, and a doubling of the percentages above should represent an upper bound on the estimate of the role of foreign firms in Japan.[8] By this calculation, foreign firms represented no more than 1.8 percent of corporate assets and 2.4 percent of corporate sales.

If one keeps in mind the possible lack of complete consistency over time in the MITI survey, the results show little change in the relative presence of foreign firms. Indeed, the small presence of foreign firms appears to have fallen over time as shown in table 3-2. The share of total assets represented by firms replying to the questionnaire was 2.1 percent in 1980, slipping to 0.9 percent by 1990, where it remained in 1995. The same trend of decline from 1980 to 1990 and subsequent leveling off also characterizes the percentages of sales and employment for the total corporate sector, manufacturing and nonmanufacturing.

Similar data for the United States indicate that the share of foreign-affiliated firms is much higher than in Japan. For 1995 foreign affiliates (firms in which foreign ownership of total equity is 10 percent or greater) represented 10.8 percent of total sales by corporations, and 4.9 percent of employment. In the manufacturing sector the figures come to 12.4 percent of sales and 11.4 percent of employment.[9]

However, all sources of data published by the Japanese government on the presence of foreign-affiliated firms are flawed in ways that understate the true presence of firms. How serious are the flaws in the data? Two issues have already been mentioned in this chapter—the reliance on notifications to the Ministry of Finance (MOF) and the incomplete nature of the MITI survey. The only economist to look seriously at the problems with the Japanese investment data has been David Weinstein. He argued that several other factors may artificially reduce the reported level of foreign investment in Japan. First, the widely used MITI survey only covers firms in which foreigners have a 33 percent stake or higher, while the United States counts those with 10 percent or higher foreign ownership. Second, Japanese data collected by the Ministry of Finance until recently measured inward investment in dollar terms rather than yen (which undervalues the current yen worth of those investments if one simply takes the current dollar cumulative total and converts it into yen (since a dollar invested in Japan in the 1960s when the exchange rate was ¥360 per U.S. dollar acquired far more yen-denominated local assets than today). This dollar valuation problem, though, does not seriously affect the flow data reported in figure 3-1 since the flows in each year are converted at the exchange rate of that year. Third, neither the Ministry of Finance nor the Bank of Japan (BOJ) bothers to collect statistics on small investments (less than ¥30 million in the case of the MOF and less than ¥5 million in the case of the BOJ), although this error may not have much impact. Finally, neither the MOF nor BOJ investment numbers measure reinvested earnings, whereas the U.S. government data do. Taken together, these serious flaws in the Japanese data could imply that foreign direct investments in Japan are much higher than reported.[10]

Weinstein worked with two private surveys of foreign firms in Japan to attempt to construct a better estimate of the presence of foreign firms. Even these databases are incomplete, so his final estimate rests on a variety of assumptions about the probable sales and employment characteristics of missing firms. His estimates suggest that the overall sales of foreign-affiliated firms in Japan could be 5.7 percent of total corporate sales or even as high as 6.0 percent.[11] This share is five times larger than reported by the MITI survey, representing a much larger upward adjustment than suggested earlier to compensate for the incomplete coverage of the MITI survey. Weinstein's estimate should be considered an upward bound on the range of possible adjustments. But even this figure is much lower than the role of foreign firms in the United States, and Weinstein notes that it is lower than other OECD countries by a factor of two or three.

Any adjustment to the official data rests on assumptions. A separate way to evaluate the data is to contrast U.S. and Japanese data. The Commerce Department reported cumulative American direct investments in Japan to be $40 billion in 1996, or 2.2 times larger than the $18 billion reported by the Ministry of Finance. The Commerce Department data deal with most of the problems that plague the Japanese data, but the resulting adjustment factor is less than half that estimated by Weinstein. Therefore, his estimate should be considered a generous upper bound on the possible size of foreign direct investment in Japan.

Adjusting for problems in the Japanese data, therefore, leaves the conclusion that foreign-affiliated firms in Japan generate a much smaller share of economic activity than they do in the United States or other major countries. Even the Weinstein estimate leaves a large difference between Japan and other countries, and that disparity widens if his estimate is overly generous. The disparity may be higher when the question of effective corporate control is considered. While in theory a foreign firm may be able to exercise some influence over a foreign affiliate in which it owns as little as 10 percent of the shares, this is rarely the case in Japan. On rare occasion, a foreign firm with a more sizable minority stake may gain a major role in the firm's management (as happened with Ford's minority stake in Mazda in the mid-1990s when Mazda experienced serious financial difficulties). But even in some of the 50-50 joint ventures in Japan, the foreign owners have felt that their voice in decisionmaking has been minimal. Therefore, a more effective picture of what constitutes truly foreign-controlled firms would come from looking at the subset of foreign-affiliated firms with 50 percent or greater foreign ownership. Here the disparity between Japan and the United States widens dramatically.

The preference for majority ownership has been long-standing, characterizing the global behavior of American and Japanese firms.[12] Majority ownership generally clarifies corporate control and can bring efficiencies through enhanced intra-firm transactions as the majority owner can treat the joint venture more like a direct subsidiary. In the United States, majority-owned affiliates of foreign firms represent 86 percent of total assets of all foreign-affiliated firms, 86 percent of total sales of foreign affiliates, and 82 percent of employment of foreign affiliates. Similarly, for American firms invested abroad in 1995, majority-owned firms represented 86 percent of assets of all cumulative direct investments, 84 percent of sales, and 81 percent of employees.[13] Clearly, foreign firms choosing to invest in the United States and American firms abroad have a strong preference for majority ownership.

In Japan, the MITI survey found that 72 percent of the *number* of foreign-affiliated firms surveyed in 1996 were majority owned by the foreign firm but provided no data on the share of capital, sales, or employment that these firms represent among all foreign-affiliated firms surveyed.[14] U.S. data on American-affiliated firms in Japan provide one way around this problem. In 1995 majority-owned American-affiliated firms in Japan represented 68 percent of the total assets of American-affiliated firms in Japan, 53 percent of their sales, and 41 percent of their employees.[15] Thus foreign-affiliated firms in Japan that are affiliated with American parents demonstrate considerably lower shares of majority-ownership than do

American-affiliated firms on a global basis or foreign-affiliated firms in the United States.

Assume that the experience of American firms investing in Japan is typical of those of other parent countries. This may be a conservative assumption; presumably American firms have somewhat more clout in negotiating with potential Japanese partners on joint-venture shares and, therefore, may actually have a higher proportion of corporate assets, sales, and employment in majority-owned operations. Offsetting this prospect is the possibility that more American firms than those of other countries entered Japan in the early postwar period when majority-owned opera-tions were generally not permitted (though even these firms have had ample time over the past two decades to alter their ownership relationships in these joint ventures). Taking Weinstein's high estimate of 6 percent for the share of foreign affiliates in total corporate sales in Japan, then using the American experience on majority ownership yields an upper-bound esti-mate of 3.7 percent for the share of domestic corporate sales originating in majority-owned, foreign-affiliated firms. The alternative, lower estimate provided earlier of the total presence of foreign-affiliated firms yields an estimate of 1.8 percent of corporate sales for majority-owned firms. In con-trast, majority-owned foreign-affiliated firms in the United States account for 9.4 percent of total corporate sales, almost triple the high-end estimate for Japan.

This bleak picture of foreign direct investment in Japan may seem odd. Foreigners visiting Japan discover quickly that they can eat at McDonald's around the country, order home delivery of Domino's Pizza in Tokyo, shop at the world's largest Tower Records in the trendy Shibuya district of Tokyo, and stock up on daily necessities at Seven Eleven. But appearances can be deceiving. The visible presence of a handful of brand-name food or retail outlets does not necessarily imply that foreign firms are heavily invested in Japan. In fact, Seven Eleven in Japan has no American ownership anymore, nor does Denny's, both of which were joint ventures from which the Amer-ican partners withdrew. McDonald's has been enormously successful, but its business is franchising; the actual restaurants are locally owned small busi-nesses. Tower Records does have its largest store in Tokyo but has relatively few stores across Japan (eighteen in 1996) and can compete on price only on its foreign recordings (since Japanese recordings are subject to legal retail price maintenance set at a high level by Japanese recording companies).[16] Recently the Gap and Eddie Bauer have entered Japan but in only a modest way and with joint venture partners for individual outlets. Toys R Us may be the most successful American retail operation entering Japan (now with more than sixty stores), but its entry required tough negotiations between the two governments. The point is that seeing a recognizable name on a store does not provide any real insight on the extent of the presence of foreign firms.

An emerging partial exception may be the financial sector. Acute problems in the 1990s implied that the antipathy of the government toward the presence of foreign-affiliated institutions fell. The presence of foreign financial institutions had been making modest inroads from the 1970s to the 1990s, helped by repeated bilateral negotiations. Foreign investment banks, for example, had been barred from acquiring seats on the Tokyo Stock Exchange until 1988. And foreign insurance companies had been relegated to a niche market when they tried to enter in the 1970s, with two rounds of difficult negotiations in the 1993–96 period necessary to provide them a better chance to break into the mainstream life and property casualty markets. Even as foreign institutions expanded their presence, though, acquisition of domestic institutions remained an elusive goal until 1997–98. Merrill Lynch purchased retail branch offices from bankrupt Yamaichi in 1998. GE Capital made several acquisitions including Toho Mutual Life and two small consumer credit companies.[17] Overall, the situation in 1998 appeared to be much more open and receptive to foreign institutions, but how far this trend would proceed was uncertain.

The relative lack of investment matters for the flow of merchandise trade is discussed in chapter 2. A great deal of trade takes place in the form of flows from home countries to subsidiaries abroad. For the United States, 26 percent of global U.S. exports in 1994 were to the foreign subsidiaries of American firms. But for U.S. exports to Japan, only 16 percent were intrafirm transactions of American firms.[18] Both the relatively low level of American investment into Japan (relative to Japan's economic size and importance) and the lower degree of American ownership of those affiliates provide explanations for the lower intra-firm shipments among American exports to Japan.

Japanese data confirm the importance of investment for trade flows. The MITI survey indicates that surveyed foreign-affiliated firms in Japan in fiscal 1995 had imports of ¥4.0 trillion ($42 billion at 1995 exchange rates), and on balance imported ¥1.7 trillion ($19 billion) more than they exported. American-affiliated firms in the sample had total imports of ¥2.1 trillion ($21 billion) and brought in ¥750 billion ($8 billion) more than they exported.[19] The one major exception to this picture is transportation

Figure 3-2. *Bilateral Trade Handled, by Firms of Partner, 1992*

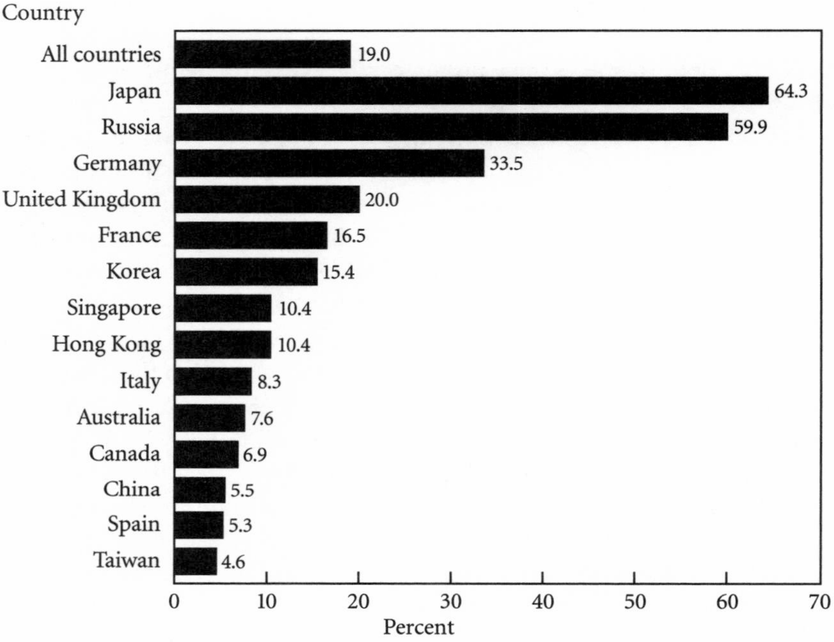

Country

Source: Department of Commerce, *Survey of Current Business,* vol. 77 (February 1997), pp. 32–33.

equipment (largely automobiles), probably because of large exports from Japan by Mazda (with minority ownership by Ford). Even that relationship might change in the future if Mazda becomes increasingly integrated into the Ford structure and becomes a corporate mechanism for importing and distributing Ford cars. Thus in a year when Japan generated a large total trade surplus, foreign-affiliated firms provided a small offset.

These trade balances for foreign-affiliated firms imply that the nationality of firms engaged in bilateral trade matters. This point can be generalized in the context of U.S.-Japan trade, using U.S. data shown in figure 3-2, which shows the percentage of American merchandise trade with a number of different trading partners that is handled by the firms of the partner country. In 1992 a high 64.3 percent of the two-way flow of goods between the United States and Japan was handled in the form of intra-firm transactions of Japanese firms. This stands in sharp contrast to the pattern with most other U.S. trading partners. Despite all the talk about ethnic Chinese "capitalism," with its preference for insider trading, rather little of U.S. trade with China, Hong Kong, Singapore, or Taiwan takes place in the form of intra-firm transactions within firms affiliated with those countries. Even the Republic of Korea, which emulates Japan in several respects, does not engage in bilateral trade through its own firms to the extent that the Japanese do. The only country that comes close to the Japanese pattern is Russia, a nation with which most Japanese would prefer not to be compared. If more of U.S.-Japan trade transpired between American firms and their affiliates in Japan, with their propensity to import more into Japan than they export, then the pattern of bilateral trade would look quite different. But this does not happen because of the relatively low number and size of American investments in Japan.

Why is foreign investment into Japan so low? This is a subject that has attracted great interest over the years.[20] Earlier in the postwar period the answer lay in government controls that made direct investment by foreign firms extremely difficult. But those controls were gradually relaxed and eliminated between the late 1960s and the early 1980s.[21] Since that time, presumably the explanation cannot lie in official investment barriers. Some suspicions remained that requirement for prior notification of investment opened the way for potential obstructionist policy, but even that requirement was changed to ex post notification in the 1990s.

Economists argue that firms engage in investment because of a set of organizational, locational, and internal factors (often dubbed the OLI model) that provide an incentive to invest in other countries.[22] Firms invest directly abroad when they possess organizational and technological advantages that competitors in the foreign country do not possess, when the foreign location provides some advantages that can be exploited only by being present there (such as low wages or a particular set of labor skills), and when investment is a superior corporate choice over the alternatives of exporting or licensing production to local firms. These three factors provide a convenient way to analyze the question of low investment in Japan.

One possible explanation is that all three of these motivating factors worked against foreign firms. By the time formal investment barriers were gone, foreign firms had lost much of their organizational advantage over Japanese firms. By the 1980s, in fact, foreign firms were busily studying and trying to adapt what was loosely labeled "Japanese management." Therefore, foreign firms might have had no particular organizational advantage in entering Japan, the home of efficient competitors.[23] This is the equivalent of the proposition explored in chapter 2 that intra-industry trade is low because Japanese manufacturers have strong comparative advantage across a wide array of products or industries.

Masaru Yoshitomi, the former Economic Planning Agency economist, implicitly believes in the validity of this notion of loss of organizational advantages by non-Japanese firms. He has argued that Japanese firms possess certain organizational advantages (at least when operating in their home market), including principally: *keiretsu* relationships, cross shareholding patterns among domestic firms, and the practice of lifetime employment. These are core features of the Japanese economy that he feels are both legitimate and economically efficient relative to business practices in other countries. Therefore, the failure of foreign firms to enter is not a problem to be explained or corrected but simply something that foreign firms must solve by becoming more accepting of local conditions and learning patience.[24] This is a disingenuous and discouraging view because it means that foreign firms will simply not be a greater presence in Japan and should accept that inability. *Keiretsu* relationships have been exclusionary to the long-term disadvantage of foreign firms; cross shareholding patterns imply that domestic firms are simply not for sale to foreign firms; and lifetime employment practices have made labor procurement more difficult for foreign firms. Foreign firms that accept local conditions and practice patience are doomed to never making much of a dent in Japanese markets. In the context of the organizational explanation, foreign firms face organizational disadvantages in Japan that they are unlikely to overcome.

Location could be explained in a similar fashion. In the earlier postwar period, Japan was perceived as advantageous for sourcing manufacturing production because it had a supply of low-cost skilled labor. But by the 1980s Japan had high wages, as well as high land costs. Therefore, foreign manufacturing firms were no longer interested in Japan, and perhaps more interested in other Asian countries that possessed low-wage skilled labor forces reminiscent of Japan in earlier years.

Finally, consider the possible anti-investment bias stemming from internal factors. The skill and adaptability of Japanese firms in the past fifty years put them in a position to effectively absorb foreign technology, and they eagerly did so. Therefore, for many foreign firms, licensing technology to Japanese firms provided a convenient and feasible alternative to attempting to invest in Japan. One recent study noted that American firms selling to Japan derive 18 percent of their revenue from licensing fees, whereas they derive only 2 percent of their income from Britain in this fashion, and 3 percent from Germany.[25] One could conclude that owing to the organizational and locational disadvantages, and the ready market for licensing, rational American firms with technology advantages simply chose to engage in business with Japan through licensing.

This benign view of the low level of investment is inconsistent with a broader set of facts. First consider organizational advantage. Certainly some Japanese manufacturing firms in the 1980s in some industries exhibited leading edge behavior, and there were certainly lessons on the organization of factory production for Western firms to absorb.[26] However, those advantages did not characterize all firms or all industries even within manufacturing. Motorola, for example, possessed superior technology for cellular telephone systems in the early 1980s, was strongly invested in Japan (including some manufacturing capability), but faced a prolonged struggle against Japanese government efforts to favor the inferior technology of its captive, government-owned telephone company Nippon Telegraph and Telephone (NTT).

Furthermore, the Japanese advantages pertained primarily to the technical issue of production organization (encompassing interrelated issues of engineering design for ease in manufacturing, production flow, parts supply, and quality control). Japanese firms do not appear to have been particularly efficient at a broader level of corporate management, such as corporate decisionmaking or financial control. And organizational advantage can also come from proprietary hard technology. In this case, Japanese firms were at the lead in certain industries or products within industries, but American firms have also had strong advantages in other industries and products.

One of the major flaws in assuming that foreign firms had no organizational advantages comes from the implicit assumption in many studies that direct investment is all about the manufacturing sector. But according to Japanese data (admittedly with all the caveats discussed earlier), only 55 percent of foreign direct investment in Japan was in the manufacturing sector, as of 1994.[27] Even if one assumes that Japanese manufacturing firms in some parts of manufacturing in the 1980s and 1990s represented the leading edge of technology and efficiency, this is not at all true in other sectors. In construction, financial services, accounting, legal services, civil aviation, management consulting, telecommunications, retailing, and other service sectors, American firms appear from casual observation to have far stronger technology and organizational skills than most or all of their Japanese competitors. So why is foreign investment in these industries not higher? As table 3-2 shows, the share of foreign-affiliated firms in the service sector was even lower than in manufacturing, a puzzling outcome if foreigners are supposed to have comparative advantage in this sector.

Several Japanese firms have done so well in international competition that they must possess significant organizational advantages themselves. The danger lies in generalizing from this small subset of firms to the overall situation. The generalized view that foreign firms had lost their earlier organizational advantages over foreign firms is simplistic and unrealistic.

A slightly different argument pertains to locational advantage or disadvantage. High labor costs and land costs are frequently cited as a factor limiting foreign investment into Japan and cannot be denied as a problem. By the mid-1970s Japan was no longer a low-wage economy, and the sharp appreciation of the yen after 1985 made Japan an unattractive location for new manufacturing production (unless production located geographically close to the customer is a characteristic of the particular product or industry). But the rise in the yen made Japan a more attractive location for exports from the United States and other countries. If foreign manufacturers needed a local investment to handle marketing, after-sales service, and research as suggested earlier, then the higher labor and land costs would not be a conclusive reason for manufacturing firms to avoid investment. Higher local costs caused by yen appreciation decreased the locational advantage of investment but simultaneously enhanced organizational advantages (that is, possession of products that now had a much stronger price advantage in the Japanese market) that could be realized through these distribution-related investments in Japan. Therefore, although some aspects of what one could consider traditional locational factors—wage and land costs—worsen for foreign firms, the impact was not clearly negative.

Perhaps the notion of locational disadvantages should be viewed more broadly. Although high wages and land costs may be a problem, one remedy is to invest away from the major urban centers of Tokyo and Osaka (which have the most developed markets for Western style housing, the international schools, and other amenities). Land is cheaper in the countryside, but very basic aspects of business infrastructure are missing in some of these locations. For example, Oita prefecture in the northeastern section of Kyushu Island, has been the location of a Texas Instruments semiconductor factory since the 1970s. Oita would like to attract further investment—both domestic and foreign—and can offer a largely rural setting with lower prices for land, housing, and food. But in Oita, only 27 percent of the population lives in dwellings connected to a sewer system. What foreign company, headed into the twenty-first century, wants to invest in a mature, industrial nation where there is a high probability of putting up with non-flush toilets at home? Of the seven prefectures in Kyushu, only Fukuoka (59 percent) is at or above the national average for percentage of population in dwellings connected to a sewer system (which is only 53 percent).[28]

It is possible to have a flush toilet without a sewer connection (using a septic tank), but applying the national average for flush toilets not connected to a sewer system brings the percentage of dwellings with flush toilets in Oita up only to 49 percent, meaning that just over one-half of all dwellings still had an old-fashioned nonflush facility.[29] Of course, even nationwide this remains a problem as well, with only 75 percent of all dwellings reported to have flush toilets. The point is that, at least away from the major urban centers, some very basic pieces of public infrastructure are poorly developed in Japan despite years of high levels of spending on public works, making these areas less attractive to foreign firms (and to domestic firms). This is the result of government policy, not just market outcomes. The central and local governments could have invested in better infrastructure but did not. Indeed, the point extends well beyond the odoriferous problem of sewage. Areas away from Tokyo and Osaka, for example, lack international airports (and even Tokyo's premier Narita Airport still has only one runway) and other business-related infrastructure important to foreign-affiliated firms.

Consider also a 1991 survey of American firms in Japan by the American Chamber of Commerce about their perceptions of problems of operating in Japan. The list included the high cost of establishing a business (largely a matter of the high cost of land, rental space, and housing), difficulties in recruiting local staff (essentially Yoshitomi's lifetime employment argument), complex or intricate methods of doing business, complex distribution systems, existence of *keiretsu* relationships, and nontransparent government regulations and policies.[30] This is an interesting list of obstacles as perceived by American businesses, since the problems apply broadly to the question of selling to Japan, not specifically to the establishment and operation of local subsidiaries. But what is most interesting about this list is that it is far broader than the traditional locational problems of labor and land cost. Essentially this list implies that American business continues to believe that a physical presence in Japan through direct investment will not necessarily enhance success in penetrating the market. Regulation, nontransparency, and other problems remain important. These are not simply the outcome of a benign and efficient but unique economic system. Many of these obstacles are the result of deliberate government policy. Even labor practices are the outcome of fifty years of government policy favoring long-term employment (that is, lifetime employment) and discouraging mechanisms to create a broader market for job switching.[31]

A few of the traditional locational problems eased somewhat after 1995. The continuing debacle in real estate markets meant that foreign firms could acquire land or rent space at a more reasonable price than in the late 1980s and early 1990s. By 1997 urban real estate in the six largest urban centers was down 56 percent from the peak in 1991, and commercial real estate in these cities was down 72 percent.[32] Simultaneously, the sizable decline in the value of the yen against the dollar reduced the dollar-denominated costs for real estate, as well as the cost of maintaining expatriates in Japan (food, transportation, children's education in private international schools, and other items). Falling costs may help account for the modest uptick in inward investment in 1996.

But other locational problems may still be operative. Too much has been made of the notion of "complexity" of distribution and other aspects of doing business in Japan. If business dealings are complex, the complexity applies equally to Japanese and foreign firms, and any diligent foreign firm can learn how the system works and adjust to it. What really matters are locational factors that work to the disadvantage of foreign firms. Of these factors, the core issue is acquisition of local firms. Acquisitions provide a primary method for foreign firms to enter other national markets. Acquisition of existing Japanese firms, in particular, provides a potentially successful strategy for overcoming some of the barriers perceived by foreign firms, because the acquiring firm gains the existing labor force, distribution and service relationships, political connections, local reputation, and other tangible and intangible assets of the acquired firm. If business practices are intricate or obscure, and government policies nontransparent, acquisition of a Japanese firm already accustomed to maneuvering in this environment would be helpful. And if lifetime employment means that foreign firms newly entering the market are at a disadvantage in recruiting employees, an acquisition solves the problem instantaneously. Nevertheless, foreign acquisitions of Japanese firms remain relatively infrequent.

Table 3-3 shows the number of foreign acquisitions in comparison to other merger and acquisition activity in Japan, as well as in comparison to the United States. Although the data indicate that it is not entirely impossible to acquire a local firm, the frequency remained low until into the 1990s. In numbers of firms acquired, the data show a big increase after 1991, from

Table 3-3. Mergers and Acquisitions in Japan and the United States

Nation and type[a]	1985	1986	1987	1988	1989	1990	1991	1992	1993	1994	1995	1996	1997
Japan													
Domestic–domestic					271	304	259	259	240	244	280	304	421
Domestic–foreign					411	463	262	199	134	204	212	257	199
Foreign–domestic					19	17	13	36	31	46	56	56	80
United States[b]													
Domestic–domestic	1,369	2,041	1,952	2,211	2,712	3,074	2,540	2,686	3,525	4,176	4,584	5,202	
Domestic–foreign	91	111	162	223	347	392	402	455	197	207	317	364	
Foreign–domestic	259	345	365	536	693	773	504	361	n.a.	n.a.	80	73	

Sources: Daiwa Securities, "M&A Shiryō 1998"; and Department of Commerce, *Statistical Abstract of the United States, 1994*, p. 551, and *Statistical Abstract of the United States, 1997*, p. 550.

a. "Domestic–domestic" refers to acquisition of domestic firms by other domestic firms; "domestic–foreign" is acquisition of foreign firms by domestic firms; and "foreign–domestic" is aquisition of domestic firms by foreign ones.

b. The domestic–domestic figures for the United States in 1993 and 1994 include foreign acquisitions of American firms because separate figures for foreign acquisitions are not available for those years.

less than twenty a year to eighty in 1997. Although this was far below the pace of foreign acquisitions of American firms in the 1980s and early 1990s, there was an unusual drop in foreign acquisitions in the United States in the mid-1990s (perhaps because Japanese firms became less active in the U.S. market), so that foreign acquisitions in Japan and the United States appeared more equal in the 1996–97 period.

However, the data in table 3-3 should be treated very cautiously. The Japanese data are based on informally gathered information on publicly traded corporations that publicly announce mergers and acquisitions. Acquisition activity in Japan is much larger than shown here. All mergers and acquisitions must be registered with the Japan Fair Trade Commission (JFTC). In 1993 the JFTC reported 1,917 mergers and 1,153 acquisitions. Most of these mergers were small; 83 percent of acquired firms had total assets of less than ¥5 billion ($45 million at 1993 exchange rates).[33] Unfortunately, the JFTC does not record the nationality of the firm carrying out the acquisition, so the Daiwa Securities data are the only source available. If one assumes that the Daiwa data have captured most acquisitions by foreign firms, then the low number of foreign acquisitions appears even lower relative to total merger and acquisition activity in Japan. More important, the fairly high number of mergers and acquisitions belies one piece of conventional wisdom about Japan. That is, Japanese firms are often described as averse to mergers and acquisitions in general, so that the paucity of foreign acquisitions is simply an outcome of local business custom. However, the data paint a rather different picture. Mergers and acquisitions do not appear to be infrequent within Japan according to the JFTC data. And according to the Daiwa Securities data, as Japanese firms began to move abroad in the 1980s, they very quickly learned to use acquisitions abroad as part of their own investment strategy.

Not all firms included in the Daiwa Securities data set reported the size of assets involved in the acquisition. However, financial data are available for forty-three of the acquisitions in 1997. For these acquisitions, the average total assets of acquired firms were ¥10 billion ($83 million at 1997 exchange rates), and this average fluctuated sharply over the years (from a low of ¥2 billion in 1992 to a high of ¥30 billion in 1995). In comparison, the average value of the seventy-three American firms acquired by foreign firms in 1996 was $40 million. (But this average also fluctuated greatly from year to year and was as high as $100 million in 1989). The most that can be concluded from these incomplete data is that the average size of acquisitions of Japanese firms by foreign firms does not appear unusually low in comparison to foreign acquisition activity in the U.S. market.

The upward trend in foreign acquisitions during the 1990s is somewhat encouraging. With the decline of the yen against the dollar after early 1995, acquisitions became less expensive from the perspective of foreign firms. And the continued poor economic performance in the Japanese economy during the 1990s may have led to an increased supply of firms willing to be purchased by foreigners. But the high level of foreign acquisitions in Japan in 1996–97 may equally represent a cyclical peak. The relevant comparison would be to the cyclical peak in foreign acquisitions of American firms in the late 1980s, when several hundred a year were occurring (peaking close to 800 in 1990). As a result the picture remains somewhat mixed; the upward trend is encouraging, but the level of foreign acquisitions in Japan as of 1997 is not yet high enough to imply that the problem is over.

Finally, consider the question of internalization in the OLI model as a cause of low direct investment in Japan. That foreign firms choose to interact with Japan through licensing rather than exports or investment does not necessarily reflect the preference of those firms. Firms, perceiving that barriers to exports exist, and that investment is difficult, may opt for licensing as the only realistic means for profiting from the Japanese market. This reasoning was certainly true in the early postwar period when trade and investment obstacles were overt and serious. That American firms still engage more heavily through licensing in Japan than elsewhere in the world in the 1990s is surprising. For many American manufacturing industries, Japanese firms are their primary competitors, which would suggest that American firms would be less inclined to license technology to Japanese firms than to other foreign companies out of concern for enhancing the competitiveness of their competitors. Rather than viewing licensing as an efficient economic choice, therefore, it is yet another manifestation of the difficulties of participating in Japanese markets by other means coupled with the aggressive pursuit of licensing contracts by Japanese firms.

This discussion implies that the OLI factors involved in producing foreign direct investment do not justify the low level of investment into Japan. Foreign firms, even in manufacturing and certainly in services, do have organizational advantages. Some locational factors worked against foreign firms after 1985, but mainly in terms of making Japan a less desirable location for manufacturing production. The main locational problems were the difficulty of acquiring domestic firms and the perception that a local presence would not necessarily enhance market access. And in terms of internalization, there is no reason to suppose that foreign firms prefer licensing over alternative strategies. The core issues are really the acquisition problem and the nature of market access barriers.

In recent years, the Japanese government expressed some concern about the low level of inward direct investment, admitting it as a problem or at least an embarrassment. The 1997 government White Paper on Trade expresses these sentiments. Noting that inward investment in 1995 was only 0.1 percent the level of investment entering the United States that year, the report pondered what the problems might be. Based on a survey of foreign firms in Japan, it turned up the usual suspects of high real estate costs, high corporate taxes, high wages, and administrative red tape, all producing a "high cost structure" environment.[34]

Although Japan certainly has a high cost structure, the government's focus on these issues missed the core problems identified above. As a result, the government has done little to modify the real factors that have limited inward investment and concentrated instead on a variety of small promotional programs beginning in the early 1980s. As reported by MITI in the summer of 1997, the array of policies included:[35]

—A package of measures enacted in 1992 intended to help firms overcome the initial cost of establishing a presence in Japan. This included extension of the loss carryforward provision in corporate income tax laws from five years to ten years (that is, losses incurred in any year can be applied against profits up to ten years in the future, a significant issue in Japan where subsidiaries can take a long time to reach a break-even point in their operation). In addition, this package included establishment of an organization to assist foreign firms called the *Tai-Nichi Tōshi Sapōto Sābisu* (called officially in English the Foreign Investment in Japan Development Corporation, or FIND).

—Expansion of below-market-rate financing for foreign firms from government financial institutions. The Japan Development Bank (JDB) had several programs, which first began in the early 1980s. In fiscal 1995, the JDB had a small total of ¥1.2 billion ($11.2 million) in loans outstanding to foreign-affiliated companies for promotion of direct investment (though this was down substantially from ¥27.9 billion in fiscal 1992).[36] In addition, a regional lending institution, the *Hokkaidō Tōhoku Kaihatsu Kōko* (scheduled to be merged into the Japan Development Bank in 1999), also has a lending facility for foreign firms. These programs also included eligibility for supporting infrastructure, such as loans to international schools for facility expansion.

—A variety of small programs run by the Japan External Trade Organization (JETRO) to help incoming foreign firms. These are focused mainly on seminars, lectures, and other meetings to educate foreign business people about investment in Japan. JETRO also has business support centers in Tokyo and four other cities (Osaka, Yokohama, Nagoya, and Kobe) that provide assistance to foreign firms new to the market (including temporary office space).[37]

—Changes in the Foreign Exchange Control Law at the beginning of 1992. Although virtually all controls over inward direct investment had been eliminated by 1981, this change shifted a prior notification requirement on investment to ex post notification. The change also included some other measures intended to increase transparency in administrative procedure.

—Other business support facilities in Tokyo and elsewhere. These centers provide seminars on doing business in Japan as well as language training and cultural education for foreign business people.

How should all these measures be evaluated? On the surface it is encouraging that the government at least acknowledged a problem and attempted to devise a policy response. Anything that affects the profitability of foreign firms in Japan, such as the change in tax provisions and subsidized business support, is a positive rather than a negative step. But the above measures will make little difference. Foreign firms in the 1990s were no longer as ignorant of conditions in Japan as in the past, and the private sector market of consulting firms to guide foreign corporations through the initial entry stage has become rather well developed. Change in loss carryforward provisions in the tax codes was helpful, but that provision was never a key obstacle to foreign investment. Subsidized government bank loans represented another small improvement, but loans from government banks no longer carried the sense of government acceptance (thereby opening other lending doors and business opportunities) that was the case in the past, and those intangible benefits might not accrue to foreign firms in any case. Foreign business support and promotion centers were a small useful addition, but as noted above the private market of management consulting services (including through American consulting firms operating in Japan) was well developed, so that the addition of a small array of government-subsidized services would not make a critical difference. Furthermore, many of the support facilities were placed in inconvenient locations that had far more to do with local politics and payoffs than any real intent to promote the inroads of foreign firms.

The only organization on the MITI list of promotion policies that came at all close to addressing an important issue was the *Tai-Nichi Tōshi Sapōto Sābisu* (FIND), which was created in 1993. FIND was intended to assist foreign firms in finding partners in Japan or possible acquisition targets. This organization was a so-called third-sector organization, blending government and private ownership. The largest shareholder was the *Sangyō Kiban Seibi Kikin* (Industrial Structure Improvement Fund), a subsidiary organization of MITI, which owned FIND jointly with a collection of approximately 100 Japanese firms and trade associations.[38] However, FIND has been criticized because its advice is limited to recommending tie-ups with its member firms (for which FIND receives referral fees). Furthermore, as a government organization it was not really an independent voice for merger and acquisition advice.[39] Foreign firms were less in need of advice or introductions to potential business partners than in a dismantling of the real obstacles to acquisitions.

Unfortunately, this kind of minor policy response—in which the list of individual actions by the government appears extensive but fails to address any of the core problems—is all too typical in Japan. Creation of programs and organizations (which can provide additional landing spots for retiring government officials—a problem addressed in chapter 5) takes precedence over substance. Furthermore, remarkably, the listing of investment promotion programs issued by MITI in the summer of 1997 was almost identical to that contained in a report issued five and a half years earlier at the beginning of 1992.[40] Neither the intensive bilateral Structural Impediments Initiative (SII) talks pursued by the Bush administration nor the part of the Framework talks of the Clinton administration focused on improving the climate for investment produced much of real substance in Japanese investment policy. Most of what the Japanese government has done must, unfortunately, be honestly labeled as trivial and irrelevant.

One must reluctantly conclude that the investment climate in Japan remains unattractive. Certainly some improvement has occurred over the past decade. Small programs by the government do not hurt, and recent developments in exchange rates and land prices eased some of the problems of the late 1980s. But at the core are two large problems: the perception that investment within Japan does not necessarily overcome the market entry problems foreign firms believe exist, and the difficulty of acquiring domestic firms. As a result, Japan is not an attractive location for investment in most sectors. As global firms plan their international allocation of investment, Japan is unlikely to be high on the list in most cases. This paints a discouraging picture.

Japanese Investment in the Rest of the World

During the past decade, a remarkable change has occurred in Japan's investment position in the world. Japanese manufacturing firms strongly preferred to produce at home until the mid-1980s. Thereafter, a combination of the sharp rise in the value of the yen against the dollar and fears about protectionism abroad (driven especially by the "voluntary" restraints on automobile exports to the United States that were binding during the 1981–85 period), Japanese direct investment abroad expanded very rapidly.[41] Meanwhile, service-sector firms were either constrained from going abroad by regulation (such as most financial institutions until the 1980s) or had little knowledge of foreign markets until the 1980s. The change was clearly visible in figure 3-1, which indicated the sharp increase in the annual flow of direct investment overseas compared with the continued low inflow of investment. Even though the collapse of the bubble in the early 1990s decreased the overall outflow temporarily, it was rising again in the second half of the 1990s.

Unfortunately these data have the serious measurement problems discussed earlier, which may cause official data to be overstated. However, the MOF does not attempt to measure either reinvested earnings of overseas subsidiaries or investment financed through local debt. This would result in underestimation of investment. A large share of investment in expanding Japanese affiliates abroad comes from retained earnings and thus does not show up in the Ministry of Finance data. For fiscal 1996, the ratio of reinvested earnings to total capital investment at overseas affiliates was 48.4 percent, based on the MITI survey.[42]

Table 3-4 attempts to sort out the impact of these measurement issues. The U.S. Department of Commerce bases its foreign direct investment data on surveys of foreign affiliates and includes investment from parent companies, reinvested earnings, and local debt financing. The table compares MOF data on Japanese direct investment in the United States with U.S. Commerce Department data on investment in Japanese-owned affiliates in the United States.

Table 3-4. *Japan's Direct Investment in the United States*

Billions of U.S. dollars

Year	Ministry of Finance	U.S.
1985	5.4	3.4
1986	10.2	7.3
1987	14.7	7.5
1988	21.7	17.8
1989	32.5	17.4
1990	26.1	19.9
1991	18.0	5.4
1992	13.8	2.9
1993	14.7	2.1
1994	17.3	2.7
1995	22.7	3.6
1996	22.8	8.8
Cumulative total 1996	240.0	118.1

Sources: Ministry of Finance, *Ōkurashō Kokusai Kin'yūkyoku Nempō*, 1990 ed., p. 443; 1992 ed., p. 480; "Statistical Profile: International Transactions of Japan in 1996," JEI Report, no. 45A, (December 5, 1997), p. 16; and Department of Commerce, *Survey of Current Business* (August 1990), p. 52; (July 1996), p. 106; (July 1997), p. 39; (June 1998), p. 43.

In every year in the twelve years reported, the Ministry of Finance recorded a higher flow of new investment into the United States than reported by the Department of Commerce, and in some years the disparity is startling. In 1993, for example, the MOF data indicate new investments in the United States of almost $15 billion, while the Department of Commerce finds only $2.1 billion. The probable cause is the lack of disinvestment in the Japanese data; stung by large losses, Japanese investors in real estate and finance appeared to be retreating from the U.S. market in the mid-1990s. As a result, by the end of 1996 (or March 31, 1997, in the MOF data), the cumulative value of Japanese investments in the United States as reported by Japan ($240 billion) was double that reported by the United States ($118 billion).

These measurement problems with the Japanese data are serious. However, assume that errors are reasonably constant across industries and locations (with some exceptions noted below). Then the MOF data may give at least a reasonable picture of overall trends in the flow, as well as geographic and sectoral composition, of Japanese direct investment overseas. As was

Table 3-5. *Japan's Foreign Direct Investment, by Geographical Region*

Percentage of total investment

Year	North America	Latin America	Asia	Middle East	Europe	Africa	Oceania
1985	45.0	21.4	11.7	0.4	15.8	1.4	4.3
1986	46.8	21.2	10.4	0.2	15.5	1.4	4.4
1987	46.0	14.4	14.6	0.2	19.7	0.8	4.2
1988	47.5	13.7	11.8	0.6	19.4	1.4	5.7
1989	50.2	7.8	12.2	0.1	21.9	1.0	6.8
1990	47.8	6.4	12.4	0.0	25.1	1.0	7.3
1991	45.3	8.0	14.3	0.2	22.5	1.8	7.9
1992	42.7	8.0	18.8	2.1	20.7	0.7	7.0
1993	42.4	9.4	18.4	0.6	22.0	1.5	5.6
1994	43.4	12.7	23.6	0.7	15.2	0.8	3.5
1995	45.2	7.5	24.0	0.3	16.7	0.7	5.5
1996	47.9	9.3	24.2	0.5	15.4	0.9	1.9
Cumulative total	44.2	11.3	17.8	0.9	18.8	1.5	5.5

Sources: Ministry of Finance, *Ōkurashō Kokusai Kin'yūkyoku Nempō*, 1990 ed., pp. 443–447; 1992 ed., pp. 480–483; and "Statistical Profile: International Transactions of Japan in 1996," p. 16.

shown earlier in figure 3-1, Japanese outflows of FDI peaked during the "bubble" years of the late 1980s. After bottoming out in 1992, however, the amount was once again rising. This pattern shows up in table 3-4 as well, although the drop in investment in the 1990s was much more pronounced in the U.S. data and did not turn up significantly until 1996. The point, however, is that despite the economic stagnation in the Japanese economy, Japanese firms, and particularly manufacturing firms, did not entirely abandon the trend of investing abroad. One motivation was the renewed appreciation of the yen from 1993 through 1995, causing more manufacturing firms to seek lower-cost production bases. The weaker yen in 1997 and 1998, plus uncertainty about the rest of Asia in 1998, though, will probably have a strong dampening effect on direct investment.

Table 3-5 presents the Japanese investment flows by region, showing the relative share of investment flowing to different geographical regions. Several features stand out in these data. First, by far the largest share of Japanese foreign direct investment has gone to the United States (or North America, of which most is in the United States), with the annual flow fluctuating between 42 percent and 50 percent over the period from 1985 to 1996. Second, the share destined for the rest of Asia increased in the 1990s, from a 10 to 11 percent level prevailing in the 1980s to a 23 to 24 percent level in the mid-1990s. Third, offsetting this increased share destined for Asia has been a falling share of investment in Europe. Finally, other parts of the world have attracted very little Japanese investment—the Middle East, Africa, and Oceania have received very little investment and a once sizable share to Latin America diminished. At the end of the 1980s, Europe had attracted increased investment as Japanese firms sought to invest prior to the formation of the European Union, but that interest waned after the EU was formed in 1992. Asia attracted increased investment as Japanese firms became increasingly focused on reducing labor costs as the yen appreciated in value against the dollar. Presumably this enthusiasm for investment in Asia was dealt a severe blow in 1997–98 by the economic turmoil in some Asian countries, but certainly Asia should continue to have strong attractions for Japanese business in the future (principally because of lower-cost labor and geographical proximity to Japan) and will be a favored location.

Perhaps the most interesting aspect of these data is the fact that Japanese firms continued to focus so heavily on the United States even as their enthusiasm for Asian investment increased. This apparent continued emphasis on the United States might be less than indicated in the Japanese data if disinvestment has been substantial and pertains more to investments in the U.S. market than elsewhere. However, Japanese firms were likely to have undertaken increased disinvestment in other regions as well, including Asia and Europe. Despite the high wage costs, Japanese firms were probably still worried about possible protectionism in their largest overseas market or had reasons to be geographically close to their customers (as has been the case for Japanese auto parts manufacturers following the major auto companies to the United States).

Data on Japanese investment by industry inject additional concerns about the accuracy of the MOF data. Table 3-6 shows Japanese investment in several selected major sectors—manufacturing, services, and within services the industries of trade (wholesale and retail—mainly investments by the large Japanese general trading companies), finance, and real estate.

People often assume that foreign direct investment is primarily a story of manufacturing (and the effort to find lower-cost labor). However, these data show that Japanese manufacturing investment has been a minority of total investment activity. The share of manufacturing rose in the 1990s as

Table 3-6. *Japan's Foreign Direct Investment, by Sector*

Percent of total investment

Year	Manufacturing	Services			
		Total	Trade	Finance	Real estate
1985	19	78	13	31	10
1986	17	80	8	32	18
1987	23	75	7	32	16
1988	29	69	7	28	18
1989	24	75	8	23	21
1990	27	71	11	14	20
1991	30	69	13	12	21
1992	29	69	11	13	15
1993	31	68	14	18	17
1994	34	65	11	16	12
1995	37	61	10	11	12
1996	42	56	10	16	13
Cumulative total (March 31, 1997)	30	68	11	18	15

Sources: Author's calculations based on Ministry of Finance, *Ōkurashō Kokusai Kin'yūkyoku Nempō* (Tokyo), 1990 ed., pp. 448–449; 1992 ed., pp. 484–485; and "Statistical Profile: International Transactions of Japan in 1996," p. 16.

the desire to relocate production to countries with lower wage costs increased with appreciation of the yen against the dollar. However, even in 1996 (when the effort to move production out of Japan was arguably at its peak, motivated by the very strong value of the yen against the dollar that prevailed from 1995 through most of 1996), the share of manufacturing was 42 percent, and for cumulative investment abroad through fiscal 1996, the share was a lower 30 percent.

Among other industries with significant investment abroad, wholesale and retail trade has traditionally been important because this sector includes the large Japanese general trading companies that have dominated the handling of international trade. But these data indicate that for the decade from the mid-1980s to the mid-1990s, finance and real estate also occupied significant shares of new investment flows. As financial regulation was eased in the 1980s, Japanese financial institutions rushed to establish a presence abroad—creating substantial operations in major money centers such as New York and London, as well as acquiring local financial institu-

Figure 3-3. *Japan's Overseas Production*

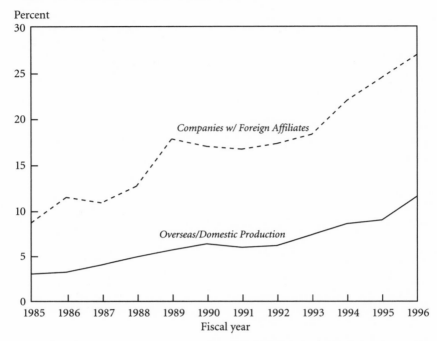

Percent

Companies w/ Foreign Affiliates

Overseas/Domestic Production

Fiscal year

Sources: Ministry of International Trade and Industry, *Wagakuni Kigyō no Kaigai Jigyō Katsudō* (Survey of Overseas Business Activities of Japanese Companies), no. 26 (1998) p. 36; and data for 1996 from MITI website www.miti.go.jp/stat-j/h2c4003j.html.

tions (including retail banks in California, for example). Similarly, in real estate investors rushed into purchases of American, Australian, and other foreign properties in the late 1980s, so that real estate peaked at 21 percent of total foreign direct investment in 1989 and 1991. However, the data for the 1990s must be misstated because of the failure to record disinvestment. These data do indicate that the share of direct investment going into finance and real estate declined in the 1990s (with finance down from a peak of 32 percent in 1987 to 16 percent by 1996, and real estate down from its 1991 peak of 21 percent to 13 percent in 1996). By 1996, though, Japanese investors were liquidating some of their overseas real estate holdings, and Japanese financial institutions also appeared to be in retreat. Since the MOF data do not record disinvestments, the picture presented by the official data is distorted. American data for net investment by Japanese-affiliated firms show negative flows (that is, disinvestment) in real estate in a few years after 1990, and generally smaller investments in finance than during the 1980s.[43]

Figure 3-3 puts Japanese manufacturing investment abroad in a different context, showing the ratio of production overseas to domestic production. From only 3.0 percent in 1985, this ratio rose slowly but steadily to 11.6 percent in 1996. Similarly, the percentage of manufacturing firms with affiliates abroad rose from 8.7 percent to 27.0 percent. While still lower than similar ratios for the United States or European countries, these data indicate a substantial change for Japan. These data come from the flawed MITI survey, with voluntary returns to a mailed questionnaire. Therefore, the ratio of overseas production to domestic production is underestimated because the overseas figure includes only the production reported by those firms responding to the questionnaire. Estimating the probable underestimation is impossible since firms with foreign affiliates within the sample might have been more likely to complete the survey form than those with no foreign affiliate (so that the reported data represent more than 60 percent of firms with affiliates)—a distinct possibility that also implies the data for the proportion of firms with foreign affiliates are overestimated. Despite all the problems with the accuracy of the data, the trends over time are likely to be valid: both the ratio of production overseas to domestic production in the manufacturing sector and the percentage of Japanese firms that have foreign affiliates have been rising.

Among manufacturing industries, the same MITI survey indicates that 64 percent of the sales of overseas affiliates came in only two industries in fiscal 1995: electric machinery and transport machinery (mainly the auto industry).[44] Another way to demonstrate the importance of these two industries is through the ratio of overseas production to domestic production, presented in figure 3-4. At 16.8 percent for electric machinery and 20.6 percent for transport equipment, the overseas production ratios were far ahead of the 9.0 percent average for manufacturing as a whole in fiscal 1995. If the caveats about the MITI data are kept in mind, it is reasonable for one to assume that the problems in the sample do not vary significantly across industries. That is, while the ratio of overseas production to domestic production is underestimated, the degree of underestimation does not vary significantly by industry. If this is the case, then the concentration of overseas investment in electric machinery and transportation equipment is correct.

All of these data, despite the major data problems, imply that a major change has occurred since the 1980s. Japanese manufacturing firms that had

Figure 3-4. *Ratio of Overseas to Domestic Production*

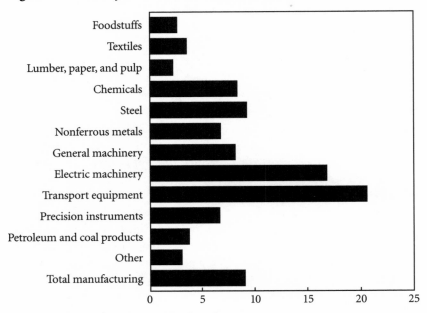

Source: MITI, *Wagakuni Kigyō no Kaigai Jigyō Katsudō*, p. 38.

previously preferred to center their production entirely at home rapidly relocated production overseas. Service sector firms other than the traditional general trading companies moved abroad too, motivated by both competitive pressure and reduction in regulatory restrictions. Even with the dampening of investment flows in the wake of the collapse of the "bubble" of the late 1980s, there is no mistaking the fact that a fundamental shift had occurred and was continuing in the mid-1990s. Rapid investment abroad then raises the question of impact on trade flows. If Japanese firms relocated manufacturing investment abroad, what happened to the output from those subsidiaries?

Data in the annual MITI survey of subsidiaries of Japanese firms abroad indicate that 11.2 percent of imports in 1996 were from foreign affiliates of Japanese firms, a ratio that has risen considerably from a 4.0-4.6 percent range in the 1986 to 1990 period—shown in figure 3-5. From 1992 to 1996, the absolute value of these imports from affiliates increased by ¥2.6 trillion (from ¥1.5 trillion in 1992 to ¥4.1 trillion in 1996). Over the

Figure 3-5. *Imports from Affiliates*

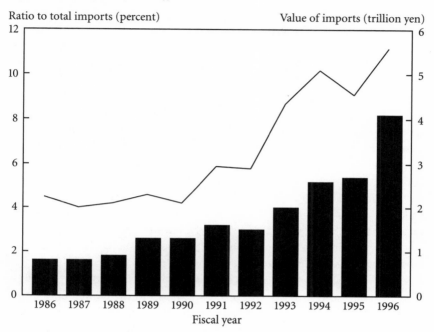

Sources: MITI, *Wagakuni Kigyō no Kaigai Jigyō Katsudō*, p. 63; and data for 1996 are from MITI website, www.miti.go.jp/stat-j/h2c4011j.html.

same period, total Japanese customs-clearance imports increased by ¥8.4 trillion, so that the share of increased imports in the 1992–96 period coming from affiliated firms was a high 31 percent. This is a conservative calculation, assuming that firms reported to MITI the landed cost of goods coming from their overseas affiliates. If the values represent the cost of goods exclusive of the cost of moving them to Japan, then the ratio increases 32 percent.[45] Either way, the data suggest that a modest but substantial portion of the net increase of Japanese imports from the early to mid-1990s came from affiliates of Japanese firms. Also keep in mind that the MITI survey reports only the numbers for the firms answering the survey, which also makes these ratios conservative.

A noticeable portion of increased imports coming through intra-firm transactions reinforces the point that rising imports in the 1990s did not necessarily mean Japanese markets were more open. With existing domestic distribution channels, political or bureaucratic connections, and products already meeting domestic standards, Japanese manufacturing firms faced fewer problems in relocating production abroad and bringing products back home. Non-Japanese firms could easily continue to face serious access problems while imports were actually rising. This occurrence implies that the distinction between foreign goods and foreign firms is important. The term "imports" in trade data refers to a geographical location of production, which might be produced by firms of any nationality. With a portion of increased imports coming from Japanese-owned firms, foreign-owned firms did not benefit quite as much in the 1990s as the data in chapter 2 would indicate. However, this point should not be carried too far. Imports coming from Japanese-affiliated firms did not account for the majority of the total increase. And as chapter 4 discusses, exports from the United States to Japan did rise rapidly in the 1990s. Relatively few of them represented products from Japanese-owned subsidiaries in the United States.

A somewhat related question is the impact of Japanese subsidiaries abroad on sales by Japanese firms to the U.S. market. The MITI survey of 1995 showed that Japanese-affiliated firms in Asia (China, ASEAN 5, Hong Kong, Taiwan, and Korea) exported ¥843 billion to the United States during 1994.[46] Not all of the sales of these firms were identifiable by destination; assuming that the unallocated portion of sales flowed in the same geographical pattern, sales to the United States would be ¥1.6 trillion. Assuming that surveyed firms were representative of all Japanese-affiliated firms in Asia (70.1 percent of whom responded to the survey), exports to the United States from all affiliated firms to the United States would be ¥2.2 trillion. At 1994 exchange rates, this sum comes to $21.0 billion. In that year, the United States imported $146.7 billion from these countries, making imports from Japanese affiliates 14 percent of the total. The MITI survey notes that exports from Asian affiliates to the United States increased 2.4 times in the period from 1986 to 1994, confirming the notion that this flow of Japanese-firm-affiliated goods to the United States has expanded very rapidly.[47] Over the same period, U.S. imports from these countries rose 2.4 times, or $86.7 billion, from $60 billion in 1986.[48] If one accepts the MITI survey result on the increase in exports from Japanese-affiliated firms during this period, exports in 1986 would have been ¥916.7 billion, or $5.4 billion at 1986 exchange rates. By this estimate, goods from Japanese-affiliated firms accounted for only $15.6 billion of the $86.7 billion increase in U.S. imports from these countries.

This exercise implies that U.S. imports from Japanese affiliates in Asia are substantial and have grown rapidly in the past decade. However, the numbers are not sufficiently large to justify the common perception that the deteriorating American trade balance with the rest of Asia is due entirely to growing imports from Japanese firms in those countries. American firms also invest in Asia and ship products back to the United States, as do firms of other nationalities. And for South Korea and some other Asian countries, purely domestic firms are major participants in exporting to the United States too.

Conclusion

Analyzing the direct investment dimension of the U.S.-Japan economic relationship is difficult because of the very poor quality of the Japanese data. Although these data provide extensive interesting detail, the flawed collection techniques practiced by both the Ministry of Finance and Ministry of International Trade and Industry severely limit the validity and usefulness of the numbers. But even with all the caveats, cautions, and efforts at estimation in mind, the analysis of the preceding pages yields several important conclusions.

First, the striking disparities between high levels of Japanese investment abroad and low levels of foreign investment into Japan that were evident in the late 1980s continued virtually unabated in the 1990s. Whereas Japanese firms invested heavily abroad in the past decade, foreign firms remained a small presence in Japan relative to the situation in other industrial nations. Even when generous assumptions are made about the underestimation in the official investment data, foreign firms have a far smaller presence in Japan than is true in other industrial nations.

Second, the low level of investment in Japan does not seem to be simply the outcome of corporate preference. Among the explanations for this disparity in investment flows is the rapid rise of the yen after 1985, which made Japan a less desirable production base (for both Japanese and foreign manufacturing firms). But this is not a complete explanation. By the 1980s, official investment barriers were gone, and foreign firms should have had strong organizational reasons to increase investment into Japan. Even in manufacturing, Japanese firms' competitive strengths did not extend to all industries or products. Furthermore, even though the appreciation of the yen made Japan a less attractive location for manufacturing production, the need for foreign manufacturing firms to invest in distribution and after-sales service continued. In the service sector, the advantage of foreign firms is more pronounced, and often investment is an essential ingredient of market participation. Therefore, the level of foreign direct investment in Japan is lower than what one would expect, related to the problems of acquiring local firms, the nature of market access barriers, and the lack of strong supporting infrastructure relative to other countries.

From the standpoint of direct investment theory, one could argue that foreign firms have not had distinctive advantages that would lead them to invest in Japan, but this chapter has demonstrated that this notion does not hold up to scrutiny. Even firms that do appear to have strong corporate advantages have felt disadvantaged in Japan. And in the service sector, where American firms are well ahead of their Japanese counterparts in several industries, there is also a record of access problems and low investment.

Third, the low level of foreign investment into Japan is directly related to market access issues. In the straight economic sense, the low level of investment implies a lower level of imports into Japan. Foreign firms in Japan import more to Japan than they export, in the context of an economy that has had an overall large trade surplus. Meanwhile, the presence of American firms in Japan, and the existence of trade between American parents and subsidiaries in Japan, is far less prevalent than in other bilateral relations of the United States. The data suggest strongly that American firms would prefer to be more heavily invested in Japan and to be able to conduct more sales to Japan that are routed through their own subsidiaries. In a broader sense, the unwillingness of foreign firms to invest more heavily in Japan is another manifestation of the perception that market access is limited in ways that cannot be overcome by a stronger local presence through investment. Firms will invest when they perceive that a physical presence will contribute to penetration of the market and generation of corporate profits. That perception relates more to perception of market barriers than land prices or the high cost of maintaining expatriates in Japan.

Fourth, the increasing presence of Japanese manufacturing firms abroad has contributed to a situation in which trade numbers in the 1990s improved somewhat but benefited foreign firms less extensively than raw data imply. Japanese firms have obvious advantages exporting back to their own country; the same insider advantages they have been able to use to keep foreign firms at bay gives them an advantage in bringing their own products in from abroad. Thus it is possible for the trade numbers to show a large growth of imports, giving the impression of a change in the conditions of market access without much fundamental shift. Foreign firms unaffiliated with Japanese firms still face market barriers.

Overall, the investment dimension of the relationship confirms and extends the picture formed from analyzing the trade data in chapter 2. Problems of access to Japanese markets remained through the mid-1990s. Although Japan was certainly not "closed" to foreign firms, the trade and investment patterns together imply that access to Japanese markets has been more difficult and more obstructed than in other nations. This conclusion leads directly to the next chapter, which explores what the U.S. government has done in the 1990s to deal with these problems.

CHAPTER FOUR

Trade Negotiations
in the 1990s

Bilateral trade relations in the first half of the 1990s were characterized by a continuation and intensification of the tensions that had developed in the 1980s. Data presented in chapters 2 and 3 provide a strong explanation for why this American pressure on Japan occurred. Modest improvement in import penetration and intra-industry trade levels took place from the mid- to the late 1980s, but those changes plateaued or retreated, while wide price differentials and low levels of foreign investment into Japan continued unabated. First the Bush administration and then the Clinton administration sought to accelerate improvement in market access through intensive negotiations. The Bush administration created the Structural Impediments Initiative, a series of negotiations concerned with structural or generic issues pertaining to many industries rather than dwelling only on narrow problems raised by individual firms or industries. The Clinton administration created the Framework Agreement, a broad agreement with the Japanese government that laid out an ambitious negotiating agenda, including structural and sectoral negotiations, macroeconomic discussions, and cooperation on global issues.

This chapter analyzes these trade negotiations of the 1990s, with a special focus on the Framework talks of the Clinton administration. Although the objectives of both the Bush and Clinton administrations were laudable and ambitious, the accomplishments were modest and the negotiating environment difficult. This negotiating record demonstrates that no magic bullet exists that will yield rapid improvement in access to Japanese markets. Besides reviewing the negotiating history of this period, this chapter discusses a number of the problems characterizing the negotiating process.

The most visible development of the 1990s was the contentious period in bilateral relations during the first term of the Clinton administration. Opponents were highly critical at the time of the administration's handling of the bilateral relationship. This chapter concludes that the picture was far more complex; the administration certainly made some early mistakes, but other important factors beyond the control of the administration helped create tension. Along the way, much of what was happening was rather distorted in the press. The modest successes and problems of both the Bush and Clinton administrations provide useful lessons for how to (and how not to) pursue bilateral negotiations.

U.S. government efforts to negotiate improved market access in Japan have a much longer history, dating back to the 1960s. Through the Kennedy and Tokyo rounds of multilateral negotiations in the GATT, plus bilateral negotiations, U.S. government officials had achieved agreement from the Japanese government on substantially eliminating quotas and lowering tariffs from the early 1960s through the 1970s. But during the 1980s, the Reagan administration pursued a collection of tariff, quota, and other non-tariff issues with the Japanese government. Limited success on some of these problems and the highly public opposition of the Japanese government led to rising tension as the decade wore on. Trying to accelerate progress, the Reagan administration created the Market-Oriented Sector Selective (MOSS) negotiations in 1985, a process that involved intense negotiations on a number of impediments in four industries (forest products, medical equipment and pharmaceuticals, electronic products, and telecommunications equipment and services).[1]

Unsatisfied with the administration's efforts, a Democratic-controlled Congress passed the Trade Act of 1988. This legislation required the administration to identify countries that were "unfair traders" and then engage in negotiations addressing identified problems (through a provision in the law known as Super 301). This action by Congress reduced the discretion of the White House in deciding what priority to attach to trade negotiations with Japan and what tactics to employ. Although Congress acted out of a partisan dissatisfaction with the Reagan administration's trade policies, many within the administration were also increasingly frustrated in their dealings with Japan. In this atmosphere of heightened awareness of continuing access problems in Japan, increasing frustration at the slow pace of progress in making markets more open, and rising discontent in Congress, the Bush administration took office in 1989.

The Bush Administration and the
Structural Impediments Initiative

From 1989 through 1992, the Bush administration pursued a vigorous, multipronged agenda of trade negotiations concerning Japan. Its efforts included pursuing some issues through the Uruguay Round of multilateral negotiations in the GATT as well as bilateral talks. At the bilateral level, the administration pursued specific sectoral issues and created a new approach to solving generic or structural problems.[2]

The Bush administration was faced immediately with enforcing the Super 301 provision of the Trade Act of 1988. Frustration over Japan had been a principal reason why this clause was added to the Trade Act of 1988, so the new administration had little option but to name Japan as an "unfair" trading partner and specify a negotiating agenda to resolve identified problems. Partly to take the sting out of being named under Super 301, the administration picked only three product areas for negotiation (government procurement of satellites, government procurement of supercomputers, and technical barriers in forest products), picked two other countries as "unfair traders " so that Japan was not the sole target, and simultaneously proposed a parallel set of discussions called the Structural Impediments Initiative (SII).[3]

The Structural Impediments Initiative focused on generic problems rather than those identified as obstructing a particular firm or product, and the scope included both macroeconomics and microeconomic problems. At the macroeconomic level, the talks focused on structural features of the economy (such as land policies and tax policy) that might increase the level of savings in society, thereby contributing to Japan's large current-account surplus. At the microeconomic level, they focused on problems such as weak antitrust enforcement and the restrictions on expansion of large-scale retail stores as generic obstacles to increased imports. Intense meetings progressed over the next year, resulting in a variety of agreements announced in a joint report in 1990.

As a concept, SII had some appeal as a mechanism to move away from contentious industry-specific struggles and to cast issues in a way that might have appeal to the Japanese public. At the time, some observers felt the SII approach had tapped an existing desire among business and individuals in Japan to reform and deregulate the economy.[4] The heady days of the economic "bubble" when the economy was growing at a 5 percent annual rate were certainly a time of domestic discussion of the need to deregulate, and in the SII process, the U.S. government used the analysis and policy proposals emanating from that domestic discussion. In retrospect, the extent of real reform sentiment in Japan was exaggerated, and the image of public support for the U.S. government's positions was short-lived. As discussed in chapter 5, deregulation and structural change remained on the domestic policy agenda through the 1990s, but substantial progress in most areas were not achieved.

Whatever its worth, the Bush administration stuck with the SII approach for only a year before largely losing interest. Furthermore, one of the most successful pieces of the talks turned out to be very closely tied to a specific industry or firm-based problem (the Large-Scale Retail Store Law and its negative impact on the entry of Toys R Us into Japan). Only when the distribution issue was tied to the problems facing Toys R Us did negotiations make real progress. After the summer of 1990, the administration's overall enthusiasm for SII faded, and the Japanese bureaucracy resisted negotiations more stoutly.[5]

Officially the SII process continued beyond the initial year of 1989–90 but achieved relatively little additional progress. The initial sense of public and business willingness to endorse American pressure for regulatory change faded rapidly, and the Japanese government became doggedly resistant. As part of its increased resistance, the Japanese government opposed further commitments on change in Japan on the grounds that the U.S. government had not implemented recommendations in the joint report for change in America. Since the SII process had been a two-way one, the Japanese government had recommended various structural reforms in the United States. As noted by one U.S.-government participant, the next joint report issued in 1992 was far less ambitious than the 1990 report as a result of this resistance.[6]

SII had other problems. Although the exercise may have offered useful education to American officials with little background on Japan, many of the issues were simply too difficult or complex to yield much progress in a relatively short period, and many of them were somewhat peripheral to American concerns about market access. Consider the land policy issue, which was part of the SII discussion of structural reasons for the domestic excess of private savings over investment. Complex land use rules, skewed

taxes related to real estate, and taxes on land transfer intersected to produce a real estate market in which transactions were relatively few and the
price of land very high. Arguably, the high price of land forced people to
save more money to meet down-payment requirements to purchase a
home. Those higher savings then contributed to the imbalance between savings and investment in the domestic economy and the emergence of large
current-account surpluses. But the regulations and tax policies were complex and had produced strong vested interests in society that would be disadvantaged by changes. In any society, changing policies that strongly affect
large parts of the population is difficult politically. Trying to make much
progress in the space of a year of SII talks was simply not possible and even
more difficult when momentum was lost after 1990.

This appraisal of the limitations of the SII process differs from some
recent academic analyses, which have viewed SII relatively favorably, notably
in the research of Leonard Schoppa and Norio Naka.[7] Both authors chose to
define "success" in the SII process by whether bilateral agreements were
reached and the extent to which those agreements resembled the initial
American demands (or perceptions of the initial demands as portrayed by
the press). Press perceptions, especially the Japanese press, can be exaggerated or focused excessively on some elements of initial bargaining positions to the exclusion of others. Governments often include a basket of
requests or demands at the beginning of a negotiation, knowing that many
of them are expendable. Evaluating success by comparing final outcomes
to press perceptions of initial demands, therefore, can be misleading without knowing which demands were serious.

More important is whether agreements made a difference in making
markets more open. By that standard, the SII talks were not particularly successful. As detailed in chapters 2 and 3, the end of the 1980s and early 1990s
were years in which indicators of foreign success in entering Japanese markets were not improving. As with most negotiations in the past twenty years,
the best one can say is that SII chipped away a bit at the problem of market
access and structural distortions. Accomplishments were certainly positive
but modest. One of the principal U.S. government participants in the SII
process has expressed a similarly modest assessment of the outcome.[8]

The late 1980s may have represented an unusual point in time for
Japan. After several years of rapid economic growth, the sense of confidence
in Japan was high. Economic success engendered discussion of tackling
difficult structural economic questions and produced a receptive attitude
toward foreign pressure in that direction. Perception that structural reform

was under active discussion encouraged the incoming Bush administration to undertake the SII approach. That the talks had such modest results despite the seemingly favorable mood toward change should be a sobering lesson in the difficulties of achieving substantial progress in any limited period of bilateral negotiations. By the time the Clinton administration arrived in office, attitudes were again changing in Japan. Despite extensive talk of deregulation, the economy was entering a period of relative stagnation, and concern was rising about the possible implications of real deregulation and structural change on employment.

Assumptions of the Incoming Clinton Administration

When the Clinton administration took office, one goal was to raise the priority attached to the economic relationship with Japan. The bilateral relationship with Japan has two somewhat separate sides: security and economics. The two countries are tied by a bilateral mutual security treaty that includes the stationing of American soldiers on bases in Japan, as well as an extensive web of trade and investment activities. Throughout the postwar period, the security relationship has been dominant in American thinking about the overall relationship with Japan, but this dominance was increasingly challenged during the 1980s by academics, business people, and members of Congress. The incoming Clinton administration embraced a shift in the relative priority of the economic and security sides of the relationship.

Consider the communiqué of the Bush-Miyazawa meeting in Tokyo in January 1992 as an example of the traditional approach. The overarching theme was "Global Partnership," conceived mainly in terms of political and security cooperation plus joint efforts to promote global economic growth. Discussion of the political and security aspects of the bilateral relationship preceded the text on economic issues in both the communiqué and the attached details or action plan.[9] Such an approach was quite traditional and fit the postwar notion that the political-security relationship defined the overall relationship, within which economics and business was accorded a supporting role. Even though the purpose of the Tokyo Summit was viewed as heavily economic, the rhetoric of the administration stuck to the traditional formulation. Emphasis on a close partnership, common visions of the world, and security cooperation presumably provide cover for often contentious trade negotiations. But the dominance of security also means that when trade negotiations do become contentious, those involved with the security side of the relationship play a moderating or dampening role, leading U.S. administrations to lessen pressure.

The incoming Clinton administration wanted to alter this set of priorities. The Framework Agreement of July 1993 dealt only with the economic relationship, and the bilateral summit meeting from which it emerged produced no broad written statement on political or security affairs. In his opening statement at his confirmation hearings, Ambassador Walter F. Mondale turned to economic issues first in his summary of the administration's policy goals. As he put it, "First, our most pressing need at this time is to correct the imbalance in our economic relationship."[10] In later speeches, Ambassador Mondale continued to reflect a strong emphasis on economics, even though he was always careful to cover all aspects of the relationship in general policy presentations.[11]

This decision to give high priority to the economic relationship lasted only for the first term of the administration for a variety of reasons. The subsequent move back to a more traditional stance took place after resolution of the automobile negotiations in the summer of 1995 and the occurrence soon thereafter of a horrendous rape incident involving U.S. soldiers stationed in Okinawa. With the completion of the automobile negotiations, all the principal elements specified in the Framework Agreement had been negotiated, leading to a natural decline in priority. And by the fall of 1995, the security relationship needed some attention and not simply because of the rape case. By April 1996, when President Clinton met with Prime Minister Hashimoto, both of them clearly and deliberately emphasized the primacy of security issues in their opening press statements after the meeting.[12] This shift in relative emphasis was not lost on the Japanese media. One newspaper report of the summit meeting had as its sizable headline the news of a shift from economics to security.[13]

Although the shift in emphasis back to a traditional stance is understandable, it had some unfortunate consequences. The change in relative emphasis fed into an environment of less success in opening Japanese markets. Believing that the U.S. government no longer cared as much about economic issues, the Japanese government was prepared to slow down its response to American requests on measures to make Japanese markets more open. Focused closely on the relationship with the United States, Japanese government officials have long believed that the tendency of the Americans to emphasize the security relationship provided opportunities to delay or diminish responses on trade negotiations, and judging from the record of negotiations thereafter, they seemed to interpret the shift in 1995 in these terms.

Besides initially assigning trade relations a higher relative priority when it came to office, the administration also intended to adopt a more aggressive stance on trade negotiations. Even in a speech before the 1992 election President Clinton stated, "Although the U.S. has negotiated many trade agreements, particularly with Japan, results have been disappointing. I will ensure that all trade agreements are lived up to." Thus he reflected a desire to do something more aggressive motivated by a belief that many agreements had not worked as intended—either at a micro level (meaning that agreements had not solved access problems in the specific market) or a macro level (to reduce the bilateral deficit).

Note that this expression came from the president himself. Any president faces a broad array of domestic and international issues, within which economic relations have rarely garnered much time on the presidential agenda. The interest of President Clinton in spending time on these issues in speeches and meetings represented a change. So the incoming administration chose to shift the emphasis on Japan from security to economics and assigned these issues a higher priority on the crowded presidential agenda.

In articulating a desire to pursue a more aggressive strategy, President Clinton was reflecting the frustrations of American business, frustrations that had been building throughout the 1980s and early 1990s. By 1993 business was calling for something beyond the usual trade negotiations and agreements to make access to Japanese markets more open. The Advisory Committee on Trade Policy and Negotiations (ACTPN), a private sector group reporting to the U.S. Trade Representative (USTR), issued a report on relations with Japan in February 1989 that had endorsed a vague concept of "results-oriented" negotiating strategies.[14] In January 1993, just as the Clinton administration was about to take office, ACTPN issued a new report. This report endorsed the notion of using temporary quantitative indicators (TQIs) to measure progress toward outcomes that would reasonably result from an open market. This concept assumed that some neutral analysis could be made on what foreign market share in Japan would be for a particular product in the absence of trade barriers, a quantative outcome to which both countries could agree at an official level. This market share indicator would become a goal, presumably to be removed once reached.[15]

This approach, essentially endorsing the market share indicator approach of the semiconductor agreements of 1986 and 1991, raised the specter of managed trade. The ACTPN report tried to draw a distinction between its proposal and managed trade, arguing that such indicators were not intended to produce cartelized outcomes in Japan, would not be an automatic trigger for American retaliation when not realized, and should simply be thought of as a "benchmark" in the tradition of Total Quality Management in corporations. Failure to achieve the TQI level, would, however trigger review within the U.S. government to determine what additional measures (including the option of retaliation against Japanese exports to the United States) might be appropriate. The report assumed that such indicators would be acceptable to the Japanese government, since both sides were interested in solving problems rather than political posturing.[16]

This distinction between indicative benchmarks based on an estimated open-market outcome, and managed trade in which government forces the agreed outcome, proved to be a difficult concept to define or articulate convincingly. However, the ACTPN report, which represented the opinion of a sizable group of American corporate executives, including many who were not associated with radical ideas concerning Japan, provided intellectual input for the notion of "objective criteria" that eventually emerged in the Clinton administration.

Similarly, this document alerted the Japanese government (just as the earlier ACTPN report in 1989 had done at the outset of the Bush administration) to a concept that it would have to work against. Having signed the semiconductor agreements, out of the practical spirit recognized by the ACTPN group, the Japanese government was unwilling to generalize this approach. Why? Market share agreements might have been acceptable to Japanese government officials when agreement was reached in private (covered by a public pretense of open trade) or under extreme duress, but when adopted broadly and publicly, they represented an embarrassing acceptance of the notion that access to markets in Japan was obstructed and that, given the deeply collusive nature of markets, simply changing the official rules of access would not make much difference. Furthermore, the semiconductor agreement was widely regarded as having made a real difference in market outcomes, and to extend a truly successful strategy to a number of other markets would have been inimical to the desires of the Japanese government and industry.[17] Therefore, the assumption of both the ACTPN report and the incoming Clinton administration that a results-oriented approach of TQIs would be acceptable to the Japanese government was badly mistaken.

Is this cynical view of the Japanese government's motives in resisting the notion of TQIs overdrawn? Based on international trade theory, economic efficiency, and the overall goals of multilateral trade negotiations in the GATT, one can argue that TQIs would represent an unfortunate departure from the rules-based effort to make markets more open. However, the commitment of the Japanese government to genuine market liberalization was very weak, and the possibility that they were genuinely concerned by this theoretical concept is very doubtful.[18]

Rather than being worried about a departure from general principles of rules-based market liberalization, the Japanese government was more likely to have been motivated by the more practical concerns just laid out—embarrassing exposure of the disparity between principle and reality in Japanese government policy, as well as the fear of real increase in market access. Although the government's response may be characterized in these practical if cynical terms, the American academic economics community cared much more deeply about principle.

The Framework Agreement

Once in office, the Clinton administration quickly put together a basic strategy for economic relations with Japan. The centerpiece of the administration's new trade policy was completion of the Uruguay Round negotiations, achieved by December 1993. The Uruguay Round agreement lowered tariffs, tightened language on technical and phytosanitary standards, and created the new World Trade Organization. Japan was part of those negotiations, and in that sense, trade relations with Japan were bound up in the successful effort to complete the Uruguay Round. Some elements of the WTO negotiations involved certain concessions by the Japanese government, such as the limited opening of the domestic rice market. However, as was true in the Bush and other previous administrations, trade policy toward Japan proceeded at a multilateral and bilateral level.

At the bilateral level, the new administration sought to create a new framework to guide negotiations on both macro- and microeconomic issues. This effort led to bilateral negotiations before the meeting between the president and Prime Minister Miyazawa at the G-7 summit meeting in Tokyo held at the beginning of July 1993. The concepts pressed by the administration in this initial negotiation would define the nature of bilateral dialogue on economic issues. The result was the so-called Framework Agreement signed on July 10, 1993.[19]

Most of what was included in this document represented little real change from the past, but some of the language was different. One objective of the agreement was to move away from the pattern of the 1980s, when economic issues had often been kept off the summit agenda. Therefore, the agreement mandated that economic issues would be "anchored" in biannual meetings of the two leaders. The president and prime minister already met at least twice a year anyway (for the G-7 and APEC meetings), so the number of meetings was not an increase, but the emphasis on holding bilateral discussions on economic matters was a new stipulation. Although this may have been unnecessary, since discussing economic matters at summit meetings had become more routine from the time of the Bush administration, the Clinton administration still preferred to put this commitment to paper, partly because of the continuing desire of the Japanese government to keep these issues off the summit agenda (as they later tried in the planning for the April 1996 meeting).

The agreement covered several aspects of the relationship, including macroeconomic policy discussion, microeconomic market access issues, and a common approach to global problems. At the macroeconomic level, the agreement aimed at producing a reduction of Japan's then rapidly growing current-account surplus. The agreement states, "Japan will actively pursue the medium-term objectives of promoting strong and sustainable domestic demand-led growth and increasing the market access of competitive foreign goods and services, intended to achieve over the medium term a highly significant decrease in its current account surplus."[20] The United States, meanwhile, pledged to pursue a goal of substantially reducing its domestic fiscal deficit, promoting domestic savings, and strengthening its international competitiveness.

At the microeconomic level, the agreement mandated negotiations in several areas, aimed at increasing global access to Japanese markets. The purpose of these negotiations was to "deal with structural and sectoral issues in order substantially to increase access and sales of competitive foreign goods and services through market-opening . . . measures."[21] Specific product or structural areas designated for negotiation were government procurement (of computers, supercomputers, satellites, medical technology equipment, and telecommunications equipment), financial services, insurance, competition policy, transparent government procedures, deregulation, distribution, the automotive industry (vehicles and parts), intellectual property rights, access to technology, and long-term buyer-supplier relationships.

On global issues, the agreement established a Common Agenda for Cooperation in Global Perspective.[22] This Common Agenda was meant to create collaborative efforts to deal with issues pertaining to the environment, technology, development of human resources, population, and AIDS. The Common Agenda provided a deliberate effort to demonstrate that bilateral economic relations included government-to-government cooperation as well as disputes.

What was new about this agreement was the insertion of language referring to the direction of change expected in economic variables. As noted, the macroeconomic commitment called for a "highly significant decrease" in Japan's current-account surplus. For government procurement, the agreement noted that measures negotiated should "aim at significantly expanding Japanese government procurement of competitive foreign goods and services." On autos and auto parts, the eventual agreement was to achieve "significantly expanded sales opportunities to result in a significant expansion of purchases of foreign parts by Japanese firms in Japan and through their transplants."[23]

Furthermore, the two governments agreed to formalize a process of monitoring the outcomes of agreements. The agreement states, "The two governments will assess the implementation of measures and policies taken in each sectoral and structural area . . . based upon sets of objective criteria, either qualitative or quantitative or both as appropriate."[24] Thus, without specifying market share targets or other specific numbers for imports, this language committed the Japanese government to the principle of accepting rising sales by foreign firms as an outcome of greater openness and to a bilateral monitoring process to review progress. This language was the administration's attempt to insert its concept of "results-oriented" policy into the agreement. On the one hand, this language got the Japanese government to admit that agreements ought to result in observable differences in market access, as expressed in the language on significant increases in sales of foreign goods and services. On the other hand, the administration avoided specific numbers or targets that could have been identified as representing "managed trade" and accepted additional qualifications on "competitive foreign goods and services." Nevertheless, the subsequent attempt to embody the concept of results-oriented policies into bilateral agreements on specific sectors proved very difficult and controversial.

Even this rather vague language on the objectives of agreements was difficult to obtain, with the negotiating process following a familiar pattern of last-minute resolution. Negotiations had broken down on several occasions, and then lasted literally through the final night of President Clinton's visit to Tokyo, and at one point involved a physical altercation between two members of the Japanese delegation who disagreed with each other on the wisdom of allowing such language in the agreement.[25] Since both sides make concessions in any negotiation, presumably the Clinton administration had initially asked for language stronger than "significant increase" on particular sectoral issues. It is also widely known that the U.S. Treasury Department had wanted the Ministry of Finance to accept stronger language calling for a reduction of the current-account surplus below 2 percent of GDP by the end of 1996. Deputy Treasury Secretary Roger Altman wrote in early 1994 that the U.S. government interpreted the framework language of "highly significant" to mean "a fall in those surpluses from 3.5 percent of GDP to below 2 percent . . . in three to four years."[26] This quotation suggests the language that Treasury had probably wanted written into the Framework Agreement itself, but when the agreement was signed, the administration had settled for the more mild language of "highly significant," a retreat from an initial desire for stronger or more precise language that would characterize all of the subsequent specific trade agreements.

The Framework Agreement incorporated the structural approach emphasized in the Bush administration's SII talks (through inclusion of such structural issues as intellectual property rights, distribution, and competition policy) and sectoral issues (such as insurance and automobiles). Thus the common perception that the Clinton administration abandoned a structural approach is not correct, and several structural issues were part of the active agenda. The deregulation issue, for example, included periodic bilateral meetings and submission of lists of desired changes for the Japanese government to consider as its deregulation process (which has emphasized list making—discussed further in chapter 5) moved forward. Certain structural areas were later subject to considerable attention and negotiation, including import clearance procedures (which continued from the SII Working Group on Import Procedures to the Framework's Deregulation and Competition Policy Working Group), and eventually brought progress on some of the issues involved (especially improvement in cumbersome, time-consuming, and expensive import processing for air cargo).[27]

Other structural areas addressed by the Clinton administration included government procurement (mainly in the two industry-specific categories of telecommunications equipment and medical equipment), inward direct investment, intellectual property rights, and harbor services practices. Negotiations on intellectual property rights, for example, resulted in two agreements in 1994 designed to reduce time and idiosyncratic procedures in Japanese patent processing that disadvantaged foreign firms.

The reality is that all recent administrations have engaged in both sector-specific and structural negotiations, and often the line between the two is obscure. The Bush administration, although devoting much energy to the SII talks, also conducted negotiations related to several specific industries. The Bush administration reached bilateral agreements on wood products (1990), supercomputers (1990), government procurement of general purpose computers (1992), government procurement of satellites (1990), public works construction contracting (1991), semiconductors (1991), cellular phones and radio communications (1989), digital network channel termination equipment (1990), international value-added network services (1990 and 1991), paper (1992), flat glass (1992), automobiles and auto parts (1992), certain agricultural products (corn and dairy products, 1992), and amorphous metals (1990).[28] Altogether, the Bush administration negotiated thirteen bilateral industry or sectoral agreements with Japan in its four years, as well as several informal "understandings" that were contained in the January 1992 action plan.[29]

What the Clinton administration dropped or deemphasized were structural issues such as land policy (including taxes and zoning), *keiretsu* practices, and competition policy, areas that showed little opportunity for progress at that time. Nor did these areas have any industry-specific problems that could be used as a means to broach the broader structural issues. On competition policy, for example, the Bush administration had been instrumental in getting the Japanese government to strengthen antitrust penalties and increase the staffing and budget for the Japan Fair Trade Commission. As a result, the Clinton administration observed the implementation of these changes and evaluated their impact but did not press for further changes.

The point of stressing the inclusion of structural issues is to counter the conventional wisdom that the Bush administration adopted a useful and novel structural approach that the Clinton administration abandoned. Although the Bush administration highlighted the SII talks, it engaged in extensive sectoral negotiations. Some of these were part of the Super 301 mandate, but most of them were not. And the Clinton administration, whose sectoral negotiations on issues such as automobiles attracted the most attention, actively pursued structural issues too. The distinction between the two administrations and their approaches, therefore, is over-done. The relative merits of structural and sectoral approaches are considered further in chapter 6, suggesting that in most cases a structural approach is unlikely to be successful unless anchored to the specific problems of an American firm or industry.

Once the Framework Agreement was signed, serious negotiations on all the different issues began. Initial expectation was that some agreements would be ready for signing at a bilateral summit in Washington, D.C., scheduled for February 1994. Language to this effect was included in the Framework Agreement, which called for "utmost efforts" to reach agreement on government procurement, insurance, and automobiles in time for the first bilateral summit in 1994.[30] This goal proved illusory. Sparring over a variety of issues took place, including both the substance of rules-based changes in regulations and other aspects of market access, and disagreement over language on expected outcomes. Rather than resulting in last-minute compromises after all-night bargaining sessions just before the February summit meeting, the negotiations failed to produce any agreement on any of the individual trade negotiations. For the first time in the postwar period, the usual use of deadlines had failed to provide sufficient incentive to reach agreement. President Clinton and Prime Minister Hosokawa somewhat stiffly announced continued disagreement while others expressed disappointment. The press focused on missed signals and other negotiating mistakes on both sides.[31]

Following the February summit, bilateral negotiations were in abeyance for several months while the Japanese government attempted to create a new set of concessions on its own. The new package was announced by the Japanese government on March 29, 1994, but deemed by the U.S. government to be of insufficient content to warrant resuming real negotiations.[32] With the Japanese side not bringing sufficiently new proposals forward, the administration chose to increase the sense of pressure by announcing a revival of the Super 301 provision of the Trade Act of 1988 and saying that a determination of priority problem areas under its provisions would be announced September 30. This effectively established a new deadline for negotiations.[33]

This time the implicit deadline produced some agreements. Over the summer agreement was reached on one of the less controversial areas of negotiation—intellectual property rights. And with the traditional all-night bargaining, October 1 brought agreement on four issues: government procurement of medical equipment, government procurement of telecommunications equipment, procurement by Nippon Telegraph and Telephone (NTT), and insurance (which was actually only "an agreement to agree" by December pending additional negotiations on remaining disputed points). Negotiations on financial services other than insurance were resolved by January 1995.

By the end of 1994, the only major remaining trade area specified for negotiation in the Framework Agreement was automobiles and auto parts. At issue were several somewhat separate problems: access in Japan for foreign cars (including the allegation that domestic Japanese manufacturers actively discouraged existing dealers from carrying foreign automobiles), the market for auto parts for new cars (including sales to Japanese transplant factories in North America, plus sales to factories in Japan), and sales of parts into the replacement part market in Japan.

All three involved matters of regulation or enforcement of antitrust law in Japan. Sales of foreign automobiles rested mainly on existing dealers. As in the United States, most dealers are independent businesses with the right to handle more than one brand of automobile (a fact that eased the entry of Japanese automobiles into the U.S. market). But the argument was that dealers were afraid to exercise this right because of pressure from their existing Japanese suppliers, and that the government had not enforced antitrust laws in this case. Parts for new cars involved problems of tight *keiretsu* relations between parts manufacturers and the major car companies. The issue of replacement parts was regulatory in nature, involving a system of car inspection and licensing of repair garages that was alleged to result in a car repair system biased toward use of the original manufacturers' parts. But besides antitrust and regulatory remedies, the administration was hoping for something akin to the forecasts made in 1992 by the Japanese automakers about their plans to purchase foreign parts that they made.[34]

The negotiations leading up to the October 1 deadline produced no resolution on autos, and the U.S. government responded by initiating a regular section 301 investigation (rather than invoking the more politically visible Super 301 provision). Bilateral negotiations resumed in December, but relatively little progress occurred in the next several months on either the substantive issues on deregulation or the language on the objective criteria for evaluating the outcome, even though the completed negotiations on the other issues pointed the way to what should have been acceptable language on autos.

Automobiles and auto parts represented the largest of the American industries involved in the set of Framework negotiations. Autos also represented a sector that had been at the heart of bilateral tensions since the beginning of the 1980s, including the "voluntary" export restraints on Japanese auto exports to the American market in place 1981–85, as well as the 1992 Bush administration agreement on increased market access in Japan and "forecasts" of auto parts purchases. Believing that more could be accomplished than the Bush administration had achieved and aware of the political importance of the industry, its union, and the states where it was located, the Clinton administration was determined to press these negotiations vigorously. But the lack of progress from the beginning of negotiations in September 1993 through the spring of 1995 presented a serious problem.

At this point, the administration chose to raise the stakes again. As the result of its self-initiated section 301 investigation, President Clinton announced on May 10 two new steps: retaliation against Japanese exports to the United States and initiation of a WTO case.[35] The retaliation took the form of a punitive 100 percent import duty on thirteen models of luxury cars from Japan announced several days later, effective immediately but with actual collection of the import duties postponed for one month.[36] With the WTO, USTR sent a letter of intent to formally file a case within forty-five days.[37] Although the WTO case would take time, the imposition of the tariff provided an early deadline.

This time, the Japanese government responded in kind, filing its own WTO trade case against the United States, arguing that the unilateral imposition of tariffs on Japanese luxury cars was a violation of WTO rules. That is, the Japanese government argued that regardless of the merit of any case the United States might bring about conditions of access to Japanese markets for automobiles and auto parts, the choice of raising tariffs prior to any authorization from the WTO was a violation of WTO commitments.

On the one hand, the Japanese automobile industry faced a serious blow should its government fail to reach agreement by the deadline because the duty was sufficiently high to effectively knock Japanese cars out of the luxury car market in the United States. Because profit margins on luxury cars are typically higher than for less expensive models, and because these models were generally manufactured in Japan and exported to the United States (rather than manufactured at Japanese transplant factories), this measure had the potential of lowering profits for Japanese auto manufacturers. This could have been especially serious for Nissan, which had an operating loss in both fiscal years 1994 and 1995.[38] On the other hand, the unilateral imposition of a tariff against a single trading partner was, in the view of many observers, a violation of U.S. obligations under the WTO.

Having that question tested by a WTO dispute resolution panel decision was not very attractive to the U.S. government.

In this highly charged atmosphere, negotiations resumed. Indicative of the high-pressure atmosphere, President Clinton focused two public speeches (one delivered at an auto assembly plant) on his determination to follow through with the punitive tariffs if no reasonable negotiating outcome materialized by the June 27 deadline.[39] In June the Japanese government bargaining position began to soften on some of the difficult regulatory issues, and the Japanese auto manufacturers began to announce their parts purchase plans.[40] Just hours before the U.S. government would have begun collecting the retroactive tariff, agreement was finally reached and announced on June 28. Most of the text dealt with changes in regulations and clarification of the rights of existing car dealers to carry additional lines of foreign cars under Japanese antitrust law, but it also contained language on objective indicators for the follow-up evaluation by the two governments resembling that used in the agreements reached on other issues in 1994.[41] The Japanese car manufacturers individually issued forecasts of their future demand for foreign parts, as well as announcing capacity expansions at their North American plants (to which American and other foreign parts producers had been more successful in selling than to car factories in Japan), developments that the two governments officially "welcomed" in the agreement.[42] However, the two governments viewed the outcome differently, with the joint announcement including separate statements. USTR Mickey Kantor included estimates of the impact of the agreement and the forecast by Japanese auto firms on purchases of American-made auto parts for use in transplant factories, production of vehicles in the United States, purchase of American auto parts for use in Japan, and the hoped-for increase in the number of existing dealers in Japan who would add American cars to their existing sales lines (to 1,000 outlets by the year 2000). MITI Minister Ryutaro Hashimoto made clear that the Japanese government had no involvement in any of these calculations.[43] (See appendix B for the text of the agreement. This agreement is of central importance to bilateral trade relations in the 1990s.)

With agreement reached, the U.S. government canceled its proposed WTO case and the 100 percent import tariffs, while the Japanese government canceled its WTO case as well. But there were two problems with the agreement. First, the scope for disagreement in interpretation seemed wide, a point that the press emphasized immediately.[44] Second, some wondered if the actual agreement was worth the pressure applied, or whether the import tariffs should have been imposed because the deal was not good enough.[45] The regulatory and other changes in the agreement were only a modest step in the long-running effort to open the auto and auto parts markets. What is most interesting about the modest outcome of the negotiations, however, is that the threat of punitive tariffs had become necessary to achieve even this outcome, indicative of the depth of the opposition to change in this industry in Japan. A final question is whether the resolution of the negotiations without actual implementation of the 100 percent tariffs lowered the reputation of the administration. Those who felt that the agreement was very modest could argue that rather than settling for this agreement, a better outcome would have been to impose the retaliatory tariff. By not imposing the retaliation, the administration furthered a Japanese view that this American bargaining tactic was only a bluff. This dilemma is considered further in chapter 6.

Outcomes

One of the ironies of the 1990s was that the heightened tensions of 1993–95 came when U.S. exports to Japan were increasing rapidly. The overall economy was close to stagnant, with 0.3 percent growth in 1993, 0.6 percent in 1994, and 1.5 percent in 1995, followed by a temporary rebound in 1996 to 3.9 percent in 1996 before heading back into recession.[46] Economic stagnation usually works against imports, but the 1993–95 period was one of rapid and strong yen appreciation that gave imports an added price advantage despite economic stagnation. From ¥125 per dollar at the beginning of 1993, the yen appreciated against the dollar to a peak of ¥84 in April 1995, and even in August of 1996 it was still ¥108.[47] As the yen rose against the dollar, foreign goods and services gained price competitiveness against domestic ones.

Figure 4-1 shows the rise in the yen-denominated value of imports from 1993 through 1996. After falling from 1990 to 1993, total imports grew 41 percent from 1993 through 1996. Manufactured goods rose 56 percent, and some product areas such as electric machinery imports exploded by 127 percent. This is the increase that produced the modest upward movement in the import penetration and intra-industry trade statistics analyzed in chapter 2. One could argue that this outcome indicated that exchange rates matter far more than trade negotiations in producing higher sales of foreign goods and services. However, that conclusion would be at least an exaggeration of what was really happening.

Figure 4-1. *Japan's Yen-Denominated Imports*

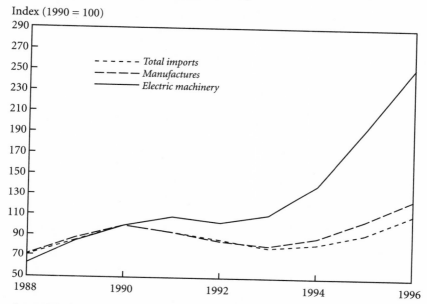

Index (1990 = 100)

Total imports
Manufactures
Electric machinery

Source: Author's calculations based on Organization for Economic Cooperation and Development, *International Trade by Commodities Statistics, H.S. Rev. 1, 1988–1996* (Paris, 1997), on CD-ROM.

Part of the growth in imports was the result of the extreme level to which the yen appreciated. Consider the hypothetical demand curve presented in figure 4-2. When the currency is weak, import demand drops quickly because imports are not price competitive with domestic goods (shown as line segment AB). But once they become price competitive, over a wide range of exchange rates demand may be very inelastic in collusive markets (shown as line segment BC). That is, the volume of sales does not change much as the currency continues to appreciate because of problems such as collusion in the domestic industry or discriminatory regulations that keep imports relegated to a niche in the domestic market, even as foreign goods gain what should be a considerable price advantage. But even in protectionist or collusive economies of this sort, there must exist some exchange rate at which the price disparities between domestic and foreign products are so wide that collusion or the zeal to maintain discriminatory rules and regulations begin to fray (shown as line segment CD). This appears to represent what happened in Japan in the 1993–96, though the

Figure 4-2. *Demand for Imports*

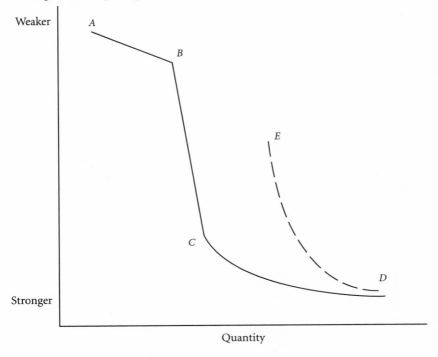

record of difficult negotiations suggests that the impact was more on reducing domestic collusion to keep out foreign goods rather than any reduction in the desire of government to stick to discriminatory rules and regulations. Anecdotally, this period was one during which firms were questioning their long-term relationships with domestic suppliers.

A second outcome of the appreciation of a currency is the decision of domestic firms to relocate production overseas. As discussed in chapter 3, this was also happening. A large part of the growth in electric machinery imports, therefore, was the result of imports from new production subsidiaries abroad rather than from foreign firms. In this sense, the rise of imports provides an image of structural change in domestic markets that exceeds the reality.

What was true of Japan's global imports, however, was also largely true of American sales to Japan. Figure 4-3 shows U.S. exports to Japan. Since

Figure 4-3. U.S. Exports to Japan, 1989–96

Index (1990 = 100)

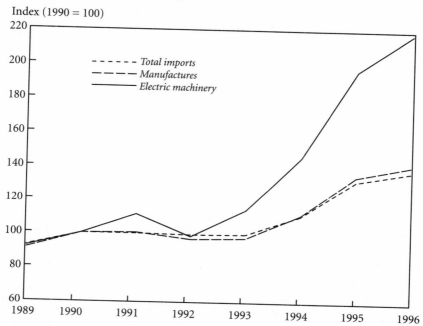

- - - - - - Total imports
- - - - - Manufactures
———— Electric machinery

Source: Author's calculations based on OECD, *International Trade by Commodities Statistics*, H.S. Rev. 1, 1988–1996, on CD-ROM.

these data are dollar denominated, they are somewhat different from Japan's import data but provide a better picture of the real sales of American firms since the 1993–95 yen appreciation meant each yen could purchase a greater quantity of foreign products. After being flat from 1990 to 1993, total U.S. exports to Japan rose about 40 percent by 1996; manufactured goods rose by the same amount, and exports of electric machinery jumped almost 120 percent. Thus, even though electric machinery imports from Japanese subsidiaries in Asia were a substantial part of what was occurring in this period, imports from the United States rose rapidly too.

Do these rapid increases in Japan's imports from the world and from the United States imply that the trade negotiations and attendant tensions of the 1990s were inconsequential? No, for two reasons. First, the increases could not occur unless or until other aspects of market access had improved. The 1993–96 increase was at least in part the legacy of the trade negotiations of the 1980s and early 1990s, which cleared away some of the thicket of obstacles facing imports so that domestic purchasers could buy foreign products should the move in the exchange rate make them exceptionally attractive to domestic buyers. Put in terms of the demand curve in figure 4-2, if regulatory or standards barriers were not cleared away, then demand would remain constrained even when imports have a strong price advantage. The negotiations of the first term of the Clinton administration had a somewhat smaller impact on the trade data in figures 4-1 and 4-3 since most of the agreements were not completed until late 1994 and 1995, with implementation to occur over a period of time after the signing. By 1996, though, the Clinton first-term agreements should also have been contributing to the rise in American sales to Japan.

Second, trade negotiations affect the composition of increases in exports to Japan. Without efforts to make markets more open, only those products not facing serious market barriers would benefit from the movement in the exchange rate. This would skew American exports to Japan, generally in an undesirable direction. If the market for logs is open while that for wood products (lumber, plywood, and other composite materials) is not, then an appreciation of the yen would increase sales of American logs (which gain price competitiveness against Japanese timber) while not affecting sales of wood products even though they gain price competitiveness as well. Therefore, trade negotiations to make those markets in which American firms are competitive on a global basis more open leads to a more efficient outcome.

These same trade data also provide a strong explanation for the decline in political priority on trade negotiations with Japan in the second term of the Clinton administration. Having experienced a rapid rise in sales to Japan for three years, American manufacturing firms were less inclined to press Washington to negotiate vigorously over further improvements in market access. Even though firms may have felt that they still faced unusual problems in Japan that were at odds with Japanese government commitments under the WTO or bilateral agreements, the desire to pursue those issues diminished, at least temporarily.

The trade data presented above extend only through 1996. With the return of economic stagnation, coupled with the depreciation of the yen in 1997 and 1998, the situation shifted once again. In 1997 real GDP growth was only 0.9 percent, and 1998 was expected to result in an actual contraction of the economy. From ¥108 per dollar in August of 1996, the yen sank steadily to ¥140 in the summer of 1998 before rebounding. In these circumstances, foreign goods and services faced both a stagnant economy and decreased price competitiveness. The big question would be whether what economists call hysteresis would come into play. Having achieved some breakthroughs in Japanese markets, with new profitable relationships established, would the fall in the yen drive domestic buyers back to their previous domestic sources of supply, or would they stick with their new foreign suppliers? As shown in figure 4-2, the question is whether demand for imports would slide back to the niche range (line segment BC), or whether real structural change in demand had occurred (represented by dashed line DE). Loss of some price competitiveness would naturally lessen demand for imported goods, but the new demand curve would leave foreign products with higher sales at any given exchange rate than before.

Problems

The two years of negotiations under the Framework Agreement from 1993 to 1995 proved exceptionally noisy and difficult, although the end result was signed agreements in all areas negotiated. Why did this period of time prove so difficult? The answers are important for understanding the continuing problems of designing and implementing successful strategies for negotiating with the government of Japan explored later in chapter 6.

Several major problems impeded progress. First, as noted earlier, the Japanese economy had been growing rapidly in the late 1980s (with an average annual real economic growth rate of 5 percent from 1987 through 1991), and society, business, and government appeared to be in the mood to accept some change, deregulation, and market opening. As a result, the Bush administration faced a positive attitude on at least certain portions of the SII agenda in the 1989–90 period. But by 1993 the economy was stagnant, worries about the future were rampant, and the government was in no mood for greater market openness. The movement in the exchange rate provided a serious prod on domestic firms to lessen their dependence on long-time domestic suppliers, but this desire did not translate into any shift in the behavior of government negotiators.

Many in the United States thought the political change occurring in the summer of 1993, when Prime Minister Morihiro Hosokawa became the first non-Liberal Democratic Party (LDP) prime minister since 1955, would bring a change in the stance of the Japanese government toward market liberalization. Just after Hosokawa's ascension to the prime ministership, Thomas R. Reid, the Tokyo bureau chief for the *Washington Post* at the time, reflected this optimism when he described the Hosokawa cabinet as a "striking infusion of new blood into a political system that had previously been strongly resistant to change" and commented that his coming to office was a "political earthquake."[48] This reporting typified the enthusiasm of Americans for the new government in Japan. A reform government pursuing deregulation and structural change ought to have made bilateral trade negotiations easier. But the Japanese government desires to preserve Japanese markets to the maximum extent possible for Japanese-owned firms. Its policy since the early 1960s has consisted of the three "D's"—Deflect, Delay, and Diminish the pressures for change coming from the United States and other countries. Advent of the new Hosokawa government made no discernible difference in this basic attitude.

When the LDP returned to power in 1994 (albeit in a coalition with the Socialist Party in which the Socialists were permitted to hold the prime ministership to provide a facade of involvement), the same patterns continued. Ryutaro Hashimoto served as MITI minister during the brinkmanship of the auto negotiations in 1994–95, and later as prime minister permitted the frustrating backtracking and renegotiation of the insurance agreement. And in 1998, Japanese government officials under both the Hashimoto and Obuchi governments pursued an unhelpful and obstructionist position by being the only country to oppose a regional trade liberalization package on nine product areas within APEC.[49]

Second, after twelve years of Republican administrations, the Japanese government and press seemed to believe that Republicans represented free trade and (therefore) Democrats represented protectionism and managed trade. As a result, the Japanese government was ready to react negatively even before Clinton assumed office. As stated by then-Foreign Minister Michio Watanabe one day before the 1992 U.S. presidential election, "The Democratic Party has been supporting trade protectionism and attempting to put a brake on the sale of cheaper Japanese goods."[50] And Kazuaki Harada, vice president of the Sanwa Research Institute at the time commented, "It's going to be difficult times."[51] Certainly Democrats in Congress during the 1980s had used trade policy with Japan as a means of attacking the Reagan administration, culminating in the Trade Act of 1988 with its Super 301 provision. And some in the two parties differed on political rhetoric, with a greater tendency for Republicans to use terms like free trade. But Japanese perceptions exaggerated the difference between Republicans and Democrats. Assuming that the new administration would be protectionist and would pursue a hard-line version of managed trade, the Japanese government began from an exceptionally antagonistic position.

Third, the government of Japan may have been worried that the Americans had learned the essentially managed nature of markets in Japan. The emphasis on results indicated a rising American understanding that problems often were not resolved by signing documents to modify rules to provide easier market access. The traditional strategy of deflect, delay, and diminish was under serious challenge if this recognition led to insistence on either targets or serious periodic review of negotiating outcomes. Even without specific targets, the notion of reviewing statistics with the expectation that the role of foreign firms should increase if market barriers fall was a direct threat to the bilateral bargaining game pursued by the Japanese government and industry for the previous thirty years. Certainly not all bilateral agreements had failed to achieve their objective of more open markets in Japan, but the frequent perception among American business people was that little had changed in markets where conditions of participation had presumably been improved through bilateral negotiations. Therefore, if the Clinton administration recognized this problem and was determined to do something about it, then the Japanese government faced a serious challenge to its past strategy of minimizing real change while satisfying American negotiators with the image of greater openness.

Fourth, after almost fifty years of playing a relatively low-key, passive, conciliatory role in bilateral affairs, the Japanese government was beginning to show signs of increased willingness to be more assertive in responding to American pressures. In the exchange of letters at the time the Framework Agreement was signed in July 1993, Japan's ambassador to the United States, Takakazu Kuriyama, stated clearly that Japan would reserve the right to withdraw from any negotiation in which the United States resorted to use of section 301 or other sections of American trade law to take action against Japanese exports.[52] Although Japan did not exercise this option in the fall of 1994 when USTR announced a decision to proceed with a section 301 investigation of the automobile and auto parts issue, the case filed against the United States at the WTO in the spring of 1995 concerning the 100 percent tariffs on luxury cars from Japan was a sharp departure from the past. These were Japanese government actions that would not have happened just a few years earlier and appeared to result from changed attitudes within the Japanese government about how to respond to American trade policy. An era of Japanese passivity in the bilateral relationship had come to an end.

This shift was further aided by the new WTO itself. By restricting the ability of nations to block dispute panel decisions, and by creating doubts about the WTO-compatibility of section 301 of the U.S. Trade Act (discussed further in chapter 6), the new WTO framework provided the Japanese government with a viable option to counter American market-opening pressures that dovetailed with this new-found assertiveness.

Fifth, results-oriented policies proved to be very difficult to define and equally difficult to get the Japanese government to accept. Anything that was not explicitly "free trade" could be described as managed trade, and defining an intermediate position was virtually impossible. This complex issue is considered further later in this chapter.

Besides these large issues that contributed to greater difficulty and increased tension in the negotiating process, various smaller factors specific to the 1993–95 period mattered. Consider, for example, that in the first year of negotiations between the Clinton administration and the Japanese government under the Framework Agreement, Japan had four governments. Bureaucrats carry out the bulk of actual negotiations, but they need direction from politicians—even in bureaucrat-dominated Japan. But from July 1993 to July 1994, Japan had four different prime ministers— Miyazawa, Hosokawa, Hata, and Muryama. The swirl of arriving and departing cabinet officials and political power brokers complicated the bilateral relationship.

Furthermore, the Hosokawa and Hata cabinets were the first non-Liberal Democratic Party (LDP) cabinets since 1955. During the nearly forty years of LDP governments in Japan, the bureaucracy developed close personal ties with party leaders. When politicians needed to enforce political decisions on a ministry, a network of personal connections could be brought into play to bring compliance from the bureaucrats (or the reverse, with bureaucrats using networks to get support for their policies from politicians). Some politicians began their careers within the bureaucracy (Prime Minister Miyazawa began as a Ministry of Finance official, for example) and other LDP Diet members built ties with bureaucrats when they were serving as minister or parliamentary vice minister of particular ministries. These ties have been an important part of making the wheels of government work in a society in which personal relationships are an important feature of political and economic behavior. Imagine the shock to the system when the first non-LDP government since 1955 came into office in 1993. Many of those carefully nurtured relationships presented bureaucrats with a problem. Although the new ruling coalition included some who had been climbing the rungs of power within the LDP before bolting the party in July 1993, many of the new crop of cabinet ministers had no webs of personal ties to the bureaucracy on which to rely. Worse, successful personal relationships are a means of building trust and loyalty. All of those ties had been between bureaucrats and LDP politicians. Should a bureaucrat be helpful and compliant toward the new non-LDP coalition? What would happen if the LDP were to return to power (as it did in 1994)? Would compliant behavior toward the new coalition result in destruction of ties of trust with the LDP when that happened? These serious questions led to confusion, anxiety, and attenuated ties between the political and bureaucratic levels during the Hosokawa and Hata governments, complicating relations with the United States.

Political change also led to a problem of political leadership. Under LDP dominance, political power was relatively easy to identify. Politicians moved up over the years within the LDP hierarchy, and figuring out which ones represented the major sources of power on particular issues was not difficult. A cabinet minister might be weak or ineffective, but somewhere within the LDP would be a senior figure with whom both bureaucrats and foreign negotiators could work quietly to resolve problems. But the Hosokawa and Hata governments and the initial Hashimoto government were all coalitions involving complex new relationships. Even with the LDP more firmly in control in the Hashimoto and Obuchi governments, the party was more fractured, alliances more fluid, and the role of traditional power brokers less certain. Figuring out where the centers of political power lay became far more difficult from 1993 on. If Japanese bureaucrats had difficulty in identifying the locus of leadership, imagine the difficulty for foreign trade negotiators. To whom should they turn for decisions to break negotiating deadlocks? In a few cases this question could be answered. In the case of the 1994 negotiation on cellular phones, the informal "godfather" of the Ministry of Posts and Telecommunications was Ichiro Ozawa, the leader of the group that broke with the LDP in 1993 and led the formation of the coalition government.[53] Since he had built his relationship with the MPT during his long LDP career, he could use his network of personal ties. That negotiation was resolved quickly and successfully. But such cases were rare. More typical was a problem of political weakness of the cabinet ministers and relative mystery as to "back" channels that could be pursued.[54]

One should also recognize that the new Clinton administration had its own new officials, who needed time to learn their jobs and were prone to early mistakes. Many of the people coming into the administration had little or no background on Japan, trade, or diplomacy, leading to early missteps. By trying to establish an ambitious agenda toward Japan in the spring of 1993, the new administration moved too quickly. At that point in time, some jobs were still unfilled (Undersecretary of Commerce for International Trade Administration Jeffrey Garten, for example, was not confirmed until the fall). And those who were in place had not yet learned their jobs or had little notion yet of what tactical approaches would or would not work with the Japanese government. Equally important, the new administration had not really reached internal agreement on how it wanted to proceed on issues such as how to define the vague notion of results-oriented negotiations.

All of these factors contributed to a particularly difficult negotiating environment from 1993 to 1995 when the Clinton administration chose to push its trade agenda vigorously. And some factors continued into the late 1990s—including the basically uncooperative stance of the Japanese government on market opening and its new assertiveness in resisting American pressure.

Seeking Managed Trade?

The most serious criticism the Clinton administration faced was that its trade policy toward Japan represented a "managed trade" approach. The administration had endorsed the ill-defined notion of getting "results" from trade agreements. Whatever the administration might develop as a real policy based on that concept, it was liable to the accusation that it was endorsing managed trade, in which the U.S. government would negotiate market shares for American industries in the Japanese market rather than focusing on removal of market barriers. The administration did not believe it was endorsing managed trade, and none of the agreements worked out with Japan over the next several years came close to managed trade (with the partial exception of pressing for forecasts from the individual Japanese auto firms on their expected purchases of local parts in North America and imported parts in Japan).

Rather than managed trade, the Clinton administration generalized the approach begun by the Bush administration. Each bilateral agreement included both language concerning the presumption of a "substantial" increase in opportunities and sales by foreign firms and a clear bilateral review or monitoring process in which the two governments would meet periodically to discuss implementation and outcomes. This represented a modest change in approach or expansion of the Bush administration approach that sidestepped the issue of managed trade. But along the way the administration was sharply criticized by outside observers.

Early in the administration there was imprecise discussion about the new "results-oriented" approach to trade negotiations. The semiconductor agreements (of 1986 and 1991) and the 1992 auto parts "understanding" certainly motivated the interest in a results-oriented approach. Those agreements were widely perceived as representing a successful model that had useful lessons. The principal lesson was that these agreements included targets for foreign sales in Japan toward which the two governments agreed market outcomes should move.[55]

Those trade agreements, however, also included a variety of traditional rules-based measures aimed at easing market barriers. What the administration appeared to be seeking initially was a somewhat similar path, one in which the primary purpose of trade negotiations would be to work out an easing of explicit access obstacles but with the added feature of some target, goal, or benchmark by which the success of the agreement could be judged afterward. It was hoped that the numbers included in the agreement would provide a pressure point on the Japanese government, leading it to implement the changes in rules and regulations in good faith so that markets would operate more freely.

Alternatively, such agreements might involve the Japanese government using administrative guidance to cause domestic buyers to cease informal biases that had disadvantaged foreign firms. At least theoretically, guidance from the government to buy from foreign firms would represent a cessation of previously biased or collusive behavior that had artificially limited or excluded foreign goods and services. In this way, guidance could be viewed as a form of affirmative action—an artificial outcome to offset the equally artificial existing situation in hopes that once established, new beneficial relationships with foreign firms would drive corporate behavior in Japan toward something akin to rational market outcomes. This view was articulated by incoming head of the Council of Economic Advisers Laura Tyson in a 1992 book: "Paradoxically, in Japan something akin to managed trade is often required to achieve something akin to a market outcome."[56] Expanding on this theme that quantative targets for foreign products in Japan could be beneficial, she noted that forced additional presence of foreign products encouraged American firms to undertake the necessary local investment in sales and service to underwrite a stronger presence in the market and could "destabilize the institutional and informal arrangements that impede foreign access."[57] That is, Japanese firms would be sufficiently enamored of the business benefits of their initially forced (or officially encouraged) relationship with foreign firms that they would continue to make business deals on rational criteria (such as price, quality, and delivery time) rather than reverting to their *keiretsu* or national preferences of the past. Just like the objective of affirmative action in domestic American social policy, therefore, managed trade could be a temporary step that would permanently break the causes of the original problem.

The distinction between this positive, promarket view of temporary market share targets and that of distortionary managed trade was obviously subtle at best. As the difficulty in defining that distinction became more clear, the administration backed away from precise targets in favor of language concerning general trends. In backing away, though, deciding and then explaining what it really wanted was difficult, and the administration was not very successful in providing convincing explanations. And in the absence of internal agreement, different officials were saying different things. As one critical Washington observer put it, "Despite all of the administration's convoluted arguments, the Clinton trade team persuaded everyone that the United States wanted to allocate markets. This impression upset our trading partners and many markets."[58]

On September 27, 1993, Professor Jagdish Bhagwati sent a letter, representative of the criticism, signed by thirty-nine other academic economists (including several Nobel laureates) urging the administration to abandon a course of managed trade. The letter stated, "We urge you to abandon the new course on which your administration has embarked, in seeking managed-trade targets." And "The imposition of quantitative targets as in the case of semiconductors and now sought in other sectors would be a retrograde step."[59] The letter went beyond attacking the administration for a managed trade policy to questioning the underlying premise that access to Japanese markets was impeded. These accusations were made with limited knowledge of the administration's position, and many of the signers had little or no knowledge of Japan. The administration had already retreated from early thinking based on the semiconductor agreement and was seeking language concerning qualitative and quantitive indicators that was very mild.

The problem primarily was another failure to communicate effectively. In a sharp reply to the Bhagwati letter, then-Undersecretary for International Affairs at the Treasury Department Lawrence Summers admonished the signers for not having sought out and discussed their concerns with professional colleagues in the administration. He strongly denied that the United States was seeking "managed trade" with Japan and argued that the Framework Agreement reflected a commitment by both governments to allow market forces to work and thereby avoid managed trade.[60] Summers's comments reflected the mainstream of Clinton administration officials and the direction that the internal discussion of how to define a results-oriented trade policy was taking within the administration.

In similar fashion, a study group convened by the Carnegie Endowment sent an open letter to President Clinton and Prime Minister Hosokawa in March of 1994, decrying both the strained nature of trade relations and the presumed trend toward managed trade. The letter stated, "The United States should set aside demands for quantitative indicators for Japanese imports which suggest that the Japanese Government can or should control market results." At this point in time, the administration was not pressing for quantitative targets of the sort envisioned in this criticism. The administration's failing was not to adequately communicate its evolving policy concepts to its American critics. And both letters may have reflected the administration's inattention to the active public relations efforts by the Japanese government to convince American policy elites that the administration had goals of achieving managed trade.

Both the Carnegie letter and the Bhagwati letter also illustrate a common problem in American academic thought regarding Japan. As put in the Carnegie letter, "Japan, however, cannot just say 'no.' It should come forward with a credible multiyear . . . concrete program for meaningful deregulation of its economy." Similarly, the Bhagwati letter stated, "The sins are those of commission by the U.S. in seeking quantitative trade and surplus-reduction targets, and of omission by Japan in not exercising bolder leadership on more appropriate ways to deal with the problems that prompt the U.S. to embrace these unwise policy options." Many policy recommendations from bilateral academic and policy-oriented groups tend to take this approach of declaring that the United States should not deviate from a strict interpretation of free trade policy, while Japan should unilaterally dismantle trade barriers. The dilemma is that without strong and credible pressure from the United States, often the Japanese government and corporate behavior do not change. That dilemma remained in the 1990s; as noted earlier, little was happening to materially ease the conditions of market access, and the negative, defensive posture of the Japanese government was unchanged.

Exercises such as the Bhagwati letter successfully fed into the Japanese government public relations effort to put the administration on the defensive. The Japanese government realized quickly that any departure from the scripted rhetoric of free trade exposed the Clinton administration to potential criticism from American academics, partisan political opponents, and other nations around the world. Great effort went into building a public relations campaign to paint the administration as advocates of managed trade and protectionism, in contrast to a stalwart defense of free trade by Japan. As amazing as this characterization of the two countries might seem, the above discussion of the criticisms of the administration indicate that the campaign reached sympathetic ears. Prime Minister Hosokawa's reply to the Bhagwati letter, released the following January, noted that he was "very gratified and encouraged . . . that your opposition to managed trade coincides with our views." By protesting against managed trade, the Japanese government continued to spread the view that the administration was indeed seeking managed trade outcomes.[61]

Japanese scholars joined the criticism of the administration. In late January 1994, just before a summit meeting between Prime Minister Hosokawa and President Clinton, a group of leading Japanese economists wrote a letter similar to but stronger in tone than the Bhagwati letter. They stated that under the U.S. proposals for negotiations in the various sectoral talks mandated by the Framework Agreement, "The Japanese government is obliged to allocate market shares or sales of U.S. (or foreign) imports in the Japanese market." One wonders how these economists could be so certain of what the Clinton administration wanted.[62]

Some of these scholars were also part of a committee in Japan, organized by the Japanese government to rebut the Clinton initiative. This group, the Subcommittee on Unfair Trade Policies and Measures under the Uruguay Round Committee of the Industrial Structure Council (which is an official advisory body to MITI with academics and others appointed by MITI) issued a report on January 19, 1994, decrying managed trade and arguing that the Japanese market was open. They made a standard theoretical economic argument that managed trade would, in principle, result in a situation in which "Japanese companies are required to suppress their share of the domestic Japanese market," while foreign firms "are able to avoid competition with Japanese companies."[63] As noted earlier, it is this artificial distortion from what would be a market-based outcome that troubles economists about truly managed trade. And since the subcommittee argued that access problems did not exist in Japan, managing trade would necessarily drive markets away from equilibrium.

So what was the administration seeking, if not managed trade? One of the problems was that incoming officials in the administration did not have a clear concept of how to take the notion that results "matter" and translate it into policy initiatives that would be different from some form of managed trade. If access to a market is impaired, then presumably those alleging impairment have some notion of what would happen to market shares absent impediments. But incorporating that vision of the free market outcome into a signed agreement provides a commitment to a specific outcome that implies government coercion on industry to generate it. The dilemma was to define what, if anything, could be put into agreements to emphasize the need for real improvement in foreign market shares in Japan as evidence for greater openness without sliding into managed trade.

Pessimists on the question of access to markets in Japan wanted managed trade, and a few incoming Clinton administration officials gave vent to such views before any policy was decided. Believing that agreements designed to reform the regulations and other rules governing access to markets were ineffectual, this group believed that negotiations should be focused on outcomes rather than rules. Derek Sherer, who served briefly as Deputy Undersecretary for Economic Affairs at the Department of Commerce in the spring of 1993, was an advocate of managed trade on the grounds that most Japanese markets were managed anyway and that it was unrealistic to expect that the Japanese government would truly liberalize access through meaningful changes in rules and regulations. This pessimism was, and is, fairly prevalent among experienced American businessmen working in Japan in industries characterized by access problems.

The appointment of Laura Tyson as chair of the Council of Economic Advisers was taken by many in Japan as another signal that the administration would endorse managed trade as its strategy toward Japan. This image came from the 1992 book cited above on U.S.-Japan competition in high-technology industries in which she sketched the case for managed trade as affirmative action. But Tyson had not endorsed managed trade as a general principle for dealing with Japan; she cautiously stated that such "voluntary import expansion" policies were "sometimes" better than doing nothing.[64] Perhaps reflecting that caution, she was not known as an advocate of managed trade in dealing with Japan once she entered government.

As the administration began to work out its policy toward Japan, the promanaged trade approach of specific market-share targets for particular products quickly lost, since mainstream members of the administration realized that this objective would be too controversial or represented an undesirable general principle. Instead in the fall of 1993, the USTR initially proposed using at least vague references to the level of foreign penetration of particular markets in other industrialized countries. At a press conference at the U.S. Embassy in Tokyo in December 1993, Deputy USTR Charlene Barshefsky stated that in the drafts for individual agreements, the U.S. government proposed that "Japan's receptivity to global imports in these sectoral areas should be akin to those of other major industrialized economies. Surely not identical, but in the range . . . representative of the competitiveness of foreign producers and in the range representative of consumer demand in Japan."[65] Barshefsky and others were well aware of the potential for criticism about managed trade, having already received the Bhagwati letter, and had hoped that language concerning "in the range of other major industrial nations" would be acceptable.

Deputy Treasury Secretary Roger Altman, writing in early 1994, reinforced this idea, when he wrote that the administration's intent was "to negotiate a series of long-term goals and objective standards against which progress can be judged. The overall goal should be convergence toward international standards of market openness."[66] The intent at that point was to include a set of numerical indicators or benchmarks to be evaluated by the two governments as a package, thus attempting to avoid the direct charge of managed trade in which individual or specific market shares for foreign products would be the subject of measurement.

Such language was hoped by the U.S. government to skirt the question of managed trade, but it brought only further outrage from dedicated free trade advocate Jagdish Bhagwati. Responding to Altman, he charged that "benchmarks are only a weasel word for targets (that is, quotas), and these import targets quickly turn into export protectionism: they work to guarantee for American firms a share of the foreign market just as conventional import protectionism gives firms a guaranteed share of the domestic market."[67]

Unsure exactly how these ideas of benchmarks could be translated into specific language, initial drafts of American bargaining positions were vague. The initial draft of the U.S. negotiating position on automobiles and auto parts, for example, contained language that called for use of quantitative indicators that the governments would review but went on to state, "Regarding the above quantitative indicators, specific expectations shall be included in the Arrangement pending further discussions between the two governments."[68] The initial draft also called explicitly for the government of Japan to use "administrative guidance" to encourage the industry to buy more foreign auto parts, and that the firms should submit data, their projected purchase plans, and corporate initiatives to meet those plans to the two governments for review. This draft, and its discovery by the press, did much to give the image of an administration seeking managed trade, even though this early language was cautiously phrased, and the U.S. government moved away from this initially proposed language very quickly.

By January 1994 the administration had suggested language for the auto agreement that called for continuation of recent trends in parts purchases of foreign auto parts by Japanese auto manufacturers (which had been growing roughly 20 percent annually in the preceding several years), with sufficient flexibility for fluctuations in business conditions that the U.S. government could deny the formula represented a market share target. The U.S. government also proposed an expectation that sales of foreign automobiles in Japan would rise to around 100,000 a year.[69] The Japanese government refused to agree to any such language.

Once again, the administration was caught by the dilemma of trying to define a results-oriented agreement without specific market shares. The trend-line approach was believed to avoid the precision of market share targets. One could argue that without knowing where the overall market is headed, but recognizing that the foreign market share had been unusually or artificially low in the past because of market access barriers, then agreement that a relatively high rate of increase in sales (such as had characterized the previous three years) would be a positive development and would move Japan closer to a pattern likely to represent a market-determined outcome. But the dilemma was that the trend-line approach could be interpreted as a market share. If one develops an estimate for the total market size in the future, then maintenance of the trend line for foreign purchases would yield an estimate of foreign market share. The other suggestion of a goal for foreign auto sales in Japan was a rather explicit number, but it was not a serious negotiating demand (since outcomes for consumer product sales where millions of individual consumers make decisions cannot be managed like producer products where the number of buyers is limited) and was dropped quickly.

This latter point is important. A major difficulty in assessing the administration's strategy in these early phases of the negotiations stems from the nature of the negotiating process. Negotiators begin with requests that they know will be unacceptable to the other side. Which parts of the initial negotiating drafts represented core parts of the administration's agenda and which were fluff to be discarded as negotiations became more serious is often difficult to disentangle. The sales goal for foreign cars was rather obviously not a serious demand (and proved embarrassing when the Japanese press continued to claim that it was an American demand late in the negotiations after it had been long discarded).

By late spring of 1994, the U.S. government had moved away from trying to insert language on trends or industrial country averages. The eventual agreements settled for even more vague language borrowed from the Framework Agreement itself to the effect that the purpose of each sectoral agreement was to produce "significant increase" in market access and sales of "competitive" foreign goods and services. This put on record the Japanese government's acquiescence to the concept that greater market openness should result in some real increase in the foreign presence in the market, without attaching any numerical dimensions. For example, the cover letter from the government of Japan to Commerce Secretary Ron Brown that was part of the agreement on government procurement of medical equipment acknowledged that "annual evaluation [will occur to measure] progress in the value and share of procurements of foreign medical technology products and services covered by the Measures and Guidelines to achieve, over the medium term, a significant increase in access and sales of competitive foreign medical technology products and service." The agreement further specified five quantitative indicators and five qualitative indicators to be reviewed at the annual meeting. But the indicators and follow-up meetings did not constitute the core of the agreement, which consisted of 20 pages of detailed changes in government procurement procedures intended to make procurement more transparent and objective.[70]

This language was quite similar to what the Bush administration had obtained in some of its agreements—vague references to increased sales of foreign goods coupled with a bilateral review process.[71] It seems ironic that after Clinton campaigned against Bush in 1992 and came into office determined to pursue a more active and effective strategy toward Japan, the end result for his administration was about the same as it was for the Bush administration. After toying with the intellectual concept of emphasizing targets for foreign products in various Japanese markets, the administration chose to adopt only a small change. Those who advocated managed trade were few in number, and the administration was not willing to move away from mainstream views on trade policy when it became aware of how controversial such a move would be. Even by the time the Framework Agreement was signed, it was clear that the administration did not want to pursue import targets of the semiconductor sort and thereby be painted as abandoning the ideology of free trade. But thinking about alternatives was unclear, and early attempts, such as Deputy USTR Barshefsky's notion of moving toward import penetration levels in the range of other industrial nations appeared to many Japanese and Americans as being too close to managed trade. A U.S. trade newsletter quickly labeled the initial U.S. position on autos and auto parts as a "market share arrangement."[72] The administration was sensitive to such criticism and kept searching for alternative language until it finally settled upon the vague language endorsing increased market penetration.

One can sympathize with the dilemma faced by the administration and those who had genuinely wanted strong provisions on targets or benchmarks. Access problems in some industries in Japan have persisted despite repeated efforts to liberalize the rules of access, including years of negotiations that resulted in quota elimination, tariff reduction, and investment liberalization in the 1960s and 1970s, as well as changes in standards, testing procedures, and other nontariff issues in the 1980s. Semiconductors represented one such problem area, and a number of American analysts agree that the setting of indicative targets for foreign semiconductors in the Japanese market was instrumental in breaking down barriers in the market, as noted earlier in this chapter. But the intellectual and ideological commitment to the concept of free trade is very deep in the United States, and the administration was unwilling to challenge the orthodoxy very much. What emerges from this review of the concept of results-oriented bargaining strategies in the Clinton administration is the intensity of the American commitment to a strong version of free trade, to which many advocates wish to admit no practical or expedient departures.

In retrospect, the effort of the Clinton administration to implement a results-oriented bargaining strategy with Japan was doomed to heavy criticism and probable failure. But keep in mind the basic problem that policymakers were trying to address. Many of the markets subject to negotiation had been characterized by opaque and strong collusive relationships that had not responded much to previous attempts to make the rules on market participation more clear and fair. Semiconductors, paper and other wood products, flat glass, government procurement of general and supercomputers, and procurement of telecommunications equipment by the government-owned telephone company were all subject to repeated negotiations during the 1980s and 1990s with only limited success in making these markets open. Given this history, changes in rules without any benchmark against which to measure the impact of those changes after implementation was perceived as an invitation to further failure. The changes in rules are usually implemented, but other opaque factors come into play to prevent those changes from having a real impact. American firms in some industries had experienced this problem. Thus, the adamant refusal of the Japanese government to accept any language on outcomes raised strong concerns about the commitment of the Japanese to making markets more open.

Ex post, the administration declared that the language it negotiated in each agreement fulfilled its original aim. As stated in USTR's annual report to Congress in 1997, "Under the Framework, the Administration has sought agreements with distinctly defined commitments from Japan that can be measured using objective criteria, both quantitative and qualitative. This approach, which assesses the implementation and success of agreements through 'tangible progress,' has been successful in creating and expanding opportunities for imported products in the Japanese market."[73] In reality, the phrase "substantial increase" was not very precise or distinctive, so that the administration did not have any clear definition of "success" in carrying out its assessment of agreements. Nevertheless, the institutionalization of a review or assessment process based on a basket of qualitative and quantitative indicators was an important innovation of the 1990s, with due credit to the Bush administration.

This conclusion that the Clinton administration had at least modest success in pressing a trade agreement formula that acknowledged the expectation of real improvement in market access and engaged the governments in a review process has been labeled a failure by others. For example, Leonard Schoppa has written, "It is my evaluation that the Clinton team failed to achieve its most critical aim of securing a Japanese commitment to 'results' which would be explicit enough to allow the U.S. to hold the Japanese government accountable under U.S. trade law."[74] This conclusion erred in two respects. First, it assumed that the "most critical aim" of the administration lay in the vague notions of "results" expressed early in 1993 before officials had hammered out internal consensus on negotiating goals.

The second error lies in the excessively legalistic notion that numerical targets were necessary to trigger use of section 301 retaliation against Japan. The 1987 retaliation over semiconductors was indeed triggered by a U.S. government determination that Japan failed to abide by the 1986 semiconductor agreement (including the market share goal expressed in the secret side letter to the agreement). But section 301 is sufficiently broad in its language that numerical targets are not necessary in any agreement. Even without explicit language about targets, the USTR would be well within the letter and spirit of the law if it determined that a foreign government had not effectively carried out its obligations under a trade agreement if mysterious new problems cropped up that obstructed foreign products, even if that government had implemented the specific measures in the agreement. Inclusion of "targets" could presumably make the 301 determination easier, but it was certainly not a necessary precondition. The notion that including language on market outcomes would put Japan into jeopardy under section 301 (and therefore must be resisted) seems to have been a part of the Japanese government's public relations strategy that was favorably received by the academic community. As discussed in chapter 6, this point may be moot, since many believe that under the rules of the new World Trade Organization, opportunities for the U.S. government to use section 301 without provoking retaliation from trading partners are limited.

How then to judge what the administration achieved? As formulated by early 1994, and ultimately incorporated in the specific trade agreements signed, the administration did accomplish at least a modestly useful step. The Japanese government officially recognized in a string of specific sectoral agreements that market opening measures ought to yield significant increases in foreign market share—representing a substantial admission that access had been impeded in the affected markets. This language provided a useful reference point for American trade negotiators. If little change took place in market behavior, the immediate result would be review of the situation and possible strong criticism from the U.S. government. Should the subsequent discussions be unsatisfactory, there is little doubt that the aggravated sense of bad faith could be enough to justify (in American minds) some form of retaliation against Japanese economic interests if necessary and feasible. In addition, the review process using qualitative and quantitative indicators decreased the ability of the Japanese government to play a game of superficial implementation. This review process certainly did not ensure full compliance but at least exposed implementation policies and market behavior to bilateral argument on a regular basis. Given the nature of past problems, this was a modestly useful step.

Special Deals for American Firms?

Because the United States has often exerted bilateral pressure on Japan, the bilateral negotiating process has raised concerns among other countries that the common outcome is a special deal for American firms, at the expense of firms of other nations. With the ambitious agenda of the first term of the Clinton administration, and with a new rhetoric about results, such concerns arose again. At the 1994 meeting of the GATT Council, both the European Community members and Australia expressed concern about whether bilateral agreements with Japan would be truly applied on a most favored nation basis.[75]

The reality is that bilateral agreements negotiated by all American administrations in the past thirty years have produced changes in the rules of access to Japanese markets which apply on an MFN basis, and the Clinton administration was no exception. Obviously the U.S. government negotiates on matters of particular concern to American firms or where it believes American firms have a strong competitive advantage. But "deals" that only give an advantage to American firms are rare. The United States bore the brunt of negotiations with Japan during the 1970s and 1980s to ease and then end the quotas on beef imports to Japan; in 1988 the United States supplied 54 percent of total beef imports in Japan (combining fresh and frozen beef) and in 1996 a modestly higher 61 percent. For auto parts, an area subject to long and difficult negotiations in both the Bush and Clinton administrations, the United States was the source of 26 percent of Japan's imports in 1988 and 36 percent in 1996. In both cases the share of imports sourced from the United States rose modestly over this eight-year period but not by a sufficient amount to imply that bilateral negotiations benefited only American firms. More important, in both of these examples, the primary benefit was to produce a rapidly expanding level of imports (with beef imports up 2.3 times and auto parts imports up 3.8 times over this period), benefiting all countries exporting to Japan. The modest rise in the market share of American-sourced products, therefore, still enabled a substantial rising amount of exports by other nations.[76]

More broadly, the American share of Japan's imports of manufactured goods has not changed appreciably. From 26.7 percent in 1988, the United States supplied an almost identical 26.4 percent of Japan's total imports of manufactures in 1996, and the share remained in a rather narrow 26 to 29 percent range throughout this time period.[77] Thus all of the negotiations aimed at easing import barriers for manufactured products in Japan did not seem to have materially affected the overall competitive position of firms exporting to Japan from the United States relative to those from other countries.

Geographical origin of products may not entirely reflect the nationality of the companies providing them, with American subsidiaries of Japanese manufacturers, for example, possibly expanding exports of auto parts from the United States back to Japan. But even for semiconductors, a product area where the governments collect data by nationality of company rather than geographical location of the products, American firms have not gained all the benefits. From 1985 (just before the initial bilateral semiconductor agreement) through 1996, the share of foreign firms in the Japanese semiconductor market rose from 8.6 percent to 25.5 percent. Of foreign firms, the share of American firms rose from 8.5 percent to 20.2 percent, while other foreign firms expanded from 0.1 percent to 5.3 percent.[78] Thus, while American producers continued to be the dominant foreign supplier of semiconductors to the Japanese market, other foreign suppliers had gained share too, from a truly insignificant level before the agreement.

Given the collusive or managed nature of many Japanese markets, there is always the possibility that the outcome of some agreements could be to skew purchases toward American firms even under MFN rules and a supposedly open market. Under the "squeaky wheel gets the grease" notion, Japanese markets characterized by extensive collusion may choose to provide the noisiest American firms with increased (but carefully controlled) access, rather than becoming more open to all foreign firms. But this problem is the result of Japanese market behavior and the lack of antitrust enforcement (or even explicit government approval of collusive behavior), not the agreements negotiated by the U.S. government. By sticking to rules-based agreements, the thrust of American negotiating behavior has been to diminish the ability of Japanese firms and government to continue such collusive or managed behavior.

The more interesting implication of the examples above is that the U.S. government was consistently willing to engage in bilateral negotiations with Japan and bear the brunt of pressing Japan for market liberalization measures in industries or product areas where American firms would not be the sole or even dominant suppliers to Japan. In theoretical terms, one would expect that when a number of countries export to Japan, the more logical route would be for multilateral negotiations. However, large multilateral rounds of negotiations are infrequent and slow. When such negotiations are not under way, bilateral negotiations are necessary, and Japan has been more responsive to pressure from the United States than from other trading partners.

The Second Clinton Term

The signing of the bilateral agreement on automobiles and auto parts in the summer of 1995 marked the conclusion of the principal trade issues included explicitly within the Framework Agreement of 1993. Thereafter, the Clinton administration chose to reduce the public visibility of its trade negotiations with Japan, a decision that continued into the administration's second term. Despite the reduced visibility, a reasonably active relationship continued, involving further bilateral negotiations on specific problems and bilateral meetings for the monitoring of existing agreements.

Specific Bilateral Issues

After the automobile agreement, the administration concluded negotiations with Japan involving semiconductors, the insurance sector, telecommunications equipment procurement, civil aviation, and harbor services. Meanwhile, cases pursued at the WTO on liquor taxes and copyright protection resulted in outcomes favorable to the United States. But in early 1998, the United States lost a major case at the WTO on access to the consumer market for photographic film and paper in Japan.

The Bush administration agreement on semiconductors expired in the summer of 1996. After an initial refusal to consider an extension, negotiations led to a replacement agreement reached at the end of July that eliminated the numerical indicators. But the new agreement did leave in place a process of monitoring and bilateral consultations. It also called for creation of a Global Government Forum in which all semiconductor-producing countries are invited to join (nations that eliminate tariffs on semiconductors are eligible for membership in the council). The new forum thus provides an explicit expansion of discussion of government-level semiconductor issues from the bilateral arena to a multilateral one.[79]

Insurance proved difficult and contentious. The October 1994 agreement did not result in the regulatory changes anticipated by the U.S. government, and negotiations were reopened in the fall of 1995. This was particularly frustrating to U.S. negotiators who felt they were covering the same issues that had supposedly been settled in 1994. But a renegotiated "supplementary measures" pact was finally signed in December 1996. These two agreements were supposed to result in substantial deregulation of the life insurance sector and property/casualty markets, followed by liberalization of entry by Japanese firms into the so-called third sector (a small segment of the insurance market where foreign firms have a 40 percent market share).[80] Even this new commitment, however, did not proceed smoothly.

International civil aviation is not covered by the WTO and falls instead under the jurisdiction of bilateral treaties. The U.S.-Japan bilateral treaty established a managed trade framework in 1952, discussed in chapter 2. The Clinton administration pressed for an "open skies" agreement, which would essentially remove government from managing this market. This approach continued a consistent policy dating to the late 1970s of renegotiating aviation treaties with bilateral partners that had resulted in a number of open skies agreements by the mid-1990s. However, the effort with Japan failed, and the administration finally settled in January 1998 for a continued managed outcome that permitted some increases in flights, clarified the issue of "beyond rights" (the right to stop in Japan and then fly on to third countries, including the issue of picking up passengers in Japan for the second leg of the trip), and permitted code sharing (in which airlines in the two countries could cross-list and coordinate times for flights).[81]

Only occasionally did bilateral trade negotiations rise to media prominence. One of these occasions involved a long-standing dispute on Japanese harbor service practices. A cartel of harbor-service firms authorized by the Japanese government—the Japan Harbor Transportation Association—controlled all stevedore work. This comprehensive cartel maintained high prices for stevedore work and administered a rigid work allocation system to the disadvantage of shipping companies with time-sensitive schedules.[82] Repeated failure to make progress on this set of problems led the Federal Maritime Commission (FMC) to propose fining Japanese vessels in retaliation for continuation of discriminatory practices in Japan in November 1996, with a fee of $100,000 per vessel calling at any American port. The FMC then issued a ruling effective April 1997 confirming the fees but delaying implementation for further negotiations; actual sanctions were imposed at the beginning of September (with the retroactive collection date postponed to October 15).[83] When the Japanese firms refused to pay the accumulated fines on the specified date, the FMC requested the Coast Guard to impound Japanese vessels. The prospect of armed Coast Guard vessels denying entry to arriving vessels and detaining ships in port had the intended result of moving negotiations forward at last, and the fee was not actually enforced—representing a tactical approach considered further in chapter 6.[84] Thereafter, trade negotiations returned to a quiet approach.

The color film case was more substantive in terms of bilateral importance. Kodak had filed a section 301 complaint with USTR concerning access problems in the Japanese market in May 1995. At issue were allegations of government administrative guidance promoting collusive behavior in the market for consumer color film. Beginning in the late 1960s (when the Japanese government was committed in the GATT to lowering tariffs on film and in the OECD to lowering direct investment barriers), the government encouraged the existing wholesale dealers to move into an exclusive relationship with Fuji film and promoted other actions to limit Kodak's inroads in the market. A year later, USTR completed its own analysis of the situation and under section 301 chose to pursue the case through the WTO, mainly because the Japanese government had pointedly refused to engage in bilateral discussions. After filing the case in the summer of 1996, USTR and MITI submitted documents and analysis to a WTO dispute settlement panel beginning in early 1997. The WTO panel issued a preliminary finding in December 1997 and its final decision in January 1998. The U.S. government lost on all the substantive allegations made, winning only a small moral victory on some of the theoretical issues (concerning the possible WTO-illegality of administrative guidance).

Loss of the color film case at the WTO could have triggered a strong reaction in the administration and Congress. The case represented a major effort to expand the scope of the WTO beyond traditional, simple trade barriers to encompass the complex and often informal world of Japanese industrial policy (explored further in chapter 6). The loss was an obvious disappointment, but the reaction was very restrained. USTR, while expressing disappointment with the decision, also emphasized the value of the WTO and the fact that all seven other cases brought by the U.S. government up to that point had been decided in favor of U.S. petitions.[85] By the time the final report of the WTO panel was issued, the U.S. response had become even milder. In testimony on March 4, General Counsel Susan Esserman began with extensive praise for the WTO, noting that by then the United States had won on nine panel decisions and achieved favorable outcomes on eight other WTO cases prior to a panel decision. Instead of protesting the decision, the government chose to closely monitor Japan for discrepancies between government or market behavior and the Japanese government's claims during the case.[86]

Reluctance by USTR to pursue the color film loss may have been partly because of other cases pending at the WTO. In October 1998, the U.S. government won a favorable decision against phytosanitary standards on several agricultural products (including apples, nectarines, cherries, and walnuts). This case was built upon the new WTO phytosanitary standards accord, arguing that the requirement for testing each variety of these fruits and nuts was scientifically unjustified and served as a significant barrier to entry.[87]

Deregulation Initiative

Although the overall tenor of bilateral trade negotiations was reduced to a lower level of visibility and rhetoric, the administration chose to emphasize negotiations on deregulation, dubbed the Enhanced Initiative on Deregulation and Competition Policy, adopted at a bilateral summit meeting in June 1997. Discussion of deregulation had proceeded under the Framework Agreement, with the U.S. government submitting periodic lists of requests for deregulation items as part of the overall process of deregulation being pursued by the Japanese government (discussed in chapter 5). But this engagement had not been very fruitful, and the administration chose to give it greater emphasis in the second term. Rather than continuing only a scattergun approach, the discussions narrowed to several areas in which the administration deemed regulatory measures particularly important in disadvantaging foreign goods and services: telecommunications, housing, medical devices and pharmaceutical products, financial services, competition policy, distribution, and transparency of government practices.[88]

This Enhanced Initiative resulted in a bilateral announcement of progress in the spring of 1998 that represented further modest progress. Most of the deregulation actions were sector specific, including reduction in fees for completion of international telephone calls from abroad, an increase in the number of channels satellite broadcasters can provide, a move to internationally accepted standards on housing materials, acceleration of approval of medical devices and pharmaceuticals, permission for more innovative financial products, and repeal of the large-scale store law. As is typical with such lists of changes, though, the real impact would lie in the details of implementation. For example, while the Large-Scale Retail Store Law was repealed (to take effect in April 1999), MITI encouraged prefectural and local governments to pass their own laws (though supposedly confined to issues such as environmental damage, traffic congestion, and noise issues related to large stores). Local laws could, therefore, undo some or all of the gains from eliminating the national law. In announcing the package, USTR Charlene Barshefsky noted that these measures "now must be followed by further meaningful reform in these and other markets."[89]

Table 4-1. *Status of Monitoring Effort as of Summer 1998*

Issue or agreement	Date agreement signed	Status of monitoring or review
Automobiles and auto parts	1995	Semiannual monitoring report issued by USTR August 1998. Identified continuing problems, and urged the Japanese government to take additional deregulation steps. Auto exports to Japan falling (and losing market share), but parts sales to transplants and exported to Japan rising.
Insurance	1994, 1996	Bilateral review meeting June 1998 on status of implementation. U.S. government charged inadequate Japanese action on opening the life and property/casualty markets.
Flat glass	1995	Bilateral review meeting May 1998. No gains by foreign firms, and Japanese government rejected U.S.-proposed plan for combating anticompetitive practices.
Construction	1994	Bilateral review meeting summer 1998.
Semiconductors	1986, 1991, 1996	U.S. calculation of the foreign market share in Japan released in June 1998 was 33.3 percent, up 5.8 percentage points from 1996 (and well above the now-expired 20 percent target included in the 1986 and 1991 agreements).

Sources: Office of the U.S. Trade Representative, "Administration Calls on Japan to Make Progress under Auto Agreement, despite Recession," press release, August, 12, 1998; "U.S. Pressing Japan to Adopt Flat Glass Antitrust Enforcement Plan," *Inside U.S. Trade*, May 15, 1998, pp. 11–12; "USTR on Foreign Computer Sales to Japanese Public Sector," *USIS Washington File*, June 11, 1998, www.usia.gov/cur...washfile/newsitem.shtml; "Commerce 6/3 News Release on Japan Semiconductor Market," *USIS Washington File*, June 4, 1998, www.usia.gov/cur...washfile/newsitem.shtml; "USTR Continues to Place Japan on IPR Watch List," Kyodo News as reported by FBIS-EAS-98-121; Office of the U.S. Trade Representative, *1998 National Trade Estimate Report on Foreign Trade*

The administration continued this quieter approach centered on deregulation through 1998. For the second round of this initiative, the administration raised a new set of issues along with existing ones related to telecommunications, housing, financial services, medical devices and pharmaceuticals, energy, and automotive sectors. Also included were more generic areas of competition policy, distribution, and transparency of government processes.[90] Meanwhile, discussion of structural issues such as the difficulty of mergers and acquisitions proceeded under the working group on direct investment that was part of the Framework Agreement.[91] Though not dramatic, these initia-

Table 4-1. *(continued)*

Issue or agreement	Date agreement signed	Status of monitoring or review
Medical devices and pharma- ceuticals	1994	Bilateral review meeting March 1998. Continuing U.S. concerns on regulation, especially proposed implementation of a reference pricing system for pharmaceuticals as well as the incremental pace of regulatory change.
Government procurement of general computers and supercomputers	1992	Bilateral review meeting summer 1998. U.S. government expressed "concern" at the decline in foreign market share of general computer procurement (from 13.7 percent in 1994 to 9.3 percent by 1996), and a similar drop in personal computer procurement.
Film	1998[a]	The first U.S. monitoring report issued August 1998. Analysis indicated need for further Japanese government actions to bring its efforts in line with its claims before the WTO panel.
Intellectual property rights	1994	Japan placed on the "watch list" of the Special 301 provision of the Trade Law of 1988 in an annual review, May 1998, because of continuing concerns on software and trade secrets plus operation of the patent system.

Barriers, pp. 197–198; Office of the U.S. Trade Representative, "Administration Releases First Monitoring Report on Foreign Access to Japan's Film Sector," press release, August 19, 1998; and "U.S.-Japan Bid to Resolve Insurance Fight Stalls as July Date Passes," *Inside U.S. Trade*, July 10, 1998, p. 10;

a. No bilateral agreement on color film exists, but the U.S. government announced its intent to monitor the situation in Japan for compliance with the Japanese government's claims concerning market openness made during the WTO case.

tives implied that the administration was trying to pursue a continuing agenda of structural problems beyond the initial year of the Enhanced Initiative.

Monitoring

The final bilateral focus in the second term was the monitoring of existing agreements—including those signed in the Bush administration with a continuing bilateral mechanism, those signed in the Framework negotiations, and the unilateral monitoring announced for color film. Table 4-1 presents the status of this effort on nine issue areas as of the summer of 1998.

Out of this list, only one issue appeared to be largely resolved. With the share of foreign semiconductors reaching a 30 percent market share in Japan by the end of 1997, there seemed to be little cause for concern that domestic collusion would cause the foreign share to decline once the 20 percent market-share target was ended (when the 1991 agreement ended in 1996 and was replaced with the new agreement containing no such numerical goal). All other areas subject to monitoring included U.S. government concerns that regulatory and other problems persisted.

By devoting resources to this monitoring process, the U.S. government remained engaged on a continuous basis with the issues involved. However, monitoring is not a complete solution. Table 4-1 includes only comments on the U.S. government concerns. At bilateral review sessions the usual routine is presentation of American concerns and Japanese government denials. Thus, while the Japanese government is appraised of American concerns or complaints, the situation is no different from a contentious trade negotiation and forward movement by no means the likely outcome.

This fact points to a broader dilemma for monitoring. What happens when the review process leads the U.S. government to believe substantial problems remain or that implementation has been faulty but that the Japanese government will not alter policies? In the eight areas subject to review in the first half of 1998, the dominant theme was an American sense of lack of progress on regulatory changes, collusive arrangements, or penetration of markets by foreign firms. But on none of these issues did the U.S. government appear to be willing to raise the stakes by a return to concentrated negotiations or use of retaliatory tools. For a monitoring process to be truly effective, the Japanese government needs to know that a demonstrable lack of progress will have some consequence or cost, but that element appeared to be lacking in 1998.

Clearly the administration had lost its appetite for the high-profile, tense negotiations that characterized the 1993–95 period, especially as other issues became more important in the bilateral agenda (problems in the security relationship and deep concern over Japan's macroeconomic performance and financial problems in the second half of the 1990s). Chapter 6 endorses the notion of reducing the visibility and rhetoric on trade issues and avoiding overarching themes that raise unrealistic expectations about improvement in market access. But at the same time a steady level of attention to problems and a willingness to press issues seriously when necessary must continue.

Conclusion

The record of trade negotiations in the 1990s illustrates the high-profile approach taken on trade born of the continuing frustrations of American firms and U.S. government officials dealing with Japanese market access problems. The frustrations were consistent with the statistical evidence of chapters 2 and 3. Penetration of manufactured imports remained low, intra-industry trade patterns did not improve until the mid-1990s, and inward direct investment remained very low. Business pressure on both the Bush and Clinton administrations to pursue an active negotiating agenda designed to improve market access, therefore, was no surprise. The activist agenda, though, provides several lessons.

The first lesson is that large thematic efforts to push Japan on trade liberalization provide only limited results relative to the energy expended. The Bush administration made a show of the Structural Impediments Initiative and achieved some modest progress but largely lost interest after the first year. The Clinton administration put strong emphasis on the Framework talks, and pursued them vigorously for two years, but also lost interest after that point. The dialogue on deregulation in the second term of the Clinton administration achieved modest results in 1998, though it would take several more years to see the results.

Intense negotiations on a variety of issues over a relatively short period certainly produce some results in the form of signed agreements that ease some market barriers, but often the results are disappointing. The political problems on the Japanese side (a strong voice for opponents of liberalization) are often deeply embedded, and a short negotiating period simply does not permit sufficient time to wear down the opposition. Meanwhile, Japanese government officials are well aware that these enthusiasms are likely to wane, and they try to outlast their American counterparts at the bargaining table. And on the American side, the act of creating a highly visible theme or framework carries a political commitment to producing a positive outcome by a certain date, thereby creating a dynamic in which the U.S. government is willing to settle for very modest outcomes in order to meet the demands of its own rhetoric.

The second lesson is that departures from a rather strict interpretation of free trade ideas are extremely difficult for the United States. The Clinton administration struggled to find a path between strict free trade and managed trade. The final outcome of this struggle, the incorporation of vague language about significant increases in foreign penetration of Japanese markets coupled with an explicit bilateral review process, was a modestly useful development. But the criticism the administration received during this period was a sobering lesson in the deeply ingrained American belief in the principle of free trade and the ability of the Japanese government to play upon those American beliefs to the disadvantage of the U.S. government. This may seem at odds with obvious American departures from free trade in the form of tariffs, quotas, and other protectionist policies at home. But to negotiate with another country for better access to its markets on any terms other than an improvement in the rules of access proved very controversial. As much as some American business people believe that a stronger results-oriented approach to Japan is the only feasible way to achieve true progress toward something akin to a free-market outcome in Japan, this approach seems politically infeasible. If the business community is correct, however, then the ultimate lesson is that the ability to open up Japanese markets will remain limited as long as the Japanese government chooses to deflect, delay, and diminish the negotiating and implementation processes.

A final lesson is that even when Japan was presumably favorably disposed toward change and deregulation, progress on trade issues proved slow and difficult. The Bush administration faced a confident Japan experiencing strong economic growth and generating considerable domestic talk about major structural change, encouraging the administration to propose the SII talks. The Clinton administration faced a breakdown in the dominance of the Liberal Democratic Party, which had long had very close ties with constituencies opposed to market liberalization. The subsequent coalition governments in 1993–94, and even the LDP when it returned to power, espoused deregulation and structural economic change. But both administrations faced difficult and often tense negotiations that produced only modest outcomes. This dilemma is the topic of chapter 5.

A Changing
Japan?

What has been happening in Japan
during the 1990s? It is important for the U.S. government to answer this
question before deciding what it should do in the future. What policy and
behavioral environment did U.S. negotiators face in Japan, or will they face
in the near future? Was the Clinton administration wrong in adopting a
high-profile and contentious trade policy toward Japan? Was Japan entering
a period of internally generated, rapid deregulation or market opening?
Belief that this move was occurring in Japan was prevalent in the United
States in the 1990s, beginning in 1993 when Morihiro Hosokawa became
the first non-Liberal Democratic Party (LDP) prime minister since 1955.
Even when the LDP regained the prime ministership in 1996, Prime Minister Ryutaro Hashimoto made a strong rhetorical stand in favor of deregulation and administrative reform that appeared on the surface to lead
toward a more open market-oriented economy.

Japan was certainly characterized by a great deal of discussion about the
need for change during the 1990s and was rocked by an unusually large
number of scandals involving politicians and bureaucrats, which undermined public trust of government and its traditional strong role in the
economy. The scandals and the discussion of change gave the impression
that real deregulation and restructuring were under way.

Despite all the discussion, however, relatively little real change occurred
in the role of the government in the economy, and the reluctance to liber-

alize markets to access by foreign firms remained strong. Even in the late 1990s, after almost a decade of slow economic growth and scandal, great uncertainty remains as to whether fundamental change will occur. As in any society, some changes were occurring, and these were generally in the direction of modest deregulation. But will the desire of government to influence economic outcomes through regulation, administrative guidance, and other aspects of industrial policy fade away? Probably not.

Deregulation became a buzzword in Japan beginning in 1993. The dramatic slowdown of the economy, from an average annual growth of 5 percent in the late 1980s to under 1 percent in 1993 led some Japanese analysts to believe that the problems confronting the economy were structural and that only thorough deregulation would enable the economy to escape from its sluggishness. Proponents of change generated studies showing that deregulation would be good for Japan in terms of increased economic growth and job creation.[1] Defections from the Liberal Democratic Party took place, ending its majority in the Diet. The subsequent formation of a non-LDP coalition with Morihiro Hosokawa as prime minister lent further encouragement to those favoring deregulation because he had been associated with reformist ideas. One of his initial actions in the fall of 1993 was to create an advisory group to make recommendations on a deregulation strategy, producing the so-called Hiraiwa report that December.

Discussion and some action on deregulation proceeded for the next several years. Although the outcome was certainly not a negative one, substantial reasons lead one to doubt the overall significance of the measures taken in the 1993–97 period or the significance of probable measures to emerge in the rest of the decade.[2] Some change and deregulation were occurring, but the pace was slow and the impact on easing conditions of market access uncertain. The partial exception to this assessment is the financial sector, where the seriousness of the structural problems produced a more ambitious agenda (dubbed the "Big Bang" deregulations). Nonetheless, several important structural problems hinder deregulation.

Vested Interests

Fifty years of peace and rising prosperity produced a number of strong vested interests in Japan. The construction industry thrived on a collusive noncompetitive bidding process for public works projects. Politicians depended—to an extent unknown in the United States—on disbursement of pork barrel public works projects, encouraged by legal and illegal donations from the construction sector. Farmers lived on subsidies, enjoyed a wall of protectionist barriers for rice and some other agricultural products, and heavily supported the LDP. Throughout the postwar period small shopkeepers had sufficient political clout to have the government seriously hinder the advance of larger, more efficient retail firms. An overlapping maze of tax regulations, zoning rules, and transfer costs resulted in a very inefficient use of land and produced a nation of property owners benefiting from existing rules. Bureaucrats operated in an environment of great power, reinforced by the fact that they drafted most of the legislation defining the scope of their own authority, and by a system in which the private sector depended on currying favor with the bureaucracy.

Vested interests such as these may well have been a cause of the deceleration of Japanese economic growth over time. The major cause of Japan's declining growth rate after its spurt of high growth in the earlier postwar period was the result of the end of a century of catching up with the advanced industrial nations. Once Japan had largely eliminated the technology gap between itself and the advanced nations, the potential growth rate of the nation diminished.[3] And the economic stagnation in the 1990s was the direct outcome of the stock and real estate asset bubbles of the late 1980s and their subsequent collapse. However, as Japan's economic performance deteriorated in the 1990s, one additional factor was the debilitating impact of these various entrenched interest groups. Some inefficient or declining sectors of the economy needed to shrink (agriculture, construction, and small retail shops among them) and new sectors to grow, but vested interests have slowed both the contraction and the expansion.

Mancur Olson's theory of special interest groups in society provides a useful way of conceptualizing the dilemma facing Japan in the 1990s. Olson posited that long periods of peace and political stability breed rising numbers and influence of interest groups in society. These groups often seek to redirect resources in society to their own benefit rather than acting to promote the benefit of the whole society. He argued that wrenching political change in the 1930s and 1940s in societies such as Japan, Germany, and France swept away many previously existing interest groups. Absent these stifling influences, these societies were able to generate rapid growth in the first decades following World War II. In Japan, new institutions, such as the prevalence of enterprise-based unions (which were more likely than craft unions to accept productivity-enhancing change in the corporation) aided this process.[4]

Olson's thesis can be challenged as an explanation for the acceleration of growth in postwar Japan. The Occupation-era reforms did not exactly sweep away vested interest groups in the economy (other than the military as a purchaser of economic output). And the predominant explanation of high growth rests on macroeconomic factors (such as high savings and existence of a technology gap) and social factors (such as an emphasis on education). One can argue, though, that some groups often viewed as hindering growth (especially organized labor) were weak in postwar Japan.

But Japan has now had ample time to develop new entrenched interests that might be detrimental to the goal of economic growth and efficiency. Indeed, one can go further and argue that some groups that might have been beneficial in the 1950s were counterproductive by the 1990s. Agricultural cooperatives helped reduce economic uncertainty for the newly formed sector of small, landholding farmers in the early postwar period (most of whom had been poor tenants before the war). But the quickly emerging political power of farmers and their co-ops subsequently led to inability to alter the structure of farm land ownership as labor costs began to rise sharply in the 1960s, leaving Japan with an extraordinarily inefficient agricultural sector of tiny farms, supported in part by protectionist barriers on some agricultural products (rice, beef, oranges, and some other fruits among them).

Small retail shops were economically efficient and rational when wages were low and few people owned cars, and their organization into tight vertical relationships with wholesalers and manufacturers may have brought some economic efficiencies. But their organized political power also led to the Large-Scale Retail Store Law of 1973, which limited the expansion of more efficient, large discount stores in Japan (which would also be more likely to carry independent foreign products than the small shops that were dependent on close and carefully nurtured relationships with domestic suppliers).

Small business in general, not just retailers, received substantial economic benefits over the years. Doctors, *ryokan* (traditional inns), coffee shops, and public bathhouses all benefited from special legislation passed in the 1960s and 1970s, with astute politicians like Kakuei Tanaka playing a major role in catering to their special, narrow interests.[5] Extensive state support through both finance and regulation (which often restricts entry or innovative change) provides part of the explanation of why Japan has so many small firms. In 1994, for example, 22 percent of employment in manufacturing was in firms with fewer than 20 employees, and 71 percent in firms with fewer than 300 employees. By way of contrast, in the United States, only 8 percent of employment was in firms with fewer than 20 employees, and 66 percent in firms with firms with fewer than 500 employees (with no data available for a comparison of the fewer than 300 employees category).[6]

Other sectors, including telecommunications, construction, harbor stevedoring services, and even tourism have all fallen under the control of rent-seeking groups that have subverted the needs of the broader economy. Telecommunications had been granted to a state-owned monopoly, which the government has only reluctantly and slowly deregulated beginning in the mid-1980s. The large size of the construction industry (employing 10 percent of the total domestic work force) and its strong political connections resulted in a heavily entrenched system of public works spending, complete with large amounts of corruption and poorly chosen projects. The graft, corruption, and collusion in construction, in turn, supported collusive behavior in industries supplying construction materials—including steel, cement, aluminum, and wood products.[7] Harbor services were organized into an umbrella group in the 1960s in a successful compromise to end labor strife, but the power of this group then proceeded to hinder efficiency (as well as to disadvantage foreign shipping firms). Tourism was dominated by large tour operators, a pattern that represented another rational economic choice when society was poor (and people could not afford higher-cost individual travel), but the tour companies skewed pricing rules for travel services in their favor, hindering individual travel in favor of a continuation of tours as society became affluent.

Having had fifty years to develop (and some of these groups date to the efforts of the government to tightly organize industry in the early war years), these groups have proven very difficult to dislodge. Without a revolutionary change, such as the Meiji Restoration of 1868 or the defeat in 1945, society has difficulty mustering sufficient political force to oppose or eliminate these groups and their excess economic rents. The general rhetoric of deregulation in the 1990s, therefore, clashed with the political strength of these entrenched groups and their anxiety about the loss of their sizable economic benefits.

Group Society

In Japan's group-oriented society, deregulation represents a large departure from past societal norms. The essence of deregulation is to enhance individual choice, freedom, and responsibility in ways that can be unsettling. Within a group setting, individual members are taught to temper their own "egotistical" desires to blend or coordinate with others for the sake of group goals.

This notion of group orientation extends to economic organization.[8] Industries, for example, are viewed as akin to social groups by both industry participants and the government. Regulation and administrative guidance by government has been an important means for preventing the excesses of individual corporate competitive action from damaging the fortunes of others in the group. And in this model those firms possessing some technical or other competitive advantage should be cajoled into sharing their innovations with others in the industry, to the benefit of the group as a whole. Trade associations act as the formal group mechanism to adjust or coordinate industry behavior, and the government works closely with trade associations in transmitting its industrial policies.[9] Although Japan has an antitrust law, enforcement has been weak, and industry collusion that would be prosecuted in the United States has been either approved or implicitly tolerated under the Japanese law.[10]

Large parts of Japanese government policy toward the economy in the past fifty years have reflected these ideas about appropriate group behavior. The "convoy" system in the financial sector, in which the Ministry of Finance kept competition sufficiently at bay that the most inefficient financial institutions could earn a profit is certainly one major example. The liquor distribution industry operated for decades with fixed geographical territories for retail outlets determined by the government to protect the livelihood of small liquor shop operators. Retail prices for a variety of products were fixed by manufacturers, also inhibiting price competition among retailers. Policy on intellectual property emphasized limitations on protection for individual innovations and the need to license innovations to others in the industry rather than on protection of intellectual property rights. Cement, steel, petrochemicals, and other basic industries have operated under de facto cartel structures for decades, keeping prices high and stifling competition from lower-priced foreign products.

Deregulation is diametrically opposed to this general organization of economic society. Rather than punishing those firms or entrepreneurs who deviate from the agreed group behavior of limiting competition to strengthen the group, deregulation permits and encourages competition by individual firms and entrepreneurs. Although this is an obvious and simple point to anyone used to the American economy, it remains a troubling notion in Japan. Consumers flock to stores advertising bargain prices when they are available, but the broader notion that this practice may be damaging to the welfare of others in the industry remains strong.

The notion of group society hinders deregulation in another manner. The dynamics of decisionmaking in Japan are very different from the United States, with far greater emphasis on consensus. It is not sufficient to decide that deregulation is more efficient, build a political movement in its support, and alter the regulatory structure. Those opposed to deregulation cannot be simply defeated politically, they must be cajoled and won over, usually with some form of compensation.[11] Although this dynamic is not fundamentally different from the United States, the catering to the interests of opponents is far stronger than in the United States. The vested interests described previously are strong, are present in many sectors needing deregulation, benefit economically from the existing system, and are a major force against change. Obtaining agreement from those opposed to deregulation in this consensual group setting can be debilitatingly slow and often leads to small, piecemeal changes. Thus, at best deregulation becomes diluted and delayed, and at worst it is blocked.

Hierarchy

In Japan's hierarchical society, government has occupied a privileged position, and entering the bureaucracy has long attracted the brightest of university students. But the long history of privileged status, deference, and delegation of authority to bureaucrats makes changing the system difficult. People may be dissatisfied with the regulated state of the economy and the pettiness of regulatory behavior, but mounting a successful challenge to the bureaucrats upsets the social balance. The issue is succinctly summarized by an anonymous Ministry of Finance official in 1997: "If you think the state can be run without elite bureaucrats, just try it."[12]

The 1990s brought some change in public attitudes toward the bureaucracy, resulting from the sluggish performance of the economy and the emergence of a number of scandals involving graft and corruption within the bureaucracy. Weekly magazines, generally more willing to deal with scandalous stories than the newspapers, joined the antibureaucratic fray. *Shūkan Posuto* (the *Weekly Post*) ran a series of stories in 1997 showing that some 200 bureaucrats were on the controversial Nomura Securities "VIP" list (people for whom Nomura provided special treatment in handling their investment portfolios) and that since 1992 transactions in their accounts appear to have profited from insider information about government efforts to prop up stock market prices.[13] Even Bank of Japan (the central bank) officials have been implicated in providing advance notice on Bank market operations to the private sector.[14] And Ministry of Finance officials told banks when their "surprise" inspections would occur, and those inspections were often perfunctory as the officials responsible were entertained by the banks being inspected.[15] Scandals have been a frequent occurrence in Japan, but before the 1990s they usually involved politicians or corporate executives rather than bureaucrats. For years the mythology prevailed that government officials were selfless servants of the nation who were above bribery, but the scandals of the 1990s punctured this myth.

However, to what extent has this change in attitudes been a fundamental one? It is one thing for society to believe that bureaucrats have behaved badly and should be chastised, indicted, and generally taught to behave in a more sincere fashion. It is quite a different thing to believe that the problems of the economy should be solved by simply sweeping away significant portions of the function of government. Some Japanese obviously believe in this latter, strong view of change, but one wonders whether this group is more than a vocal minority.[16]

With the power and privilege still accorded to the bureaucracy, that is the only group that can bring about changes in government rules and regulations despite the recent damage to its reputation. In the longer run, even the bureaucracy cannot buck determined public opinion on deregulation. But when the business sector or households press for change, they must still work through the bureaucracy to get the new legislation written and to implement it once passed. Furthermore, the bureaucracy has worked over the years to influence the public or business voice in its own direction.[17] The bureaucracy is likely therefore to retain a significant role, including a strong involvement in economic affairs, largely accepted by the public.

Risk Aversion

A major obstacle to thorough deregulation comes from conservative, risk-averse attitudes in society that go well beyond the detrimental impact of simple political pressures of special interest groups. A core feature of the postwar economic system as it evolved by the 1950s was an emphasis on job security. This security was provided principally through "lifetime" employment in large corporations. This system was reinforced by the quasi-permanent linkage of small firms to the large firms through vertical relationships (*keiretsu*), both upstream (as parts or service suppliers) and downstream (as distributors), thereby giving employees at many smaller firms at least some of the security prevailing among large corporations. That is, while small firms might not formally practice lifetime employment, working at a parts supplier with *keiretsu* ties to one of the leading manufacturers would provide a greater sense and reality of employment security. Furthermore, lifetime security of those in large firms was enhanced through these vertical relationships, because the smaller contractors and distributors became providers of employment for those reaching the (early) mandatory retirement age in large firms.

One of the major fears of deregulation is the breakdown of this system of relative employment security. Certainly not all workers were ever covered by this ideal of lifetime job security, but coverage was sufficiently broad and the concept sufficiently ingrained in the national psyche as a desirable norm that its potential demise or diminishment raises concerns in society. For example, two influential articles appeared in a leading policy magazine in 1994 arguing that deregulation in the United States produced a variety of ills, with the emphasis placed on job losses. The first article focused heavily on the job losses when Eastern Airlines went bankrupt, including tales of hardship among those who lost their positions, with anecdotes presented as representing the broader ills of deregulation. The authors quoted one of the principal academic advocates of deregulation in the United States, Alfred Kahn, as saying that deregulation would lead to the end of lifetime employment in the affected industries.[18] Their analysis was subsequently challenged by two leading academic proponents of deregulation in Japan (professors Iwao Nakatani and Takatoshi Ito of Hitotsubashi University), but their counterarguments based on standard economic analysis did not carry the personal punch of stories of unemployed workers.[19]

The employment issue becomes especially salient because the existing system amounts to a privatization of unemployment issues. Rather than tolerating higher unemployment and socializing the cost by providing generous unemployment benefits financed by taxes (the European approach), large firms have borne much of the cost by not laying off workers. The government does provide unemployment compensation, but the benefits are rather limited in amount and duration. Although large firms have long touted the benefits of lifetime employment (low turnover rates producing lower training costs and continuous increase in firm-specific worker skills), their ability to keep redundant workers on the payroll also depended on the profits accruing from regulated or collusive markets at home. Meanwhile, the other element of the privatized safety net was the ease of entry into small business (though at highly flexible wages that fall in recessions), especially the retail sector. Workers who could not enter the large firm sector or who were forced out could open a small shop or find employment in a small business. Vigorous deregulation would undermine both parts of this privatized unemployment safety net. Large firms would experience stronger competition in their markets, lowering profit margins, and thereby diminishing their ability to subsidize redundant workers during economic slowdowns. And real competition in retailing, construction, and other small-business sectors would reduce their ability to act as an employment shock absorber. Therefore, deregulation needs to be accompanied by creation of a better public safety net in the form of improved unemployment benefits and retraining programs if the public is to view deregulation less fearfully.

This risk aversion and conservatism can also be related to concepts of group society. In the Japanese economy, the ideal is to be in a situation wherein the group looks out for the interests of individuals. Successful individuals attend leading universities (where large companies recruit new employees) and build relationships with professors who recommend their students to firms with which they have connections. Once hired by a large corporation practicing lifetime employment, the individual gives up a great deal of individual freedom in return for job security, and when the time comes to retire, the firm will place the individual in a postretirement job with a subsidiary. Throughout this lifetime of employment, the successful individual is dependent upon the benevolence and assistance of others in his reference group—school and corporation. But in a deregulated environment, one of the unsettling images is an increased burden on the individual to act alone. To return to the story of Eastern Airlines, its employees were left on their own to find jobs because the corporation was gone. Again, what seems normal in an American context—individuals seeking employment largely on their own—can sound excessively insecure and uncertain in a Japanese context.

Perhaps employees are rightfully frightened at the prospects of finding jobs on their own because the job market—especially for managerial employees—is not well developed. With the prevalence of lifetime employment, large firms hire managers almost exclusively from new school graduates. The prospects for a mid- or upper-level manager suddenly stuck looking for a job independently could be poor unless a larger market develops for midcareer job seekers.

The Diversion of Bureaucratic Pettiness

Much of the desire to pursue deregulation has been less about economic efficiency and more about irritation over bureaucratic pettiness and slowness. At a personal level, people seem concerned that their daily life requires conforming to useless regulations or that the bureaucratic process is slow or irrational in responding to requests—a phenomenon not unknown in the United States. Just before becoming prime minister, Hosokawa published a book in which there was a prominent anecdote about his travails as a governor in getting the Ministry of Transportation to move a bus stop by ten meters (a process that took six months).[20] His lament is typical of attitudes about deregulation.

Willingness to criticize the regulatory or bureaucratic process clearly increased in the 1990s. Masao Miyamoto, an American-trained psychiatrist who returned to Japan to work for the Ministry of Health and Welfare, published a series of articles and books providing a scathing description of the often dysfunctional behavior patterns within the bureaucracy. His description of bureaucratic power in drafting legislation, a rigid approach to precedent, emphasis on demonstrating extraordinarily long hours of work rather than substance or efficiency, and the endless emphasis on hierarchy appealed to many people, though his writings eventually led to termination of his government employment. What Miyamoto described is a bureaucratic system that is more concerned with internal power struggles and factions than with the economic, social, or medical rationality of the resulting policies.[21]

Some bureaucratic decisions began to attract anger from the media in the 1990s, who were dismayed over the lack of economic or other rational justification for decisions. The Ministry of Transportation, for example, approved substantial increases in regulated taxi fares and highway tolls in 1994 despite generally falling prices in the rest of the economy. During 1994, the government also decided to raise local telephone charges, subway fares, and public housing rents. This decision was widely decried in the press (but to little avail—some of the increases were postponed, but only by six months to early 1995).[22] Dissatisfaction arising from such individual episodes has led to a general sense of "get the government off my back."

All of this criticism of the bureaucracy, which emerged in the 1990s, should have been an encouraging sign in favor of deregulation. However, note that the concern was often focused on the behavior of certain individuals within the bureaucracy or on particular decisions rather than with the system as a whole. The implication often was that bureaucrats should make better decisions and be more honest. Prime Minister Hosokawa's experience with the bus stop was egregious, but the presumed solution was for the Ministry of Transportation to have made the decision more quickly out of a concern for efficiency, rather than to simply eliminate the role of the central government in such small decisions. The bureaucracy can respond to such pressures through small technical changes or special exceptions in cases that become publicized, leaving the broader features of government's role in the economy unaltered.

Process

The process created to achieve deregulation in the 1990s was exceptionally weak, for reasons that reflect the factors discussed previously. As dissatisfaction with regulation surfaced, the Japanese political process responded. Prime Minister Hosokawa established a special committee of private sector representatives to report on overall structural reform of the economy (commonly known as the Hiraiwa Commission, after Gaishi Hiraiwa, who was committee chair), which reported in December 1993. Deregulation was a major piece of the commission's mandate, rooted in the commission report's advocacy of overarching principles of transparency, consumer orientation, and harmony with the outside world. The commission adopted a vague principle for regulation that "economic regulations should be eliminated in principle with only exceptional areas regulated," reversing the implicit standard in the postwar period that everything is regulated unless specifically exempted. The report called for deregulation in land use, housing construction and related areas, distribution and "other inefficient industrial sectors," agriculture, import processing, and emerging industries (such as information and telecommunication). The report called for creation of a "third party" with authority to oversee the deregulation process by issuing recommendations to avoid the problem of bureaucratic dominance.[23]

Unfortunately, the outside body representing nongovernmental interests to oversee the deregulation was given only a weak advisory role. It could comment on government plans or make suggestions but had no authority to approve, reject, or devise its own policy. This left the process of deregulation firmly in the hands of the bureaucracy with only very soft oversight by politicians or those outside government. What some had hoped would be an effort by a reform government to wrest power from the bureaucracy failed. The bureaucracy succeeded in maintaining its centrality in this process despite what appeared to be strong support for the principle of deregulation in the media and business groups (such as Keidanren, the organized voice of business).

The subsequent Hata, Murayama, and Hashimoto administrations moved forward with policy changes within this overall framework of assigning responsibility for deregulation to the bureaucracy itself. After the Diet elections in the fall of 1996, Prime Minister Hashimoto (president of a somewhat strengthened Liberal Democratic Party) renewed the call for vigorous deregulation over the rest of the 1990s, with a special emphasis on the financial sector. However the process for implementing deregulation remained the same. This bureaucratically centered process bore little resemblance to the process in the United States. These differences reflect the underlying nature of public debate, political structure, and social expectation.

The mandate given to the bureaucracy in early 1994 by the Hosokawa government was vague, stemming from fairly general concerns such as a recognition of bureaucratic arbitrariness in many regulatory areas, the notion of overregulation slowing the economy, and the observation that prices were higher than abroad in many areas. Given a mandate for action, the bureaucracy focused on numbers. If the economy is "overregulated," then the solution is to reduce the number of regulations. Therefore, the bureaucracy issued a list of items to be considered for deregulation or modification in March 1995 and invited lists of requests from the Japanese business community and from foreign governments or businesses. Further announcements of lists of regulations for which action would be taken or "studied" appeared later in 1995, 1996, and 1997. This process was slated to continue for five years (later accelerated to be accomplished in three years, ending in March 1998), dominated by the bureaucracy acting on its own with only cursory oversight.

The fundamental problem with this process was the inherent weakness of any process of deregulation controlled by career officials. Faced with a mandate to reduce the number of regulations, any well-trained bureaucrat can discover a variety of small, inconsequential items to stick on the deregulation list that do not change regulation in any meaningful sense. No bureaucracy dominated entirely by career officials would move very far in deregulation because the competent officials are those whose *raison d'être* depends on the existence of regulations. Between 1994 and 1998, the predictable response of various bureaus of the different ministries tasked with producing lists of items to deregulate was resistance on the basis that most regulations were vital.

Consider, for example, an interim progress report from MITI issued at the end of December 1996. This report claimed that of 446 requests submitted to it for review from domestic and international sources, 186 had been acted on favorably, 88 were still under consideration, 87 were "difficult to remedy," and 85 were discarded for various reasons (such as being based on "mistaken information").[24] A subsequent detailed report issued in March 1997 had 384 pages of brief descriptions of individual actions taken (often with nothing more informative than announcing that change for a particular regulation was being studied).[25] This is hardly a realistic approach to deregulation. Such lists convey absolutely no sense of relative significance, or how changes combine to affect the overall framework for a particular industry, nor do they convey any sense of what constitutes favorable action. MITI and other government ministries wished to show simply that they had taken a lot of action and had acted favorably on many of the regulatory issues considered for action.

Having defined a bureaucratically centered process, other participants were bound to engage within the government's parameters. Keidanren, the organized voice of "big business" in Japan, for example, periodically submitted lists of requested deregulation items. A January 1997 "wish list" included 699 requests for deregulation and a further 187 requests for easing licensing application procedures, for a total of 886 individual items. One wonders how serious Keidanren was in really pressing for change given the conflicted position of much of Japanese business on deregulation. Although some Keidanren member firms would benefit from deregulation through lower prices for their inputs (such as lower electricity or telephone rates), others were at the core of industries benefiting from deregulation (such as steel or construction). Perhaps reflecting a lack of seriousness, the January 1997 Keidanren report praised government efforts to date as "a giant leap for actual deregulation."[26] Given the rather poor record of the government efforts on deregulation by early 1997, one wonders why Keidanren would offer such praise. The probable answer is that since many of its members did not truly want deregulation, behaving in a mild, supportive, deferential manner would get favorable attention for their favorite issues. In itself, this form of behavior spoke volumes about Keidanren's inability or lack of interest in fundamentally breaking the traditional framework of government-business relationships.

Eventually even the numbers-counting game ran into some problems. The 1997 government white paper on deregulation claimed success for deregulation since 91 percent of the 1,797 regulations targeted for review had been acted upon (although "action" did not necessarily mean elimination). Nevertheless, the report had to admit that the total number of regulations in force had risen by 223 to 10,983! Although some bureaucrats were making a show of easing existing rules and regulations, others were busily creating new ones.[27] Note that the very notion of counting regulations in force in society is suspect because of the vague definition of what constitutes a single regulation. Japan surely had far more than 10,983 regulations in effect. But despite the inaccuracy of this exercise, the fact that the government had to admit that several years of deregulation had left a society with more regulations in effect than before was an eloquent commentary on the weakness of the process.

The contrast with the United States is striking. Some regulatory change in the United States originated in the regulatory agencies themselves, aided by the ability of federal and state administrations to appoint commissioners to commissions when terms expired—and in so doing pick outsiders (not retired career bureaucrats) who might bring in new and innovative ideas. Similarly, for health, safety, and social regulations administered directly by federal departments, the ability of administrations to put political appointees in place provides an opportunity to move the bureaucracy in new directions. With Japanese regulation centered inside a career bureaucracy (rather than in quasi-independent regulatory commissions), and with only a marginal political presence in each ministry in the form of the minister and political vice minister, the possibility of innovation from within is greatly lessened. The career bureaucrats are certainly not totally inflexible, and changes in attitude do occur over time, but the system is less likely to move vigorously toward deregulation than the U.S. regulatory commissions or the U.S. bureaucracy.

Furthermore, the process of deregulation in the United States has relied heavily on legislative action. Even in the somewhat more flexible bureaucratic system of the United States, the scope and speed of regulatory change from within the commissions and bureaucracy were constrained because of past legal mandates or bureaucratic inflexibility. The legislative process produced important new laws revamping the regulatory framework for various industries, buttressed by an informed political debate and detailed economic analysis. In Japan very little of this has happened. Since the bureaucrats control much of the relevant information about the industries, the politicians have very limited staffs, and many of the knowledgeable academics serve on ministry advisory commissions, it is unlikely that an independent, politically driven effort could dislodge the bureaucrats from their dominance of the deregulation issue.

During the past two decades, a few episodes of legislative action have occurred that give the appearance of movement in the direction of deregulation. In the mid-1970s, the Diet voted to delegate railroad rate approval from itself to the Ministry of Transportation, a move that shortened the process of granting approvals but left basic regulatory control in place.[28] The "privatization" of the Japanese National Railways (JNR), Nippon Telegraph and Telephone Public Corporation (NTT), and Japan Tobacco in the 1980s was also brought about by legislation, but the changes in legal status of these three organizations did not involve significant deregulation (nor any decisive move from public to private ownership). The process of railroad rate approval remained unchanged, and the only significant accomplishments were to weaken the power of the railroad's unions and to fob off all JNR pension obligations on a new JNR Settlement Corporation (which was mired in financial problems a decade later). NTT remained largely owned by the government. (As of March 31, 1997, the central government owned 65.5 percent of total outstanding shares.) And the overall state of deregulation of telecommunications remained far behind the United States (with the 1999 breakup of NTT into three companies, proposed in late 1996 as a deregulation measure, arousing much skepticism). Privatization of Japan Tobacco provided a means to allow foreign firms independent access to retail cigarette outlets in Japan, but ownership of the corporation remained in the hands of the government. Overall, legislative action in the Diet had a very small role in the overall process of deregulation in Japan.

What the Japanese government defines as deregulation also often falls short of complete change or elimination of needless regulatory obstacles. For example, Japan has had throughout the postwar period retail price maintenance on some consumer products, with the list dwindling slowly over time. The 1996 report on progress in deregulation called for elimination of retail price maintenance for pharmaceuticals and cosmetics but was very unclear on copyrighted materials (promising only to "limit and clarify" the scope of the retail price maintenance system by March 1998.[29] Two years later, on March 31, 1998, the decision was made to retain retail price maintenance for copyrighted materials (while promising further "study").[30] This issue, which applied only to Japanese copyrighted materials (not foreign products) had led to a huge price differential between domestic sound recordings and imported recordings (with foreign compact disks selling for roughly one-half the price of domestic recordings at major retail outlets in Tokyo such as Tower Records, in one of the rare examples of a regulation that has benefited foreign products relative to domestic ones). Even with such a startling price disparity, this obvious candidate for elimination remained in place.

Despite the general weakness in the deregulation process, international developments provide one small bit of optimism. As chapter 6 discusses, the deregulation process is helped somewhat by the new World Trade Organization (WTO) phytosanitary and technical standards agreements. Although these multilateral agreements do not necessitate deregulation—that is, outright removal of regulations—they do impose an international obligation on Japan. If implemented as intended, the WTO agreements imply that transparency in the standard-setting process must increase, regulations must be based on better or more clear scientific evidence, and there must be greater acceptance of foreign products that meet functionally similar but different standards in their own countries. If Japan does not alter its standard-setting practices and testing procedures to fit the letter and spirit of the WTO, then it is liable to face American and other foreign challenges within the WTO. A set of deregulation measures adopted in 1996 (following periodic negotiations with the United States over a number of years) for wood products and other housing materials included acceptance of U.S. softwood lumber grade marks for two-by-fours. Further progress occurred on housing materials in the first joint report in May 1998 under the bilateral Enhanced Initiative on deregulation issues (including an intent to amend the Building Standards Law by fiscal 2000 to bring about performance-based standards), discussed in chapter 4.[31] This progress, coming after years of discussions, may have been motivated in part by the new WTO rules.

Even on this issue, however, the relative importance of internal moves toward deregulation is difficult to discern. Negotiations on housing materials had been one focus of the Reagan administration's Market-Oriented, Sector-Selective (MOSS) talks in 1985–86 (or at least wood products, producing an agreement in January 1986), then the subject of Super 301 negotiations in the Bush administration (resulting in an agreement in June 1990), then part of the Framework negotiations in the first term of the Clinton administration, and also part of the Enhanced Initiative on Deregulation in the second term of the Clinton administration.[32] Therefore, wood products and other housing materials had been the object of repeated negotiations over a prolonged period. After the WTO had come into effect, the Japanese government announced a more positive stance, with Prime Minister Hashimoto declaring an initiative to reduce housing costs through deregulation affecting imported building products. Given the appearance of a more progressive attitude, the U.S. government continued to press for changes in standards and testing that would bring Japan into closer conformity with international practice, resulting in the progress that occurred in the May 1998 settlement in the bilateral Enhanced Initiative.[33]

For housing materials, it is possible that at least the modest recent progress is related to Japanese government recognition of its weakened ability to pursue idiosyncratic standards and testing procedures under the new WTO rules. Should progress be sufficiently slow, the U.S. government has the option of taking these standards issues to the WTO to increase the negotiating pressure on Japan as it did in 1998 on testing requirements for agricultural products (discussed in chapter 4).

Continuing Corporate Connections

Close connections between Japanese firms and their suppliers and distributors have long been a problem for foreign (and domestic) firms attempting to enter a market. This system of close long-term contracting ties, known as vertical *keiretsu* ties, has some economic efficiencies.[34] But the closeness and rigidity of existing ties goes beyond the needs of long-term contracting efficiencies to produce a considerable barrier to trade. Similar allegations have been made about horizontal *keiretsu* ties as well, the loose grouping of firms across industries that have been such a distinctive feature of Japan.[35]

Some have argued that *keiretsu* ties are loosening as firms have been forced by the more competitive environment of the 1990s to jettison or relax some of their long-standing corporate ties in their quest to seek lower cost suppliers. Particularly in the period from 1993 to 1995, when the yen strengthened against the dollar, the cost of sticking with domestic suppliers in the face of lower cost alternatives from overseas increased. Firms appeared to be willing to consider switching to foreign suppliers because of the cost disadvantage of maintaining loyalty to their traditional domestic suppliers. Press stories were prevalent about the automobile industry, which was also under pressure from the United States during the Framework talks to increase parts procurement from non-*keiretsu* foreign suppliers. But the pressures were complex—sometimes resulting in purchases from foreign firms (such as Nissan purchases of airbags from TRW, touted in one article) and sometimes just resulting in lower prices paid to existing suppliers.[36] By 1998 Nissan declared that it would no longer give preference to its traditional parts suppliers, a decision reportedly under consideration by other auto manufacturers as well.[37] Nissan's plan was far short of an elimination of its parts supplier *keiretsu*, amounting more to a reorganization within which outside suppliers would be given more opportunities than in the past while the *keiretsu* members would face more pressure to cut costs.[38] Beyond these anecdotes, though, there is little evidence on the strength or extent of such changes—and official announcements by firms should be treated with at least some skepticism.

For the broad horizontal *keiretsu* little change is evident. Table 5-1 shows mutual shareholding levels and the share of total bank borrowing from the group's banks for each of the six main horizontal *keiretsu* (with membership in each group defined by membership in a presidents' club). For shareholding, the percentages represent the share of total equity of the core members of the group owned by other members of the group. For lending, the percentages represent the share of total bank borrowing by group members that comes from the banks associated with the group. In the case of the Sumitomo group, a long-term trend toward diminished ties is clearly visible, while the Fuyo, Sanwa, and Dai-Ichi groups show a more minor downward drift. But both equity and lending ties within the Mitsui and Mitsubishi groups were little changed through the mid-1990s. Overall, these data do not suggest a major loosening of horizontal *keiretsu* ties, at least as manifested in these two visible dimensions of the relationships.

By 1997 and 1998, banks were in such weak financial positions that they were rumored to be selling some of their long-held shares in other *keiretsu* members. But given the tenacity of these ties over prolonged periods of time, it was doubtful that a major shift would occur. The data in table 5-1 for March 31, 1996, certainly show little change from 1995, with just a slight drop in intra-group equity ties and a marginal increase in bank-loan ties on average. Rather than further reducing ties, some news reports in 1998 suggested that equity ties might rise. Banks, saddled with large amounts of nonperforming loans, needed to improve their capital basis. In the case of the Mitsui group, the nonfinancial firms agreed to purchase new shares in Sakura Bank to shore up its capital base.[39] The Fuyo group also cooperatively purchased new shares in Yasuda Trust Bank.[40]

As a general conclusion, the limited evidence on both vertical and horizontal *keiretsu* suggests the system was under pressure in the 1990s but

Table 5-1. *Trends in Intercorporate Ties within the*
Six Large Horizontal **Keiretsu**

	Equity ties[a]					Loan ties[a]				
	Percent equity within group					Percent of loans from group				
Group	1978	1985	1990	1995	1996	1978	1985	1990	1995	1996
Mitsui	17.9	17.9	16.5	16.3	15.8	20.6	21.2	19.6	20.5	20.6
Mitsubishi	26.9	25.2	26.9	26.9	26.8	26.3	22.4	19.4	19.3	20.8
Sumitomo	27.2	25.0	24.1	22.3	22.3	28.1	27.7	21.5	20.4	22.7
Fuyō	15.8	15.8	15.4	14.1	13.9	20.4	18.4	17.4	16.9	17.9
Sanwa	16.9	16.8	16.4	15.7	15.7	21.7	20.3	18.2	17.4	16.2
Dai-ichi Kangyō	14.4	13.3	12.1	11.5	11.2	12.7	12.1	12.5	13.9	14.1

Source: Tōyō Keizai, *Kigyō Keiretsu Sōran* [Survey of Business Keiretsu] (Tokyo: Tōyō Keizai Shinpō Sha),
1980 ed., pp. 42–53; 1987 ed., pp. 22–33; 1992 ed., pp. 40–49; 1997 ed., pp. 38–47; 1998 ed., pp. 32–41.
   a. Dates are for March 31 of each year.

without any fundamental changes. At the margin, vertical groups may have
loosened somewhat, permitting foreign firms to make inroads as suppliers.
Horizontal groups degraded their formal ownership and lending relationships modestly. In neither case does the available evidence suggest that these
basic relationships have attenuated to the point that they should not be considered a problem for new entrants to the Japanese market. Long-standing
horizontal and vertical relationships are still providing a bias against doing
business with newcomers, foreign firms in particular.

Continued Industrial Policy

At the same time that the government was actively discussing deregulation
in the 1990s, it was also pursuing new industrial policy initiatives. Despite
the rhetoric of deregulation, the government had little intent of altering
fundamental concepts about the relationship between government and the
economy; the desire to use industrial policy tools to promote and protect
domestic industries continued. The heavy-handed and direct controls that
government had used in the 1950s and 1960s to guide the economy were
long gone. But although the tools were more indirect and fewer in number,
the intent to play a role remained, leaving the situation in Japan in the 1990s
quite different from the United States.

   The major example in the mid-1990s came in the form of a new industry promotion law passed in 1995, the Temporary Law for Smooth Improve-

ment in Designated Industries.[41] In format, this law was very traditional, giving MITI broad and vaguely defined powers to promote industries affected by changing domestic and international conditions. MITI's advisory council on industrial structure had completed a study recommending fourteen broad industrial sectors for promotion.[42] Based on this recommendation, MITI originally designated 165 more narrowly defined industries and modified this list to reach 190 industries.[43] These represented industries in which firms were eligible to apply for benefits under the new law. On the list of eligible industries were several of particular interest from a bilateral perspective. Consider, for example, that building materials were on the list, the area discussed earlier as one in which idiosyncratic standards and testing procedures had protected the domestic industry.

Among the support measures available to firms applying under the law were special depreciation tax measures, reduction of some other taxes, access to subsidized loans from the Japan Development Bank and other government financial institutions, and loan guarantees—all standard industrial policy measures. As is often the case in Japanese industrial policy, some of the tax provisions became extraordinarily precise. Among the 104 items designated for special depreciation, for example, was equipment for manufacturing TFT computer screens with a diagonal size greater than 350 millimeters.[44] The Japanese economy and the public would be better served by fully opening the market and simply forcing domestic firms to meet the competition rather than concocting new schemes to promote and grow the domestic industry. Infant industry arguments that could be used in the 1950s to justify these kinds of promotional schemes simply did not apply to Japan in the 1990s.

Semiconductors represented another area of new and active industrial policy in the mid-1990s. With a fear of falling behind the United States in semiconductors, industry and government launched new programs in the 1994–96 period. With what began as a private sector initiative in 1994, MITI developed its own government initiative, resulting in the establishment of the largest-scale research and development project on semiconductors since the VLSI project of the 1970s. As with other projects, this one brought together all the major Japanese semiconductor firms in a cooperative framework, and with many of the same aims as the 1994 private sector initiative. More important, the core research programs were restricted to the Japanese firms. Foreign firms were participating, but they were restricted to the more peripheral parts of the program. This approach perpetuated the tradition of blurring government-industry boundaries, pursuing narrow nationalism, and devising new informal or opaque relationships—the kind of relationships that deregulation and administrative reform were presumably diminishing.[45]

The kind of government-sponsored joint R&D project under way in semiconductors has had a mixed record in the past twenty years. Some view many of these exercises as ineffective or inefficient.[46] But even projects that do not lead to pathbreaking new technologies can still result in collusive outcomes whereby the domestic participants in these projects are protected from superior foreign technologies (through, for example, sweetheart procurement deals from government or government-controlled entities like NTT). And for new projects, such as the current semiconductor one, foreign firms are justifiably concerned that it might be successful, to their future detriment in the market.

Another area of continued active industrial policy has been small and medium enterprises. Small and medium businesses include those with up to 300 employees in manufacturing, 100 employees in wholesale, and 50 employees in the retail and other service sectors.[47] Japan is not unique in providing financial and other government assistance to smaller firms, but the potential certainly exists for promotion and protection of these firms to conflict with efforts to make markets more accessible. Smaller manufacturing firms serve as subcontractors to larger manufacturers in vertical *keiretsu* relationships, so that policies to support them can be detrimental to efficient foreign firms attempting to enter the market. Similarly, support for smaller wholesalers and retailers slows the shift toward a less convoluted distribution system and larger retail outlets that are more likely to carry foreign consumer goods.

Much of the government policy framework to support small and medium enterprises was established in the early postwar period (with the basic support law enacted in 1963). However, the 1990s brought new supportive activity by government. Table 5-2 lists eight laws enacted in the 1990s affecting small and medium enterprises. Of these, the 1995 law for financial assistance to small firms devastated by the Hanshin earthquake seems unremarkable. But the others continue the tradition of protecting and promoting small and medium businesses in the face of economic pressures such as the strong yen and inroads of competitive foreign goods and services. In fact, these eight laws represented a great deal of legislative activity since they represented a quarter of the thirty-three laws in force affecting small and medium businesses in 1997. Rather than backing away from an

Table 5-2. *Laws for Small and Medium Enterprises Enacted in the 1990s*

Year	Law	Title (abbreviated)	Translation
1991	57	Chūshō Kigyō Rōdōryoku Kakuho Hō	Law to Promote Maintenance of Employment at Small and Medium Enterprises
1991	82	Tokutei Shōgyō Shūseki Seibi Hō	Law for Promotional Facilities for Designated Businesses
1992	65	Chūshō Kigyō Ryūtsū Gyōmu Kōritsuka Sokushin Hō	Law to Promote Efficient Distribution by Small and Medium Enterprises
1993	51	Shōkibo Jigyōsha Shien Sokushin Hō	Law to Support Small Scale Businessmen
1993	93	Tokutei Chūshō Kigyō Shinbunya Shinshutsu Enkatsu Hō	Law to Smooth Entry of Designated Small and Medium Enterprises into New Business Areas
1995	16	Hanshin Daishinsai Taisho Zaisei Shien Hō	Law to Finance and Support Recovery from the Hanshin Earthquake
1995	47	Chūshō Kigyō Sōzō Katsudō Sokushin Hō	Law to Promote Establishment of New Small-Medium Enterprises
1997	28	Chiiki Sangyō Shūseki Kasseika Hō	Law to Invigorate Consolidation of Local Industries

Sources: Small and Medium Enterprise Agency, *Chūshō Kigyō Shisaku Sōran Shiryōhen* [Overview of Small and Medium Enterprise Policy] (Chūshō Kigyō Sōgō Kenkyū Kikō, 1997), pp. 75, 90, 94, 103, 116, 118; Ministry of International Trade and Industry, *Tsūshō Roppō* [Compilation of Industry and Trade Laws] (Tsūshō Sangyō Chōsakai, 1997), pp. 1897–1901, 1969–1971.

activist industrial policy role, the government (MITI in this case) was moving forward aggressively with new initiatives.

To what extent these new laws have increased or changed the nature of government support for small businesses is less clear. Table 5-3 shows government funding for small business in the 1990s. The budget for direct government expenditures to support small business has fluctuated sharply with no clear trend in either direction. The initial budget for fiscal 1997 was ¥195 billion ($1.6 billion at 1997 exchange rates). Subsidized lending through government lending institutions shows outstanding total loans of ¥27.5 trillion ($217 billion at 1992 exchange rates) in fiscal 1992, rising and then

declining slightly to ¥26.8 trillion ($246 billion at 1996 exchange rates) by
1996. Thus the additional legislative programs in the 1990s did not result
in any clear increase in financial support for small business. But neither
did support decline in any appreciable way. At least the new burst of legislation helped maintain an active program of policy support.

How does this evidence of continued industrial policy initiatives fit
with the rhetoric of deregulation in the 1990s? As put by one observer, the
government was trying to "change the system, . . . but not fundamentally
abolish the elite-managed, catch-up system with its focus on the maxi-
mization of producer welfare and its use of managed markets to promote
political, social, and economic stability and overall national economic well-
being."[48] Something was changing in the 1990s, and certainly some deregulation was part of that change. But the government had no intention and
no desire to alter its basic relationship toward the private sector. Belief in
market failure and the need for the government to extend a guiding hand to
gently mold the shape and progress of Japanese industries remained strong.
Foreign firms would find modest progress in access where the United States
and other governments had pressed negotiations, but the essence of industrial policy remained the promotion of Japanese-owned firms.

Amakudari

An important feature of the government's ability to pursue industrial policy
in the 1990s even as deregulation was supposedly proceeding was the continuation of a practice known as *amakudari* (literally "descent from
heaven"). This is the practice of government officials moving into postretirement jobs in the private sector or in the quasi-public sector upon retiring from their ministries. *Amakudari* is a subset of general labor market
practices, since employees at large corporations also generally move to
arranged postretirement jobs when they reach the mandatory retirement
age in their corporation. The *amakudari* system provides a substantial reason to be skeptical of the extent of deregulation and unilateral market opening in Japan because of the manner in which this practice establishes a
broad web of personal ties between government and Japanese firms.
Although these patterns had come under criticism in the press as the result
of scandals related primarily to the financial sector, little was happening to
alter or end the system during the 1990s.

Several features of the *amakudari* system are worth emphasizing. First,
the practice is broad. Mandatory retirement ages in government are early

Table 5-3. *Government Support for Medium-Small Business*

Fiscal year	Government budget for medium-small business programs (Yen billions)	Outstanding government loans to medium-small business (Yen trillions)
1992	¥269	¥27.5
1993	416	29.3
1994	286	29.2
1995	646	27.7
1996	213	26.8
1997	195[a]	n.a.

Source: Small and Medium Enterprise Agency, *Chūshō Kigyō Shisaku Sōran Shiryōhen*, 1997 ed., pp. 16, 32.
a. Initial budget; often subject to major increase through supplements later in the fiscal year (as much as 200 percent in 1995).

(still set at age 55 or slightly above) and have not advanced as they have in the private sector over the past two decades. Virtually all government officials take a postretirement job when they officially retire. For those on the top career track, a maximum of only one employee in each age cohort in any single ministry will remain after age 55, promoted to the top post of vice minister. All other members of the age cohort leave at some point between 45 and 55 as the management pyramid in the ministry narrows; if an official is not promoted, he "retires" since the ministries maintain a rather strict seniority ranking so that an older official should not serve under a younger one within this top career group. But relatively early retirement characterizes all segments of the bureaucracy (including those not in the elite career track), and as they retire by their mid-50s, all these people need jobs.

Most of the attention of the scholars who have studied this phenomenon has focused only on those bureaucrats in the top career track for whom the Japanese government releases information on their *amakudari* positions. This approach is flawed because it ignores the much broader flow of people from the bureaucracy to the private sector.[49] Those officials on the top career track may be the most important in the sense that they receive high-level positions in the private sector and are in the strongest position to interact at a high policy level with their former colleagues in the ministry. But on issues concerning access for foreign firms, the use of domestic firms as landing spots for officials of all levels is important.

Second, the process of moving into a postretirement job is organized by each ministry. Retiring officials do not go out independently into the job market to find a position; they are placed by their ministry. One Japanese press report alleges that as much as 90 percent of the Secretariat Division at the Ministry of Finance is devoted to arranging jobs for retiring officials.[50] This practice makes *amakudari* fundamentally different from the American "revolving door," which at least relies on individual behavior. Even the individual revolving door process is a perennial topic of concern in the United States because it creates possibilities for favoritism and skewed government policies as former government officials work their contacts in government. Imagine then, the possibilities for bias, favoritism, and skewed policies if the flow of people from government to the private sector were organized and operated on a systematic basis by the ministries. That is the situation in Japan. The very act of ministries negotiating with the private sector over placement of officials introduces an additional element of favor swapping; firms may agree to take (a possibly unwanted) official in exchange for other favors (such as protecting its domestic market share against foreign competition). Even without explicit negotiation of favors, a ministry would certainly be loath to have deregulation or inroads of foreign competitors jeopardize the ability of the ministry to continue placing of postretirement officials.

Third, there are several destinations to which government officials can descend, including the private sector, politics, and government-related organizations.[51] Any presumed impact of *amakudari* on trade policy should be tempered by realization that not all officials pour into the private sector. But even here the picture is blurred. For those officials on the top career track, some restrictions do apply to their ability to shift smoothly into industries related to their work in the ministry. Existence of a wide variety of government-related organizations provides a place to park these officials until they can legally move into industry. In addition, some of these quasi-governmental organizations have an economic function that may include either interacting with the private sector or engaging in services for the private sector (such as product testing) that can have trade implications.

For those going into the private sector, the prevalence of *amakudari* varies by industry. Some sectors, such as construction, are particularly affected. Consider, for example, the role of former government officials on the boards of construction firms. Most Japanese corporations fill their corporate boards predominantly with managers of the firm, with only a few outsiders. The top 100 construction firms in Japan have 2,995 directors, of whom only 1,121 (37 percent) are from outside the company. Of the outside directors, 517 are *amakudari* officials—amounting to 46 percent of outside directors and 17 percent of total directors.[52] Even this figure understates the presence of *amakudari* in construction firms because it does not identify other officials who are serving in capacities other than as a member of the board.

This practice is a good example of the kind of special interest group building that Mancur Olson pointed to as gradually harming national economic interests. *Amakudari* is largely a postwar phenomenon, but its evolution over the past half century reinforced the role of the bureaucracy and strengthened the bonds between government and industry in ways that were not necessarily good for the economy and have been increasingly difficult to dislodge. Although there are examples of officials retiring prior to the war into private sector jobs, the prewar system did not have mandatory retirement ages.[53] The large flow over the past several decades has now created a set of personal ties among government, firms, trade associations, and think tanks. A government that must manage or manipulate a system to find landing spots for its retirees each year is likely to deviate from the public good in order to meet its narrow interests in finding jobs for all those retirees.

Why would private sector firms willingly accept retiring officials from government? These people have spent their careers in government, with no knowledge or experience in a private sector setting. Several theories have been advanced on this question. Some of those explanations have emphasized benefits within a system in which the government wields considerable regulatory power, a power often exercised through informal "administrative guidance." Smaller firms in an industry may wish to improve their chances of being favored in government regulatory decisions, while others may see acceptance of *amakudari* officials as the route to government contracts (especially in the corrupt allocation of construction contracts for public works projects), or as a way to get the ministry to listen to the firm's concerns when new regulatory measures are pending.[54]

The system of *amakudari* placements in the private sector matters in Japan's relationship with the rest of the world because foreign firms do not have the same access to the system as Japanese firms. A few foreign firms have taken on *amakudari* officials, but their experience has been mixed. Meanwhile, the existence of these extensive personal ties between the ministries and Japanese firms simply strengthens the lack of transparency in government-business relations and the probability of favoritism for those domestic firms with which the government has a connection. From the ministry's perspective, it must vigorously protect its existing landing spots, and foreign competition in an industry may jeopardize this function, as noted earlier. Furthermore, those government officials engaged in trade negotiations must think about their personal future; they know with absolute certainty that they will retire at an early age and that the biggest plums for postretirement jobs are with private sector firms. Therefore, any action to open markets perceived as detrimental by the domestic industry damages the future employment prospects of the official responsible. If officials do make concessions, they at least have to demonstrate that they tried their best to avoid doing so, creating one reason for the difficult and protracted nature of trade negotiations with Japan.

The impact of the *amakudari* system on trade policy extends beyond placement of officials in firms. Some officials end up working at trade associations and testing authorities, increasing the probability that foreign firms will be disadvantaged in product approval processes. It is difficult to separate general problems (high testing fees for all firms to enhance the revenues of the testing group and salaries of its retired government officials) versus problems only for foreign firms (discrimination against foreign products, enhanced by *amakudari* connections to ministries with little interest in seeing foreign products in the market), but testing issues have certainly been one of the problems that foreign firms face, and the *amakudari* connection may supply part of the answer for those problems.

Elimination or drastic modifications of the scope of the *amakudari* system would be a highly significant, positive development in promoting greater market openness. During the 1990s, scandals erupted about the relationship between bureaucrats and the private sector. Some of them involved connections through *amakudari* officials.[55] But negative media attention did not result in much real modification, and elimination of the system was not on the deregulation agenda in any realistic sense. Some ministries lengthened the time before officials could take positions in a related industry, but this small change was not a serious constraint on government-business relations. In the summer of 1997, the Jinji-in (National Personnel Authority) recommended in its annual report that rules on *amakudari* placements be strengthened by prohibiting any official in the upper ranks of ministry posts (director general or above) from taking any private sector positions in an industry covered by the ministry for two years after retirement.[56] Even this proposal, if it were enacted, would result in only a mild tightening of the rules. The basic system was not under challenge, and the two-year prohibition would simply put more pressure on government-related organizations to absorb these people until they could be recycled to the private sector.

Far more important, no change in the early retirement ages for the ministries was under discussion during the 1990s. If the retirement age does not change, then the government will maintain its organized placement of officials in the private sector. Given the social norms in Japan, it is virtually unthinkable that government agencies employing lifelong career officials would not play a role in finding them postretirement positions since this is a widely accepted practice in Japanese labor markets. The only realistic means of diminishing the extent and role of *amakudari*, therefore, lies in postponing the retirement age of government officials. That this possibility was not under discussion in the 1990s implies that no real change in the system was likely to occur.

At a broader level, it is also important to recognize that *amakudari* is but one of a number of mechanisms for reinforcing interpersonal bonds within the decisionmaking elite in Japan, generally in a manner that is opaque and informal. As one scholar of government-business relations notes: "The blurring together of professional and personal ties gives government-business relations their distinctively Japanese flavor. This phenomenon might be described as the 'personalization' of professional interactions, or the intrusion of affective bonds into the domain of public policy-making."[57]

One important mechanism in constructing this web of personal relationships is the use of *shingikai* (generally translated as "advisory council" or "deliberative council") and other consultative bodies used by government to discuss policy issues with the private sector. These bodies ostensibly provide a means for submitting policy proposals to a form of public scrutiny, thereby reducing arbitrary bureaucratic control and reinforcing democratic decision making. Vetting proposals with such groups is a substitute to the American system of public hearings and comment periods. But government agencies control appointments to these consultative bodies, and many of these organizations have been widely criticized as doing little more than providing legitimacy to ministry proposals. The *shingikai* have a statutory basis to advise ministries on specified matters, lending them at least a modicum of independence and authority.[58]

The formality of the *shingikai* has led to a proliferation of other advisory bodies appointed and paid by government agencies: *kondankai* (discussion group), *kenkyūkai* (research group), *benkyōkai* (study group), and *uchiawasekai* (coordination group). None of these formats has official standing, while (as with the *shingikai*) government agencies select participants, pay them, and staff the secretariats.[59] During the 1980s and 1990s, the

U.S. government pressed for foreign firms to be allowed to have their representatives chosen to sit on some of these formal and informal bodies. Although some progress has taken place in this direction, especially on some of the *shingikai*, the general practice of using consultative bodies still permits arbitrary government decisions to exclude foreign interests or to carefully choose only those foreign representatives deemed least likely to raise difficult questions.

School ties have also provided a form of interpersonal connections between government and industry. To a far greater extent than in the United States, going to the right school has been the ticket to a good job. Once hired, common school background—especially with people from the same graduating class—helps build ties between government and business or across firms. Of the various school ties, the most important are the ties among the graduates of the University of Tokyo. In the 1990s, University of Tokyo graduates continued to dominate the elite corps in the bureaucracy. Of those successfully passing the entrance exam in 1996 (including both top track administrative officials and technical officials), 27.6 percent were from the University of Tokyo, by far the largest single source (followed by the number-two-ranked national university, Kyoto, with 14 percent). Private universities in total supplied only 18 percent of the incoming class. If one narrows the pool by looking only at the administrative elite (leaving out the technical hires) actually hired by administrative, legal, and economic ministries, the share of the University of Tokyo rises to 50 percent. And at the prestigious Ministry of Finance, 74 percent of the entrants were from the University of Tokyo, as were 71 percent at MITI.[60] Coming after a number of years of publicized intent to reduce the heavy reliance on University of Tokyo graduates, these data show little real change. Thirty years earlier, University of Tokyo graduates occupied 53 to 73 percent of upper level career slots in major ministries, as well as the chairmanship of many major banks, steel firms, and other major firms.[61]

Only a small percentage of graduates of the University of Tokyo enter the bureaucracy. Those who do, therefore, have many classmates in the private sector, with whom they have a predisposition for close, cordial relations based on their elitist academic background. These relationships are sufficiently important that business people and government officials are well aware of the academic affiliation and year of graduation of those with whom they deal.

One of the means to bring together people periodically is the use of informal study groups—*benkyōkai* and *kenkyūkai*—ad hoc groups of friends and acquaintances to meet over drinks or dinner and discuss current issues. Informal, often short-lived, and with diverse shifting memberships, these groups bring together people from many sectors—government, academe, business, and media. They can serve as additional means of building personal bonds, diffusing information across groups, and helping in the process of getting important individuals and groups to coalesce upon a consensus view of problems or issues. Because these groups are informal, some of them include foreigners as members (and some have been organized by foreigners working in Japan as a means of reinforcing their own information flow with the Japanese). But primarily these function as a means of reinforcing bonds among Japanese individuals and groups.

Although the *amakudari* system constitutes the most important formalized flow of people between government and the private sector, a small amount of reverse flow occurs as well—private sector individuals entering government. These outsiders are usually appointed to limited-term, mid-career assignments on secondment from private sector firms. Keidanren career staff people, for example, have occasionally served within the Japanese Embassy in Washington, and private sector businessmen serve in some of the consulates around the United States. Between 1988 and 1996, some 177 private sector people are reported to have spent time assigned to the Ministries of Finance, Construction, and Foreign Affairs.[62] At the Ministry of Finance alone, some 83 people from the twenty-one leading banks in Japan served on a temporary basis from 1986 to 1995—often in sections of the ministry closely related to supervision of various aspects of banking.[63] This system is very different from the American flow of private sector individuals into and out of government. As is the case with *amakudari* officials, these individuals from corporations are placed in the government on the basis of corporation-government negotiations, not on the basis on individual initiative. And when they leave government, they return to the corporations from which they came.

Secondment also occurs across government ministries. To build personal ties across bureaucratic divisions, and to keep lesser agencies under scrutiny or control, the Japanese government has an extensive system of dispatch of career personnel to other ministries or agencies. In 1994, MITI had 229 (125 administrative, 104 technical) officials assigned temporarily to other agencies. The listing of those seconded officials organizes the names by year of entry to MITI, undergraduate school, and the agency to which they have been assigned—all useful pieces of information in a Japanese context. Furthermore, 103 of the 125 administrative personnel assigned to other agencies were from the University of Tokyo, 82 percent of the total.[64]

The Japan Fair Trade Commission (JFTC), the government's competition policy enforcement agency, exemplifies the potential implications for secondment. The JFTC is relatively weak within the pantheon of government agencies, and some members of its staff are on loan from other government agencies. This provides a means for those other agencies to undermine the JFTC's efforts to enforce the antitrust law if those efforts are deemed detrimental to the agencies' industrial policy goals. As of 1998, the director general (Sōchō) of the commission's secretariat was occupied by a seconded official from MOF and two directors, one of the economic research division in the Economic Affairs Bureau, and the other in the Trade Practices Department from MITI. Consider also the makeup of the commissioners themselves. The JFTC has five commissioners. Although they are not on detail from other ministries, all five are retired officials, of whom only one in 1998 was a career official of the JFTC. The others were from the Ministry of Justice, MITI, Ministry of Finance, and Foreign Ministry. Both the MITI and Finance commissioners had been involved with medium and small business policies in their last posts at their ministries, a policy area where concepts of cooperation and suppression of competition are dominant.[65] The ability of other agencies to eviscerate the JFTC role in this manner is a principal reason why pursuit of antitrust cases is not a promising route for foreign firms to solve their market access problems in Japan.

Scholars studying Japan have tended to look for positive aspects of all these practices. Within the context of Japanese society, and with the conscious decision to operate an economic system in which government wields great influence over the private sector through industrial policy, creation of multiple ties between government and the private sector was important. As put by one scholar, the existence of this network of ad hoc, informal ties "gives industrial policy and government-business interactions the resilience and adaptability for which Japan is renowned."[66] Scholars have generally been looking for organizational explanations for Japan's phenomenal economic growth and development in the past fifty years. They did not ask many questions about either the tendency for these ties to become less productive over time (Mancur Olson's thesis) or the implications for international trade and investment. A system characterized by dense, multifaceted organizational and personal relationships between domestic firms or industries and government is very difficult for foreign firms to penetrate. Foreign firms are outside the system and have great difficulty moving inside.

Even if they take on some of the trappings of "belonging," such as taking an *amakudari* official on to their payroll, foreign firms tend not to react to administrative guidance or other pressure moving through the pipelines of personal ties in the same manner as Japanese firms. Fear of larger numbers and greater importance of such foreign firms becomes a powerful reason for the government to resist changes that would make markets more open.

Financial Sector Exception?

The financial sector in the late 1990s has been the one partial exception to the general thesis of weak deregulation and structural change. Finance has been one of the most heavily regulated industries of the postwar era since influence over the allocation of credit was critical to the government's pursuit of industrial policy. Foreign entry into this sector was also limited until recently. *Amakudari* ties to the Ministry of Finance have been extensive. The 1990s brought distress to this sector in the form of a mountain of bad debt and scandals involving unethical and illegal behavior. Despite the legacy of regulation, tight government-financial sector ties, and limited entry for foreign institutions, the distress appeared to bring more rigorous deregulation action and new opportunities for participation by foreign institutions.

Slow, piecemeal deregulation had characterized financial sector policy from the mid-1970s to the mid-1990s. That twenty-year effort left Japan with a financial sector that was still heavily regulated and less open to foreign participation than was the case in the United States or major European nations. But in 1996, Prime Minister Hashimoto called for a "Big Bang" financial sector reform (borrowing his rhetoric from the "Big Bang" deregulations of British financial markets in the 1980s). The proposed elements of this deregulation are shown in table 5-4.

Changes in regulations concerning foreign exchange transactions, removal of the holding company ban, and partial decontrol of brokerage commissions all occurred in 1998, the other moves hopefully following in the next three years. On the surface, this list of proposed changes is ambitious and would seem to drive the financial sector in the direction of greater competition. The change should provide opportunities for foreign financial institutions, since they have operated in less controlled environments outside Japan and have expertise in asset-backed securities and other innovative products that will finally appear in Japan.

Whether this ambitious agenda will be implemented fully or whether it will transform the financial sector is not yet clear. Through 1998 the

Table 5-4. *Proposed "Big Bang" Financial Deregulation:*
Principal Components

Foreign exchange. From April 1998, eliminates the limitation on foreign exchange business to licensed commercial banks; eases rules on nonfinancial firms netting out exchange positions internally; permits firms to use foreign exchange in domestic transactions; eases limitation on individuals maintaining foreign currency accounts abroad.

Brokerage commissions. Deregulation of stock brokerage commissions, beginning with large-lot transactions (April 1998) and eventually extending to all transactions.

Off-exchange trading. Eases rules concerning trading shares off-exchange.

Over-the-counter trading. Eases rules concerning the over-the-counter market with the intent of increasing the liquidity of the market.

Securities transaction tax. To be eliminated.

Financial holding companies. To be permitted, with certain restrictions on size and market share of the total entity and the individual companies held.

Asset-backed securities. To be legalized and encouraged.

Derivatives. Rules to be eased including those pertaining to trading on the exchanges and over-the-counter.

Insurance. Price competition and product design competition to be allowed, along with a removal of the separation between life and nonlife segments of the market. Other changes include greater flexibility in marketing (permitting telemarketing, for example).

Segmentation. Through the financial holding company format and other means, restrictions among different forms of financial business will be lessened. This includes permission for commercial banks and nonbank financial firms to issue bonds.

Accounting standards. Will move accounting practices closer to international standards, including requirements for reporting on a consolidated basis and use of current market values.

Source: Based on descriptions in the Financial System Research Council, *Regarding the Reform of the Japanese Financial System: Contributing to the Vitalization of the National Economy,* June 13, 1997.

Ministry of Finance and the Liberal Democratic Party continued a pattern of nontransparent policies to prop up weak or insolvent banks that were antithetical to the concept of the deregulation agenda.[67] Some of the changes, such as deregulation of foreign exchange in 1998, were also largely symbolic (since foreign exchange transactions had been largely deregulated by the early 1980s so that the changes in 1998 were fairly minor). As the creator and enforcer of the existing regulatory framework, the Ministry of Finance had powerful reasons to resist this package of deregulation measures that would diminish its role in supervising or guiding the sector. The ministry's resistance was under political attack in 1998, especially by the opposition parties after their political voice increased when they won control of the upper house of the Diet in July 1998. But the eventual outcome—whether substantial deregulation would occur, or whether the Ministry of Finance would find ways to subvert, delay, or offset the intent of reform—remained unclear.

Even with obstruction by the Ministry of Finance, clearly a process of deregulation was in process. Changes such as the ending of fixed (and high) commissions for brokerage fees had the potential to eliminate pockets of high profit and thereby unleash competitive forces and industry restructuring that the Ministry of Finance could not undo. Foreign participants in Japan's financial sector appeared quite aggressive, poised to take advantage of their own competitive strengths as deregulation took place. The final outcome might not converge on an American model, but something that went beyond the record of deregulation in nonfinancial sectors seemed to be in motion.

The other aspect of change in the financial sector was the extreme nature of distress for some domestic financial institutions and the revelations of unethical and illegal behavior that occurred in the mid-to-late 1990s. Whereas the Ministry of Finance and domestic financial firms had resisted penetration efforts by foreign financial institutions from the early 1970s to the mid-1990s, some cracks appeared in this facade after the mid-1990s. In some cases, foreign institutions were the only savior for failing domestic institutions. After Yamaichi Securities declared bankruptcy, for example, Merrill Lynch acquired fifty Yamaichi retail offices and their 2,000 employees. In other cases, foreign institutions had gained reputation as safe or as possessing superior portfolio management skills. Citibank, for example, made inroads into retail banking on the basis of its enhanced reputation.

How far this newfound receptivity to foreign financial institutions would go was uncertain. Opportunities unthinkable as recently as 1995 or 1996 were opening up to foreign institutions in 1998. But even in 1998 the opportunities were not unlimited. As the record of contentious negotiations and further problems in the follow-up process indicate, the insurance industry was not part of this more optimistic picture for the financial sector (discussed in chapters 4 and 6). The major changes were in investment banking and secondarily in commercial banking. Even in these two parts of the financial sector, foreign institutions could bump against new, informal constraints should their market share in Japan expand beyond a modest level.

Conclusion

In the 1950s Japan had an economic system characterized by a strong government operating a vigorous and extensive industrial policy in which regulations and controls were endemic. Strong import and inward investment barriers made the system workable by excluding disruptive foreign influences. Dense networks of personal relationships among the major domestic players eased the problem of coordination and policy formation. Since the early 1970s, this system has undergone slow change in the direction of reducing the scope of explicit government power through a process of deregulation. With the economic malaise of the 1990s and the advent of a non-LDP government in 1993, the impetus for deregulation appeared to strengthen.

Hopes that substantial change would emerge from these new domestic forces proved disappointing, at least through the late 1990s. Broadly speaking, the reasons for the disappointing lack of change can be divided into two causes: vested interests and social preference. Most companies and individuals have a vested interest in the existing system, having worked so hard in the past either to construct the system or to adapt to it and benefit from it. Dislodging them after a half century is difficult. Reinforcing this problem is the strong web of ties among the elites at the core of the existing system. Through *amakudari*, school ties, study groups, and secondment (to other agencies or from the private sector into government), those who are at the core of managing and benefiting from the existing system are closely knit in mutually reinforcing relationships.

The other set of problems stems from social preference. Americans see a smaller role for government through extensive deregulation as the logical choice for Japan. Deregulation is widely perceived as a positive development within the American economy, and the arguments that might have once justified a strong government role in Japan (promotion of infant industries in a developing country context) are no longer valid. But the existing system in Japan is consistent with a variety of social behavior patterns, which few in society want to undermine. The notion of fairness within a group-oriented society militates against leaving firms and industries entirely at the mercy of a cold and uncaring market mechanism. Notions of deference in a hierarchical society imply that the general public has misgivings about truly challenging the role of career government officials. And the generally risk-averse nature of society implies that individuals prefer the problems of the system they know rather than to gamble on a set of unknown benefits and costs that would result from a deregulated economy. No voices were raised in protest as the government devised new industrial policy initiatives to promote industries in the mid-1990s; these were normal developments and the obvious contradiction between industrial policy and the rhetoric of deregulation bothered few in Japanese society.

The combination of vested interests and social concerns explains the very weak process of change, in which the bureaucracy was detailed to manage deregulation. By the end of the 1990s, this weak process will produce as much deregulation as society finds acceptable or comfortable, but this outcome will be far short of what American observers think is necessary or desirable.

Furthermore, little in the internally generated muted process of change was likely to benefit the interests of foreign firms trying to do business in Japan. Foreign governments could use the existing process to raise their own regulatory and other market access issues, capitalizing on the rhetoric of change and openness. But negotiations were generally no easier than they had been during the 1980s. In some cases, those negotiations did bear fruit and became significant parts of what the Japanese government subsequently claimed to be the result of its efforts at deregulation. Several years of tense negotiations in the insurance sector led to significant measures to deregulate prices and design of new products, which were then folded into the "big bang" financial reforms touted by the government. And many years of negotiations over wood products and other housing materials resulted in some progress on standards that ought to permit wider use of non-Japanese materials in the housing construction industry. But these successes do not appear to have been appreciably accelerated or magnified by the overall domestic rhetoric about deregulation.

The one major exception to these patterns has been the financial sector (other than insurance). Extreme stress within the domestic industry stemming from the mountain of bad debt after the collapse of real estate and stock market prices, plus the exposure of unethical and illegal behavior, created a less hostile environment for foreign firms. Helped also by the more extensive deregulation in this sector, foreign financial institutions were suddenly able or even encouraged to participate in some domestic financial markets to an extent unimaginable just a year or two earlier. But even in this major exception, how long the receptivity will last or how far it will proceed were uncertain in 1998.

Given the weakness of the domestic process of change outside the financial sector, American and other foreign government efforts to generate greater market access in Japan remain necessary in the late 1990s. Even where some domestically generated deregulation was occurring, the impact on foreign firms was likely to be limited. The purpose of domestic change was to promote the efficiency of the domestic economy; the rallying force was often the concern that Japanese-owned firms had fallen behind foreign competitors in cost structure or other dimensions of competitiveness. Diminishing the attention on trade relations with Japan out of an optimistic view that market-opening change would occur on its own, driven by domestic political or policy dynamics in Japan, is simply not a realistic option. Most real improvement in market access will continue to come from a process of negotiation.

CHAPTER SIX

Dealing with
Japan

Amerian trade negotiators have been chipping away at Japanese trade and investment barriers for the past thirty-five years. At times, as in 1993–95, the bargaining process has been very public and tense. Gradually, official barriers to both trade and investment have fallen, and negotiators have worked out many agreements on other policies, including procedures on government procurement, standards, testing, customs, and others. But success is incomplete. Japan in the late 1990s still seems to be a less hospitable environment for foreign corporations than other industrial or even some developing countries. Japan has been moving in a more open direction more slowly than other nations.

This situation leads to several important questions. Should the United States care? Do these remaining differences in market access matter sufficiently to pursue policies aimed at their reduction? Second, what policies should be pursued—are there viable alternatives to the trade policies of the recent past that would be more successful? The answer to the first question is that barriers do matter sufficiently to warrant attention—though not the kind of high-profile attention of the 1993–95 period. The second question has a somewhat more discouraging answer. Some modest modification of the trade policy approach to Japan should make a difference, but no magic solution exists. A realistic future is one of continued problems and tensions, largely for the reasons presented in chapter 5. The most practical approach is an eclectic one. The World Trade Organization (WTO) provides a strengthened multilateral framework, but it is not the appropriate venue for all problems. Multilateral and bilateral pressure should be focused primarily on individual problems when clear American corporate interests are at issue. Additional government personnel resources are needed to ensure the capability of dogged attention to detail in both negotiations and postagreement monitoring.

Significance

Problems of access to Japanese markets matter for several important reasons related to both economics and politics. The first and most obvious explanation is size; the Japanese economy is huge and, therefore, is important to American firms involved in global competition. At nominal exchange rates, Japanese GDP was $5.2 trillion dollars in 1995, second only to that of the United States ($7.2 trillion). Although nominal exchange rates overstate the size of the Japanese economy owing to high domestic prices, even a purchasing power parity exchange rate leaves Japan as the second largest economy in the world, coming to 40 percent the size of the United States and still 64 percent larger than the next largest economy in the world (Germany).[1]

Actual and potential business opportunities relate to market size. As the largest national market abroad facing American corporations, access matters enormously. As a matter of negotiating priority, size also matters. If a negotiation to deal with a trade barrier takes a fixed amount of effort, pursuing that negotiation with a large trading partner provides a larger payoff in terms of the value of improved business opportunities than pursuing it with a small nation.

In general this simple fact reflects U.S. government priorities. Casual observation suggests that the Office of the U.S. Trade Representative (USTR) devotes much attention to negotiations and discussions with the Japanese government, and the chapter on Japan in its annual report to Congress always has more pages than that of any other single nation.[2] But sometimes this focus is redirected. In the 1994–96 period, the Department of Commerce created a new trade promotion initiative focused on what were labeled "big emerging markets," a set of large, rapidly industrializing nations. As a matter of priority among developing economies, this was a sensible strategy. But the shift in emphasis also came at the expense of resources devoted within the Commerce Department to trade promotion and negotiation with Japan.[3] This relative shift of human and fiscal resources was not appropriate given the huge size of the Japanese economy relative to any set of developing countries.

Second, Japan matters because it a very affluent nation. Despite what one might expect on the basis of a simple comparative trade theory, much of global trade is among affluent nations. China, for example, has a huge population but is not yet a large market for consumer durables such as automobiles. Overall, 55 percent of American exports go to the affluent developed countries of Europe, Canada, and Japan.[4] At purchasing power parity exchange rates in 1995, per capita GDP in Japan was 82 percent the level of that of the United States, putting Japan slightly ahead of Germany (78 percent) and France (75 percent).[5] The rankings are less important than the fact that Japan is one of a small number of very affluent nations in the world. As a result, the Japanese economy consumes more of the sophisticated, high value-added goods and services in which American firms are globally competitive. Therefore, access to Japanese markets and improvement in that access should be a high priority for American trade negotiators.

Third, access to Japanese markets matters because it sets a precedent for other markets. If developing countries perceive that the Japanese government can keep domestic markets less open than is the case in other industrial nations, they may be encouraged to follow the same path. One major element of the "Japanese model" of development was heavy trade and investment barriers. If a more open global market is a goal of the U.S. government, then letting the Japanese government maintain barriers is the wrong signal to send. Conversely, opening markets in Japan sends a signal to other governments and may encourage them to act to lessen barriers to their own markets before facing similarly determined pressure from the American government.

This point about Japan as an example also matters in a multilateral setting; few efforts to establish broad multilateral agreements can succeed unless the Japanese government is willing to join. If not, why should others? The generally recalcitrant behavior of the Japanese government in the Uruguay Round of GATT negotiations, or in the 1998 effort by the Asia Pacific Economic Cooperation (APEC) council to expedite concessions on certain products, was discouraging. Given the importance of the Japanese example, therefore, access issues in both a bilateral and multilateral setting deserve serious attention.

Fourth, access to Japan matters for domestic American political reasons. A simple version of economic theory implies that unilateral free trade is sufficient for a nation. That is, an American decision to open its own markets should not depend on reciprocal action by its trading partners. The economic gains to a nation in the simplest version of trade theory depend on the existence of differences in relative prices between a country and the outside world. Why those prices might be different (whether they represent differences in relative costs of production elsewhere in the world, or subsidies, collusion, industrial policy, and other government-induced distortions of markets) does not matter. Even Paul Krugman, who is often associated with the notion of strategic trade theories, agrees that the U.S. choice to be open should not be conditional on others.[6] But the politics of trade complicate the picture. As attractive as the simple theory of free trade may be to some people, it has always been a difficult concept to pursue politically.[7]

As markets become more open, domestic firms face increased competition from abroad. Some firms or industries will succeed in meeting the competition, some will fail. Why should they be willing to accept the risk of failure? One reason is because the foreign market is also becoming more open, creating new business opportunities. If those opportunities do not exist, then domestic firms and workers can more easily argue that the process of liberalization is unfair. If movement toward open markets is good for the U.S. economy, therefore, then pressing for more open markets abroad is critical for building the necessary domestic political support for the process. Within this process, Japan stands out because of its size and visibility. Since Japanese firms are the main global competitors to American firms in some industries, the sense of lack of access to Japanese markets undermines political support for American openness. Access need not be on the basis of a strict product-by-product reciprocity; the thrust of the past half century has been to pursue reciprocity in a broad sense. That is, if Japan has overwhelming reasons to keep its rice market closed, that is acceptable, but only if other markets are open. The problem with access to Japan is that the sense of obstructed access applies to such a wide variety of goods and services. The progress in changing this situation has proceeded too slowly, leading to the disparity in market openness between Japan and other nations detailed in chapters 2 and 3.

Fifth, negotiating better access to Japan matters because of strategic corporate considerations. As a large, affluent economy, Japan is the home base of many of the major global competitors to American firms. In autos, nonelectric machinery, electric machinery (including electronic components like semiconductors), and many other goods, Japanese firms are strong global competitors. As part of global corporate strategy, American firms need to be in the home markets of their key competitors. This presence prevents competitors from reaping excess profits at home (that can be used to subsidize penetration of other markets around the world) and keeps American firms in close touch with the technological or product advances of their competitors. Therefore, as a matter of corporate strategy, American firms should have a special interest in being in Japanese markets and in soliciting U.S. government negotiating support in that effort.

This point on corporate strategy relates directly to the general concept of industrial policy in Japan. As an industrializing nation, the government pursued an active industrial policy over the past century, attempting to guide or encourage the growth of particular industries. The debate over the effectiveness of Japanese industrial policy has been long and contentious, but what matters for this chapter is less the macroeconomic consequences (of whether industrial policy produced faster growth in Japan) than the microconsequences (of whether the Japanese government created advantage for particular domestic industries at the expense of foreign industries). The answer is a clear yes; in a variety of industries—steel, semiconductors, automobiles, color film, and others—the government has clearly fostered domestic firms through all the available policy tools.[8]

A critical element of industrial policy has been protectionism. The government shielded many industries from international competition, some that succeeded and some that did not. Protectionism, justified by explanations about fostering infant industries, is not unusual for a developing country. But protectionism in Japan lasted well beyond that stage. After the mid-1970s, the continuation of major access barriers falls into the category of strategic trade policy rather than just a latecomer development strategy.

Strategic trade theory postulates that a nation can create comparative advantage for its economy through protectionism, subsidies, tax benefits, and other industrial policy measures in industries characterized by economies of scale and positive external economies. In industries characterized by economies of scale, closure of the domestic market enables domestic firms to increase their sales and production, reducing their average cost of production. Economies of scale can occur either because the size of fixed investment in plant and equipment is very large and the marginal cost (the direct cost associated with producing an additional unit of output) low, so that every unit of additional output distributes the fixed costs across more units of production, or because marginal cost itself is declining as production increases. In some industries so-called learning by doing can cause direct production costs to decline as production levels rise. Or an industry may be characterized by changing technologies, such that the next generation of technology reduces production costs, but the technology is the result of experience gained through production. In any of these cases, artificially increasing domestic market share (by erecting trade and investment barriers) lowers the average cost of production and raises profit levels for domestic firms. Those higher domestic profits then enable firms to expand their market shares abroad—either because they can cross-subsidize their foreign sales or because denial of the domestic market has burdened their foreign competitors with smaller production scale and higher average production costs.[9]

Besides specific economies of scale affecting the targeted industry itself, some industries have important spillover effects or positive external economies of scale on the rest of the domestic economy. Knowledge or technology generated in one industry may have positive applications to others. For example, Ford's development of the manufacturing assembly line had enormous implications for the rest of manufacturing and arguably spread faster in the United States than in other nations because the innovation originated there.[10]

The theory of strategic trade has not gained broad support among economists as an accurate model of actual or preferred national behavior for several reasons. First, governments have difficulty in correctly picking winners and losers in choosing industries to subsidize or otherwise support. Second, if all governments choose to follow the same model, no individual nation can achieve an advantage because all would tend to protect and promote the same industries, canceling out the individual advantages a nation might gain. Third, since such policies amount to "beggar-thy-neighbor" policies, other nations are likely to retaliate.[11] Finally, the effects on national welfare—even assuming rationality in choice of industries and lack of retaliation from trading partners—are ambiguous according to economic theorists.[12]

Despite these doubts and objections, part of continued Japanese industrial policy since the 1970s resembles what one would expect from a government pursuing a strategic trade policy. The long effort to enhance competitiveness in semiconductors, continued effective closure of the domestic automobile and auto parts markets, the use of procurement by the government telephone company to build competitiveness of domestic telecommunications equipment manufacturers, and other aspects of policy in the past quarter century fit many of the characteristics of strategic trade policy. In these industries, partial closure of the domestic market arguably enabled higher profits, higher research and development spending, and subsidization of penetration of foreign markets.[13]

How could the Japanese government succeed at this policy given the generally negative interpretation by economists? Consider the proposition that if one nation practices strategic trade, others will either imitate it or retaliate, thereby negating the potential gains. This line of reasoning assumes that other nations understand what the strategic trade country is doing and have both the will and means to retaliate or imitate. Within the GATT-WTO system, however, opportunities for a nation to cheat abound, especially through the use of nontariff barriers as tariff cuts take place. The logical deterrent to cheating is "tit-for-tat" responses. That is, a nation cooperates with its trading partners in lowering trade barriers until cheating is perceived and then retaliates.[14] But there are several problems with this assumption. If country A has a hard-nosed strategic trade policy while country B has had a benign vision of the rest of the world, A may be able to pursue its policies without incurring serious retaliation. Or country A pursues its policies but under such a cloud of obscurity that B faces difficulty in proving that cheating is occurring at a quasi-legal forum like the WTO. Firms in B may even face problems convincing their own government of problems in A's market if government officials adopt an ideological view (for example, adopting the simple theoretical view that no nation actually practices strategic trade because all countries understand its ultimate futility) or are relatively unversed in the intricacies of A's policies. As should be obvious at this point, these possibilities describe the U.S.-Japan relationship quite well over the past two decades.

For those industries with economies of scale or rapid technological change, therefore, protectionist policies in Japan matter in global competition. In general, these do not appear to be life-and-death issues for American businesses. Despite all the fears expressed in the 1980s about the Japanese juggernaut, American firms in high-technology industries and others characterized by economies of scale or rapid technological change seem to have done well in coping with pressures from their Japanese competitors.[15] But even if Japanese government efforts to promote leading industries do not result in the failure of their American competitors, the outcome is certainly a shift in corporate market shares and profits that give an advantage to Japanese firms. Therefore, trade negotiations with Japan matter because attempts to artificially give an advantage to Japanese firms and industries in competition with other industrial nations distorts market outcomes and holds the potential for unfair harm to American industries.

However, Japanese government protectionist policies are far broader than picking and protecting "winners." Indeed, much of protectionism in the past quarter century can be described on average as shifting toward protecting "losers."[16] Construction, cement, manufactured wood products, petrochemicals, pharmaceuticals, financial services, retailing, and other industries all stand out as relatively inefficient in international comparison. But protectionism has been high in many of these industries, with domestic prices well above international levels and domestic profits that have often enabled exports at lower international prices.[17] In these cases protectionism has not resulted in globally competitive industries.

Accept for a moment the notion of Japanese international comparative advantage in a core of manufacturing industries—autos, nonelectric machinery, and electric machinery—although chapter 2 rejected this hypothesis in its strict form. If Japanese comparative advantage lay with these industries, then comparative disadvantage lies in other industries, such as the ones listed in the previous paragraph. A comparative advantage model for international trade, therefore, would yield relative success in exporting (and resisting imports) in those industries characterized by comparative advantage, and less success in exporting and higher inroads by foreign products at home in those industries characterized by comparative disadvantage. For some agricultural products, such as wheat and soybeans, this has been the case; barriers are gone and reliance on imports is high. But many industries in which Japanese firms have a comparative disadvantage are characterized by strong protectionist barriers and low imports. Japanese government policies, therefore, obstruct the functioning of comparative advantage. In reality, an open market in all goods and services would demonstrate that Japanese manufacturing firms in the leading manufacturing industries have less comparative advantage than commonly supposed, and other sectors (forced to compete against foreign firms) would turn out to have less of a comparative disadvantage. The main point, though, is that trade negotiations matter because access policies in Japan obstruct economic efficiency by hindering the operation of comparative advantage.

Protection of inefficient firms can have a further damaging impact on foreign economies. By pursuing protectionist policies at home, inefficient firms can still generate excess profits, and in a world of mobile capital, are in a position to enter foreign markets or even purchase foreign competitors. In such a manner, an inefficient producer can conceivably gain control over more efficient foreign operations, and then use the ensuing market power to raise prices. At the very least, the inroads of inefficient firms protected at home can be very galling for American companies. Japanese construction firms, for example, gained some business in the United States during the 1980s, and in the 1990s the government-affiliated telephone company became increasingly interested in making acquisitions in the United States. Although these advances are not life threatening to most American industries, the sense of unfairness that comes across in conversations with American business people is palpable.

Besides damaging the interests of foreign firms, protection of inefficient industries harms the Japanese economy. Thus, besides all the reasons why pursuit of more open markets should matter for American policy, it matters for the Japanese economy too. With a more efficient allocation of productive resources, and competitive pressures to force inefficient sectors to improve their performance, the Japanese economy would be more productive and the population more affluent. This basic argument against protectionism has rarely succeeded on its own to bring about change in Japan, but at least it provides American negotiators with a useful public argument.

Furthermore, a more efficient, productive Japanese economy matters to American firms; they are better off with a strong, productive, growing Japanese economy. Some American firms may be satisfied with a partially closed market into which they can sell a limited amount at high prices. But overall American and other foreign firms benefit from a more open market that drives their Japanese competitors to become more efficient themselves because a more productive and affluent market will buy more goods and services from foreign firms.

As a final consideration, the United States has noneconomic reasons for pursuing market openness in Japan. Greater penetration of Japan by foreign firms through both exports and investment is a means for embedding Japan more deeply in the fabric of international ties. As the world heads into the twenty-first century, it is not in the interest of the United States to have a Japan that perceives itself as separate from the currents of the rest of the world—at least not to the extent many Japanese have believed during the past century. Embeddedness has many dimensions, but trade and investment are certainly central. Japanese exports and investment abroad provide one aspect of embeddedness, but it is equally important that imports and inward investment in Japan provide the other half of the connection. Japan's relationship with the world has been distressingly one-directional, with Japan penetrating the outside world through exports, direct investment, loans and portfolio investment, and travel, while the reciprocal flows have been severely limited.[18]

The bilateral security treaty with the United States is an important part of the ways in which Japan is embedded in a global framework. The U.S. government continues to value that security relationship (although it has been subject to some doubts or calls for modification from the non-government policy community in recent years). However, the security relationship can be undermined by the negative attitudes stemming from frustration on trade issues. Politicians and voters could wonder why the United States maintains a close security relationship with a country that has such a record of grudging access to its markets. In the late 1990s, these attitudes did not appear to seriously threaten the existence of the security relationship, but they could in the future (especially if the immediate regional security threat on the Korean peninsula were to wane). Therefore, a continuing policy to open markets in Japan removes or reduces the possibility of economic frustrations adversely affecting the security relationship. This conclusion is exactly opposite of that often advanced by those who focus on security affairs. The common concern in the past was that excess tension in negotiating increased market access could poison the atmosphere for the security relationship, by creating negative publicity among American voters and politicians or by diminishing Japanese desire to be allied with the United States. But this formulation of the interrelationship between economics and politics confuses short-term tension over negotiations with the long-term corrosive effect of protectionist behavior.

Finally, all of the problems of access to Japanese markets are in direct contradiction to the international commitments the Japanese government has made through the GATT-WTO in the past thirty-five years and inconsistent with the rhetoric of the government and private sector, which have touted the principles of free trade. Notions of facade, in which reality may deviate from appearances, are a part of Japanese society. However, the Japanese government's relations with the rest of the world would be smoother if other countries could believe what they hear and the commitments they see on paper. Distinguishing reality from rhetoric is important in any society, but the distinction appears to be particularly wide in Japan in general, and especially so on trade policy. Simply recognizing that distinction is important for American business and government, but so, too, is pressing the Japanese government to truly stand behind its international commitments on trade and carry through on its rhetoric. The Japanese government also gains from this process; its international reputation has been tarnished in the past two decades by the perception that it does not take seriously its international commitments to opening domestic markets. The U.S. government is thoroughly justified, therefore, to press hard on the Japanese government to abide by the letter and spirit of its written and oral commitments.

As an enormous, affluent market, Japan is an obvious focus for American firms and government negotiators, and rightfully so. The strategic need for American firms to be in the home market of their competitors reinforces that importance. Japanese firms may derive strategic advantage in some industries where active industrial policies continue. Adding protection of inefficient industries in which Japanese firms have not gained international competitiveness also denies comparative-advantage benefits to American firms that should accrue with open markets. Both countries would be better off with a more open Japanese market. Embedding Japan more firmly in an international fabric has broader economic and political benefits. And holding the Japanese government to its commitments is both justifiable and important. The question is how to persuade a nation that has been resistant to opening its markets to change its behavior.

Structural versus Sectoral Approaches

Some debate has occurred over the relative merits of structural versus sectoral approaches to trade negotiations. A sectoral approach is one in which governments negotiate specific problems related to an industry or firm. In a structural approach, governments negotiate a generic problem only loosely connected to specific problems faced by a particular industry or firm trying to sell a certain good or service. Intellectual property rights (affecting any company with intellectual property), retail distribution (affecting all firms manufacturing consumer products), or customs procedures (affecting all firms exporting to Japan) are examples of a structural approach. Structural issues were the focus of the Structural Impediments Initiative (SII) talks pursued by the Bush administration in 1989–90 (as discussed in chapter 4). Rather than dealing with the specific problem of Toys R Us, for example, the SII process pressed Japan on general changes in the Large-Scale Retail Store Law to make it easier for any firm (foreign or domestic) to obtain permission to open new stores.

This concept of structural negotiations has received a favorable response from some academics. Leonard Schoppa and Norio Naka, for example, have each argued that the Japanese public and business communities would be more willing to support such generic changes, thereby making foreign pressure more likely to succeed.[19] The rationale for such success rests on the view that structural or generic changes take the specificity out of negotiations and permit a more theoretical argument about improving economic efficiency. That is, a discussion of removing the restrictions on large-scale retail stores can be cast in terms of the benefit to Japan from greater efficiency in distribution rather than being put into antagonistic terms of benefit to a particular American firm or industry in competition with particular Japanese firms.

But this conclusion is neither obvious nor necessarily correct. The American Chamber of Commerce in Japan, in an extensive review of bilateral negotiations from the beginning of the 1980s through the mid-1990s, spoke rather favorably of the SII in some respects. However, the review noted that the SII was not very effective in improving access to Japanese markets, and that cases of success occurred only when generic issues became very specific. The study concluded: "One of the lessons learned from the SII, therefore, is the need for the U.S. Government to be specific in making its requests to the government of Japan. Generalities about 'liberalization' or 'deregulation' are likely to be ignored by the Japanese government or, if heeded, largely benefit Japanese firms unless the U.S. emphasizes specific and concrete American firms that are trying to gain market access."[20]

Even the retail deregulation issue, aimed at loosening or ending the restrictions on large-scale stores, made little progress until the issue was connected to the problems encountered by Toys R Us when it attempted to enter the Japanese market in the late 1980s (at which point it ran into the delays in the small retailer-dominated approval process that promised to indefinitely delay or even block the ability of Toys R Us to enter Japan).

Some issues, however, are obvious structural ones. Although the specificity of Toys R Us provided the focus and leverage to press Japan successfully on retail distribution regulation (though with only modest change in the regulations), the issue was still a structural one. The required solution for Toys R Us was not an exemption or special treatment for the company under the existing rules but a change in the generic rules governing establishment of large retail outlets. More broadly, the contrast between sectoral approaches and structural ones may be exaggerated—the boundary between the two is unclear. Is the copyright protection issue within the structural discussion of intellectual property rights really a structural issue or a sectoral issue applying to the recording industry (since copyright protection of audio recordings has been the main problem)?

Furthermore, the distinction between a supposedly structural approach pursued by one administration and a sectoral approach adopted by different administrations is overdone, as argued in chapter 4. The Clinton administration, for example, did not completely abandon the structural approach of the SII talks. The Clinton administration pursued negotiations on intellectual property rights and inward direct investment in Japan as structural issues during its first term, both of which resulted in structural agreements.[21] Nor did the Bush administration focus entirely on structural issues.

During the second term of the Clinton administration, the overarching theme of trade negotiations moved more in the direction of emphasizing structural talks under the rubric of the Enhanced Initiative on Deregulation. Such an approach has some rhetorical advantages because it is easier to cast the issues in terms of economic benefit for the Japanese economy. Assistant Secretary of State for Economic and Business Affairs Alan Larson, for example, gave a detailed and forceful speech in the spring of 1997 in Washington on the value of deregulation for increasing productivity and efficiency in the Japanese economy.[22]

However, as an organizing principle for U.S. policy toward Japan, deregulation has two problems. First, the concept is too broad. As a bilateral topic, the government of Japan will try to keep much of the discussion focused on generalities and principles, which will have little impact on the specific problems facing U.S. firms. Second, issues in deregulation are difficult to prioritize. Japan was considering changes in many different areas after 1993 under the deregulation movement discussed in chapter 5, and the established process called for foreign governments and business groups to submit long lists of their desired changes. In response the U.S. government submitted lengthy requests of specific deregulation items under the bilateral dialogue that was part of the Framework Agreement. An initial list was delivered in November 1994, followed by additional documents in April 1995, November 1995, and November 1996. These documents were lengthy compilations of desired changes organized by industry or topic. The list of November 1996 came to forty-seven single-spaced pages even though each individual request was limited to a single summary sentence. Even with this long list, the U.S. government noted, "This submission is not intended to be an exhaustive list of deregulation, administrative reform and competition policy issues in Japan of concern and/or interest to the USG."[23] This process, which did not establish priorities, enabled the Japanese government to act only on minor requests and then declare success on the grounds of the number of specific deregulation actions taken.

U.S. government officials involved in the process had not been encouraged by four years of discussion and submission of such lists. As put by one official in charge of the bilateral discussion of deregulation in the spring of 1997: "We have noted that each year there seems to be less and less willingness on the part of our Japanese counterparts to address in a serious way the concerns and recommendations we have raised."[24] Many of the items included by the Japanese government in its long lists, it turned out, were those on which action had already been decided before the official deregulation process began or when "action" was defined as nothing more than a promise to study the possibility of change.[25]

The Clinton administration attempted to surmount these problems in its second term through the Enhanced Initiative on Deregulation, discussed in chapter 4. In the new format, the U.S. government largely limited its interest to four sectoral areas (telecommunications, housing, medical devices and pharmaceuticals, and financial services) and process issues in deregulation and competition policy.[26] Even these areas, however, were broad, and they included so many narrow areas of regulatory concern that the probability of dramatic success was relatively limited. Housing materials, for example, are affected by regulations related to lumber, processed wood materials, other construction materials (insulation, wallboard and other nonwood materials), plumbing fixtures, electrical fixtures, tools, roofing materials, and glass.

Furthermore, while the U.S. government wanted to regard the enhanced bilateral arrangement for deregulation as "a series of negotiations," the Japanese government adamantly insisted that the process was "enhanced dialogue" that was "about providing friendly advice."[27] Rarely has "friendly advice" had much impact in bringing about significant regulatory change in Japan. The Japanese government wanted a vaguely defined process intended to keep U.S. officials busily engaged without producing significant results.

Within the context of this new initiative, the USTR submitted another set of requests to the Japanese government in November 1997 on deregulation, restricted to financial services, housing, medical devices and pharmaceuticals, and telecommunications, with emphasis on priority regulatory changes and desired dates for implementation. Even this restricted list identified many regulatory problems connected with restricting foreign access and could not entirely limit the petition to the five identified sectors.[28]

Negotiations on housing materials produced some progress in the agreement announced in June 1998 (considered in chapter 4). But this movement meant reducing the generic housing materials deregulation issue to the specificity of standards affecting certain products (thus reducing a supposedly structural issue to a collection of sectoral issues). These requested changes related to problems faced by individual American firms with an interest in selling particular goods to Japan. What began as a supposedly structural issue of deregulation progressed by being reduced to detailed sectoral problems.

On more diffuse deregulation issues progress was minimal. One of the other topics in the Enhanced Initiative was improving the climate for foreign investment in Japan. This generic issue was on the bilateral agenda throughout the 1990s, with very little outcome. For example, an agreement on investment was signed in July 1995, but two years later, one of the American officials who participated labeled Japan's efforts to promote inward investment "poor and ineffective."[29] The factors discussed in chapter 3 that discourage foreign direct investment in Japan are either too deeply embedded in the social and political fabric of Japan, too complex, or too disconnected from tangible problems of American firms for easy resolution. Rather than tackling fundamental issues, such as the difficulty of corporate acquisitions, the Japanese government approached the issue through offers of largely ineffective or irrelevant investment promotional programs.

Even when negotiations yield progress, there is no guarantee that structural problems facing American firms will be resolved. For example, Japan has been a signatory to all the GATT agreements on government procurement. Nevertheless, Japan managed to manipulate the system so that bilateral negotiations on government procurement of telecommunications equipment and medical equipment were needed on several occasions in the 1980s and 1990s to get at features of the procurement process peculiar to these products. Even in the late 1990s problems remain. The principle of fairness embodied in the GATT government procurement code was sufficiently imprecise that the Japanese government could pursue policies that undermined the spirit of the agreement while claiming that its behavior met its international obligations.

What does all this imply about the relative merits of structural and sectoral approaches? The U.S. government should and will engage in both sector-specific and structural negotiations. Some issues are truly structural, affecting a broad range of foreign goods or services, while others are product or industry specific. The major mistake to avoid is to believe that a structural approach is superior to a sectoral one. The negotiating record of the 1990s on structural issues is modest and mixed. Those issues that could be reduced to rather specific sectoral components were the ones on which the most progress occurred. Casting sectoral issues in a broader structural framework, as in the Enhanced Initiative, may provide some useful rhetorical cover. But structural issues unconnected to specific problems should be avoided or approached with great caution.

Making *Gaiatsu* Work?

One of the notions advanced recently by academics has been that American trade policy toward Japan has been flawed because it misunderstood the notion of *gaiatsu* (foreign pressure) in the context of Japanese decision-making. American pressure on Japan is much more likely to succeed when it is applied on issues that already have a recognizable domestic constituency in Japan.[30] Relaxing the rules of the Large-Scale Retail Store Law to the benefit of Toys R Us and other American retailers worked because both the public and some domestic retailers (large chain stores) also favored these changes. Therefore, American officials should carefully pick and choose among issues to focus only on those with existing support in Japan that can be mobilized to produce change. The general point that pressure works when a domestic constituency favors the change is painfully obvious. If all relevant actors in Japan on a particular trade issue were adamantly and unalterably opposed to change under any conceivable conditions, then negotiations would fail. But as an operational guideline to trade relations with the Japanese government, this view is both naive and unworkable for several reasons.

First, discovering what the real positions are on the opposite side can be very difficult. Those who appear to favor change and those who appear adamantly opposed may not be revealing their real positions, or those positions may change unexpectedly as the negotiations proceed, with presumed supporters evaporating or supposed opponents canceling their objections. Expressions of support for change at a general level often mask real opposition to the specific changes American negotiators seek. Analyses of the SII talks or other previous negotiating episodes have the advantage of investigating the record of a completed set of negotiations where the outcomes are known and domestic support easier to ascertain. But developing an accurate analysis of support and opposition prior to a negotiation is practically impossible.

Second, such an approach could be easily highjacked by the Japanese government. Every Japanese government official involved in bilateral relations would redouble efforts to steer American pressure away from important trade issues to trivial areas in which these officials will allege that great support for change exists in Japan. Since the analysis of what issues have the most domestic support and, therefore, chance of success would necessarily depend heavily on impressions received from personal contacts at the embassy level in Tokyo and in Washington, the opportunities for the Japanese government to skew the process are excellent. Many American officials are sophisticated enough to recognize such efforts to skew or deflect perceptions of what issues are feasible. But others are not, especially in Washington where many agencies and individuals with little previous experience with Japan become engaged in bilateral issues. At the very least the process of separating fact from fancy becomes more difficult in such an environment. Obviously an effort to search for potential sources of support for American negotiating positions among various policy-relevant groups in Japan should be pursued as part of any trade negotiating strategy. What is extremely doubtful is whether any declared intent to base the choice of issues on an initial analysis of which issues have domestic support in Japan would yield a workable outcome.

Finally, the entire issue is somewhat sophomoric. Of course negotiations are more likely to succeed if significant players on the other side already agree to the proposed changes. And, at the extreme, pressure for changes that are a complete anathema to all players on the other side will not result in a successful negotiation. Trade negotiations occur between sovereign nations, the governments of which presumably do not make decisions that are fiercely opposed by politically important domestic groups. But the essence of negotiation is to press the other side toward changes that it does not want initially. Tactics along the way can include mobilization or encouragement of those private sector or government groups on the other side most likely to bend or which already hold favorable positions. No one can know with any certainty in advance how the complex political relationships on the other side will work out. Abandoning potential issues on the presumption that progress is unlikely is silly except in extreme cases.

The most that one can take from this notion of tailoring the negotiating agenda to the preferences of the Japanese side is to form a somewhat more realistic view of which negotiations will be easy, difficult, or just not worth trying. As was the case in discussions about deregulation, it is not difficult to conclude that negotiations over housing materials standards and regulations were more likely to yield progress than discussion of inward direct investment in the late 1980s and 1990s. Certainly American negotiators should enter into negotiations with realistic views as to how far and how easily the Japanese side will bend during the negotiations. Even this calculation can be difficult, however, replete with false information conveyed informally to American officials as to the "bottom line" on the Japanese side. The reality is that trade negotiations are a complex game, which defies simplifications such as tailoring the choice of issues to those for which *gaiatsu* is perceived to be the most successful.

Gaiatsu also raises the politically divisive and controversial issue of how to apply pressure. Cultivating domestic groups in favor of change is certainly one method of trying to put pressure on the government, and obviously this should be done when feasible. U.S. government officials tell the Japanese public in speeches and the media that negotiations and proposed changes provide benefits. Embassy officials and officials in Washington should do more of this outreach, and they should more actively cultivate groups that seem favorably disposed to proposed changes. But the notion that friendly speeches about benefits to the public will change Japanese government negotiating positions is naive. This idea relates to the notion that the SII talks were successful because the public supported the U.S. government position of positive benefit to the Japanese economy stemming from the proposed changes. The broad public has little if any input on policy formation. Organized interest groups—farmers and industries—do have input, and their positions are usually narrowly self-interested, as they are in any country. They may be amenable to friendly cooperation on some issues of direct interest or benefit to their group but not on matters of general principle.

But in other cases, there is no positive support or mutually reinforcing desire for change expressed by relevant parties in Japan. In this case some other form of pressure is necessary. A mild form of action consists of making public speeches or statements to the press about displeasure with the lack of progress in a negotiation. Particularly in the Japanese press, such expressions by American officials are often highlighted. But what happens when such statements have no impact? Ultimately pressure, if it is to be pursued, must involve a realistic possibility of imposing a real cost on the other side. In the U.S.-Japan context, this choice involves punitive action against Japanese economic interests in the United States. Even without visible signs of support for change before a negotiation, the threat of retaliation alters the perception of costs and benefits on the Japanese side. Even a group initially opposed to change may prefer the change over the costs that would be imposed in the absence of change.

Are such threats or actual punitive actions a viable negotiating tactic? No one likes such an approach, and most groups outside government that have made recommendations on appropriate trade tactics decry threats of sanctions. However, the harsh reality is that the Japanese government has often been strongly resistant to changes to make markets more open. In the absence of some expectation of a cost imposed against Japanese business interests in the United States, little progress takes place at the bargaining table on these difficult issues.

The theoretical concept of using retaliation is incorporated in the GATT/WTO framework. The mechanism for dispute resolution provides authorization for a nation to retaliate should its trading partner fail to make changes upon losing a disputed case. At one level, one can think of this retaliation as a simple tit-for-tat response since a country is authorized to impose costs on its trading partner equal in value to the losses imposed by the partner's failure to live up to its WTO obligations. But WTO retaliation is also a tactical tool in two ways.

First, the possibility of losing a case before the WTO and having retaliation imposed may cause negotiators to be more forthcoming at the negotiating table. In 1988, for example, the Japanese government finally agreed to replace its beef import quota with a tariff because the USTR was preparing a case to take to the GATT that Japan would almost certainly have lost.[31] Thus, the very possibility of multilaterally sanctioned retaliation may produce progress at the negotiating table. Indeed, the GATT-WTO appears to have intended that permission for retaliation have exactly this tactical use. One of the implementing documents of the WTO states that "neither compensation nor the suspension of concessions or other obligations is preferred to full implementation of a recommendation to bring a measure into conformity with the covered agreements."[32] If the United States were to win a case against Japan, for example, Japan could refuse to alter the offending behavior, leading to WTO-sanctioned American retaliation (compensation for the loss to American economic interests imposed by Japan), but the WTO is clear that this is not the satisfactory outcome, and this sense of moral obligation to actually accept WTO rulings could be useful in proceedings with Japan, since the government and public consider their nation's international reputation important.

Second, the actual loss and the imposition of penalties may provide sufficient real economic costs to produce a new negotiating position (if, for example, the industry whose interests are damaged mounts pressure on its government). Retaliation can be levied against products other than those being disputed. The firms affected by this retaliation, resenting the costs imposed on them, may be more willing to lobby their own government in favor of compliance or concessions since their own interests were not at stake in the original dispute.

Although the WTO has some advantages as a means of using retaliation as a tactical negotiating tool, unilateral action is also possible. Any American administration dealing with bilateral issues must be willing to use this form of tactical retaliation even though its use is controversial. The reasons for doing so are explored in greater detail in this chapter in discussing policy on non-WTO issues.

Overall, *gaiatsu* is an important part of the negotiating process. It cannot be fine-tuned to preselect issues for which a presumed domestic constituency for change exists in Japan. Nor can polite, friendly, and nuanced efforts to build upon the support of such groups be assumed to always work to advance American negotiating interests. The real essence of *gaiatsu* in many cases revolves around the credible threat of retaliation against Japanese economic interests in the United States to move a reluctant Japanese government to be more forthcoming in negotiations when the rather dysfunctional policy formation dynamics in Japan (even when some groups are in favor of change) fail to produce acceptable negotiating offers. The WTO offers a means to pursue this option in an internationally approved manner, but unilateral action is also a necessary option. A blunt tool that all would prefer to avoid, retaliation as a negotiating tactic remains an unfortunate but necessary option.

Bilateral Dispute Resolution Mechanisms

In the 1990s, the notion of a special bilateral dispute resolution mechanism or arbitration panel was proposed as a means of resolving bilateral trade disputes in a less contentious manner. In separate position papers Senator Bradley and a policy group sponsored by the Carnegie Endowment endorsed versions of such a plan in 1994 and in 1995 (with the Carnegie proposal being for a weaker nonbinding process).[33] The model for this approach was the dispute resolution procedure built into the U.S.-Canada Free Trade Agreement and then the North American Free Trade Agreement. Like taking disputes to the WTO, this approach results in decisions reached by a presumably nonpartisan panel, removing the stigma of unilateral American pressure on Japan.

This concept has some serious problems, despite its surface appeal. First, the entire notion of arbitration by a neutral party presumes the existence of an enforceable contract or agreement, the enforcement of which is in dispute. Many of the contentious issues in the bilateral relationship are about the negotiation of new agreements themselves, not their subsequent enforcement. Arbitrators cannot make policy decisions about issues such as the deregulation of Japan's insurance market, opening the rice market, or creating new rules for government procurement. To the extent that American pressure on Japan means negotiation of new agreements to make markets more open rather than disputes over interpretation of existing agreements, therefore, a bilateral dispute resolution mechanism would not be suitable.

Second, an arbitration process is based on agreement by the two parties in a dispute that a neutral third party is capable of rendering an impartial decision that both sides are willing to accept. In a bilateral process, the panelists must be drawn from individuals in the two countries. In Japan, the names proposed as panel members would come from the ranks of retired government officials holding *amakudari* jobs in the private sector and academics who are close to the government. Therefore, American firms would not believe that the panels could be fair or impartial and would not be very willing to use the process. With an odd number of panelists, panels would presumably alternate between those with a majority of American and a majority of Japanese panelists; in at least those with a majority of Japanese panelists, American firms would be skeptical of obtaining an impartial hearing. Foreign firms already have more than a decade of experience dealing with the Office of Trade and Investment Ombudsman System (OTO) in Japan, a government agency set up to provide a "neutral" party within the Japanese government to aid in the resolution of problems. American business believes strongly that the OTO has been virtually useless, and this experience shapes opinions on the inability of Japanese panelists to be neutral.

Third, a dispute mechanism might be able to make a determination of whether the letter of an agreement had been followed, but it is very doubtful if broader questions of abiding with the spirit of an agreement could be addressed. Japan is rarely in technical violation of the language of an agreement, while often wide of the mark of the intended outcome. Government agencies, for example, are bound by the WTO to abide by open rules for procurement on purchases above a certain threshold but can avoid them by dividing annual procurements into individual monthly or quarterly orders that remain below the threshold. This has been the nature of Japan's response in bilateral negotiations concerning government procurement issues discussed earlier; Japan has abided narrowly by its formal commitments to the GATT-WTO without making government procurement much more open in real terms.

Finally, the U.S.-Canada dispute settlement mechanism on which this notion was based exists in the context of a bilateral free trade area to settle issues that fall under the jurisdiction of that agreement. No such agreement exists with Japan (nor is one likely to come into existence). From time to time, proposals for a bilateral free trade area (FTA) with Japan have surfaced, which would provide a legitimate jurisdiction for a bilateral dispute resolution mechanism. However, this idea never garners much support. The cause for this lack of support is American skepticism of the ability of such an agreement to encompass the array of nontariff barriers that prevail in Japan. Or, even if an agreement could deal with many of the existing, known barriers, others would probably come into existence outside the scope of the agreement. Could, for example, such an agreement realistically include language bringing about an end to *amakudari* ties or ministerial informal encouragement of business collusion? The U.S. government is also committed to the Asia Pacific Economic Cooperation (APEC) forum as a means for accelerating market access liberalization in the region, and creating a special bilateral relationship with Japan would harm the broader regional process. Therefore, creation of a bilateral FTA with Japan remains very unlikely.

In the absence of an FTA, a bilateral dispute resolution mechanism has no clear jurisdiction. Virtually all U.S. bilateral agreements with Japan are on a most favored nation basis. What is the justification for a purely bilateral dispute resolution mechanism in this case? Those bilateral negotiations that result in most favored nation agreements in areas covered by the WTO provide the opportunity to take disputes over interpretation to the WTO. For those bilateral agreements outside WTO coverage, which are also on a most favored nation basis, why should only American firms have a bilateral dispute resolution panel for appeal while other foreign firms in the market do not? The obvious path to pursue is to expand the scope of the WTO so that more of the disputes over implementation or interpretation of agreements for all foreign firms can be handled. Until WTO coverage does encompass an issue, such disputes are better handled on a bilateral negotiating basis, backed by the possibility of unilateral retaliation, rather than through an artificial, restrictive, and unworkable bilateral dispute panel.

Using the World Trade Organization

The WTO is a potentially more effective arena for resolving problems of market access than a bilateral dispute panel. This approach is attractive for two reasons. First, the multilateral nature of the WTO protects the U.S. government from the negative imagery of unilateral pressure or retaliation. Second, the changes wrought by the Uruguay Round make this multilateral approach somewhat more viable than in the past—more industries are covered, and some of the language has been strengthened. The General Agreement on Tariffs and Trade (GATT) began by covering the issues of tariffs and quotas on merchandise trade. The Uruguay Round created the WTO, which extended the scope of the previous GATT to include language on how governments should behave in setting technical and phytosanitary standards. And some service sector industries are now covered (including telecommunications), but many remain outside the scope of the WTO.

Review of how the WTO can be used is important, but an awareness of its limitations is equally important. Even though coverage has been extended, it simply does not apply to all sectors. Harbor practices and civil aviation, for example, are two recent areas of dispute that were outside the boundaries of the WTO. Second, language defining violations of the WTO has been interpreted narrowly, limiting its usefulness in dealing with often informal or opaque problems in Japan. Third, the WTO dispute procedures, just like a bilateral dispute mechanism, apply only to disputes about existing agreements and not to the negotiation of new agreements. If the U.S. government wants improved rules of access in a market in Japan, it cannot go to Geneva to get resolution of the issue. To be sure, the GATT-WTO has provided a backdrop or organizational framework for large multilateral rounds of trade negotiations (even though these are not mandated as a procedure in either the GATT or WTO treaties). At the level of negotiating new agreements, the large multilateral negotiating rounds are infrequent and lengthy; absent such rounds, the WTO presumes that nations negotiate bilaterally and apply most favored nation treatment to their agreements. As a result, the U.S. government should use the WTO to deal with Japan when possible, but with the recognition that this approach is no panacea, presents some liabilities, and is not relevant to all access problems.

These cautions about the limitations of the WTO route matter because official Japanese government policy since 1995 has been to force the United States to Geneva rather than deal with issues bilaterally.[34] Although the

Japanese government denied that it intended to force all issues into a WTO arena, subsequent statements reaffirmed the basic approach, out of a belief that the Uruguay Round agreement placed a significant limit on the American ability to act unilaterally.[35] That is, the Japanese government views the WTO as a buffer or mechanism to slow down or obstruct pressures to make its markets more open. It is rather ironic that a multilateral institution viewed by many Americans as embodying the principle of free trade and fostering movement in that direction would be viewed by the Japanese government as having precisely the opposite effect.

To the extent that the WTO does provide a useful vehicle for pursuing at least some disputes with Japan, though, the most relevant sections are article 23 (nullification and impairment), article 10 (transparency), article 3 (national treatment), and language on technical and other standards.

Article 23 states: "If any contracting party should consider that any benefit accruing to it directly or indirectly under this Agreement is being nullified or impaired or that the attainment of any objective of the Agreement is being impeded as the result of (a) the failure of another contracting party to carry out its obligations under this Agreement, or (b) *the application by another contracting party of any measure, whether or not it conflicts with the provisions of this Agreement,* or (c) the existence of any other situation, the contracting party may, with a view to the satisfactory adjustment of the matter, make written representations or proposals to the other contracting party or parties which it considers to be concerned." The article specifies that if bilateral discussion fails to resolve the issue, a panel may be requested.[36]

Article 23 provides a potential means for countering Japanese government industrial policy measures designed to protect and promote domestic industries, whether or not the specific policy measures taken violate GATT-WTO rules. As long as Japan has agreed within a GATT-WTO negotiation to remove quotas, lower tariffs, or take other market opening measures, then its trading partners have a reasonable expectation that their access to the market will improve. This expectation was clarified in a seminal GATT panel decision back in the 1950s, which stated that "the main value of a tariff concession is that it provides an assurance of better market access through improved price competition. Contracting parties negotiate tariff concessions primarily to obtain that advantage. They must therefore be assumed to base their tariff negotiations on the expectation that the price effect of the tariff concessions will not be systematically offset."[37] A substantial portion of Japanese industrial policy from the late 1960s through the 1990s has been aimed at finding means to impede entry of the products of foreign-owned firms despite lowering or eliminating official access barriers to which government committed itself in successive GATT multilateral negotiating rounds. Such policies should be violations of article 23.

However, this approach to dealing with bilateral trade problems has some problems that became more evident when the United States lost its major case on access to the color film market in Japan. First, it is necessary to demonstrate that protectionist policies were deliberately intended to off-set concessions made in the GATT and that such policies were unknown or unanticipated (by the U.S. government) when the tariff concessions were negotiated. That is, if a nation convinces its trading partner to lower tariff barriers in an industry and is aware at that time of other potential market access obstacles that it fails to include in the negotiations, it cannot subsequently claim nullification and impairment on the basis of those obstacles. As clearly specified in another GATT panel case, it is necessary to prove that "the measure[s] could not have been reasonably anticipated by the party to whom the binding was made at the time of the . . . tariff concession."[38]

This requirement significantly narrows and complicates the use of article 23 in cases with Japan. If firms are confronted with one set of problems that effectively keep them out of the market, then they may be unaware of other policies or may miscalculate or misunderstand the impact of those other policies because they had no experience dealing with them. But under such circumstances, an article 23 case would fail since the Japanese government could argue that the American side should have been aware of the situation.

Second, the formal structure of Japanese policies generally conforms to international standards. Indeed, the government argued in the early 1980s that its industrial policies were consistent with OECD principles (so-called positive adjustment principles, or PAP).[39] Even if the application of industrial policy measures may have a negative effect on foreign products, the government may be able to make a case to the contrary before a WTO panel. Indeed, this was one avenue pursued in the color film case. In its initial response to the American submission in Geneva, the government of Japan argued that "all the alleged measures taken by the Japanese Government are fully consistent with the GATT rules."[40] The WTO panel essentially accepted this argument in its final decision.[41] Barriers that seem obvious to American firms and U.S. government officials close to the action in Japan may not seem so obvious in Geneva to a panel of trade law specialists unfamiliar with Japan. At the very least, use of article 23 (or other aspects of the GATT-WTO) implies a much greater burden of proof than in a bilateral setting.

Third, the GATT-WTO deals only with government actions and policies. Much of what happens in Japanese industrial policy is of sufficient informality that the government can deny direct involvement. Again as stated in the response to the American submission in the color film case, MITI argued that "many of the alleged 'measures' are in fact reports of the advisory councils, etc. and not government measures that the WTO panel can examine."[42] In the color film case, this defense by the Japanese was also accepted by the panel. WTO rules and their interpretation in the color film case represent a very Western view of the distinction between government and industry. In Japan that boundary has been blurred in many ways, including through the web of ties such as *amakudari,* advisory councils, and industry associations closely linked with government ministries discussed in chapter 5. Also at issue is the means by which government influence is communicated or exercised. If the connection is indirect or unwritten, so that one sees only the outcome in quasi-government reports and speeches, the WTO is currently unwilling to deduce the connection. Only those government actions involving clear written documents issued by direct government agencies meet the test. If the WTO sticks to its narrow view of what constitutes government-mandated action, then many of the industrial policy actions detrimental to foreign firms in Japan will escape unchallenged.

The second major possibility for dealing with Japan comes through Article 10, which deals with transparency of government process. Article 10 states as follows:

> Laws, regulations, judicial decisions and *administrative rulings of general application,* made effective by any contracting party, pertaining to the classification or valuation of products for customs purposes, or to rates of duty, taxes, or other charges, or *to requirements, restrictions or prohibitions on imports or exports* or on the transfer of payments therefore, or *affecting their sale, distribution, transportation, insurance, warehousing, inspection, exhibition, processing, mixing or other use, shall be published promptly* in such a manner as to enable governments and traders to become acquainted with them." And: 3.(a) *Each contracting party shall*

administer in a uniform, impartial and reasonable manner all its
laws, regulations, decisions and rulings of the kind described in para-
graph 1 of this Article.[43]

Through the mid-1990s, little real use had been made of article 10 with respect to Japan or other countries. In those cases where article 10 had been cited in complaints, the panel decisions were made on the basis of other GATT articles, with the panels noting that this outcome meant that no decision need be rendered on the article 10 aspects.[44] In the color film case the U.S. government argued that many of the relevant policies toward the industry were opaque: "The Government acted behind a shield of opacity, deputizing or instructing industry to carry out policies, with incentives and leverage from the government standing behind private industry behavior. In this context, foreign film and paper manufacturers encountered impenetrable market restrictions of imperceptible origin."[45] This allegation applied to both the 1970s restructuring of the wholesale industry (stripping Kodak of access to the dominant wholesalers), and an array of rules and arbitrary regulations on other marketing practices (such as advertising and promotional activities) administered by a government-authorized industry group that has continued to the present time. There may be opportunity for pursuing this approach with some problems since the informality of administrative decisions violates at least the spirit of article 10, but this effort in the color film case failed.

To grasp how informality or unwritten rules can govern actual policy implementation, consider the Large-Scale Retail Store Law. As initially enacted, the 1973 law specified a simple administrative process. Those desiring to open a large store were required to notify MITI, which then had four months to evaluate the proposal, including solicitation of opinion from local councils (representing local merchants, consumers, and others). But this rather straightforward process was changed in a series of steps by the early 1980s through ministry guidelines requiring that applicants engage in their own private consultation with local groups and reach agreement with those groups on adjustment of the proposal (floor space, operating hours, pricing of merchandise, and so on) before even notifying MITI of their intent to open a store.[46] Thus, what was supposed to be a clearly defined regulatory process became a private consultation process with no rules whatsoever, opening the way for abuses of blockage, delay, or bribery and other special deals cut privately between prospective stores and local merchants. Since MITI would not accept applications without assurance that local interests had been placated, the way was opened for indefinite denial of licenses to open stores, without any legal recourse. Only after the SII negotiations did these procedures change. The frequency with which procedures are left to the quiet discretion of bureaucrats or delegated to private groups raises a problem if the WTO is unable or unwilling to accept evidence on these matters.

The third route within the WTO is article 3, which addresses national treatment—the principle that foreign firms should be treated equally with domestic firms. The obvious example of discrimination of this sort is domestic excise taxes, which some countries have applied in an unequal manner to domestic and foreign products. But the scope of article 3 is quite broad. Paragraph 4 of the article states that "the products of the territory of any contracting party imported into the territory of any other contracting party shall be accorded treatment no less favorable than that accorded to like products of national origin in respect to all laws, regulations, and requirements affecting their internal sale, offering for sale, purchase, transportation, distribution or use."[47] In a 1958 decision, a GATT panel reaffirmed this broad reach in a case involving subsidized credits to Italian farmers to purchase domestic farm equipment: "The drafters of the Article intended to cover in paragraph 4 not only the laws and regulations which directly governed the conditions of sale or purchase but also *any laws or regulations which might adversely modify the conditions of competition between the domestic and imported products on the internal market.*"[48]

Given the existence of this requirement, no rational nation would deliberately promulgate regulations or rules explicitly stating that domestic firms be favored over foreign ones. But the Japanese government has been masterly in devising superficially neutral or innocent measures that have exactly that intent and impact. This is easy to do by using narrow technical specifications in defining the applicability of a regulation, specifications that favor domestic products. Annual registration fees on automobiles that vary by engine size is one example in Japan (taxing cars with engines of greater than 2,000cc displacement more heavily, thereby hitting most foreign cars and few Japanese cars). Another example is the restrictions on promotional activities by firms producing consumer goods, constrained by a variety of laws in Japan. The interpretation of promotion regulations, which has generally resulted in strong restrictions on promotional behavior, discriminates against foreign firms newly entering the market with consumer products. Without existing brand name recognition in Japanese consumer markets, these firms especially need active promotional activities to build recognition and initial sales. Therefore, rules that are putatively for the purpose of protecting consumers from unscrupulous behavior by firms actually stifle competition by disadvantaging new entrants to the market.

Article 3 accepts the notion of superficially neutral measures discriminating against foreign products, stating, "It also has to be recognized that there may be cases where application of formally identical legal provisions would in practice accord less favourable treatment to imported products."[49] This was written in the context of arguing that a formal distinction between domestic and foreign products favoring foreign products might be necessary to overcome such inherent unfairness. But the important point is that the GATT has explicitly acknowledged the possibility of situations in which supposedly equal treatment involves de facto discrimination against foreign products.

The combination of articles 23, 10, and 3 formed the core of the American case on color film. The results were disappointing. The WTO panel upheld the principles discussed here—all three articles can be construed to apply broadly to the kinds of problems alleged to exist in Japan. But the panel then decided that none of the evidence supplied by the United States was sufficient to prove the allegations. In so doing, the panel established a very high standard for proof, which may be difficult to meet in very many market access cases concerning Japan. Much of what occurs between government and business is verbal and opaque, leaving little or no paper trail of evidence. And the government-private boundary is quite indistinct. Therefore, the ability to use these aspects of the WTO in disputes with Japan remains in much doubt.

The final manner in which the WTO may be applicable to problems with Japan relates to rules on technical and other standards.[50] The language on phytosanitary standards states that members must ensure that "any sanitary or phytosanitary measure is applied only to the extent necessary to protect human, animal or plant life or health, is based on scientific principles and is not maintained without sufficient scientific evidence."[51] The rules laid out in this agreement are clear, holding members to tests of transparency, fair procedures for testing, and scientific evidence. As a result, this new measure opens an avenue for dealing with a variety of troubling issues with Japan that were generally handled on a bilateral basis in the past, including the decades-long effort to deal with regulations on apples clearly designed to protect inefficient domestic growers rather than safeguard the health of consumers.

Similarly, the WTO has a new agreement on technical standards, requiring members to use existing international standards when available, modify domestic standards when circumstances change, and restrict standards to the minimum necessary to achieve legitimate objectives (national security, prevention of deceptive practices, promotion of health and safety, preservation of plant and animal health, and protection of the environment).[52] Standards are also to be based on performance rather than design, and foreign products are to be accepted even when foreign standards differ but meet the objective of the domestic standard. These new, tighter rules on standards are important for U.S.-Japan relations since standards and testing procedures have been at the core of several bilateral disputes in the past two decades. The Japanese government, working closely with domestic industry, has often devised and used standards as a mechanism for impeding entry for foreign products—in both uncompetitive or declining industries (such as wood and paper products) and in emerging competitive industries (such as cellular phones and other telecommunications equipment where use of the radio transmission spectrum and the standardization of technologies to use the spectrum are critical issues).[53]

Neither of these provisions is a panacea, but the requirements for scientific justification, transparency, advance notification, extension to local governments, acceptance of products meeting functionally similar standards abroad, most favored nation treatment, and expeditious and fair treatment in testing open a broad array of means to challenge Japanese practices in a multilateral setting. Japan's phytosanitary and technical standards have often been opaque, different from international standards for no justifiable scientific reasons, applied with great partiality, and generally based on design rather than performance. The WTO provides a legal procedure in which the accused party has ample opportunity to defend its practices before a panel that will have little prior knowledge about the specific practices in Japan. And in that context, defendants can dispute issues such as what constitutes scientific proof or what is the minimum standard necessary for public health and safety. Many of Japan's practices on phytosanitary and technical standards of the past appear to be such blatant violations of the new rules that a clear opportunity exists, but much will depend on the strictness with which WTO panels choose to construe these provisions.

In 1997 the USTR noted that Japan's phytosanitary standards continued to be applied to very narrow varieties of plants (necessitating a complete approval process for each individual variety of apple, cherry, nectarine, and other fruits and vegetables). Fumigation policy was also characterized by a lack of transparency, and even with removal of some pests from the quarantine list, the U.S. government argued that other nonharmful pests that might have an effect on American horticultural exports to Japan remained on the list.[54] The U.S. government filed a WTO case on some of these issues (protesting the Japanese government requirement that testing be repeated for each single variety of a fruit or vegetable), and the panel decision issued in October 1998 favored the United States. This successful case suggests that the new standards code will be a useful route for pursuing some bilateral cases.

However, even in the short history of the WTO some evidence exists of problematic behavior by Japan's government. Japan blocked a European Union proposal to have the WTO committee on information technology products conduct a study intended to lead to streamlining the self-certification of information technology products. The inability of foreign manufacturers to self-certify their products for compliance with Japanese standards has long been a problem. The objections of Japan (plus Korea and Thailand) were based on procedural issues (claiming the EU proposal exceeded the mandate of the committee and infringed on areas properly belonging to other WTO committees), but the broader impression is of a continuation of the long pattern of obstructionism.[55] Thus, while the new standards codes provide an improved opportunity to pursue technical barriers to trade, the road will not be easy.

Using the WTO is also time consuming. The color film case was filed by Kodak with the USTR in May of 1995; the USTR decided to take the case to the WTO in June of 1996; the preliminary decision by the WTO panel was handed down in December of 1997 and the final decision in February of 1998, close to three years after the initial complaint to the USTR by Kodak. Deciding whether to go to the WTO, preparing long, detailed written arguments and assembling voluminous documentary evidence, selecting the panel, presentation and rebuttal of evidence, and the panel's actual consideration of the arguments cannot happen quickly. Because all of this process involves a third party unfamiliar with the details, nothing can be handled informally or quickly. What might involve a verbal exchange across the negotiating table in a bilateral negotiation becomes a formalized submission of hundreds or thousands of pages of documentation.

Even when decisions are made favoring the United States, opportunities to delay remain. Excise taxes on liquor have been sharply lower for "clear spirits" (mainly a domestic liquor called *shochu*) than for whiskey and brandy, as well as discriminating between high-class (largely imported) whiskey and other whiskey (largely domestic). Japan lost a GATT case on this issue in 1987, but its subsequent tax revision in 1989 only addressed the tax differences among varieties of whiskey.[56] This led to another case, filed under the new WTO by the EU and joined by the United States. In this case, the WTO ruled against Japan in February 1997. At that time, the WTO declared that Japan needed to implement the ruling within fifteen months (rather than by the year 2001 as proposed by Japan).[57] Thus, resolution of the liquor tax issue required more than a decade of on-again off-again activity.

Also keep in mind that many gray areas related to coverage remain. Consider the question of what entities are covered by WTO rules on government procurement. The Nippon Telegraph and Telephone Company (NTT) was a direct subsidiary organization of the Japanese government until 1987, when it was "privatized." However, although the legal designation of the organization changed, the government owned all the stock for several years. By the end of March 1997, the government had sold only 35 percent of the shares to the public.[58] And even when NTT is reorganized in 1999 into a holding company with three subsidiaries (two geographically divided domestic firms and one long-distance international service provider) government ownership of the holding company will remain at this level.[59] Nevertheless, the government insists that NTT is a private company and, therefore, not bound by Japan's government procurement obligations under the WTO. Faced with this opposition, the U.S. government negotiated two separate procurement agreements in 1994, one covering Japanese government procurement of telecommunications equipment and services, and one covering NTT. In 1997 the NTT agreement was revised (to include coverage of a few of NTT's subsidiaries) and extended, but only for the two years until the holding company was to be created.[60] The Japanese government insisted that NTT should be regarded as a private company when the 1999 reorganization occurs, for which no government-negotiated procurement agreement should apply. No analyst would agree that NTT, with approximately 65 percent government ownership, behaves or will behave like a private firm free of close government supervision, and it is extremely unfortunate to have the Japanese government using such ploys to delay and diminish foreign access to NTT's procurement process. The ability of government to limit the agreement to two years with the presumption of ending in 1999 was fully understood by the Japanese press, which emphasized this aspect as a protectionist victory (with one press report noting that "at most, the agreement will be in effect for two years and three months").[61]

Despite the problems, limitations, and caveats about working out disputes with Japan through the mechanism of the WTO, this new organization will clearly occupy a greater role in bilateral relations with Japan. Dealing with such issues imposes new demands and costs on the U.S. government. Arguing a case in Geneva before a panel unfamiliar with the minute details of the situation means a far higher level of documentation and persuasive argument than is required in bilateral negotiations. For the U.S. government to pursue an active agenda of challenges to Japanese practices will require more staff and greater effort to collect, document, and analyze information. Government must allocate these resources, and the private sector will have to work cooperatively with government to supply relevant information if the WTO option is to be exercised adequately.

Non-WTO Issues

Not all problems can be taken to the WTO. Some issues represent negotiations to create new agreements dealing with new commitments on market opening, rather than disputes over existing commitments. Such negotiations must occur on a bilateral basis unless they are postponed for inclusion in another of the infrequent multilateral negotiation rounds. From the time the Tokyo Round was completed in 1979, sixteen years passed before the Uruguay Round reached completion at the end of 1994. For many industries with outstanding issues, this amount of time to wait for creation of new agreements is intolerable. Neither the GATT nor the WTO assumes that negotiations will occur only in a multilateral round context; the principle of most favored nation status covers bilateral negotiations. Nations are expected to work out bilateral deals, but membership in the GATT-WTO implies that the outcome of those agreements must apply on a most favored nation basis. All bilateral agreements negotiated by the United States with Japan fit this requirement, whether they apply to WTO-covered manufactured products or uncovered service industries. All bilateral agreements have dealt with rules, standards, and procedures, the changes in which apply to all foreign firms, not just American ones. Even the vague language on increased opportunities and sales written into 1990s-era agreements applies to all foreign firms. The closest one can find to an exception is the forecasts by Japanese auto companies of their expected purchase of locally produced parts for use in their North American assembly plants (forecasts announced in the context of both the 1992 and 1995 auto agreements although these were private sector forecasts and not government commitments).

Other issues do not fit in the WTO framework because the industry is not covered or the behavior is not covered. The Clinton administration negotiated agreements with Japan covering deregulation of the insurance industry and financial services (largely new rules for management of pension funds) resulting in deregulation measures applying on a most favored nation basis, but the financial sector remained outside WTO coverage at that time. In other cases, the behavior involved is not specifically included in the WTO. As in the color film case, it might be possible to build an article 23 case to cover broad industrial policy problems, but limitations (including proof of lack of prior knowledge of the problem or simultaneity in substituting the new barrier for reduction of the previous barrier) suggest that much of industrial policy will remain outside the scope of the WTO. In these cases, there is little alternative to a bilateral approach.

The bilateral negotiation in 1997 concerning restrictive practices in Japanese ports is a prime example of an issue outside the WTO. The sector—stevedoring services—does not appear to be covered by the WTO, nor were the sector's arcane practices within the reach of WTO rules. At the core of the case, though, were problems akin to those that WTO tries to eliminate, such as opaque and arbitrary practices that put foreign firms at a disadvantage. The Federal Maritime Commission (FMC) ruling in this case noted that among the key problems was the fact that there "are no written criteria, explanations, or avenues for appeal given for JHTA's [Japan Harbor Transportation Association's] decisions, and that JHTA uses its control over access to the prior consultation system to suppress competition and allocate work among its member companies."[62]

As long as bilateral negotiations and agreements conform to most favored nation principles, there is no reason why such negotiations should not proceed when issues outside the scope of the WTO arise, as will surely occur. In such cases, a critical element is the leverage that can be exercised in the negotiation. With a WTO case, the leverage comes in the form of retaliation that can be levied if the defendant loses the case and refuses to alter behavior. In a bilateral case, the same need arises. Not all trade cases reach an impasse, but some do. Faced with no credible threat to impose costs on Japanese firms, why should the Japanese government make concessions when its internal incentive structure is to defend domestic industry?

Bilateral negotiations, therefore, require some form of leverage when the Japanese government is reluctant to liberalize markets. This leverage can be of two types: positive or negative. Positive leverage involves the existence of some benefit that the Japanese side would like to obtain from the negotiations. This positive sum game underlies the principles of the GATT-WTO. One country agrees to lower its own barriers in negotiations with a trading partner in exchange for concessions from the partner. The prospect of increased opportunities in the partner's market enables the government to fend off political pressures from the domestic industry whose own protection is to be lowered.

This sort of bargaining occurred in several bilateral negotiations in the 1990s. Consider insurance negotiations in the 1993–96 period. The insurance business in Japan has been rigidly separated into life insurance, property insurance, and a "third sector" that includes personal injury, cancer, and several other insurance products that were not traditionally classified as part of either of the other two sectors. Foreign firms were permitted into the third sector in the 1970s, and a few firms developed a lucrative business there (one American firm in particular in cancer insurance). In the 1990s, foreign insurance firms wanted better access to the life and property markets, especially through deregulation, which would permit them to compete on the basis of price, product design, and new marketing techniques. In exchange, Japanese insurance firms wanted access to the third sector, since they were envious of the profits they saw accruing to foreign firms. In both rounds of negotiations in the mid-1990s, the U.S. government used the Japanese desire for access to the third sector as part of the leverage to wring concessions on deregulation of the other two sectors of the insurance business.[63]

Leverage in this positive sum game is not always exercised wisely. Under the 1952 bilateral aviation treaty, the United States has had two "incumbent" passenger carriers (Northwest and United), while Japan had one (Japan Air Lines), which have unlimited rights to fly to the other nation as discussed in chapter 2 (that is, the right to choose routes and frequencies without constraint by either government). In the 1990s, Japan wanted All Nippon Airways (ANA) to be added as an incumbent carrier, while the United States wanted improved "beyond rights"—the right for American carriers to fly beyond Japan (including carrying passengers picked up in Japan to other destinations in Asia). The U.S. government proposed that the whole issue be resolved by adopting an "open skies" agreement under which all airlines would have unlimited rights. The limited agreement that emerged in 1998 fell short of open skies and traded incumbency for ANA for increased numbers of flights for nonincumbent American carriers and improved beyond rights for American carriers.[64] This outcome, however, represented a misuse of leverage. With ANA granted incumbency, the Japanese government had no further desire for future airline negotiations because ANA was the only other significant Japanese-flag international carrier. In essence, the Japanese government achieved the equivalent of open skies for its carriers, while a number of American airlines remained far short of freedom to set their routes and frequencies.

The best one can say about the airline issue is that the U.S. government stuck to its insistence that Japan reopen negotiations after four years, at which time the American negotiators would again raise the request for an open skies agreement. The agreement states that when negotiations recommence by 2001, the objective is "fully liberalizing the civil aviation relationship between Japan and the United States." Should no agreement be reached within twelve months, the 1998 agreement specifies a series of automatic expanded flight authorizations over the next four years.[65] Although the commitment to reopening negotiations and the inclusion of automatic approval of increased flights if no satisfactory settlement is reached by 2002 were certainly concessions by the Japanese government, American negotiators will discover that bargaining leverage no longer exists when those negotiations occur. Settling for any agreement short of open skies in 1998 represented a tactical mistake.

The other form of leverage in bilateral negotiations is negative in nature: the threat to impose retaliatory costs on the Japanese side. As a matter of diplomacy, governments obviously prefer the positive sum game of swapping concessions. But what if one side has no realistic concessions to swap? Most markets in the United States are already freely accessible to Japanese firms, especially in comparison to ease of access to Japanese markets for foreign firms. The essence of the negotiating game in the past two decades has been to get the Japanese government to make markets more open in a manner that would reduce the disparity of access. Swapping concessions would not yield this desired outcome. When friendly discussion or debate fails to produce progress, bilateral negotiations require the use of negative tools that take away benefits that Japanese firms already have in the American market.

As an example of the need for this approach, consider harbor services. Vague support existed in the Japanese government for reforming the institutional framework for harbor services, but neither the government nor the Japanese shipping industry was willing to move on the issue until a year of escalating threats resulted in imposition of punitive fees on Japanese vessels entering American ports. The prospect of armed Coast Guard ships impounding Japanese vessels knocked loose the negotiating process, and progress on deregulating Japanese stevedoring services occurred without any real action by the Coast Guard. Nonetheless, the episode remains an unsettling reminder of how difficult achieving progress is—even when strong leverage is applied. At the very end, the Japanese government believed that the Coast Guard would act as requested but apparently did not take the threat seriously until that point. Similarly, in the automobile negotiations in 1993–95, little progress occurred on any of the related issues until after the USTR announced its retaliation against imports of luxury cars from Japan.

What retaliatory tools does the U.S. government have at its disposal in these bilateral cases? Despite the concern over the possible inability to retaliate unilaterally given the existence of the WTO, several options are available.

First, tariff or quota barriers can be imposed despite the WTO commitments. The existence of the WTO does not prohibit any government from imposing higher tariffs or creating quotas; it only permits nations to bring complaint against those who do, with the subsequent right to erect comparable barriers should the offending nation refuse to change its behavior. This situation obviously limits the willingness of the U.S. government to proceed with a unilateral imposition of higher tariffs. However, the WTO process takes some time. If the point of the tariff is as a tactical negotiating tool, it might still be effective. Consider automobiles. The punitive 100 percent duty levied on Japanese luxury cars effectively locked them out of the market (since they would no longer be competitive on price against American or European luxury cars). Even though the Japanese government announced its intent to file a case against the United States on this action, the subsequent WTO proceedings would take up to eighteen months. During this time, the Japanese auto companies faced substantial loss of revenue. For a company like Nissan, which was operating at a loss at that time, the loss may have been unsustainable. Therefore, careful use of the unilaterally imposed tariff may still be a viable option despite WTO rules.

Second, opportunities exist for regulatory based retaliation. On at least one occasion in the past fifteen years, the U.S. government has threatened to revoke Japanese-flag airline rights to land at American airports. At the time of the insurance negotiations, Japanese insurance companies had license applications pending with a number of American state insurance commissions (since insurance is regulated at the state level in the United States). Although these applications were beyond the reach of the federal government, the U.S. Trade Representative or the Treasury Department certainly had the right to testify against the granting of licenses, especially since many states have reciprocity clauses written into their state licensing rules. In telecommunications as well, Japanese firms were eager to participate in the liberalized American market, but the USTR protested their involvement before the Federal Communications Commission in the summer of 1997 as bilateral negotiations on better access in Japan stalled. These are all examples of how American regulatory mechanisms can be used as part of the bargaining process.

Third, the U.S. government can impose nontariff fees. This was the approach of the harbor practices dispute, imposing fees on Japanese vessels entering American harbors (different from levying an import duty on the goods carried by the vessels). The same possibilities exist with landing fees for Japanese-flag commercial aircraft. For an industry covered by the WTO, imposition of fees only on Japanese firms might run afoul of WTO rules on national treatment (under which foreign firms should be accorded equal treatment with domestic ones), but the situation is certainly not clear until or unless a trading partner were to pursue a successful case against American actions.

Fourth, American antitrust law may also hold some opportunities for retaliation. Many market access cases in Japan involve collusion in the domestic market that places foreign firms at a disadvantage. If that collusion has some impact within the American market (such as raising prices or reducing competition by causing American firms to withdraw from the industry), then opportunities may exist to pursue antitrust cases. Usually antitrust actions proceed unconnected to trade policy. But an administration could signal that it is actively looking into antitrust prosecution or even initiate a case timed to play a tactical role in trade negotiations.

Finally, the murky question of "dirty tricks" arises. Although these are considered in casual conversation from time to time, they never achieve any serious consideration. Some are prohibited for good domestic reasons. Tax investigation harassment, for example, is not possible. However, others may be possible. Slowing processing or denial of business visas for Japanese business people, for example, does not seem to be a violation of U.S. law or treaty obligations (the granting of visas is by its nature a regulatory decision, and it should be within the legitimate scope of the government to deny visas or reassign processing priority to applications from other countries). The response to such tactics, however, is often that such petty behavior should be beneath the dignity of the U.S. government. Perhaps so, but such tactics have certainly not been beneath the dignity of many other countries (France and Japan come to mind). In the tough world of trade negotiations, giving more serious thought to the possibility of such tools might be worthwhile.

Occasionally threatening to diminish or end the bilateral security relationship is suggested as possible leverage, but this possibility is best avoided. This concept of an economic-security linkage assumes that Japanese security interests benefit from the security treaty (since the United States is a very powerful ally and thereby deters the possibility of hostile action against Japan), and threatening to reduce or remove that benefit would bring strong, positive action on trade. Reducing the number of troops stationed in Japan or ending the treaty itself are among the possibilities. The major flaw in this argument is that American security interests also benefit from the security relationship and would also be damaged if the Japanese side did not respond to this pressure. Even those Americans who do not believe the bilateral security relationship is vital must recognize that the support for the relationship is so strong within the U.S. government that no suggestion of using linkage is likely to survive discussion among U.S. agencies. Although explicit linkage is not possible, the point made earlier in this chapter remains: failure to make progress on trade issues feeds a long-term corrosive process undermining future political support for the security relationship. Reminding Japanese policymakers of that longer-term political possibility provides at least an informal means for bringing the security relationship into the trade process.

This list of possible forms of retaliation implies that the option of unilateral action by the U.S. government was certainly not lost as a consequence of creating the WTO. But for the tactical threat of retaliation to be effective, it must be understood by the other party and at least occasionally exercised. The report, cited earlier, by the American Chamber of Commerce in Japan on the history of bilateral trade negotiations notes that use of sanctions can be useful but that the U.S. government loses credibility when it threatens use of such sanctions too often without serious intent to carry through.[66]

Despite the perception that the United States makes frequent use of unilateral retaliation, the only occasion on which actual costs have been imposed on Japanese firms (that is, implemented and fees actually collected or restrictive rules enforced) was the use of punitive tariffs in 1987 for failure to abide by the 1986 semiconductor accord and the 1987 prohibition on bidding on U.S. government contracts for three years imposed on Toshiba Corporation in the wake of the Toshiba Machine Tool scandal (which was a security-related issue and not a trade negotiation). In most cases, action is threatened, but agreement is reached before the announced date for action. And in a few cases, such as automobiles or harbor practices, action was announced and implemented in principle but with the collection of fees postponed as negotiations continued (and with agreement reached prior to the retroactive collection date). That these cases have all been resolved without having to follow through on the retaliatory threats made is probably laudable, but the question about government resolve remains. At some point the credibility of retaliatory threats is lost if the other side does not believe they will be carried out.

Threatening retaliation can also be difficult without unified support at home. On the airline issue, the domestic industry was deeply divided over whether the U.S. government should doggedly pursue an open skies agreement. Northwest advocated a hard stance, but the others (including Delta, American, and Continental) favored settling for the usual managed increase in routes and frequencies.[67] This is a common problem; leverage implies pressure and the possibility of sanctions, behavior patterns that many businesses prefer to avoid. Threatening or imposing sanctions on a trading partner entails political or diplomatic costs, introducing tension into the relationship. The U.S. government does not embark on such tactics lightly, and only after internal debate in which some agencies usually oppose action. Proceeding with retaliation, therefore, is all the more difficult when the domestic industry is not united. No government agency wants to go through the difficulty of building internal administration agreement and face the negative diplomatic aspects of such actions only to realize that the industry is not supportive.

A broader dilemma is the fear that use of threats of retaliation will worsen the situation rather than resolve it. That is, those who favor change within the Japanese industry or government find themselves put on the defensive by domestic hard liners when the U.S. government threatens to take such harsh steps as it did in the harbor practices. In that dispute, Prime Minister Hashimoto said in February 1997 that the fines threatened by the FMC could "hamper the Ministry of Transport's efforts to correct such practices."[68] Many American businesses take seriously this negative possibility. Certainly damage to the dynamics of decisionmaking and negotiating flexibility is a theoretical possibility. But the unfortunate reality in dealing with the Japanese government is that often the dynamics do not move in a productive direction *without* leverage and threats of retaliation. Japanese negotiators are so flexible in accommodating the demands of domestic groups opposed to change that they often bring proposals to the negotiating table that represent only superficial progress (as was the case in the harbor practices dispute). Japanese negotiators may regret that the United States will not accept such compromises and argue that their own credibility is undermined if the U.S. ratchets up the level of pressure. But in the power politics of Japanese decisionmaking, such pressure usually does bring more realistic results.

This point about the need for threats of retaliation and willingness to occasionally actually impose costs on Japanese business interests as a negotiating tactic is both critical to negotiating success and controversial. The Japanese government takes its trade negotiations very seriously, meticulously seeking and exploiting weakness in the other side, motivated (usually) by a desire to protect domestic industry. Negotiators bring to this effort the degree of seriousness and dedication Americans often associate with strategic arms negotiations during the Soviet era. This is not the public message of Japanese government officials assigned to interact with foreigners, who emphasize free trade principles and American "misunderstanding" of the problem, but the internal decisionmaking dynamic militates against improving market access at the expense of the vested interests of domestic firms. The need for *amakudari* slots, the relationship with firms that do have *amakudari* officials, the years of gift-giving and partying with domestic executives, political contributions to the Liberal Democratic Party, and the general nationalistic sense of "us versus them" all come into play. Denial of problems, bluster, political exploitation of divisions on the American side, and extensive public relations campaigns are all part of the aggressive defensive tactics employed by the Japanese government in its *realpolitik* approach to trade negotiations.

In the United States, however, use of seemingly harsh negotiating tactics with an obstructionist ally remains controversial. For years scholars and others have decried this approach and called for a more gentlemanly approach.[69] As appealing as a softer approach seems, it often implies failure. The Japanese government does not follow a soft or gentlemanly style in its tactical approach to bilateral trade negotiations and often sees the American endorsement of a softer manner as just another factor to be exploited in its endeavor to minimize market access. Not all trade negotiations are so difficult that threats or use of retaliation are necessary to achieve progress. But some do, and displays of softness can damage the overall negotiating framework, so that progress in all areas decelerates when the Japanese government perceives the U.S. government as weak, disinterested, or unwilling to carry through with its threats.

Public Demeanor

At various times in the past two decades, the public perception in both countries has been one of serious bilateral tension, based on statements by senior government officials to the media about the seriousness of problems or the perfidious behavior of the other side. In line with the dictum "speak softly and carry a big stick," such behavior is generally undesirable. The Clinton administration began with strong public rhetoric that led the Japanese government to anticipate great pressure. Three years later, the view of the Japanese appeared to be one of believing the administration would do little to back up its rhetoric. It is far better to do the reverse; public demeanor should be subdued, while the leverage should be real. In this respect, the port services case was handled well. The FMC made its decision with a minimum of public fuss, but the message was sent, the determination to move forward with sanctions was clear, and negotiations progressed.

However, in a different sense, the U.S. government does a poor job of communication. Even if government keeps the general rhetoric on bilateral trade issues at a low key, there is a need for a more aggressive stance on the facts about particular trade issues. The Japanese government approaches these problems in a methodical fashion, including feeding both the Japanese and American press a constant stream of information from its own point of view, shaping the media's knowledge of the background of an issue and the evolving negotiating stances.

The Japanese government also feeds its public relations messages to American elites on an individual basis—including both the Washington policy community and academics perceived as recognized voices in policy debates.[70] Often the information conveyed is biased or misleading. But with the usually quiet or reactive stance in the U.S. government, these views circulate unchallenged in Japan and the United States. The tendency of the American government has been to focus on the narrow question of pursuing the issue at the bargaining table; in this process silence or reserve in speaking publicly can be desirable. Because negotiation involves compromise, it is best not to speak out much in public lest the compromise appear to be an embarrassing retreat from a publicly stated position. But this reticence works to the disadvantage of the U.S. government in the court of public opinion when the other side is actively spreading information and encouraging others to speak out in opposition on the basis of that information. In the United States public opinion matters. If influential voices in the media, business interests, and portions of the broader public seriously question the government's trade policy with Japan, this political pressure is likely to get politically sensitive administrations to modify their behavior. The Japanese government recognizes this possibility, and public relations campaigns have been a central part of its bilateral bargaining strategies.

Consider, for example, the story that the American car manufacturers failed to sell right-hand drive cars in Japan, presented by the Japanese government as a striking example of poor marketing by an American industry that deserved nothing but contempt for its self-inflicted failures to penetrate Japan. The reality was quite different. First, consider the simplicity: if all Americans hearing this story could wonder in disbelief at the stupidity of American car manufacturers, why wouldn't the car industry executives have recognized the need to supply right-hand drive cars to Japan? In other markets where traffic moves on the left, the U.S. companies market the appropriate cars—as in Britain or Australia. Why would they behave rationally in those countries but not in Japan? The market for all foreign cars until the beginning of the 1990s was for left-hand drive vehicles (since sitting on the wrong side of the car was part of the prestige of owning a foreign vehicle). Furthermore, as the market began to shift in the 1990s, with foreign cars finally beginning to move out of the very small luxury car niche, American manufacturers responded, although at a slightly slower pace than some of the European manufacturers. At the time the Japanese government was making its allegations of Detroit's marketing failure, the three leading companies were actually offering some fifty-nine models with right-hand drive in Japan.[71] But this piece of misleading and factually wrong information spread rapidly and continued to come up in Washington conversations long after agreement was finally reached in 1995. Japanese government officials astutely realized that the reputation of the top American manufacturers was low, especially among policy elites, and that this sort of anecdote would resonate. They were right.

The automobile example is one of relative success. Faced with the aggressive media campaign by the Japanese government, the U.S. government worked the press more aggressively and did correct some of the more egregious distortions of the facts and its policy position, at least with the Japanese media. In a continuation of this need to explain its own position, the decision to make public its filing to the WTO in the color film case did much to clarify the issues and the American position. But the need remains. Any issue that the U.S. government intends to pursue must be accompanied by an active media strategy. Failure to do so enables the Japanese government to shape public perceptions of the issues, a task that it takes seriously.

Public relations is often regarded as an issue of secondary importance in economic relations with Japan. What matters most is the negotiations, and U.S. government officials put most of their attention into devising positions and bargaining strategies. Furthermore, as noted earlier, the Japanese public has little or no policy input, so pursuing a public effort to win their hearts and minds seems pointless. But what does matter is the American policy elite in the pluralistic American political system. Any American administration that chooses to pursue a high-profile, aggressive market opening campaign is vulnerable to manipulation of elite opinion in the United States, which may undercut support for U.S. objectives and tactics. The Japanese government understands this potential and invests in both Washington lobbyists and its own efforts to make public relations a central part of its bilateral trade policy. This means introducing worries that trade problems will undermine the security relationship, pushing the notion of "misunderstanding" in American negotiating positions, or, as in the Clinton first term, claiming that the U.S. government was headed toward an ideologically incorrect managed trade policy.

Pursuit of a positive public relations strategy is aided somewhat by the concept of economic benefit to the Japanese economy from more open markets. As noted earlier in this chapter, protection of inefficient sectors harms the Japanese economy. Greater openness benefits foreign firms but also benefits the Japanese economy. American officials often make these points in speaking publicly, but they could do more to emphasize this point. The tendency of the Japanese government and media is to portray trade negotiations as a struggle in which Japan is being forced to make concessions or sacrifices that benefit American firms. Usually lost in this portrayal is the notion that greater openness is good for Japan. During the Structural Impediments Initiative talks, U.S. officials pressed hard on this point at a time when the media and public were more willing to hear the message. During the Framework talks, this message was still delivered in speeches but perhaps without as much vigor. Convincing the public that American trade negotiation positions are good for Japan will not change the course of very many negotiations, but at least it would diminish the ability of the government and media to portray Japan as a victim of American pressure and interests.

This aspect of trade relations with Japan should not be ignored. American government policies on market access problems need to incorporate public relations strategies at an early stage, with high-level participation. One institutional problem has been the relegation of press strategies in trade policy largely to the press office. For the State Department, this has meant reliance on the largely independent U.S. Information Agency. Although often well-intentioned, the agency had its own agenda that was not often explicitly coordinated with State Department or USTR policy strategies. Folding the U.S. Information Agency back into the State Department will help rectify this issue. But more broadly, the strategies and tactics should not be left to a press office but discussed and integrated into the work of principal participants with assistance and advice from the press office. To be sure, some of this happens, but the continuing disparity of the efforts of the Japanese government compared with those of the U.S. government is noticeable.

Public demeanor broadly defined includes issues other than a traditional public relations strategy. As noted earlier, trade issues involve the need to cultivate those domestic groups potentially supportive of American negotiating positions. Traditional public relations is one aspect of getting a message across to build possible support. So, too, is the process of meeting and talking with groups and individuals. Busy trade negotiators are confined largely to official relationships with their direct negotiating counterparts. However, American officials stationed in the embassy and consulates have the opportunity to deal with a broader array of pertinent domestic groups and individuals. They have traditionally fulfilled this role, but two points need to be made.

First, getting the message across to involved parties is labor intensive. American personnel resources in Japan have been limited, and more active pursuit of this aspect of trade issues is simply not possible without some increase in staffing. Officials involved in this process benefit greatly from sufficient language skills to enable them to interact well outside the narrow confines of English-speaking Japanese. They also need sufficient expense account support so that they are not dependent on their Japanese counterparts. American officials have worked hard in Japan, but the small numbers and low expense support severely limit the extent of their input on trade issues.

Second, the scope of this broader dialogue must incorporate Japanese politicians. Traditionally the dialogue with politicians has been the province

of those U.S. government officials charged with the political-military relationship with Japan, while those involved on the economic side have largely
confined their relations to the career bureaucracy and private sector. State
Department officers separate into political or economic tracks early in their
careers with relatively little crossover in their subsequent careers (though
exceptions do occur). This division of labor needs to end. Since 1993 the
political scene in Japan has become more complicated, involving coalition
politics and greater fluidity in the role of individual politicians. Politicians
have always been important in trade issues even in an environment of a
powerful bureaucracy, and as discussed in chapter 5, the 1990s created new
uncertainties in the relationship between the bureaucracy and politicians.
Given their role and the possibility that they may be important in new or
different ways in the political environment of the late 1990s, it is critical to
engage politicians in the broader dialogue on trade issues. To do this the
political officers must add economics and trade to their portfolio, the economic officers must reach out to engage the politicians, or greater interac-
tion and cooperation between the two sets of officers is necessary. This,
too, implies increased work for the U.S. Embassy and a need for increased
personnel.

Monitoring

The shift in policy that began in the Bush administration and was then
expanded in the Clinton administration to incorporate language into bilateral agreements about monitoring has been a useful innovation. As detailed
in chapter 4, managed trade never achieved much appeal as a policy, but a
major dilemma remained because of the managed nature of competition
in many Japanese markets that could not be addressed adequately through
superficial changes in rules of access. Watchfulness and the willingness to
quickly raise issues again when statistical evidence suggests little progress
has occurred may be sufficient to translate traditional rules-based agreements into more effective instruments of increased market access. Therefore, it is essential that the U.S. government engage in vigorous monitoring
of implementation and outcomes.

   As an illustration of why monitoring is necessary, consider flat glass.
The two countries signed agreements intended to improve access to the
Japanese market in January 1992 and again in January 1995. The 1995
agreement specified various measures to increase transparency and openness in a market fraught with cartel behavior and protectionism.[72] Never-

theless, the market share of non-Japanese firms remained flat after the agreement was signed, at a minuscule 1 percent. A 1997 MITI survey indicated that no change had taken place in the interest of domestic distributors in handling foreign glass.[73] And the U.S. government pointed out that virtually no increase had occurred in use of insulated glass or safety glass despite language in the 1995 agreement calling for Japanese promotion of these products (in which foreign firms hold a price and technological advantage).[74] Such outcomes were highly suggestive of a lack of progress toward a real increase in openness and rightfully trigger further negotiations or consideration of other measures.

Or consider the monitoring function on paper. The bilateral paper agreement of 1992 included various measures to make the market more transparent and accessible as well as actions by MITI to promote use of foreign paper. The agreement also specified a semiannual bilateral government-to-government meeting to review progress.[75] Informal cartel arrangements and impenetrable *keiretsu* relationships between producers and users meant that import penetration was only 3.7 percent in 1992, compared with levels ranging from 15 percent to 80 percent in other countries in the Organization for Economic Cooperation and Development. By 1996 import penetration in Japan reached 5.1 percent, which the U.S. government feared would fall thereafter since major capacity expansions were under way in Japan. Monitoring and periodic bilateral meetings built into this agreement were helpful in exposing these outcomes. But what should be done? The market share had risen but still left import penetration well below the level in other countries, and anecdotes of informal barriers continued. In 1997 the USTR chose not to act forcefully, falling back on an announcement of further review, admonishment of the Japanese government, and trade promotion efforts.[76]

Similar problems emerged quickly in implementation of the 1996 insurance agreement. Although the agreement was fairly detailed and seemed clear, Japanese government observers immediately noted that it was not precise in defining how much rate flexibility would be allowed.[77] Immediately upon negotiation, the agreement was denounced by parts of the Japanese insurance industry, indicating that internal opposition was strong—thereby providing officials with ample reason to interpret the agreement's mandate very conservatively.[78] Indeed, within six months the U.S. insurance industry was expressing concern about implementation of the agreement, especially the vague language in Ministry of Finance recommendations that appeared to leave room for the Insurance Council (a Japanese insurance industry trade group) to retain some of its supervisory authority over industry rate setting.[79]

On monitoring of auto parts sales to Japan, the U.S. government noted in 1997 that while exports from the United States to Japan were $2 billion in 1996 (double the 1992 level), Japan continued to have the lowest market share for foreign products among developed nations with domestic auto industries.[80] Meanwhile, progress had stalled on deregulating rules about auto parts—particularly brake system repairs. The 1995 agreement included a mechanism for foreign firms to petition the Ministry of Transportation to liberalize rules for other auto parts repairs. Four American auto parts trade associations filed such a petition on brake system repairs but were turned down by the Ministry of Transportation.[81] Furthermore, no progress was made in obtaining better access by foreign firms to automobile registration data in Japan for purposes of market analysis.[82] Despite raising these concerns, however, negotiations with Japan on deregulation of brake repairs made little progress in 1997.[83]

These four examples illustrate the need for close monitoring after agreements are signed. But they all illustrate two problems. First, monitoring can bog down. Any increase in sales by foreign firms can be touted by Japanese government officials as proof of significant progress no matter how trivial the change. Second, and more important, lack of progress does not always lead to action. None of the four areas reviewed moved back to active negotiations in 1998 even though progress on foreign penetration had been disappointing or nonexistent for several years. Government resources are limited; not all potential issues can be negotiated continuously. But to have real meaning, the monitoring process must demonstrate a willingness to pursue further actions, such as reopening negotiations for additional access measures, when monitoring demonstrates a lack of progress.

Monitoring need not be pursued only in a bilateral context. In fact, a conceptual problem is involved with bilateral monitoring. As noted earlier, agreements may be negotiated on a bilateral basis, but the outcomes are applied on a global most favored nation basis. As a result, other nations are justifiably concerned when the Japanese government sits down only with the Americans to monitor the outcomes. Such a process may lead to favoritism for American firms or at least worries by Europeans and others about possible favoritism. If the market involved is subject to collusive behavior or informal government guidance, and the Americans are the ones with whom Japanese officials must meet for monitoring, why not skew some sales toward American firms to keep American negotiators satisfied?

This accusation surfaced in the semiconductor industry and led finally to creation of a broader international committee to explore issues in international semiconductor trade. Without a semiconductor-like multilateral arrangement, the U.S. government can pursue monitoring on a unilateral basis and make the Japanese government amply aware that it is doing so, and other governments can and should do the same.

Conclusion

This study has argued that many of the indicators of participation in Japanese markets by foreign firms remain well below the level for other nations, with differences that cannot be adequately explained through recourse to standard economic variables. In some respects, the situation in the mid-to-late 1990s was better than a decade earlier, with Japan somewhat less distinctive in comparison to other nations. But the disparities imply that ease of access to Japanese markets remained a problem in the late 1990s.

What should the U.S. government do about this situation? One option is to do nothing. Many around the world seem to feel that the United States has had an excessive zeal for open markets. Neither the original GATT nor the new WTO presumes that free trade should be the world standard; they only represent an institutional mechanism designed to aid nations in moving toward greater openness if they so desire. But this chapter has argued that access to Japanese markets should matter to American policymakers. Japan has made official commitments in a series of multilateral negotiating rounds to greatly lower official barriers, and its government touts international access to its markets. Meanwhile, behind the facade of government rhetoric Japan can be described as pursuing a strategic trade policy that disadvantages its trading partners in some advanced high-technology industries as well as protectionism for inefficient sectors, all of which results in less penetration of markets for goods and services in Japan than is true in other countries. Given Japan's official commitment to open trade, there is no reason why American government and industry should tolerate a protectionist trade policy behind the facade of openness. Japan, by gaining in those industries where it has comparative advantage (and faces few serious trade barriers abroad) while denying its trade partners the opportunity to gain from their own areas of comparative advantage, imposes upon itself and other nations distortions in the allocation of resources. The distortions and loss of income caused by such barriers should matter to American policymakers.

But what should the U.S. government do? How does a major power convince another sovereign power to alter its trade policies? The suggestions proposed in this book may seem unsatisfying. There is no magical approach that shows promise of triumphing in the move toward free trade and investment where others have failed. Indeed, avoiding enticing but flawed "silver bullets" is most important.

First, issues of access to Japanese markets are important but do not deserve to be core parts of an administration's objectives. That is, domestic education policy, nuclear arms control, peace negotiations in the Mideast, and other issues deserve more time on the agenda of the president and high-level officials. Trade matters, but the record of the past two decades implies that the difficulty of access to Japanese markets is not usually a life-and-death issue for American industry. Economic relations with Japan will need presidential input and support on occasion (such as willingness to discuss and press firmly on trade issues at summit meetings) but need not be at the public forefront of administration policy.

Second, and related to the first point, is the need to settle for a more constant level of effort rather than adopting large themes to govern bilateral negotiations, such as the SII talks or the Framework Agreement. The political dynamic generated by creating a theme as an umbrella for an interrelated set of intensive trade negotiations almost necessarily results in only limited progress. The United States needs to show progress in eighteen to twenty-four months. Exhaustion and inattention then follow. Japan recognizes that enthusiasm will lag and that the U.S. government will settle for minor changes. Thus the effectiveness of such an approach is undermined. And among the possible themes, certainly there is no intellectual or practical advantage in adopting a structural approach compared with a sectoral one. Whether incorporated as a theme or not, both approaches are necessary. Although overarching themes do no real harm, they are certainly not a panacea, do not live up to expectations, and sometimes create a sense of tension that may not be worth the eventual outcomes. It is far better to pursue issues as they arise and devote to them a sustained effort over a long period to avoid the cycle of pressure and relaxation.

Expanding on the notion of overarching themes, the government should also reject the notion of a bilateral free trade area or bilateral dispute resolution mechanism. These mechanisms would do little to resolve real issues—either because the issues involved are simply not amenable to this approach (such as decisions to improve conditions for intellectual property protection) or because American industry would not believe that its issues would receive a fair hearing before a bilateral panel. The broader notion of a bilateral free trade area also suffers because the border barriers that are the easiest to remove in creating an FTA are not the main problem in access to Japanese markets.

What is left? First, push use of the WTO. The WTO remains a very imperfect vehicle for improving market access in Japan, but it holds more opportunities than the old GATT and is worth pursuing as long as its limitations are recognized. The loss of the color film case was an unfortunate blow to engaging the WTO on the broad array of market access problems related to industrial policy, even though having the WTO accept the principles represented in the color film case was a minor moral victory. The narrowness of the WTO ruling on color film presents a high hurdle for evidence in such cases but may still be worthwhile pursuing. More aggressive use of the phytosanitary and technical standards is a promising avenue.

Second, non-WTO issues should continue to proceed through bilateral negotiation. For these negotiations the search for leverage is crucial. With use of unilateral retaliation against Japanese economic interests in the United States under the rubric of section 301 now problematical, that search is more difficult than in the past. But in at least some cases, it should be possible to devise nontariff retaliatory measures that do not violate American commitments to the WTO. Not all negotiations result in stalemates in which the threat of retaliation becomes necessary to achieve forward progress, but some do and that threat must be credible to achieve the desired tactical goal of moving negotiations forward.

Third, the U.S. government must devise a better public relations strategy. The Japanese government takes this element of trade relations very seriously and has occasionally undermined American negotiating positions in the past by causing the administration to lose public support at home. In Japan, this effort includes engaging relevant policy groups and individuals more closely. In the past this aspect of American trade policy toward Japan has never received the attention that it deserves.

Fourth, for both WTO and non-WTO issues, the process of monitoring outcomes after agreements are signed is of central importance. Whether bilaterally or unilaterally, outcomes on both the simple matter of actual implementation of an agreement's provisions and the more complex matter of market results must be tracked carefully. The act of monitoring in and of itself may improve implementation and outcomes in some cases. But more important is the use of monitoring as a means to determine quickly whether further negotiations, or retaliatory action, are necessary to achieve the access objectives involved. Incorporating bilateral monitoring meetings, buttressed by language as to the purpose of agreements (the "significant increase" language) was a useful innovation of the Bush and Clinton administrations. But monitoring does not depend on such language. The U.S. government can and should pursue a strong monitoring function on its own.

The proposals set forth here require an increase in human and fiscal resources for bilateral trade relations with Japan. WTO cases will consume more time and energy than past bilateral negotiations because of the greater resource demands involved in preparing facts and analysis to convince panels unfamiliar with Japan. Monitoring also requires increased input to assemble and evaluate data and to review negotiations and renew pressure when needed. And engaging policy-relevant groups in Japan more closely is also a labor-intensive process. Existing resources are modest. Only a few individuals at the State Department (including the embassy in Tokyo), the USTR, the Commerce Department, and the Agriculture Department work on Japan. Even doubling the number of people involved would not represent a major reallocation of human or fiscal resources. The enormous size of the Japanese economy and the strategic need for American firms to be engaged in that market imply that the government should commit the people and fiscal resources to pursue market access issues more thoroughly. When people argue that the payoff to trade negotiations (in increased access and sales by American firms) may be too small to justify the cost, they generally refer to the political cost; the monetary cost is very small (salaries for a few dozen people) relative to the potential market sales at stake. And the political cost (potential damage to the security relationship) is generally exaggerated.

None of these proposals is exciting or sexy, and some of them represent directions in which the U.S. government is already moving. But this fact only reinforces the main point; there is no magical solution to bilateral trade problems. As long as Japan continues to doggedly resist improving the terms of access to its markets for foreign firms, no politically feasible approach other than pursuing a long, slow process of battling individual issues exists.

The Measurement of Intra-Industry Trade

Intra-industry trade involves a relatively simple concept—the two-way flow of exports and imports within industry categories in a given country. Much of global trade takes this form. Rather than simply trading along broad comparative-advantage lines, with industrial nations trading capital and knowledge-intensive goods in exchange for labor-intensive products from developing nations, a large portion of global trade consists of trade in manufactured goods among industrial nations, with considerable two-way flows of products within industries.

Although the notion is simple, how should this phenomenon be measured? The standard statistic for measuring intra-industry trade within an industry is as follows:

$$IIT_i = [1- |x_i - m_i| /(x_i+m_i)] * 100,$$

Where IIT = an index for the degree of intra-industry trade,

x = exports,

m = imports, and

i = industry i.

That is, intra-industry trade measures the absolute difference between exports and imports as a share of total trade (exports plus imports) in the industry. This calculation produces a statistic (IIT_i) for each industry that is scaled to vary over the interval [0, 100] in an intuitively obvious way. If either exports or imports equal zero, the resulting index number is zero; no intra-industry trade takes place. If exports exactly equal imports, then perfect intra-industry trade occurs and the index number equals 100. By using the absolute value of the difference between exports and imports, the emphasis is placed on that difference, rather than on distinguishing which is larger; trade in which exports are twice as large as imports yields an IIT index number identical to the case when imports are twice as large as exports.

An average index number for trade across all (n) industries within a nation can be calculated by weighting each industry by its share in total trade (exports plus imports for each industry divided by the nation's total exports plus imports):

$$IIT = \Sigma_1 \left[IIT_i * (x_i + m_i)/(X + M) \right],$$
$$\text{where: } X = \Sigma_i x_i,$$
$$M = \Sigma_i m_i, \text{ and}$$
$$i = 1,\ldots,n.$$

The resulting statistic also varies over the interval [0, 100] in the same intuitively obvious way that the statistic for each industry does.

Although the numerical calculations are simple and straightforward, the concept is not so tidy. A major problem is what to use for an industry classification scheme. Furthermore, there are different degrees of specificity in industry classifications. Most of the analysis in this study is based on the two-digit Harmonized System classification, which is now in general use among all nations. The data come from the Organization for Economic Cooperation and Development, which supplies trade data on CD-ROM for all of its member states plus a few others.

As in my previous analysis of intra-industry trade (*Japan's Unequal Trade*), the national averages for the intra-industry trade statistic are not adjusted for overall trade imbalances. If a nation runs a large overall trade surplus (or deficit), that macroeconomic fact should lower the average level of intra-industry trade (since an overall trade imbalance must consist of imbalances for individual products). However, the statistical techniques for adjusting IIT statistics for this phenomenon are arbitrary because there is no clear mathematical mapping between changing overall trade imbalances and changes in measured intra-industry trade.

Measures by the Government of Japan and the Government of the United States of America Regarding Autos and Auto Parts

I. **Goals and General Policies**

    A. The goals of the Framework for A New Economic Partnership (the "Framework") established by the "Joint Statement on the Japan-United States Framework for A New Economic Partnership" of the Heads of Governments of Japan and the United States of America (the "United States") on July 10, 1993 are to deal with structural and sectoral issues in order substantially to increase access and sales of competitive foreign goods and services through market-opening and macroeconomic measures; to increase investment; to promote international competitiveness; and to enhance bilateral economic cooperation between the United States and Japan.

    B. To accomplish these goals with respect to the Japanese autos and auto parts sector, the Government of Japan and the Government of the United States each has decided to implement the measures contained in this document, "Measures by the Government of Japan and the Government of the United States of America Regarding Autos and Auto Parts" (the "Measures") with the objective of achieving significantly expanded sales opportunities to result in a significant expansion of purchases of foreign parts by Japanese firms in Japan and through their transplants, as well as removing problems which affect market access, and encouraging imports of foreign autos and auto parts in Japan.

    C. All measures described in this document (including measures related to changes in regulations) are to be taken consistent with laws and regulations applicable to each country and international law.

D. The Government of Japan and the Government of the United States affirm the principle that vehicle manufacturers, auto parts suppliers and vehicle dealers should deal with suppliers based on the principles of free and open competition without adverse discrimination based on capital affiliation.

E. The Government of Japan and the Government of the United States reaffirm the principles of the Framework, including the principle that all measures of the Measures (including Sections II.A and IV.B.) are to be taken on a most-favored-nation basis. In this regard, the Government of Japan is prepared to take similar measures in relation to any third countries.

II. Measures to Encourage Imports and to Facilitate Market Access for Foreign Vehicles in Japan

A. *Foreign Vehicle Dealership Market Access Plan*

1. The objectives of this Foreign Vehicle Dealership Market Access Plan (the "Plan") are as follows:

   a. to demonstrate the commitment of the Japanese vehicle manufacturers to support open and competitive distribution systems for motor vehicles in Japan;

   b. to eliminate concerns that Japanese vehicle dealers may have about the consequences associated with carrying competing foreign motor vehicles;

   c. to facilitate contracts between foreign vehicle manufacturers and Japanese vehicle dealers; and

   d. to encourage foreign companies to continue to pursue market opportunities in Japan.

2. The Government of Japan welcomes and supports the Japan Automobile Manufacturers Association's (JAMA) announcement of June 28, 1995 stating the intention of its members to work to promote an open and competitive distribution system for motor vehicles in Japan.

3. The Government of Japan welcomes and supports the announcement of June 28, 1995 issued by the Japanese vehicle manufacturers that confirms that:

   a. all dealers are free to sell competing motor vehicles and that a dealer's decision to sell one or more competing motor vehicles should not be a matter of concern to the dealer regarding such dealer's ongoing relationship with a Japanese vehicle manufacturer;

b. all prior consultation requirement clauses with respect to handling competing motor vehicles that previously existed in dealership agreements have been eliminated; and

c. they support open and competitive distribution systems for motor vehicles in Japan.

4. The Government of Japan welcomes and supports the announcement of June 28, 1995 issued by the largest motor vehicle dealers through the Japan Automobile Dealers Association (JADA) publicly announcing the intention of these dealers to enter into independent franchise agreements with foreign vehicle manufacturers who offer competitive terms, conditions, and products.

5. The Government of Japan specifically in writing will inform dealers which are members of JADA that they are free to sell competing motor vehicles. The Government of Japan will attach to the notice the following sections of "The Antimonopoly Act Guidelines Concerning Distribution Systems and Business Practices" (Guidelines) issued by the Japan Fair Trade Commission (the "JFTC") on July 11, 1991, which describe types of conduct, including direct or indirect restrictions on distributors' handling of competing products, which may impede free and fair competition and violate the Antimonopoly Act (the "AMA"):

   • In chapter 4 of Part I: paragraph 2, chapeau, point 4 of paragraph 2 (i.e., circle 4), and notes 7, 8 and 9 (Restrictions on Trading Partners of Dealing with Competitors); and

   • In chapter 2 of Part II: subparagraphs 1 and 2 of paragraph 2 (i.e., parentheses 1 and 2) and notes 4 and 5 (Restrictions on Distributors' Handling of Competing Products).

   The Government of Japan's notice to JADA members will indicate that the attached Guidelines are applicable to relationships between motor vehicle manufacturers and dealers. It also will point out that any person, including a Japanese vehicle dealer, may report to the JFTC suspected violations of the AMA. The notice will inform dealers that the confidentiality of such report will be strictly protected and the report may be provided anonymously.

6. The Government of Japan and the Government of the United States will each designate an appropriate government contact person to take the steps set out in paragraph 7. In addition, the Government of Japan is pleased to note that each Japanese vehicle manufacturer has selected an appropriate senior company official who will be responsible for managing the aspects of the dealer-manufacturer relationship as set out in paragraph 7. The governments will provide the

names and phone numbers of the company and government contact persons upon request by an interested party. In addition, the Government of the United States is pleased to note that each U.S. vehicle manufacturer has selected an appropriate senior company official who will be responsible for managing the aspects of the dealer-manufacturer relationship in Japan and for taking steps as set out in paragraph 7.

7. The Government of Japan is pleased to note that foreign vehicle manufacturers may contact the Japanese company contact person and/or the government contact persons when seeking franchise agreements or other distribution arrangements in Japan.

   a. The Government of Japan is pleased to note that upon request by a foreign vehicle manufacturer, the Japanese company contact person will:

      i.   meet and explain to each dealer identified by the foreign manufacturer the Japanese manufacturer's company policy, including that the dealer is free to enter into distribution arrangements with foreign vehicle manufacturers, and that a dealer's decision to sell competing vehicles should not be a matter of concern to the dealer regarding its on-going relationship with the Japanese vehicle manufacturer;

      ii. respond to any questions or concerns the dealer may have about its continuing relationship with the Japanese manufacturer;

      iii. review the factual basis of any complaint and take appropriate steps in accordance with the company's internal AMA compliance program.

   b. The contact person of the Government of Japan will:

      i.   upon request by a foreign vehicle manufacturer or Japanese vehicle dealer, affirm that Japanese dealers are free to sell competing motor vehicles;

      ii. upon request by a foreign vehicle manufacturer or Japanese vehicle dealer, redistribute to the dealer the letter and attachments referenced in paragraph 5 above and point out that they may report to the JFTC any suspected violations of the AMA;

      iii. provide information to the JFTC where such information indicates the existence of practices that may violate the AMA, so that the JFTC can take such steps as deemed appropriate; and/or;

      iv. upon request by a foreign vehicle manufacturer or Japanese vehicle dealer, take other appropriate actions in support of the objectives of this Plan.

   c. The Government of the United States is pleased to note that upon request by a Japanese vehicle dealer, the U.S. vehicle manufacturer contact person intends to:

      i. confirm the terms under which the dealer will begin distributing the U.S. vehicle manufacturer's products; and

      ii. respond to any questions or concerns the dealer may have about the U.S. vehicle manufacturer's policies for entering into dealership arrangements, including competitive terms, conditions and products.

   d. Upon request by a Japanese vehicle dealer, the contact person of the Government of the United States will:

      i. provide the names and telephone numbers of U.S. company contact persons;

      ii. facilitate meetings between Japanese vehicle dealers and U.S. vehicle manufacturers; and

      iii. provide appropriate information about U.S. vehicle manufacturers and products.

  8. The two Governments confirm that Japanese vehicle dealers and foreign vehicle manufacturers are not bound to use this Plan, and are free to establish franchise agreements or other distribution arrangements through whatever means they choose in a manner consistent with the laws and regulations of Japan and international rules.

B. *Measures to be Taken by the Government of Japan*

  1. The Government of Japan will provide vehicle owner registration information to foreign vehicle manufacturers under the same conditions, including access to volume, detail and quality, as it provides such information to Japanese vehicle manufacturers, when they apply for such information to the Ministry of Transport ("MOT"). The Government of Japan confirms that the procedures it uses to provide the registration information will continue to be transparent. MOT will promptly respond to questions concerning the procedures from foreign vehicle manufacturers so that they can utilize the procedures.

  2. To support the development, distribution and marketing of foreign motor vehicles into Japan, the Government of Japan is to:

   a. provide financial support to the Japan External Trade Organization (JETRO) for the following activities:

    i.   exhibitions of foreign motor vehicles in Tokyo, Osaka, Nagoya, Sapporo, Fukuoka and other cities in Japan;

    ii. long term exhibitions for foreign motor vehicles in public areas such as airports and railway stations;

    iii. test driving sessions for potential customers in Tokyo, Osaka, Nagoya, Sapporo and Fukuoka; and

    iv. seminars to provide domestic dealers with basic information on handling foreign vehicles.

JETRO is expected to implement the activities set out in this sub-paragraph a. with the cooperation of relevant organizations and foreign firms upon request and as necessary.

b. provide wide-ranging financial incentives to promote the importation of foreign motor vehicles and to facilitate the establishment of manufacturing, sales and research and development facilities in Japan, including:

    i.   import promotion financing from the Japan Development Bank that is designed to provide low interest loans for activities such as constructing and equipping facilities for inspections and improving product features when a foreign company sets up a sales base in Japan that will facilitate importation and sale of foreign manufactured products, including motor vehicles, in Japan;

    ii. product import financing from the Export-Import Bank of Japan that provides funds to increase imports of manufactured products; and

    iii. loans to facilitate import sales from the Small Business Finance Corporation and People's Finance Corporation that provide the financing needed to increase sales of imported products.

C. *Measures to be Taken by the Government of the United States*

    1. The Government of the United States will provide support to the U.S. vehicle manufacturers to expand exports of U.S. motor vehicles to Japan. Among other measures, the Government of the United States will:

        a. support the participation of U.S. motor vehicle manufacturers in Japanese motor vehicle shows;

        b. encourage U. S motor vehicle manufacturers to continue to make efforts to increase exports to Japan; and

        c. provide other appropriate government support for increased exports of motor vehicles to Japan.

2. The Government of the United States will support on-going efforts of U.S. manufacturers to continue to increase their provision of competitive products under competitive terms and conditions.

III. Measures to Expand Purchases of Foreign Parts by Japanese Firms in Japan and through Their Transplants

A. *Measures to be Taken by the Government of Japan*
   1. For the purpose of promoting relationships between Japanese vehicle manufacturers and auto parts suppliers, the Government of Japan will support the Japanese vehicle manufacturers activities to:
      a. expand research and development ("R&D"), design, engineering and supplier support and outreach capabilities in foreign countries;
      b. increase suppliers' sales opportunities in Japan and other countries where they are located, without adverse discrimination based on capital affiliation; and
      c. continue to open design-in and procurement processes to foreign parts suppliers in Japan and to suppliers in other countries through the use of fair, competitive, transparent and non-discriminatory procedures.
   2. To support the importation of foreign auto parts into Japan, the Government of Japan is to:
      a. provide financial support to JETRO for the following activities:
         i. conducting exhibitions of foreign auto parts in Tokyo, Osaka, Nagoya, Sapporo, Fukuoka and other cities to promote transactions between foreign auto parts suppliers and Japanese vehicle manufacturers and to familiarize Japanese consumers with foreign aftermarket products;
         ii. facilitating design-in training by Japanese vehicle manufacturers and first-tier auto parts manufacturers for foreign auto parts engineers;
         iii. sponsoring auto parts conferences to facilitate and expand relationships between the Japanese automotive industry and foreign auto parts suppliers; and
         iv. assisting auto parts selling missions with foreign auto parts suppliers.

      JETRO is expected to implement the activities set out in this subparagraph a. with the cooperation of relevant organizations and foreign firms upon request and as necessary.

b. provide wide-ranging financial incentives to promote the importation of foreign auto parts, including:

   i.   import promotion financing from the Japan Development Bank that is designed to provide low interest loans for activities such as constructing and equipping facilities for inspections and improving product features when a foreign company sets up a sales base in Japan that will facilitate importation and sale of foreign manufactured products, including auto parts, in Japan;

   ii. product import financing from the Export-Import Bank of Japan that provides funds to increase imports of manufactured products; and

   iii. loans to facilitate import sales from the Small Business Finance Corporation and People's Finance Corporation that will provide the financing needed to increase sales of imported products.

B. *Measures to be Taken by the Government of the United States*

   1. The Government of the United States will provide support to U.S. auto parts suppliers and the appropriate organizations in their activities to promote the sale of U.S. auto parts to Japanese vehicle manufacturers and the sale of U.S. auto parts to Japanese transplant vehicle manufacturers.

   2. The Government of the United States will provide support to U.S. auto parts suppliers' activities to promote continued competitiveness of their goods through appropriate measures.

   3. The Government of the United States will encourage the U.S. auto parts suppliers to continue to provide competitive products under competitive terms and conditions.

IV. Regulatory Reform by the Government of Japan

A. *Japanese Government Procedures in the Auto Parts Aftermarket*

General Principles

   1. The Government of Japan will initiate deregulation of the auto parts aftermarket through full and effective implementation of the measures set out below. The purpose of these deregulation measures is to improve market access for competitive foreign parts suppliers in the Japanese auto parts aftermarket, while maintaining appropriate automotive safety and environmental standards.

   2. In addition to the specific measures below, the Government of Japan will continue to review its regulations affecting the auto parts after-

market, and will evaluate and respond as soon as possible to requests brought forward by foreign vehicle manufacturers and auto parts suppliers to improve market access for them in the automotive parts aftermarket.

Deregulation of Disassembling Repair Requirements (Critical Parts Requirements)

3. The Government of Japan will implement the following measures with respect to the administrative definition of "disassembling repair." Under paragraph 1 of Article 64 of the Road Vehicles Act, disassembling repairs must be inspected by MOT if not performed at a certified or designated garage. The definition of disassembling repair is determined administratively by MOT, and includes certain parts replacement operations that involve the dismounting of one or more of the following seven vehicle systems: engine system, power train system, running system, steering system, brake system, suspension system, and coupling devices. Auto parts replacement operations outside the definition of disassembling repair can be performed by anyone without requiring MOT reassembling inspection.

   a. Government of Japan will increase the transparency of the definition of disassembling repair in order to improve understanding by Japanese consumers, repair and service businesses, and foreign and domestic auto parts suppliers regarding the legal alternatives for automotive repair and servicing at certified garages or other repair and service businesses. In this regard:

      i. Annex A indicates the current status under the definition of disassembling repair of certain commonly performed parts replacement operations.

      ii. Upon request by an interested person, MOT will inform the interested person, in principle within 30 days, whether a specific parts replacement operation is or is not within the definition of disassembling repair, and will inform repair and service businesses and auto parts wholesalers and retailers. If the request is submitted in writing, MOT will respond in writing, if so requested.

   b. The Government of Japan will conduct a broad and full review of the definition of disassembling repair. The purpose of the review will be to increase alternatives for automotive repair and servicing in Japan to the fullest extent possible, through removing from the definition of disassembling repair all parts replacement operations which are not necessary to include in the definition in order to ensure safety and environmental protection. The review will be completed within one year from August 23, 1995.

c. In the review, the Government of Japan will specify each parts replacement operation which no longer will be within the definition of disassembling repair, and will inform designated, certified, and other repair garages as well as auto parts wholesalers and retailers of each decision to remove a parts replacement operation from the definition as soon as such decision is made. In this regard, the Government of Japan is pleased to note that changing shock absorbers, struts, power steering systems and trailer hitches will be removed from the definition of disassembling repair within two months from August 23, 1995.

d. In conducting the review, the Government of Japan will bear fully in mind the purpose of the review as stated in paragraph b. and will give due consideration to the progress of motor vehicle technology, regulations in other countries regarding the replacement and inspection of the particular parts under review, and requests and comments submitted by interested parties including foreign and domestic auto parts companies.

e. The Government of Japan will set up a contact point in MOT which deals with requests and complaints with regard to the definition of disassembling repair, and will establish and publish a procedure in which MOT responds to the requests and complaints, in principle within one month from receiving them. If the response of MOT is not favorable to those who made the request, MOT will provide them with the specific reason for the response and give them an opportunity to request a review of the response. The request or complaint may be submitted orally or in writing. If it is submitted in writing, MOT will respond in writing, if so requested. The review of the response will be completed in principle within one month from receiving the request for review. Any documents or materials associated with the request and complaint are open for public review, if those who made such request agree.

Deregulation of Certified and Designated Garages

4. The Government of Japan will implement the deregulation below regarding certified and designated repair garages that will create opportunities for new certified and designated repair garages.

Space Requirements

a. Effective on July 1, 1995, MOT reduced the minimum floor space required for certified garages, so that the space requirement for servicing ordinary-sized cars is the same as for servicing small-sized cars (i.e., 72 square meters as compared to 82 square meters previously for ordinary-sized cars).

Machinery and Tool Requirements
b. Effective on July 1, 1995, MOT reduced the number of tools and equipment items required for certified and designated garages, from 41 to 30 and 61 to 44 respectively. Following this reduction, MOT will continue to review the possibility of further reduction of the remaining number of tools and equipment items.

Mechanic Requirements
c. Within one year from August 23, 1995, MOT will reduce the number of government-qualified mechanics required for certified and designated garages from two to one, and from three to two, respectively. (Note: Certified garages still will be required to have two mechanics, but only one government-qualified mechanic. For designated garages, the current requirement is to have five mechanics, three of which must be government-qualified. Upon implementation of this measure, the total number of required mechanics will remain five, but the number of required government-qualified mechanics will be reduced to two.)

Special Designated Garages

5. In order to increase opportunities for repair businesses in Japan to become designated garages, the Government of Japan will implement the following measures within eighteen months from August 23, 1995.
   a. Certified garages that meet all other requirements for becoming a designated garage except the requirement of having an inspection facility, will be eligible to become special designated garages. Special designated garages will be allowed to perform repairs for *shaken* inspections, and perform the inspection at the inspection site of another designated garage.
   b. Special designated garages may form a cooperative and jointly operate an inspection site. Such garages may be eligible for Government of Japan low interest loan programs, and tax incentives for cooperatives.

Specialized Certified Garages

6. In order to allow repair and service facilities to specialize in only certain types of activities, within eighteen months from August 23, 1995 the Government of Japan will provide the option for a repair

or service facility to be certified to perform "disassembling repair" under paragraph 1 of Article 64 of the Road Vehicles Act for one or any combination of the seven vehicle systems to which the reassembling inspection requirement applies.

7. Examples of specialized repair and service facilities include certified brake repair and service facilities and certified transmission repair and service facilities. The decision of what repair or service operations to specialize in will be the decision of individual businesses. The Government of Japan will approve specialized certification for any combination of repair or service operations within the definition of disassembling repair, provided the applicant meets the appropriate requirements.

8. Specialized service and repair facilities will not be required:
   a. to have more than one government-qualified mechanic;
   b. to have floor space greater than the minimum space directly required to conduct the disassembling repair that the facilities are certified to conduct;
   c. to have tools and equipment items other than the minimum tools and equipment items directly required to conduct the disassembling repair that the facilities are certified to conduct; or
   d. to have any inspection by MOT of its certified repair work.

Deregulation of Modification Inspection Requirements

9. Within three months from August 23, 1995, the Government of Japan will deregulate requirements regarding modification inspections pursuant to Article 67 of the Road Vehicles Act. For any minor modification of the vehicle structure or configuration, the Government of Japan will eliminate the requirements to:
   a. submit the vehicle to modification inspection conducted by the MOT Land Transport Office;
   b. present the vehicle certificate of inspection to the MOT Land Transport Office; and
   c. pay the weight tax.
   "Minor" modifications of a vehicle's structure or configuration include automotive accessories attached by means other than welding or riveting. Examples of automotive accessories involved in minor modifications include those listed in Annex B.

10. The standards for passing a regular *shaken* inspection will be applied equally to motor vehicles that have, and to those that have not, undergone a "minor" modification within the meaning described in paragraph 9.

11. The Government of Japan will set up a contact point in MOT which deals with requests and complaints with regard to modification inspection and alteration to the information on the motor vehicle inspection certificate, and establish and publish a procedure in which MOT responds to the requests and complaints, in principle within one month from receiving them. If the response of MOT is not favorable to those who made the request, MOT will provide them with the specific reason for the response and give them an opportunity to request a review of the response. The request or complaint may be submitted orally or writing. If it is submitted in writing, MOT will respond in writing, if so requested. The review of the response will be completed in principle within one month from receiving the request for review. Any documents or materials associated with the request and complaint are open for public review, if those who made such request agree.

Notification of Regulatory Changes and Non-Discrimination against Foreign Auto Parts

12. The Government of Japan will immediately implement an active campaign to inform automotive repair and service facility owners, mechanics, consumers, and MOT Land Transport Offices of the regulatory changes described in paragraphs 3 through 11 above and to emphasize the non-discriminatory application of regulatory requirements. Among other things, the campaign will strongly emphasize to car dealers, repair and service facility owners, mechanics, and consumers that motor vehicle inspections and other regulatory requirements pursuant to the *shaken* inspection or other regulations do not and will not discriminate against vehicles equipped with foreign or "non-genuine" parts. In this regard, the Government of Japan will inform the public, and specifically in writing will instruct MOT Land Transport Office inspectors as well as repair garages certified by MOT that their inspections pursuant to *shaken* inspection or other regulations are not to discriminate against vehicles equipped with foreign or "non-genuine" parts.

Import Promotion

13. The Government of Japan will issue guidance encouraging the Japan Automotive Parts Association (JAPA) to endorse foreign auto parts as "superior parts" (*yuryou buhin*) based on the same criteria and evidence that is applied to Japanese auto parts.

14. To further enhance access for foreign-made aftermarket auto parts, the Ministry of International Trade and Industry sent memoranda

through business associations to their members providing guidance to auto parts distributors that:

a. they refrain from any form of discrimination when handling foreign-made parts;

b. they indicate the options available to repair businesses and customers (such options to include foreign-made parts), and that they provide their customers with opportunities to choose such parts;

15. With regard to parts purchasing by repair and service businesses, MOT sent memoranda through business associations to their members providing guidance to repair and service businesses that:

a. they refrain from any form of discrimination as to whether parts are foreign- or Japanese-made when choosing replacement parts to be used for servicing and repairs; and

b. when possible, they indicate to customers the options available (such options to include the use of foreign-made replacement parts), and that they provide their customers with opportunities to choose such parts.

16. The Government of Japan is pleased to note the statements by the replacement parts distributors group (JAPA, the Japan Federation of Auto Parts Sales Association, and the Japan Auto Accessories Manufacturers' Association) and the Japan Automobile Service Promotion Association which declared, in compliance with the guidance referred to in 14 and 15 above, their policies:

a. to be impartial with regard to parts (whether foreign- or Japanese-made) when choosing replacement parts for servicing and repairs; and

b. to indicate to their customers the options available, these options to include the use of foreign-made replacement parts.

17. The Government of Japan is pleased to note that the automotive manufacturers (including members of JAMA and the Japan Automotive Parts Industries Association) will make it fully clear to parts sales companies and joint sales companies with whom they have dealings that the handling of parts (other than genuine parts) and the handling of foreign parts are, as a general rule, to be conducted freely by each company, without adverse discrimination based on capital affiliation; that business decisions are left up to them; and that neither they nor their customers should be concerned about their business relationships with the automotive manufacturers or the parts sales companies and joint sales companies based on their decision to carry foreign parts.

18. In addition to the measures described above, the Government of Japan intends to consider or implement other possible import promotion measures related to auto parts. Among other measures, the Government of Japan will:

   a. welcome and support the establishment of contact points by auto parts distributors, auto parts sales companies and joint sales companies or related vehicle manufacturers for the purpose of facilitating contacts between foreign auto parts suppliers and those companies regarding potential opportunities in the Japanese auto parts aftermarket; and

   b. support the creation of a database and information network with such information as data matching motor vehicle types with compatible foreign replacement parts, and technical data for use by repair garages. Until the database and information network are created and working effectively, the Government of Japan will actively support foreign auto parts suppliers' activities in the aftermarket to provide information about their products through other measures such as publishing notice in automotive journals published by relevant associations and holding seminars.

B. *Japanese Government Procedures in the Area of Standards and Certification*

   1. While most automotive standards already have been coordinated among Japan, the United States and Europe, the Government of Japan continues to play an active role to achieve further international harmonization of standards.

   2. The Government of Japan intends to reach a conclusion in good faith under the consultations with the Government of the United States on the standards and certification issues raised by the Government of the United States (see Annex C) to mutual satisfaction within a period of nine months from August 23, 1995. In this regard, the Government of Japan intends to hold standards and certification expert consultations with the Government of the United States. When additional issues are raised in the future, the Government of Japan intends to reach a conclusion by mutually acceptable deadlines in the same manner.

   3. The Government of Japan will continue to facilitate importation of foreign vehicles by dispatching officials to the dealer sites to conduct inspection of automobiles imported under the Preferential Handling Procedure (PHP), and will continue to dispatch such officials on a timely basis to meet foreign vehicle manufacturers' requests.

   4. To assist efforts by foreign vehicle manufacturers to obtain Japanese Type Designation Approval (TDA), the Government of Japan is ready

to study the possibility of carrying out examinations according to Japanese testing procedures in a foreign country concerned, where appropriate, by means of utilizing official motor vehicle testing institutions of such country, or stationing an official who is in charge of conducting those examinations at the Japanese Embassy or a Consulate General in the country. In this regard, the Government of Japan will continue to station a technical official of the Ministry of Transport on a full-time basis at the Japanese Consulate General in Detroit as necessary within the limits of budgetary appropriations.

C. *Anticompetitive Practices*

1. The Government of Japan affirms its commitment to prevent and eliminate anticompetitive practices in all industries including the automotive sector.

2. The Government of Japan will support the voluntary efforts by Japanese firms to develop and implement internal AMA compliance programs and is willing to provide advice when requested by such firms.

3. The Government of Japan recognizes that the JFTC issued the Antimonopoly Act Guidelines Concerning Distribution Systems and Business Practices on July 11, 1991 (the "Guidelines"). The Guidelines are applicable to all industries including the automotive industry, and specifically describe types of conduct with respect to Japanese distribution systems and business practices that may impede free and fair competition and violate the AMA.

4. The JFTC affirms its commitment to effectively enforce and strictly apply the AMA in accordance with relevant guidelines to address anticompetitive practices in all industries including the automotive sector.

5. In June 1993, the JFTC published the results of its survey on the passenger car industry and its survey on the auto parts industry. Although the JFTC did not find any AMA violations, it pointed out several practices to be addressed from the point of view of competition policy. The JFTC recognizes the serious efforts of the relevant companies to address these practices and will observe so that the practices continue to be addressed by such companies.

6. Any person, including foreign vehicle manufacturers and Japanese vehicle dealers, may report to the JFTC suspected violations of the AMA. Suspected violations may be reported to the newly enhanced and expanded Information Management Office of the JFTC. Any information regarding suspected violation of the AMA may be reported in writing or orally. The confidentiality of such report or information will be strictly protected and such report or information

may be provided anonymously. The JFTC will review such report or information promptly and will take appropriate steps to address such suspected violations depending on the content and reliability of the information.

7. Under Article 28 of the AMA, the JFTC is to perform its duties independently.

V. Assessing Implementation of the Measures

A. *Data Collection*
   1. The Government of Japan will provide the following data for annual reviews:
      a. the number and value of new foreign vehicles sold in Japan;
      b. the number and value of new foreign vehicles sold in Japan by country of export;
      c. the number of new foreign vehicles sold in Japan by manufacturer;
      d. the number of new foreign vehicles sold through direct franchise agreements with Japanese dealers;
      e. the number of new vehicles exported to Japan from Japanese transplants; and
      f. official import statistics for auto parts.
   2. The Government of the United States will provide the following information for annual reviews:
      a. official U.S. export statistics for motor vehicles and auto parts; and
      b. other relevant national, regional, and international official statistics.

B. *Objective Criteria*
   The assessment of the implementation of the Measures, as well as the evaluation of progress achieved, will be based on the overall consideration of the qualitative and quantitative criteria set out below. These qualitative and quantitative criteria will be considered as a set, and no one criterion will be determinative of the assessment of the Measures, or the evaluation of progress achieved. These criteria do not constitute numerical targets, but rather are to be used for the purpose of evaluating progress achieved toward the goals of the Framework and the goals of these Measures.

   For purposes of this assessment, the Government of Japan and the Government of the United States are to seek and consider any available, relevant and reasonable data or information, including the data set out above, regarding the following quantitative or qualitative criteria.

Motor Vehicles

1. *Qualitative Criteria*
   a. efforts by the Japanese vehicle manufacturers to promote open and competitive distribution systems for motor vehicles in Japan;
   b. efforts of foreign vehicle manufacturers to offer competitive products in Japan under competitive terms and conditions, including with respect to price, variety of products, delivery lead time, and after-sales service; and
   c. private sector actions, including AMA compliance programs, to ensure compliance with the AMA.
2. *Quantitative Criteria*
   a. change in the number and value of new foreign motor vehicles sold in Japan in total and by country of export, and change in the number of new foreign motor vehicles sold in Japan by manufacturer; and
   b. change in the number of direct franchise agreements concluded between foreign vehicle manufacturers and Japanese dealers, and the number of foreign motor vehicles sold through such dealers.

Auto Parts

1. *Qualitative Criteria*
   a. efforts by Japanese vehicle manufacturers in Japan and their transplants to broaden suppliers' sales opportunities through design-in and supplier outreach programs, localization of R&D, and transparency in purchasing practices;
   b. procurement of parts by Japanese vehicle manufacturers and Japanese transplant vehicle manufacturers without discrimination against suppliers based on their capital affiliation;
   c. efforts of foreign auto parts suppliers to offer competitive products under competitive terms and conditions, including with respect to price, quality, and delivery lead time.
2. *Quantitative Criteria*
   a. change in the value of foreign auto parts exported to and imported into Japan as measured by Japanese and foreign country official statistics, and other available data.
   b. change in the extent of localization, as part of the Japanese vehicle manufacturers' globalization efforts, considering data on purchases of parts made in the United States and vehicle production by Japanese transplant vehicle manufacturers in the United States.
   c. change in purchases of U.S. auto parts by Japanese transplant vehicle manufacturers in the United States.

Aftermarket Parts

1. *Qualitative Criteria*
   a. the status of deregulation of the definition of disassembling repair, the standards for specialized certified garages, and of other deregulatory actions within the scope of the Measures regarding the auto parts aftermarket; and
   b. the Government of Japan's responsiveness to complaints and requests by interested persons regarding the clarification or deregulation of the definition of disassembling repair or modification inspections.
2. *Quantitative Criteria*
   a. change in the value and share of foreign parts purchased in Japan for aftermarket use; and
   b. change in the number of specialized certified garages and designated garages.

General Qualitative Criteria

   a. market conditions, including exchange rates, and
   b. the implementation of all other measures of the Measures.

VI. Consultations

The Government of Japan and the Government of the United States are prepared to hold annual consultations to assess implementation of the Measures, and to evaluate progress achieved based on the criteria in Section V(B) of the Measures. The annual consultations will be held until the end of 2000, at which point the two Governments will decide whether it is necessary to continue these consultations.

Annex A. Status of Particular Parts Replacement Operations under the Definition of Disassembling Repair

Part	Replacement not in Definition	Replacement in Definition
Service Items		
Additives, Fuel	X	
Additives, Lubricating	X	
Additives, Transmission	X	
Air Filter	X	

(continued)

Annex A *(continued)*

Part	Replacement not in Definition	Replacement in Definition
Air Fresheners	X	
Antifreeze and Coolant	X	
Brake Fluid	X	
Breather Filters	X	
Cleaner, Carburetor	X	
Cleaners & Waxes, Body	X	
Cleaners, Custom Wheel	X	
Coolant Filters	X	
Lubricating Oil	X	
Motor Oil	X	
Oil Filter	X	
PCV Valve	X	
Transmission Filters	X	
Transmission Fluid	X	
Transmission Modulator	X	
Warning Light	X	
Windshield Chemicals	X	
Windshield Wipers, Arms and Blades	X	

Repair / Replacement Items

Alternators and Parts	X	
Battery	X	
Battery Cable and Clamps	X	
Brake Springs		X
Caliper Parts		X
Calipers		X
Canister Filters	X	
Carburetors, Kits, and Parts	X	
Catalytic Converters	X	
Choke Pull-offs	X	
Clamp	X	
Clutch & Parts		X
Clutch Plate and Flywheel Resurfacing		X
Clutch Release Bearings		X
Condensers	X	
Contact Points	X	
Coolers, Engine Oil	X	

Part	Replacement not in Definition	Replacement in Definition
Coolers, Transmission Oil	X	
CV Joints		X
Disc Brake Parts		X
Disc Brake Rotors		X
Distributors and Parts	X	
EGR Control Valve	X	
Exhaust Pipes	X	
Fan Belts (including V-Belts and Serpentine Belts)	X	
Fitting and Tubing		
(Fuel Line)	X	
(Brake Line)		X
Flashers	X	
Fuel Injector Systems	X	
Fuel Pumps and Parts	X	
Fuses and Breakers	X	
Gaskets and Seals	X	
Gasoline Filters	X	
Generators and Parts	X	
Headers, Mufflers, Resonators	X	
Hose Clamps	X	
Hose, Heater	X	
Hose, Radiator	X	
Ignition Cable	X	
Ignition Coils	X	
Ignition System, Transistorized	X	
Lamp Bulbs	X	
Lining, Brake		X
Master Cylinders and Parts		X
McPherson Struts	X*	
Overload Shock Absorbers	X*	
Pads, New Lined		X
Pads, Relined		X
Power Steering Hose & Kits	X*	
Radiator	X	
Radiator Caps	X	
Sealants	X	
Sealed Beams	X	

(continued)

Annex A *(continued)*

Part	Replacement not in Definition	Replacement in Definition
Shoes, New Lined		X
Shoes, Relined		X
Shoes, Unlined		X
Solenoid and Switches	X	
Spark Plugs	X	
Starters and Parts	X	
Tail Pipes	X	
Thermostats	X	
Tie Rods and Tie Rod Ends		X
Tires	X	
Valves, Tire	X	
Water Pumps	X	
Wheel Beatings		X
Wheel Balancing Weights	X	
Wheel Cylinder		X

Items marked "" are to be classified "Replacement Not in Definition" after amendment of the related MOT ordinance based on IV.A.3.C. of the Measures.

Annex B. Representative List of Automotive Parts Involved in Minor Modifications

1. Roof Racks
2. Trailer Hitches
3. Sunroofs
4. Air Spoilers
5. Air Dams
6. Body Side Molding
7. Bumper Guards
8. Grille Guards
9. Enclosed Luggage Carriers
10. Bumper Mounted Fog or Driving Lights
11. Winches
12. Headlight / Fog Light Gravel Shields
13. Sun Visors
14. Tow Hooks
15. Mufflers
16. Exhaust Pipes
17. Truck Bed Liners
18. Antennae
19. Pickup Truck Running Boards
20. Hood Wind Deflectors
21. Hood Scoops
22. Fender Skirts
23. Bike and Ski Racks
24. Convertible Tops
25. Deflectors and Screens
26. Exhaust Pipe Tips / Extensions
27. Mirrors
28. Roll Bars
29. Louvers
30. Splash Shields and Mud Guards
31. Wheels
32. Tires

33. License Plate Frames and
    Mountings
34. Alarms and Security Systems
35. Bumpers and Push Bars
36. Window Tinting
37. Shock Absorbers and Struts

38. Tow Ropes, Straps
39. Awnings (motor homes)
40. Camper Shells
41. Covers (car, truck, fender, front end)
42. Graphics Packages and Tape Strip
    Kits

Annex C. Standards and Certification Issues

1. Acceptability of the United States Environmental Protection Agency's ("USEPA") certification to meet the requirements for the Government of Japan's engine exhaust and emissions test.
2. Elimination of the catalytic converter overheat warning systems requirement by the Government of Japan.
3. Acceptability of U.S. head restraint designs and certifications to meet the requirements of the Government of Japan's head restraint test.
4. Acceptability of front turn signal lamps that meet U.S. certification standards to meet the requirements of the Government of Japan's complete on/off function of front turn signal lamps test.
5. Acceptability of the U.S. vehicle identification number ("VIN") stamping requirement as the functional equivalent of the Government of Japan's VIN stamping requirement.
6. Elimination of the requirement for submission of FMVSS 208 data for Type Designation and acceptability of the FMVSS 203 as functionally equivalent to the Japanese steering impact test.
7. Elimination of the side-slip test requirement by the Government of Japan for vehicles imported under the Preferential Handling Procedures ("PHP").
8. Assurance of equal treatment of all manufacturers' imports and parallel imports at the MOT Land Transport Offices.
9. Acceptability of the U.S. SAE test as the functional equivalent of the Government of Japan's light alloy wheel test.
10. Elimination of rear side marker lamp spacing standard of the Government of Japan or acceptability of the European Community rear side marking lamp spacing standard as equivalent to the Government of Japan's standard.
11. Reduction of the emission audit levels for the PHP to the same level as those used in the Type Designation System ("TDS").
12. Acceptability of emission testing data and certification of two-wheel drive versions of a vehicle model to fulfill the data requirements for full-time four-wheel drive versions of the same model.
13. Acceptability of USEPA's derived deterioration factors for "trucks" in the case where those vehicles, for emissions purposes, are classified as cars in Japan (e.g. Jeep Cherokee).

14. Acceptability of vehicles that meet the lamp installation requirements of FMVSS 108 for the purposes of the Government of Japan's head lamp spacing requirements.
15. Elimination of requirement to type-designate four-lamp head lamp systems by the Government of Japan and acceptability of head lamps certified to the ECE Regulations.
16. Elimination of minimum 400 mm seat width requirement by the Government of Japan.
17. Acceptability of USEPA alternative test procedures for emission deterioration factors.
18. Either (1) adoption of a policy that front fog lamps are permitted so long as they do not impede the performance of mandated lamps or (2) adoption of appropriate, transparent specifications for front fog lamps.
19. Acceptability of final presentation of Preliminary Type Approval Test or TDS documentation in certain foreign cities.
20. Permission for manufacturer to conduct final emissions inspection under PHP.
21. Permission for manufacturer to conduct emissions and noise tests under PHP.
22. Acceptability of PHP test data for subsequent TNS application.
23. Acceptability of testing at approved foreign country testing facilities or manufacturers own approved facilities.

Notes

Chapter One

1. "U.S. Antidumping Duties Imposed on Supercomputers from Japan," *USIS Washington File*, September 26, 1997 (electronic version from USIA website).

2. See Richard Boltuck and Robert Litan, eds., *Down in the Dumps: Administration of the Unfair Trade Laws* (Brookings, 1991); and Pietro S. Nivola, *Regulating Unfair Trade* (Brookings, 1993).

3. For an example of measuring the impact of trade barriers see C. Fred Bergsten and Marcus Noland, *Reconcilable Differences? United States-Japan Economic Conflict* (Washington: Institute for International Economics, 1993), pp. 179–190; and Yoko Sazanami, Shujiro Urata, and Hirok Kawai, *Measuring the Costs of Protection in Japan* (Washington: Institute of International Economics, 1995).

4. Office of the U.S. Trade Representative, *1998 National Trade Estimate Report on Foreign Trade Barriers* (Government Printing Office, 1998); and American Chamber of Commerce in Japan, *1997 United States-Japan Trade White Paper* (Tokyo: ACCJ, 1997).

Chapter Two

1. Edward J. Lincoln, *Japan's Unequal Trade* (Brookings, 1990).

2. Detail on wine and beer imports are taken from Organization for Economic Cooperation and Development, *International Trade by Commodities Statistics, HS Rev 1988-1996* (Paris, 1997), on CD-ROM.

3. Calculation based on the World Bank, *World Development Indicators, 1998* (Washington, 1998).

4. Masaru Yoshitomi, "The Japanese Problem and Price Differentials between Home and Abroad," Japan Research Institute and Wharton School, University of Pennsylvania, September 24, 1994, p. 7.

5. Value data are from Statistics Bureau, Management and Coordination Agency, *Japan Statistical Yearbook, 1998* (Tokyo, 1997), p. 417; volume data are from Japan Development Bank, *Principal Economic and Social Indicators* (Tokyo, September 1997), p. 16.

6. Based on data from World Bank, *World Tables* (Washington, various years), on CD-ROM.

7. For an earlier review of such analyses, see Edward J. Lincoln, *Japan's Unequal Trade* (Brookings, 1990), pp. 18–25.

8. For additional analysis of low imports and the notion of trade-balance constrained imports, see Richard Katz, *Japan: The System That Soured* (M.E. Sharpe, 1998), pp. 258–71.

9. For further analysis of this point, see Lincoln, *Japan's Unequal Trade*, pp. 72–80.

10. This ratio is prominently shown by the Japan External Trade Organization in the statistics section of its web page (www.jetro.go.jp/FACTS).

11. Calculated for 1980 from data in Japan Economic Institute, *Yearbook of U.S.-Japan Relations in 1983* (Washington, 1994), pp. 111–12; and for 1996 from trade data on OECD, *International Trade by Commodities Statistics,* on CD-ROM.

12. Data on value and volume of crude petroleum imports, and total import values, are from Statistics Bureau, Management and Coordination Agency, *Japan Statistical Yearbook, 1998* (Tokyo, 1997), pp. 417, 421.

13. "'Hito-Nihonjin kara Kurinton Daitōryō e no Shokan' o Megutte" [Concerning 'A Letter from One Japanese to President Clinton'], *Kokusai Keizai Kenkyū* (Tokyo: International Economic Research Center, October 1994), p. 17. The letter referred to was written by Mitsuharu Ito, and this article included my response to his letter and his rebuttal of that response.

14. Ministry of Foreign Affairs, "Japan Is a Major Export Market for the U.S.," on MOFA web page (http:www.mofa.go.jp).

15. Philip William Lowe, "Resource Convergence and Intra-Industry Trade," 1991, Economic Research Department, Reserve Bank of Australia.

16. Lincoln, *Japan's Unequal Trade*, pp. 39–46.

17. Mitsuo Hosen, *Japan's Intra-Industry Trade*, Ph. D. dissertation, University of Pennsylvania, 1992. His results have also been published in Japanese in book form.

18. Kazumasa Iwata, "Intra-Industry Trade and the Japanese Economy," Working Paper 39 (University of Tokyo, Komaba, Department of Social and International Relations, August 1993).

19. Mark Tilton, *Restrained Trade: Cartels in Japan's Basic Materials Industries* (Cornell University Press, 1996), especially pp. 50–189.

20. Lincoln, *Japan's Unequal Trade*, pp. 106–07.

21. Lowe, "Resource Convergence and Intra-Industry Trade."

22. The results of estimation of this equation are as follows:

IIT = 9.931 + 7.75 Ln(Population) + 11.2 Ln(GDP/Population) –46.9 (Japan dummy)

t = 0.620   3.282   2.730   – 2.438

Significance = 46%   99%   99%   98%

R^2 = 0.359

Adjusted R^2 = 0.279

F = 4.476 (significant at 99% level)

Sources: Calculated using intra-industry trade index numbers reported in table 2-1. Population and GDP data are from World Bank, *World Development Indicators, 1997* (Washington), on CD-ROM; information on Taiwan provided by Taipei Economic and Cultural Representative Office in the United States; and GDP data for Germany in 1988 are from International Monetary Fund, *International Financial Statistics Yearbook 1993* (Washington).

Note: Significance figures report percentage probability that estimated coefficients are different from zero.

23. The population of Taiwan in 1996 was 21 million, compared with 126 million in Japan—or 16.8 percent. The Taiwan population figure is from Government Information Office, ROC, on its web site (www.gio.tw/info/nation/en/glance/ch_c.htm). Japan data are from Statistics Bureau, *Japan Statistical Yearbook, 1998*, p.33.

24. Lincoln, *Japan's Unequal Trade*, pp. 50–53.

25. Advisory Committee on Trade Policy and Negotiations (ACTPN), *Major Findings and Policy Recommendations on U.S.-Japan Trade Policy: Report of the Advisory Committee for Trade Policy and Negotiations* (January 1993), p. 10.

26. For an extensive discussion of the conceptual issues involved in defining and measuring service sector trade, see Christopher Findlay, "Trade in Services in the Asia-Pacific Region," *Asia-Pacific Economic Literature*, vol. 4 (September 1990), pp. 3–20.

27. Bank of Japan, *Balance of Payments Monthly* (November 1998), pp. 5, 18, and (August 1981).

28. Findlay, " Trade in Services in the Asia-Pacific Region," p. 8.

29. For an explanation of the changes see Christopher L. Bach, "U.S. International Transactions, Revised Estimates for 1986–89," *Survey of Current Business*, vol. 78 (July 1998), pp. 47–57; and see also Obie G. Whicard, "International Services: New Information on U.S. Transactions with Unaffiliated Foreigners," *Survey of Current Business*, vol. 68 (October 1988), pp. 27–34.

30. Total U.S. merchandise exports for this calculation are from Department of Commerce, *Statistical Abstract of the United States, 1990* (Washington, 1990), pp. 806, 808; and Department of Commerce, *Survey of Current Business*, vol. 78 (July 1998), p. 78.

31. *Survey of Current Business*, vol. 69 (September 1989), p. 49; and Michael A. Mann and others, "U.S. International Sales and Purchases of Private Services," *Survey of Current Business*, vol. 78 (October 1998), p. 93.

32. Ministry of Transport, *Un'yu Hakusho, 1997* [Transportation White Paper] (Tokyo, 1998), p. 12, of appendix tables, and *1994*, p. 32.

33. From statistical data from All Nippon Airways, "Nichibei Kōkū Kigyō ni yoru Nichibeikan Yusō," undated.

34. Ministry of Transport, *A Review of Aviation Relationship between Japan and the United States* (Tokyo, undated).

35. Ministry of International Trade and Industry, *Keizai Hakusho* [Economic White Paper] (Tokyo 1995), p. 241.

36. Economic Planning Agency, *Bukka Repōto '97* [Price Report '97] (Tokyo: Keizai Kikaku Kyōkai, October 1997), p. 27.

37. "Wide Price Gaps Also Seen in Services," *Daily Yomiuri*, May 28, 1995, p. 6; and "Naigai Kakakusa ga Shukushō," *Nihon Keizai Shimbun*, July 9, 1997, p. 5.

38. "Pēsu Mēkā Naigai Kakakusa: Saikō de Ōbei no 6.9-bai" [The Domestic-Foreign Price Difference for Pace Makers: At the Peak, 6.9 Times U.S.-European Prices], *Nihon Keizai Shimbun*, August 2, 1997, p. 5.

39. All data here collected personally by the author and family members in June 1994 in Japan and the United States.

40. Data collected by the author at Ishimaru Denki, June 1998, and Sears (Montgomery Mall, Bethesda, Maryland), September 1998. Ishimaru Denki had thirty-eight models on display ranging from a low of 150 liters (5.3 cubic feet) for ¥39,800 ($284) to a high of 501 liters (17.7 cubic feet) at ¥349,800 ($2,499). Sears had seventy-six models on display, ranging from 9.6 cubic feet at $338 to 29.8 cubic feet at $1,699 (with a slightly smaller 28.2 cubic-foot model at a higher $2,199).

41. Economic Planning Agency, *Bukka Repōto '97* (Tokyo, 1997), p. 29.

42. "Denryoku no Sōkyōkyū Kosuto: Nihon, Beikoku no 2-bai Ijō" [Overall Supply Prices for Electric Power: Japan More than 2 Times the U.S.], *Nihon Keizai Shimbun*, November 3, 1997, p. 3.

43. Concerns about utility company procurement were raised in Office of the U.S. Trade Representative, *1994 Trade Estimate Report on Foreign Trade Barriers* (Government Printing Office, 1994), p. 47. Further concerns were raised in the 1995 report, USTR, *1995 Trade Estimate Report on Foreign Trade Barriers*.

44. Masaru Yoshitomi, "The Japanese Problem and Price Differentials between Home and Abroad," unpublished paper for the Japan Economic Seminar, September 24, 1994, pp. 11–12.

45. Ministry of International Trade and Industry, *Tsūshō Hakusho, 1996* (Tokyo: Ministry of Finance Printing Office, 1996), p. 217.

46. Ken'ichiro Yanagisawa, "Nihon no Bukka wa Takakunai" [Japanese Prices Are Not High], *Shukan Tōyō Keizai*, June 15, 1996, pp. 120–24.

47. Organization for Economic Cooperation and Development, www.oecd. org/std/gdpperca.htm. The nominal exchange rate for 1996 was ¥108.8 per dollar, while the PPP rate was ¥172.

48. Ministry of International Trade and Industry, *Keizai Hakusho*, 1995 (Heisei 7), pp. 70–74, 86.

49. Bukka Antei Seisaku Kaigi Bukka Kōzō Seisaku Iinkai [Conference on Price Stability Policy], *Kakaku Settei ni Kansuru Kigyō Kōdō Kenkyūkai Hōkokusho: Kōzō Henka ni Chokumen suru Ryūtsū no Kadai* [Report concerning Price Formation of the Research Group on Corporate Behavior: The Topic of Distribution Facing Structural Change] (June 1997), p. 16.

50. "U.S.-Japan Price Gap Shows Yen Has Room to Fall: EPA," *Nikkei Net*, May 27, 1998 (www. nni.nikkei. co.jp/).

Chapter Three

1. Mark Mason, *American Multinationals and Japan: The Political Economy of Japanese Capital Controls 1899-1980* (Harvard University Press, 1992); and Dennis J. Encarnation, *Rivals beyond Trade: America versus Japan in Global Competition* (Cornell University Press, 1992), pp. 36-96.

2. The ACCJ reports 1,553 member firms, of which 119 are Japanese firms and 13 non-American-owned foreign firms. Data from http://www.accj.or.jp.

3. James C. Abegglen and Peter S. Kirby, "Largest Foreign Frms in Japan— The 1994 'Top 100,'" *Gemini Consulting (Japan) Newsletter*, November 1995.

4. Japan Economic Institute, "Statistical Profile: International Transactions of Japan in 1996," *JEI Report*, no. 45A (December 5, 1997), pp. 16–17.

5. Sylvia E. Bargas, "Direct Investment Positions for 1996," *Survey of Current Business*, vol. 77 (July 1997), pp. 34, 40.

6. JEI, "Statistical Profile," p. 17.

7. Japan's share of global GDP is calculated from data in World Bank, *World Development Indicators, 1997* (Washington), on CD-ROM.

8. Ministry of International Trade and Industry (MITI), *Gaishikei Kigyō no Dōkō, Dai-30kai* [Foreign-Affiliated Firm Trends, no. 30](Tokyo: Ministry of Finance Printing Office, 1998), p. 3.

9. Mahuaz Fahim-Nader and William J. Zeile, "Foreign Direct Investment in the United States," *Survey of Current Business*, vol. 77 (June 1997), pp. 54, 62; and Department of Commerce, *Statistical Abstract of the United States, 1997* (Washington, 1997), pp. 541–42. Employment ratio is for 1995, but sales ratio is for 1994.

10. David E. Weinstein, "Foreign Direct Investment and the *Keiretsu*: Rethinking U.S. and Japanese Policy," Working Paper 122 (Columbia Business School, Center on Japanese Economy and Business, June 1996), pp. 3–6.

11. Weinstein, "Foreign Direct Investment and the *Keiretsu*," p. 7.

12. Encarnation, *Rivals beyond Trade*, pp. 10–15.

13. Department of Commerce, *Foreign Direct Investment in the United States: Operations of U.S. Affiliates of Foreign Companies, Preliminary 1995 Estimates* (Washington, June 1997), table J-1; and Department of Commerce, *U.S. Direct*

Investment Abroad: Operations of U.S. Parent Companies and Their Foreign Affiliates, Preliminary 1995 Estimates, tables II.A.1 and III.A.1.

14. MITI, *Gaishikei Kigyō no Dōkō,* p. 84.

15. Department of Commerce, *U.S. Direct Investment Abroad,* tables II.A.1, III.A.1.

16. Author's conversation with Tower Records, Japan, 1996.

17. "GE Capital Will in Effect Take Over Toho Life for ¥72 Billion," *Japan Digest,* February 19, 1997; and Gillian Tett, "Braced for Invasion," *Financial Times,* July 25, 1997, p. 16.

18. William J. Zeile, "U.S. Intrafirm Trade in Goods," *Survey of Current Business,* vol. 77 (February 1997), pp. 25, 32. Bilateral figure is for 1992 rather than 1994.

19. MITI, *Gaishikei Kigyō no Dōkō, Number 30* [Foreign-Affiliated Firm Trends, no. 30] (Tokyo: Ministry of Finance Printing Office, March 1998), pp. 144, 151.

20. For a summary of explanations a few years ago, see Edward J. Lincoln, *Japan's New Global Role* (Brookings, 1993), pp. 70–77, or more recently, see Masaru Yoshitomi and Edward M. Graham, eds., *Foreign Direct Investment in Japan* (Edward Elgar, 1996).

21. For an excellent detailed history of Japanese barriers to investment from the turn of the century through the early 1980s, see Mason, *American Multinationals and Japan.*

22. The OLI view of direct investment is associated with John H. Dunning. See for example, John H. Dunning, *Multinational Enterprises and the Global Economy* (Addison Wesley, 1993).

23. This point is stressed by Edward M. Graham, "What Can the Theory of Foreign Direct Investment Tell Us about the Low Level of Foreign Firm Participation in the Economy of Japan?" in Graham and Yoshitomi, *Foreign Direct Investment in Japan,* p. 76.

24. Masaru Yoshitomi, "Behind the Low Level of Foreign Investment in Japan," *KKC Forum,* no. 5 (January 1995), pp. 1–4.

25. John H. Dunning, "Explaining Foreign Direct Investment in Japan: Some Theoretical Insights," in Graham and Yoshitomi, *Foreign Direct Investment in Japan,* p. 23.

26. For a review of the technological advantages of Japanese firms in the 1980s, see Lincoln, *Japan's New Global Role,* pp. 44–51.

27. Ministry of Finance, *Ōkurashō Kokusai Kin'yūkyoku Nempō,* 1995 ed. (Tokyo, 1996), p. 475.

28. Calculations based on data from Statistics Bureau, Management and Coordination Agency, *Japan Statistical Yearbook, 1998* (Tokyo, 1997), pp. 35, 665.

29. Calculations based on data from Statistics Bureau, *Japan Statistical Yearbook, 1998,* pp. 33, 602, 665.

30. American Chamber of Commerce in Japan, *Trade and Investment in Japan: The Current Environment* (Tokyo:1991), p. 2.

31. Recall that the recruit scandal of the late 1980s was about the efforts of a firm engaged in building a want-ad business through magazines and databases to overcome heavy regulatory obstacles by bribing politicians.

32. Statistics Bureau, *Japan Statistical Yearbook, 1998*, p. 562.

33. Japan Fair Trade Commission, *Kōsei Torihiki I'inkai Nenji Hōkoku* (Annual Report of the Japan Fair Trade Commission, 1994), appendix, pp. 21, 22, 26.

34. "Tai-Nai Tōshi: Chingin ya Zei no Takusa; Gaishikei ga Mondaishi" [Inward Investment in Japan: High Wages and Taxes Viewed as Problems by Foreign Firms], *Asahi Shimbun*, May 21, 1997, p. 15.

35. This list based on MITI, *Gaishikei Kigyō no Dōkō*, no. 30 (August 1997), pp. 73–80.

36. Japan Development Bank, *Annual Report 1996*, p. 28.

37. Japan External Trade Organization, *JETRO Business Support Center: Your Strategic Base in Japan* (Tokyo), undated brochure.

38. "FIND: Total Support for Doing Business in Japan," undated promotional brochure.

39. Based on author's conversation with Robert Grondine, a commercial attorney who has worked on these investment issues with the American Chamber of Commerce in Japan. Details on ownership from FIND brochure.

40. MITI, *Measures for Promoting Foreign Direct Investment in Japan* (Tokyo, January 1992).

41. For a more detailed review of the shift in Japanese investment abroad in the late 1980s, see Lincoln, *Japan's New Global Role*, pp. 57–68.

42. Data from MITI website. www.miti.go.jp/intro-e/images/ea225118.gif. under "Highlights of the 6th Basic Survey of Overseas Business Activities," November 1977.

43. *Survey of Current Business*, vol. 75 (August 1995), pp. 63–66; and vol. 71 (August 1991), pp. 55–58.

44. MITI, *Wagakuni Kigyō no Kaigai Jigyō Katsudō* (Survey of Overseas Business Activities of Japanese Companies), no. 26 (Tokyo, 1997), p. 38.

45. Customs clearance data record the cost of imports inclusive of all costs related to moving products from factories abroad through customs in Japan. On this basis, overall Japanese imports were ¥29.5 trillion in 1992 and ¥37.9 trillion in 1996, an increase of ¥8.4 trillion. Using balance of payments data, which measure imports exclusive of these transportation costs, imports were ¥26.3 trillion in 1992 and ¥34.4 trillion in 1996, an increase of ¥8.1 trillion. Statistics Bureau, Management and Coordination Agency, *Japan Statistical Yearbook, 1996*, p. 415, and *1998*, p. 417; and Bank of Japan, *Balance of Payments Monthly* (Tokyo, August 1997), p. 1.

46. MITI, *Wagakuni Kigyō no Kaigai Jigyō Katsudō* [Survey of Overseas Business Activities of Japanese Companies], no. 25 (Tokyo, 1995), pp. 172–73. ASEAN 5 includes Indonesia, Malaysia, Philippines, Singapore, and Thailand.

47. Ibid., p. 66.

48. Department of Commerce, *Statistical Abstract of the United States, 1989* (Washington, 1989), pp. 790–91, and 1997, pp. 803–06.

Chapter Four

1. For a review of the Reagan years, see Edward J. Lincoln, *Japan's Unequal Trade* (Brookings, 1990), pp. 142–53.

2. For an excellent review of the Bush administration's approach to trade negotiations with Japan, see Merit E. Janow, "Trading with an Ally: Progress and Discontent in U.S.-Japan Trade Relations," in Gerald L. Curtis, ed., *The United States, Japan, and Asia* (W. W. Norton, 1994), pp. 53–73.

3. Leonard J. Schoppa, *Bargaining with Japan: What American Pressure Can and Cannot Do* (Columbia University Press, 1997), pp. 49–76, describes the political calculations involved in dealing with Super 301 and the creation of SII.

4. See Janow, "Trading with an Ally," pp. 71–72.

5. Michael H. Armacost, *Friends or Rivals? The Insider's Account of U.S.-Japan Relations* (Columbia University Press, 1996), pp. 56–57.

6. Janow, "Trading with an Ally," pp. 72–73.

7. Leonard J. Schoppa, *Bargaining with Japan* and Norio Naka, *Predicting Outcomes in United States – Japan Trade Negotiations: The Political Process of the Structural Impediments Initiative* (Quorum Books, 1996).

8. Janow, "Trading with an Ally," pp. 72–73.

9. "The Tokyo Declaration on the U.S.-Japan Global Partnership," pp. 1–4.

10. United States Information Service, "Statement of Walter F. Mondale," press release, American Embassy, Tokyo, July 28, 1993.

11. The "Speech by Ambassador Walter F. Mondale," Japan National Press Club, November 5, 1993, for example, spends much more time on economic issues than on security.

12. "Joint Press Conference by Prime Minister Hashimoto and President Clinton on the Japan-United States Summit Meeting," April 25, 1997, from Government of Japan, Ministry of Foreign Affairs, web page.

13. "Keizai kara Anpo e: Nagarekawatta Nichibei Shunō Kaidan" [From Economics to Security: The Shifted Bilateral Summit Meeting], *Asahi Shimbun*, April 22, 1997, p. 2.

14. For the 1992 speech see "Technology: The Engine of Economic Growth," September 16, 1992, University of North Carolina website, http://metalab.unc.edu. See also Advisory Committee on Trade Negotiations and Policy, *Analysis of the U.S.-*

Japan Trade Problem, prepared for the U.S. Trade Representative (Washington, February 1989).

15. Advisory Committee on Trade Policy and Negotiations (ACTPN), "Major Findings and Policy Recommendations on U.S.-Japan Trade Policy," January 1993, p. 15.

16. Ibid., p. 15.

17. Kenneth Flamm, *Mismanaged Trade? Strategic Policy and the Semiconductor Industry* (Brookings, 1996), pp. 279–93; and Laura D'Andrea Tyson, *Who's Bashing Whom? Trade Conflict in High-Technology Industries* (Washington: Institute for International Economics, 1992), pp. 111–13; and C. Fred Bergsten and Marcus Noland, *Reconcilable Differences? United States-Japan Economic Conflict* (Washington: Institute for International Economics, 1993), pp. 129–36.

18. For a discussion of Japanese government attitudes toward trade liberalization in the 1970s and 1980s, see Lincoln, *Japan's Unequal Trade*, pp. 61–80.

19. "Joint Statement on the United States-Japan Framework for a New Economic Partnership," signed July 10, 1992.

20. Ibid., p.2.

21. Ibid., p.1.

22. Ibid., p. 6.

23. Ibid., pp. 2, 3, 5.

24. Ibid., p. 8.

25. David Wessel and Jacob M. Schlesinger, "Back-Room Deal: How the U.S., Japan Resolved Differences to Reach a Trade Pact," *Wall Street Journal*, July 12, 1993, p. A1.

26. Roger C. Altman, "Why Pressure Tokyo?" *Foreign Affairs,*" vol. 73 (May–June 1994), p. 2.

27. Office of the U.S. Trade Representative, *National Trade Estimate Report, 1997* (Washington, 1997), p. 191.

28. Office of the U.S. Trade Representative, *1992 National Trade Estimate Report on Foreign Trade Barriers* (Washington, 1992), pp. 137–55; and *1993 National Trade Estimate Report on Foreign Trade Barriers* (Washington, 1993), pp. 143–70.

29. Armacost, *Friends or Rivals?* p. 44.

30. "Joint Statement on the United States-Japan Framework for a New Economic Partnership," p. 6.

31. Rita Beamish, "U.S.-Japan Trade Talks Fail to Produce Breakthrough," Associated Press, February 11, 1994; and Peter Ennis, "What We Have Here Is a Failure to Communicate: Inside the Clinton-Hosokawa Summit," *Tokyo Business* (May 1994), pp. 34–38.

32. Letter from Foreign Minister Tsutomu Hata to Ambassador Walter Mondale, March 29, 1994, and its attachment, "Outline of External Economic Reform Measures (Summary)"; and Mickey Kantor, "Special Briefing on Japanese Economic Reform Measures," transcript by Federal News Service, Washington, March 29, 1994.

33. "Statement of Ambassador Mickey Kantor on the Executive Order Reinstituting Super 301," March 3, 1994 (Washington: Office of the U.S. Trade Representative).

34. For a summary of the issues, see Office of the U.S. Trade Representative, "U.S.-Japan Automotive Fact Sheet," Washington, April 1995.

35. "Statement by the President: Section 301 Determination on Japan," White House press release, May 10, 1995.

36. Masaichi Nosaka, "U.S. to Impose 100% Tariffs on 13 Car Models," *Daily Yomiuri*, May 14, 1995.

37. "U.S. to File WTO Trade Complaint on Japan within 45 Days; Text: May 10 Kantor letter to WTO Chief Ruggiero," American Embassy, Tokyo, United States Information Service, press office, May 12, 1995.

38. Nihon Keizai Shimbunsha, *Nikkei Kaisha Jōhō* (Tokyo: Nihon Keizai Shimbunsha, 1997), p. 695.

39. Al Sullivan, "Clinton: Japan Has Rigged Its Auto Market to Gain Advantage," *USIA Wireless File*, June 22, 1995; and John F. Harris, "Clinton Defends Free-Trade Record but Warns Japan," *Washington Post*, June 28, 1995, p. F1.

40. David E. Sanger, "Japan Shows Some Flexibility at Trade Talks," *New York Times*, June 28, 1995, p. 1.

41. "Measures by the Government of Japan and the Government of the United States of America Regarding Autos and Auto Parts," August 15, 1995.

42. "Joint Statement by Ryutaro Hashimoto, Minister of International Trade and Industry of Japan, and Michael Kantor, United States Trade Representative, Regarding Autos and Auto Parts," June 28, 1995.

43. "Joint Announcement by Ryutaro Hashimoto, Minister of International Trade and Industry of Japan and Michael Kantor, United States Trade Representative Regarding the Japanese Auto Companies Plans," June 28, 1995; and "Joint Announcement on Dealerships by Ryutaro Hashimoto, Minister of International Trade and Industry of Japan, and Michael Kantor, United States Trade Representative," June 28, 1995.

44. Andrew Pollack, "Agreement on Which Both Sides Disagree," *New York Times*, June 30, 1995, p. D5; and Paul Blustein, "U.S., Japan Dispute Auto Pact's Meaning: Accord Signals New Clinton Tactic on Trade," *Washington Post*, June 30, 1995, p.F1.

45. Edith Terry, "Tokyo Skeptics Question Auto Deal Benefits for U.S.," *Christian Science Monitor*, July 3, 1995; and Jim Hoagland, "A Soft Deal with Japan," *Washington Post*, July 5, 1995, p. A23.

46. Japan Development Bank, *Principal Economic and Social Indicators* (Tokyo, 1998), p. 4.

47. International Monetary Fund, *International Financial Statistics* (Washington, April 1993, January 1996, January 1997).

48. T. R. Reid, "New Japanese Cabinet Marked by Diversity; 7 Parties Represented; 3 Women Named," *Washington Post*, August 9, 1993, p. A9.

49. The Japanese government even tried to dissuade ASEAN members of APEC from supporting this trade liberalization initiative; "Yosano Fails to Induce ASEAN Resistance to U.S.-Led Free-Trade Initiative," *Japan Digest*, September 25, 1998, p. 3; and Office of the U.S. Trade Representative, "Transcript: Barshefsky/Glickman Conduct Asian Trade Roundtable," November 20, 1998 (Washington).

50. Irene Kunii, "Japan PM Ready to Work with Clinton," Reuters wire service, November 4, 1992.

51. Kunii, "Japan PM Ready to Work with Clinton."

52. Letter from Ambassador Takakazu Kuriyama to U.S. Trade Representative Mickey Kantor, July 12, 1993.

53. The author learned, during a personal conversation with a government official at MPT, that Ozawa was quite influential in MPT decisionmaking although he never served as the minister.

54. Schoppa, *Bargaining with Japan*, p. 291, notes that in interviews with U.S. government officials they expressed frustration in their efforts to discover which politicians could be engaged in the negotiating process.

55. Armacost, *Friends or Rivals?* p. 176.

56. Tyson, *Who's Bashing Whom?* p. 263.

57. Ibid., p. 265.

58. "Commentary: Douglas H. Paal on Evaluating the Clinton Team's Asia Policy at the Mid-Term Mark," *Japan Economic Survey*, vol. 19 (February 1995), p. 7.

59. Jagdish Bhagwati and others, "An Open Letter to Prime Minister Hosokawa and President Clinton," September 27, 1993. Other signers included Lawrence Klein, Paul Samuelson, Robert Solow, James Tobin, Anne Krueger, Paul Krugman, Jeffrey Sachs, and Hugh Patrick.

60. Lawrence H. Summers, letter to Jagdish Bhagwati, undated.

61. Andrew Pollack, "Japan's Chief Says U.S. Economists Oppose Trade Targets," *New York Times*, January 20, 1994, p. D2.

62. "No Numerical Targets; More Free Trade," by Scholars for Free Trade, signed by Takatoshi Ito, Masahiro Kawai, Kazuo Ueda, with endorsement signatures from 156 other Japanese economists. This letter, "*Keizai Kyōshitsu: Bei no 'Sūchi Mokuhyō' Yōkyū, Kyōsō Sokushin ni Gyakkō*," was subsequently printed in *Nihon Keizai Shimbun*, January 28, 1994, p. 29.

63. Subcommittee on Unfair Trade Policies and Measures under the Uruguay Round Committee of the Industrial Structure Council, *Position Paper on Numerical Target-Based Trade Policy* (Government Printing Office, 1994), p. 12.

64. Tyson, *Who's Bashing Whom?*, p. 264.

65. Press briefing with Charlene Barshefsky and Bowman Cutter, Friday, December 10, 1993, American Embassy, Tokyo, p. 3.

66. Roger C. Altman, "Why Pressure Tokyo?" *Foreign Affairs,*" vol. 73 (May–June 1994), p. 4. For this publication date, he would have drafted this piece in early 1994.

67. Jagdish Bhagwati, "Samurais No More," *Foreign Affairs,* vol. 73 (May–June 1994), p. 8.

68. "U.S. Seeks Market Share Arrangement to Cut Auto Deficit with Japan," *Inside U.S. Trade,* Special Report, November 1, 1993, pp. 13–14.

69. "U.S. Rejects Japanese Push for Auto Indicators Rather Than Targets," *Inside U.S. Trade,* January 21, 1994, p. 19.

70. The agreement consists of two letters—Commerce Secretary Ronald H. Brown to Ambassador Takakazu Kuriyama and Kuriyama to Brown on November 1, 1994, accompanied by "Appendix A: Measures Related to Japanese Public Sector Procurement of Medical Technology Products and Services."

71. Armacost, *Friends or Rivals?* pp. 47–48, notes the glass and paper agreements refer to "substantially increased market access for foreign firms."

72. "U.S. Seeks Market Share Arrangement to Cut Auto Deficit with Japan," Special Report, *Inside U.S. Trade,* November 1, 1993, p. 1.

73. Office of the U.S. Trade Representative, *National Trade Estimate Report, 1997,* p. 185.

74. Schoppa, *Bargaining with Japan,* p. 267.

75. World Trade Organization, *GATT Activities 1994–1995* (Geneva, 1996), p. 72.

76. Data calculated from Organization for Economic Cooperation and Development (OECD), *International Trade by Commodities Statistics, HS Rev. 1, 1988–1996* (Paris, 1997), on CD-ROM.

77. Ibid.

78. Data are from Semiconductor Industry Association, San Jose, Calif., web page,www.semichips.org/stats/shares.htm, and . . . shares2.htm.

79. Office of the U.S. Trade Representative, "U.S. and Japan Reach Semiconductor Accord," press release, Washington, August 2, 1996.

80. Office of the U.S. Trade Representative, *National Trade Estimate Report, 1997,* pp. 204–05.

81. Further details of this negotiation are considered in chapter 6. See "Highlights of the U.S.-Japan Civil Aviation Agreement," fact sheet released by the Bureau of Economic, Business, and Agricultural Affairs, Department of State, February 2, 1998, www.state.gov/www/issues/economics/fs_980202_japanair_agreement.html.

82. "FMC to Impose Sanctions for Restrictive Japanese Port Practices: Fees to Take Effect April 14, 1997," press release dated February 26, 1997, from USIA web page.

83. Federal Maritime Commission, 46 CFR Part 586 (Docket no. 96-20), "Port Restrictions and Requirements in the United States/Japan Trade," April 14, 1997;

and "FMC Imposes Sanctions on Japanese Shippers as Negotiations Continue," *Inside U.S. Trade*, September 5, 1997, pp. 1, 13.

84. "FMC Moves to Block Japanese Cargo Ships from U.S. Ports," *USIS Washington File*, October 16, 1997.

85. "Statement by Ambassador Charlene Barshefsky Regarding the WTO Dispute on Photographic Film and Paper," December 5, 1997.

86. "Testimony of Susan G. Esserman, General Counsel, Office of the U.S. Trade Representative, before Senate Subcommittee on East Asia and Pacific Affairs," March 4, 1998, and "USTR and Department of Commerce Announce Next Steps on Improving Access to the Japanese Market for Film," USTR/Commerce press release, February 3, 1998.

87. See chapter 6. Office of the U.S. Trade Representative, "Panel Finds Japanese Testing Requirements Violate WTO Rules," press release, October 27, 1998.

88. U.S. Trade Representative, *National Trade Estimate Report, 1998* (Washington, 1998), p. 196.

89. "Barshefsky Statement on U.S.-Japan Deregulation," May 15, 1998, from USIA website, www.usia.gov/abtusia/posts/JA1/wwwt2220.txt.

90. USTR, "U.S. Submits Wide-Ranging Deregulation Proposals to Japan," press release, October 7, 1998.

91. "U.S. Government Proposals for Improvement of Japan's Environment for Foreign Direct Investment," USIA press release, October 26, 1998, www.usia.gov/abtusia/posts/JA1/www.t2620.txt.

Chapter Five

1. "Rengo, Nikkeiren: Deregulation to Create 3 Million Jobs," Kyodo Wire Service, December 24, 1996 and in Foreign Broadcast Information Service (FBIS), EAS-96-248, at World News Connection, http://wnc.fedworld.gov/.

2. For other recent cautious views of deregulation in Japan, see Lonny E. Carlile and Mark C. Tilton, eds., *Is Japan Really Changing Its Ways?* (Brookings, 1998); and Frank Gibney, ed., *Unlocking the Bureaucrat's Kingdom: Deregulation and the Japanese Economy* (Brookings, 1998).

3. This aspect of Japan's changing economic growth is analyzed in Edward J. Lincoln, *Japan Facing Economic Maturity* (Brookings, 1987), pp. 41–67.

4. Mancur Olson, *The Rise and Decline of Nations: Economic Growth, Stagflation, and Social Rigidities* (Yale University Press, 1982), especially pp. 75–76.

5. Kent E. Calder, *Strategic Capitalism: Private Business and Public Purpose in Japanese Industrial Finance* (Princeton University Press, 1993), pp. 230–32.

6. Small and Medium Enterprise Agency, *Chūshō Kigyō Hakusho, 1996* [White Paper on Small and Medium Enterprises in Japan] p. 7 of statistical annex; and U.S. Department of Commerce, *Statistical Abstract of the United States, 1997* (Washington, 1997), p. 544.

7. See Mark Tilton, *Restrained Trade: Cartels in Japan's Basic Industries* (Cornell University Press, 1996), especially pp. 50–121, 169–89, for analysis of collusive behavior in aluminum, cement, and steel.

8. Rodney Clark, *Japanese Company* (Yale University Press, 1979).

9. See Leonard H. Lynn and Timothy J. McKeown, *Organizing Business: Trade Associations in America and Japan* (American Enterprise Institute, 1988), pp. 90–99.

10. Mark Tilton, *Restrained Trade*, pp. 22–49, explores the tolerance of collusive behavior of trade associations under the Antimonopoly Law and other laws. For an explicit contrast of the antitrust environment for Japanese and American trade associations, see Leonard H. Lynn and Timothy J. McKeown, *Organizing Business*, pp. 38–51.

11. This process is the subject of Kent E. Calder, *Crisis and Compensation: Public Policy and Political Stability in Japan, 1949–1986* (Princeton University Press, 1988).

12. Tadahide Ikuta, "Deep Structure of Kasumigaseki: Present State and Prospects of 'Hashimoto Administrative Reform' Already Being Foresaken by Bureaucrats," *Tokyo Shukan Daiyamondo*, March 8, 1997, in FBIS, EAS-97-047, World News Connection, Internet.

13. "The Weekly Post Special 1: MOF Involved in Insider Trading with VIP's," *Weekly Post*, June 2–June 8, 1997, Internet version. See also in the same issue, "The Weekly Post Special 2: MOF's SPKO Is Basis for Insider Trading"; "The Weekly Post Special 3: Taxpayer Money Used to Make VIP Politicians and Bureaucrats Fat"; and "The Weekly Post Special 4: Nomura's VIP Account Is a Box Not to be Opened."

14. "BOJ Exec Allegedly Gave Bankers Advance Word on Money Market Operations," *Japan Digest*, March 9, 1998.

15. "Prosecutors Charge 2 MOF Officials with Accepting Bribes," *Nikkei Net*, January 27, 1998 (in exchange for advance notification, the two officials received ¥5 million or roughly $40,000 in meals and golf outings)(www.nikkei.co.jp); and "Banks Took MoF Inspectors to Dutch Red Light District, Vegas Casinos," *Japan Digest*, January 30, 1998.

16. Committee for Economic Development and Keizai Doyukai, *From Promise to Progress: Towards a New Stage in U.S.-Japan Economic Relations*, undated report, issued spring 1994.

17. See, for example, Karel van Wolferen, *The Enigma of Japanese Power: People and Politics in a Stateless Nation* (Alfred A. Knopf, 1989), pp. 52–59.

18. Group 2001, *"Keisei Kanwa to Iu Akumu"* [The Nightmare Called Deregulation], *Bungei Shunju*, August 1994, pp. 134–46, especially pp. 140, 143. The Group 2001 was an anonymous group of journalists.

19. Iwao Nakatani and Takatoshi Ito, "Kisei Kanwa wa 'Akumu' ka 'Fukuin ka', Jiyūka ga Hirogeru Shōhisha no Rieki" [Is Deregulation a Nightmare or Good News? The Consumer Benefit of Spreading Deregulation], *Ekonomisuto*, August

30, 1994, pp. 46–54. Group 2001 responded to this criticism in "Kisei Kanwa to Iu Akumu II" [The Nightmare of Deregulation, Part II], *Bungei Shunju,* November 1994, pp. 318–30.

20. Morihiro Hosokawa and Tetsundo Iwakuni, *Hina no Ronri* [The Logic of the Countryside] (Kobunsha, 1991), pp. 19–21.

21. Masao Miyamoto, *Straitjacket Society: An Insider's Irreverent View of Bureaucratic Japan,* Kodansha International, 1994, especially pp. 73–92. His writings began as a series of articles in *Gekkan Asahi.*

22. See "Kōkyō Ryōkin, Neage Zokzoku: Kōdan Yachin, 3-Nenburi 9%" [Increases in Public Service Fees One after Another: Public Housing Rents, Up 9 Percent for First Time in 3 Years], *Asahi Shimbun,* March 24, 1994, p. 1; and Kōkyō Ryōkin Toshiake Age" [Public Service Fees Going Up after the First of the Year], *Nihon Keizai Shimbun,* July 22, 1994, p. 1.

23. The Advisory Group for Economic Structural Reform, "Regarding Economic Structural Reform," December 16, 1993, pp. 2–4.

24. Ministry of International Trade and Industry, *News From MITI: Interim Announcement of the Status of Deregulation Request Reviews,* December 27, 1996, pp. 1–2.

25. "*Kisei Kanwa Suishin Keikaku no Saikaitei ni Tsuite*" [Concerning Revision of the Deregulation Promotion Plan], March 28, 1997 (approved by the Cabinet on this date).

26. Keidanren, *Request for Deregulation, Summary,* January 1997, www. keidanren.or.jp.

27. *The Daily Yomiuri* on-line, "White Paper: Deregulation Going Well," August 27, 1997.

28. Edward J. Lincoln, "Regulation of Rates on the Japanese National Railways," in Kenneth D. Boyer and William G. Shepard, eds., *Economic Regulation: Essays in Honor of James R. Nelson* (Michigan State University, Institute of Public Utilities, 1981), pp. 143–44.

29. Ministry of Foreign Affairs, "Revision of Japan's Deregulation Action Program," 1996, www.mofa.go.jp/ju/economy/29-1.html.

30. Fair Trade Commission, *Active Implementation of Competition Policy along with the Formulation of New Three Year Deregulation Action Plan,* March 31, 1998, www.jftc.admix.go.jp/e-page/press/980331.html/.

31. "First Joint Status Report on the U.S.-Japan Enhanced Initiative on Deregulation and Competition Policy," May 15, 1998, www.ustr.gov/releases/1998/05/status.pdf, pp. 3–4.

32. For the agreements on wood products in the Reagan and Bush administrations, see American Chamber of Commerce in Japan, *Making Trade Talks Work: Lessons from Recent History* (American Chamber of Commerce in Japan, 1997), pp. 131–33.

33. "U.S.-Japan Enhanced Initiative on Deregulation and Competition Policy: Fact Sheet," White House press release, May 15, 1998, p. 2.

34. For an analysis of the economic benefits of such ties, see Michael J. Smitka, *Competitive Ties: Subcontracting in the Japanese Automotive Industry* (Columbia University Press, 1991), especially pp. 1–22, 135–74, 195–204.

35. See Robert Z. Lawrence, "Efficient or Exclusionist? The Import Behavior of Japanese Corporate Groups," *Brookings Papers on Economic Activity: 1* (1991), pp. 311–30.

36. See "Nippon no Keiei, Tabū o Koete: Keiretsu no Domino Taoshi" [Japanese Management, Overcoming Taboos: The Falling *Keiretsu* Dominoes], *Nihon Keizai Shimbun*, June 26, 1995, p. 1.

37. "Nissan, Keiretsu Yūsen wo Haishi, Kōnyū Toyota Gaishikei wo Kakudai" [Nissan Ends *Keiretsu* Preference, To Expand Procurement from Toyota Suppliers and Foreign Firms], *Nihon Keizai Shimbun*, March 22, 1998, p. 1.

38. "Nissan, Buhin Chōtatsu wo Kaikaku," [Nissan: Reform of Parts Procurement] *Nihon Keizai Shimbun*, July 22, 1998, p. 1.

39. "Sakura Bank to Strengthen Capital by Issuing Yen 300 Billion in New Shares," *Japan Digest*, August 31, 1998.

40. "Yasuda Trust to Raise More Capital From Fuyo Group," *Nikkei Net*, www.nikkei.co.jp/enews, January 23, 1998.

41. Ministry of International Trade and Industry, "Tokutei Jigyōsha no Jigyō Kakushin no Enkatsuka ni Kansuru Rinji Sochihō," [Temporary Law for Smooth Reform of Designated Industries] *Tsūsan Roppō*, 1997, pp. 358–62.

42. "Nihon Saisei 133 no Shohōsen: Sankoshin Shōi Hōkokusho" [133 Prescriptions for Reviving Japan: Report of the Industrial Structure Council's Subcommittee], *Nihon Keizai Shimbun*, November 26, 1996, p. 3.

43. Ministry of International Trade and Industry (MITI), *Jigyō Kakushinhō no Kaisetsu* [Explanation of the Business Reform Law] (Tokyo: Tsūshō Sangyō Chōsakai Shuppanbu, 1995), pp. 23–24; and MITI, "Tokutei Jigyōsha no Jigyō Kakushin no Enkatsuka ni Kansuru Rinji Sochihō Dai-2-jō Dai-1-kō no Tokutei Gyōshu wo Sadameru Shorei" [Ministry Ordinance Deciding Designated Industries under Section 2, Paragraph 1 of the Temporary Law for Smooth Reform of Designated Industries], *Tsūsan Roppō* [Compilation of Industry and Trade Laws] 1997, pp. 363–65.

44. MITI, *Jigyō Kakushinho no Kaisetsu* [Explanation of the Business Reform Law] (Tokyo: Tsūshō Sangyō Chosakai Suppanbu, 1995), p. 253.

45. Kenneth Flamm, "Japan's New Semiconductor Technology Programs," Asian Technology Information Program Report, ATIP96.091, October 8, 1996.

46. See Scott Callon, *Divided Sun: MITI and the Breakdown of Japanese High-Tech Industrial Policy, 1975–1993* (Stanford University Press, 1995), for a skeptical view of such policies.

47. Small and Medium Enterprise Agency, *Chūshō Kigyō Shisaku Sōran Shiryōhen* [Overview of Small and Medium Enterprise Policy] (Chūshō Kigyō Sōgō Kenkyū Kikō, 1997), p. 7.

48. Marie Ancordoguy, "Japan at a Technological Crossroads: Does Change Support Convergence Theory?" *Journal of Japanese Studies*, vol. 23 (Summer 1997), p. 371.

49. For example, a statistical study attempting to explain various aspects of *amakudari* by Chikako Usui and Richard A. Colignon suffers from this narrow focus. "Government Elites and *Amakudari* in Japan, 1963-1992," *Asian Survey*, vol. 35 (July 1995), pp. 682–98.

50. Susumu Mukaidani, "Ōkura Kanryō 'Amakudari Shisan Keibatsu' Zen Risuto" [The Complete List of Finance Bureaucrats—*Amakudari*, Assets, Family Connections], *Bungei Shunju*, April 1996, p. 182.

51. For a description of the various landing spots for government officials, see Chalmers Johnson, *Japan's Public Policy Companies* (American Enterprise Institute, 1978), pp. 101–02.

52. Teikoku Databank, "Gaibu Yakuin 1121-nin, Uchi Amakudari 517-nin— Zen Yakuin no 6-nin ni Hitori ga Amakudari" [Of 1,121 Outside Directors, 517 Amakudari—One in Six of Total Directors], report dated December 13, 1996.

53. Takenori Inoki, "Japanese Bureaucrats at Retirement: The Mobility of Human Resources from Central Government to Public Corporations," in Kim, Muramatsu, Pempel, and Yamamura, *The Civil Service System and Economic Development: The Japanese Experience: Report on an International Colloquium Held in Tokyo* (Claredon Press, 1996), pp. 218–19.

54. Some of the attempts to explain why firms accept these retired officials include Kent Calder, "Elites in an Equalizing Role: Ex-Bureaucrats as Coordinators and Intermediaries in the Japanese Government-Business Relationship," *Comparative Politics*, vol. 21 (July 1989), pp. 379–403; and Ulrike Schaede, "The 'Old Boy' Network and Government-Business Relationships in Japan," *Journal of Japanese Studies*, vol. 21 (Summer 1995), pp. 293–317.

55. A scandal involving wining and dining a director of the Japan Highway Public Corporation by investment banks eager for the contract to underwrite the organization's bond issues, for example, erupted in 1998. The director was a former MOF official. "10 Finance Firms Entertained Highway Exec," *Japan Times*, January 21, 1998, p.1.

56. "Jinji-in Hōkoku: Amakudari Kisei Kyōka" [National Personnel Authority Report: Strengthening *Amakudari* Rules], *Asahi Shimbun*, August 15, 1997, p. 1.

57. Daniel I. Okimoto, *Between MITI and the Market: Japanese Industrial Policy for High Technology*" (Stanford University Press, 1989), p. 157.

58. For a fairly sympathetic view of *shingikai* as consultative mechanisms between government and affected parties, see Frank Schwartz, "Of Fairy Cloaks and Familiar Talks: The Politics of Consultation," in Gary D. Allinson and Yasunori

Sone, eds., *Political Dynamics in Contemporary Japan* (Cornell University Press, 1993), pp. 217–41.

59. Ibid., pp. 237–38.

60. Material supplied from the Jinji-in (National Personnel Authority), dated August 14, 1996.

61. Chitoshi Yanaga, *Big Business in Japanese Politics* (Yale University Press, 1968), pp. 22–24. Yanaga's book is critical of the web of interlocking ties within the Japanese business and government elite. He notes that in the 1950s, 41 percent of a list of "prominent business leaders" were graduates of the University of Tokyo.

62. "Private Sector Loaned 177 Employees to 3 Ministries," *Mainichi Daily News*, May 1, 1996, p. 1.

63. "Eighty Three Employees 'Farmed Out to MOF' from 21 Banks during Past Ten Years, Reflecting Close Ties with Ministry," *Tokyo Shimbun* April 25, 1996, p. 2.

64. *Tsūshō Sangyō Shō Meikan, 1995 ed.* [MITI Directory] (Tokyo: Jihyōsha, 1994), pp. 277–87.

65. *Seikan Yōran* [Political and Bureaucratic Handbook] (Tokyo: Seisaku Jihōsha, 1998), p. 659. English titles for offices in the JFTC are based on JFTC web page www.jftc.admix.go.jp.

66. Okimoto, *Between MITI and the Market*, p. 152.

67. For a summary of some of these policies, see Edward J. Lincoln, "Japan's Financial Mess," *Foreign Affairs*, vol. 77 (May-June 1998), pp. 57–66.

Chapter Six

1. Department of Commerce, *Statistical Abstract of the United States, 1997* (Government Printing Office, 1997), pp. 838–39.

2. Office of the U.S. Trade Representative, *1998 National Trade Estimate Report on Foreign Trade Barriers* (Washington, 1998); see also earlier years.

3. Author's conversation with Marjory Searing, deputy assistant secretary for Japan, Department of Commerce, May 1996.

4. Data calculated from Organization for Economic Cooperation and Development, *International Trade by Commodities Statistics, HS Rev. 1 1988-1996* (Paris, 1997), on CD-ROM.

5. Department of Commerce, *Statistical Abstract of the United States, 1997*, p. 839.

6. Paul Krugman, "What Should Trade Negotiators Negotiate About?" *Journal of Economic Literature*, vol 35 (March 1997), pp. 113–20.

7. For a recent effort to confront fears of open trade, see Gary Burtless and others, *Globaphobia: Confronting Fears about Open Trade* (Brookings, 1998).

8. Chalmers A. Johnson, *MITI and the Japanese Miracle: The Growth of Industrial Policy, 1925–1975* (Stanford University Press, 1982), Mark Tilton, *Restrained Trade: Cartels in Japan's Basic Materials Industries* (Cornell University Press, 1996),

Phyllis Ann Genther, "A History of Japan's Government-Business Relationship: The Passenger Car Industry," Michigan Papers in Japanese Studies 20 (University of Michigan, July 1990); and Laura D'Andrea Tyson, *Who's Bashing Whom? Trade Conflict in High-Technology Industries* (Washington: Institute for International Economics, 1992), are only a few of the many studies detailing policies affecting particular industries pursued by the Japanese government in the past fifty years to promote and protect domestic industries.

9. See James A. Brander, "Rationales for Strategic Trade and Industrial Policy," in Paul R. Krugman, ed., *Strategic Trade Policy and the New International Economics* (MIT Press, 1986), pp. 32–33, for a summary of these explanations, or Michael Borrus, Laura D'Andrea Tyson, and John Zysman, "Creating Advantage: How Government Policies Shape International Trade in the Semiconductor Industry," in the same volume, pp. 91–113.

10. For discussion of spillover effects, see Paul R. Krugman, "Introduction: New Thinking about Trade Policy," in Krugman, ed., *Strategic Trade Policy and the New International Economics*, pp. 13–14.

11. For a summary of the theory and these criticisms, see Dominick Salvatore, *International Economics*, 6th ed. (Prentice-Hall, 1998), pp. 273–75.

12. James A. Brander, "Strategic Trade Policy," in Gene M. Grossman and Kenneth Rogoff, eds., *Handbook of International Economics* (Elsevier, 1995).

13. For an analysis of the implications of strategic trade policies in high-technology industries, see Tyson, *Who's Bashing Whom?*

14. See Brander, "Rationales for Strategic Trade and Industrial Policy," pp. 36–43.

15. Committee on Japan Framework Statement and Report of the Competitiveness Task Force, "Maximizing U.S. Interests in Science and Technology Relations with Japan" (Washington: National Research Council, 1997).

16. Richard Katz, *Japan: The System That Soured: The Rise and Fall of the Japanese Economic Miracle* (M.E. Sharpe, 1998), see especially pp. 165–96.

17. See Mark Tilton, *Restrained Trade*, for several basic industries for which this has been the case throughout the 1980s and 1990s.

18. These asymmetries are analyzed in Edward J. Lincoln, *Japan's New Global Role* (Brookings, 1993).

19. See Schoppa, *Bargaining with Japan*; and Naka, *Predicting Outcomes in United States-Japan Trade Negotiations*, discussed in chap. 4.

20. American Chamber of Commerce in Japan (ACCJ), *Making Trade Talks Work: Lessons from Recent History* (Tokyo, 1997), p. 144.

21. These were the Inward Investment Arrangement, July 1995; and Mutual Understanding between the Japan Patent Office and the United States Patent and Trademark Office, January 1994. See ACCJ, *Making Trade Talks Work*, pp. 83–85, 136–38.

22. "A/S Alan Larson 4/4 Remarks on Japanese Deregulation," *USIS Washington File*, April 4, 1997.

23. Submission by the Government of the United States to the Government of Japan Regarding Deregulation, Administrative Reform and Competition Policy in Japan, p. 1.

24. "Justice Department Official 4/4 Remarks on Japan Deregulation," *USIS Washington File*, April 9, 1997, p. 1.

25. Ibid., p. 5.

26. Joint Statement on the U.S.-Japan Enhanced Initiative on Deregulation and Competition Policy under the U.S.-Japan Framework for a New Economic Partnership, June 19, 1997.

27. "U.S., Japan Hammer out Details of Dereg Pact But Differ on U.S. Role," *Inside U.S. Trade*, June 27, 1997, pp. 1, 23.

28. "USTR 11/12 on Japanese Deregulation Recommendations," *USIS Washington File*, November 12, 1997 (from U.S. Information Agency web page, www. usia.gov); and "Special Report: U.S. Lays Out Demands for Structural, Sectoral Deregulation in Japan," *Inside U.S. Trade*, November 14, 1997.

29. "State Department Official on Japanese Investment Policy," USIS website, January 21, 1997.

30. See Schoppa, *Bargaining with Japan,* especially pages 301–04.

31. For an analysis of the beef and citrus negotiations, including the role of the GATT case, see Amelia Porges, "Japan: Beef and Citrus," in Thomas O. Bayard and Kimberly Ann Elliott, *Reciprocity and Retaliation in U.S. Trade Policy* (Washington: Institute for International Economics, 1994), pp. 233–66.

32. *Understanding on Rules and Procedures Governing the Settlement of Disputes* (Annex 2 of the Marrakesh Agreement Establishing the World Trade Organization), article 22, as cited in World Trade Organization, *The WTO Dispute Settlement Procedures: A Collection of the Legal Texts*, p. 22.

33. Senator William Bradley, "United States-Japan Relations: A Strategic Framework," *Congressional Record*, vol. 140, March 22, 1994; and Carnegie Endowment and GISPRI Study Groups, *Changing U.S.-Japan Relations* (Washington: Carnegie Endowment for International Peace, 1995), pp. 32–33, 64–65.

34. Yoshihiro Sakamoto, "Moving to an Era of Cooperation: The U.S. and Japanese New Relationship," speech to the Foreign Correspondents Club of Japan, Tokyo, March 15, 1996, p. 3.

35. "Former MITI Official Says Bilateral Deals Useful for U.S.-Japan Disputes," *Inside U.S. Trade*, January 10, 1997, p. 7.

36. General Agreement on Tariffs and Trade (GATT), *Guide to GATT Law and Practice*, 6th ed. (Geneva, 1995), p. 632. Emphasis added.

37. EEC—Oilseeds case, 1955, cited in Office of the U.S. Trade Representative, Japan: Measures Affecting Photographic Film and Paper; First Submission of the United States of America, Washington, February 20, 1997, p. 170.

38. EEC—Citrus products case, 1950, cited in USTR, "Japan—Measures Affecting Photographic Film and Paper; First Submission of the United States of America," February 20, 1997, p. 170.

39. Organization for Economic Cooperation and Development, *Positive Adjustment Policies: Managing Structural Change* (Paris, 1982); Japan External Trade Organization (JETRO), *Japan's Industrial Structure—A Long Range Vision* (Tokyo, 1975), p. 11; and Edward J. Lincoln, *Japan's Industrial Policies* (Washington: Japan Economic Institute, 1984), pp. 7–8.

40. Ministry of International Trade and Industry, *Statement on the Submission of the United States to the WTO Panel on the Film Case,* from the MITI home page, posted February 21, 1997(www.miti.go.jp).

41. World Trade Organization/WT/DS44/R, Japan—"Measures Affecting Consumer Photographic Film and Paper," March 31, 1998, pp. 380–464.

42. Ministry of International Trade and Industry, *Statement on the Submission of the United States to the WTO Panel on the Film Case*, MITI home page, posted February 21, 1997 (www.miti.go.jp).

43. GATT, *Guide to GATT Law and Practice,* 6th ed., p. 270. Emphasis added.

44. Ibid., pp. 271–76.

45. USTR, Japan—"Measures Affecting Photographic Film and Paper; First Submission of the United States of America," February 20, 1997, p. 181.

46. Frank Upham, "Privatizing Regulation: The Implementation of the Large-Scale Retail Stores Law," in Gary Allinson and Yasunori Sone, eds., *Political Dynamics in Contemporary Japan* (Cornell University Press, 1993), pp. 271–74.

47. GATT, *Guide to GATT Law and Practice*, 6th ed., p. 115.

48. Ibid., p. 151. Emphasis added.

49. Ibid., p. 155.

50. This possibility is emphasized in ACCJ, *Making Trade Talks Work*, p. 122.

51. GATT Secretariat, *The Results of the Uruguay Round of Multilateral Trade Negotiations, the Legal Texts* (Geneva, 1994) p. 70.

52. Ibid., pp. 139–40.

53. Brian Woodall, "Japan's Double Standards: Technical Standards and U.S.-Japan Economic Relations," in John R. McIntyre, ed., *Japan's Technical Standards: Implications for Global Trade and Competitiveness* (Quorum Books, 1997), pp. 145–61.

54. Office of the U. S. Trade Representative, *National Trade Estimate Report*, 1997, p. 6, of USIA Internet version.

55. "Japan Blocks WTO Study on Streamlining ITA Product Certification," *Inside U.S. Trade*, November 7, 1997, pp. 6–7.

56. USTR, *1993 National Trade Estimate Report on Foreign Trade Barriers*, p. 169.

57. "U.S. Keeps Heat on Japan to Implement Liquor Panel by February," *Inside U.S. Trade*, October 3, 1997, p. 9.

58. Ownership information supplied by Seiji Kawamura of NTT.

59. "U.S. Firms Mulling Bid for Renewal of NTT Procurement Agreement," *Inside U.S. Trade*, January 10, 1997, p. 9.

60. "U.S., Japan Strike Deal on Two-Year Renewal of NTT Procurement Pact," *Inside U.S. Trade*, October 3, 1997, pp. 13–14; see also "U.S., Japan Agree to Improve NTT's Procurement Procedures," *USIS Washington File*, October 1, 1997.

61. "NTT Chōtatsu Kyōtei: Nichibei, Sai Enchō de Gōi; Saihensei Kigen no 99-Nenmatsu Made" [NTT Procurement Agreement: U.S.-Japan Agree on Renewal; Only Until Reorganization in 1999], *Nihon Keizai Shimbun*, October 2, 1997, p. 7.

62. "U.S. to Retaliate against Japanese Port Practices," *USIS Washington File*, February 27, 1997.

63. Office of the U.S. Trade Representative, Executive Office of the President, press statement, December 15, 1996.

64. "U.S. Offers Compromise to Japan on Aviation Rights," Kyodo Wire Service, November 16, 1997, FBIS-EAS-97-320 (www.fedworld.gov).

65. "Memorandum of Understanding," April 20, 1998, pp. 21–22.

66. ACCJ, *Making Trade Talks Work*, p. 150.

67. U.S. Business Sharply Divided over U.S.-Japan Aviation Talks," *USIS Washington File*, September 24, 1997 (www.usia.gov).

68. "Hashimoto Criticizes U.S. Sanctions on Shipping Cargo," Kyodo wire service, February 27, 1997, FBIS-EAS-97-039 (wnc.fedworld.gov).

69. For a recent example, see Carnegie Endowment and GISPRI Study Groups, *Changing U.S.-Japan Relations*.

70. See, for example, Nancy Dunne, "Japanese Message Loud and Clear in US," *Financial Times*, June 9, 1995, p. 6.

71. American Embassy, *U.S.-Japan Automobile and Auto Parts Negotiations Media Reference Material*, Tokyo, U.S. Information Service, press office, April 27, 1995.

72. For details see American Chamber of Commerce in Japan, *Making Trade Talks Work: Lessons from Recent History* (ACCJ, 1997), pp. 93–95, 166.

73. "U.S. May Highlight Flat Glass Dispute with Japan under Super 301," *Inside U.S. Trade*, September 26, 1997, p. 7.

74. "U.S.-Japan to Consult on 1995 Flat-Glass Agreement Next Week," *Inside U.S. Trade*, October 17, 1997, pp. 15–16.

75. "Measures to Increase Market Access in Japan for Foreign Paper Products," April 5, 1992.

76. "USTR Announces Steps on Access to Japan's Paper Market," *USIS Washington File*, April 8, 1997.

77. "U.S. Claims Near Total Victory in Insurance Agreement with Japan," *Inside U.S. Trade*, December 20, 1996, pp. 10–12.

78. "Nonlife Insurance Group Leader Blasts Accord with U.S.," Kyodo wire service, December 16, 1996, FBIS-EAS-96-243 (wnc.fedworld.gov).

79. "ACCJ Urges Japan to Fully Implement Insurance Deregulation Pact," *Inside U.S. Trade*, July 11, 1997, p. 24.

80. "4/18 USTR Press Release on Japanese Auto Parts Market," *USIS Washington File*, April 18, 1997.

81. "*USTR Press Release on U.S. Auto Parts Petition to Japan,*" Washington, February 5, 1997.

82. "4/18 USTR Press Release on Japanese Auto Parts Market."

83. "U.S. Disappointed with Japan Auto Talks, Sees Few Short-Term Benefits," *Inside U.S. Trade*, October 10, 1997, pp. 1, 26–28.

Index